Nigerian Media Industries in the Era of Globalization

Nigerian Media Industries in the Era of Globalization

*Edited by **Unwana Samuel Akpan***

LEXINGTON BOOKS
Lanham • Boulder • New York • London

Published by Lexington Books
An imprint of The Rowman & Littlefield Publishing Group, Inc.
4501 Forbes Boulevard, Suite 200, Lanham, Maryland 20706
www.rowman.com

86-90 Paul Street, London EC2A 4NE

British Library Cataloguing in Publication Information Available

Library of Congress Cataloging-in-Publication Data

Names: Akpan, Unwana Samuel, editor.
Title: Nigerian media industries in the era of globalization / edited by Unwana
    Samuel Akpan.
Description: Lanham : Lexington Books, 2022. | Includes bibliographical references
    and index.
Identifiers: LCCN 2022035739 (print) | LCCN 2022035740 (ebook) |
    ISBN 9781666922851 (cloth) | ISBN 9781666922868 (ebook)
Subjects: LCSH: Mass media—Nigeria. | Digital media—Nigeria.
Classification: LCC PN92.N5 N54 2022 (print) | LCC PN92.N5 (ebook) |
    DDC 302.2309669—dc23/eng/20220726
LC record available at https://lccn.loc.gov/2022035739
LC ebook record available at https://lccn.loc.gov/2022035740

I dedicate this book to the Almighty God, the Maker of heaven and earth and the Giver of life.

Contents

Foreword

When I was asked to write the foreword to this compendium, I did not hesitate to accept the invitation because of the nature of the work in the sense that it sent me back several years during the era of emerging global attention to informatics, telematics, and geomatics. It was in Tokyo, Japan, during the 1980s at the United Nations University where I was a senior academic in the Global Learning Division, and was tasked with responsibilities, among others, to handle and manage research teams and networks in various parts of the world working on the new information and communication technologies. Just like this book, we engaged scholars from various parts of the world to provide insights into how informatics, telematics, and geomatics would impact various disciplines and sectors globally, in terms of information generation, aggregation, codification, storage, retrieval, and dissemination. The studies, in addition to others, together with concomitant policies at the national, regional, and international levels have since morphed into several aspects of digitalization today, within the wider context of globalization.

Rapid strides in digitalization and the availability of broadband technology—high speed internet access, enhanced the process of generation, aggregation, codification, storage, retrieval, and dissemination of data. With the proliferation of big data in an increasingly globalized world, policy concerns were raised on issues such as trans-border data flows. Digitalization and globalization became the fulcrum for the creation of big data and how such huge data filter through the various social media platforms. Coupled with the exponential growth in internet technology, there was an equal concern for information overload and information underuse among users of data across the spectrum.

Research teams working with the Global Learning Division of the United Nations University, for example, studied the challenges of information overload and information underuse. Africa then had major infrastructural as well as human resource problems that limited input into the global research community. Moreover, Africa's locus in the globalized world was one in which the continent was exploited rather than being part of the leadership helm of globalization. For all intents and purposes, globalization was synonymous with Westernization until China became a formidable global actor.

With the above in mind, the title of the book correctly raises the issue of Nigeria, and Africa as a whole within the context of a globalized world and digitalization, as far as media communication is concerned. Furthermore, contributions from scholars and scholar/practitioners in this compendium help to shed light on the multifarious dimensions of the digitization challenges and globalization, as far as the media are concerned in the continent. The contributions should stimulate further research into Nigeria's and Africa's locus in a globalized world. Perhaps most significantly, further research would help shed light on how digitalization could help accelerate Africa's development with the Nigerian model so as to alleviate the misery of the majority of Africans living in extreme poverty. With the availability of big data and social media platforms as well as traditional media, audiences can be targeted in a manner that would make development messages in particular more meaningful and useful for the improvement of the overall quality of life.

The media have a major role to play in this dual function, exemplified in contributions of this compendium. The current state of the art of digitalization makes it an undisputed imperative for not just Nigerians, but Africans to put it in the service of human development in the continent. In that manner, Africa can really claim to be part of a globalized world, in which the most disfavored and underserved populations in the continent will benefit. In order to achieve such a status, attention should be paid by academics, practitioners, and policy makers to the probability of information overload, a byproduct of digitalization, and how it should be managed to mitigate underuse.

This compendium, edited by a Media Scholar–Practitioner with a vast experience in the media industry, is timely, and contributes to the fund of knowledge useful not just for understanding globalization, digitalization, and Nigerian media industries, but applying such knowledge productively as well.

Professor Cecil Blake
Professor Emeritus
University of Pittsburgh, Pennsylvania, USA
Former Minister of Information
Sierra Leone

Preface

It was in 2019 as a Postdoctoral Research Fellow/Visiting Scholar in the Department of Communication, Culture and Media Studies, Cathy Hughes School of Communication and Media Studies, Howard University, Washington DC, USA, for the first time that I took my time to study the digital operations of the Western media. I compared my findings with what obtains in my dear country Nigeria, and I realized that Nigeria is very far apart from what the modern media in the developed world has. This got me concerned and thinking!

In the winter of that year, after my seminar paper presentation, I made up my mind to do a book titled *Nigerian Media Industries in the Era of Globalization*, with colleagues drawn from the various media industries.

In this book, you will find famous names synonymous with the media, medical, and cultural expertise. Therefore, this is a book for the first time in history which brings media academics and media professionals together to pen their thoughts in the area of digitization and the Nigerian media industries.

Drawing from their years of industry experience, the contributors are writing from their wealth of industry experience. The chapters capture essential areas such as digitization, globalization, changing the Nigerian narratives in the digital space, historical perspective of Nigerian media, media research, educational broadcasting, the Nigerian media, public health in Nigeria and digital media, digital production, news coverage and production in the digital era, media law, standards and ethics in the digital era, broadcast presentation, broadcast management in the digital era, Nigerian communication systems, organizational communicational, history and structure of the media, decolonization in the digital space, print journalism in the digital era, broadcast production in the digital era.

The book is organized into eight sections, with twenty (20) chapters. The first section has five chapters that look at the general Nigerian media structure, nature, and practice. Section 2 has one chapter that extensively chronicles journalism in the digital era, while section 3 has five chapters that explain the processes of digitization, media production, presentation, and management in the digital era. In section 4, two chapters touch on Nigerianness in the digital space, and section 5 has one chapter that exposes how to communicate health in the Nigerian digital space. In section 6, the three chapters discuss educational broadcasting, media theory, research, and practice in the digital era. Under section 7, there are two chapters that focus entirely on sports communication, corporate communication, and robotics in Nigeria. Section 8 discusses various outlets for organizational communication in the Nigerian digital space.

Nigerian Media Industries in the Era of Globalization is a one-stop-shop for those interested in the growth and survival of the Nigerian and African media industries.

Acknowledgments

Acknowledging with complete details everyone who inspired, encouraged and assisted me in the conceptualization and completion of this book would not only be Herculean, but almost impossible. First, I am ever and highly grateful and indebted to God for giving me the idea to assemble these great people to contribute their ideas in a book form. A big thank you to Sydney Wedbush for her guidance and support.

Professor Chuka Onwumechili, a great academic mentor to me, played a pivotal role in making sure I came up with this book, even when I almost abandoned it. In fact, every upcoming researcher and academic needs a Professor Chuka kind of mentor! Professor Carolyn Byerly, my department chair in communication, culture and media studies, Howard University, Washington DC, USA, never failed to keep a check on me on the progress of this book. Dr. Abigail Ogwezzy, the first female professor of mass communication at the University of Lagos, Nigeria, made sure I selected the best hands in the industry to pen this down. She also persuaded me to see the need to leave my position as a Visiting Scholar at Howard University to the Mass Communication Department, University of Lagos in order to contribute my quota in strengthening the broadcast sequence in the department. It has paid off! For most of my colleagues at Howard University who believed in this project and accepted to be part of it, I say a huge thank you. With much gratitude, I acknowledge the support of the *Southern Examiner* for believing in this project and throwing their weight behind it.

I thank my dear mother Mrs. Mercy Samuel Akpan, who first sowed the seed of education in me. I also thank my dear wife, Dr. Maureen, and my children, Mmekan, Medara, and Imikan for encouraging me to put together this book in the manner they would permit me to have some time to do the writing and the editing of the texts.

Thank you all!

SECTION I

Nigerian Media Structure, Nature, and Practice

Chapter 1

Mediamorphosis of Contents

Past, Present, and Future Strategic Opportunities

Unwana Samuel Akpan

In my early years of broadcasting, media contents were produced and stored in reel-to-reel, and afterwards, storage moved from reel-to-reel to cassettes, from cassettes to CDs, from CDs to flash drives, and presently, from flash drives to web links. Therefore, in the last couple of decades, the media space in the developed countries of the world has witnessed massive digital disruptions that have raised the stakes in media practices and operations globally; and this is gradually spilling onto the media landscapes of the developing world, such as Nigeria. As a result of this digital disruption in the media terrain globally, media contents have evolved and metamorphosed to digital sizes fit for global consumption. This assertion collaborates with what Cosenza, Gavidia, and González-Avella (2020) say while citing Knut and Jacobsson (2002) that "to some extent, mainstream media adapt their contents to reflect the predominant tendencies, fashionable behavior, and cultural trends in the globalized society" (p. 3). Some other scholars have also agreed media contents have been altered by digitization, and in turn, the taste buds of media consumers have not remained the same (Scholte 2005; Maldonado 2017; Orsgerby 2020; Flew, and Iosifidis 2020).

Presently, we live in a world where these digital interruptions have obviously made the world a global village, as predicted by Marshall McLuhan decades ago (Mcluhan 1964). Some scholars have equally reiterated and echoed the fact that globalization has affected virtually every sector of human endeavor (Gaëtan 2012; Wilde 2019; Neto, Ishikawa, Groenli, Ghinea 2019). Though the world has never been static, right from the days of the

Wright Brothers, Thomas Alva Edison, Aristotle, and so forth, rather, it is a world that is characterized by innovations, inventions, concepts, continuous changes in conditions and trends making it a fast-changing environment in constant digital transitions. The times are not only changing, they are changing in an unbelievably rapid way and rate in all areas of human endeavors such as the media and the way the people are now consuming media contents. These changes have also affected the shades of media contents, the way it is gathered, packaged, disseminated, processed, and consumed, as well as affected the feedback process.

Recently, there are some scholarly works that are beginning to focus attention on how messages are now consumed by people digitally via the social media in Nigeria (Nyamnjoh 2004; Von 2004; Udoette 2004; Ekeanyanwu 2009; Ademola and Okumola 2013; Omoera and Ryanga 2017; Effiong 2018; Uche, Nwosu, Okezie, Nwabueze 2020; Nyiam 2020), but no work as at present dedicates its findings on how digitization and globalization would affect traditional media practices and operation in the country when Nigeria fully switches from the analog to digital media operations, especially in the broadcast industry; hence this paper. We presently live in an era where information dissemination, consumption, feedback, and reaction is at the speed of sound; and as a result, media messages are very competitive in order to attract, lure, gain, and sustain the vast emerging audiences' attention. Those responsible for packaging these messages should understand that over time, these media contents have evolved to meet the taste and the needs of the audience, hence the need to better understand how to package it to meet the needs of the audience. Content in the age of information and new media evolution come with evolving nascent pictures of media software complexities, challenges, and uncertainties. The convergent nature of the media fuels this sudden media evolution and revolution in the media arena, and the changes it brings are here to stay because it would entirely change media dynamics, matrix, numerical, concept, and operations forever. Any media faculty that is not ready to move with the Media Convergence tide would definitely be left behind and eventually die out. Major media players, especially media owners in Nigeria, media scholars, and even observers in the media industries in Africa have doubted or been pessimistic about such changes and their impact on media content, content consumption, and even the media business model. The late Professor Ritchard Tamba M'batyo once told us two decades ago at the University of Lagos, Nigeria, when he came for his Fulbright Scholarship that if the traditional print media (newspaper and magazine) fails to embrace the new media by migrating online and change the way they structure their content, that they would not survive the emerging technological storm that is coming to African countries. I vividly remembered that most professors of journalism then doubted him, but today, we know better. All evidence staring us right now in the face suggests that the Nigerian media industries can also embrace this media evolution, as there is an emerging wealth of opportunities oozing out from the evolving media revolution. His submission that day collaborated with the postulation of some other scholars (Mcluhan and Fiore 1967; Mcluhan and Fiore 1968; Von 2004; Aririguzoh 2013) who predicted the total death of some traditional media's chores, roles, and responsibilities.

THE EARLY DAYS OF AFRICAN MEDIA

With the exception of Nigeria, Zimbabwe, and Zambia, where electronic media (radio and television) was introduced by the British before independence, most of Sub-Saharan Africa established their first television stations after independence (Bourgault 1995; Akindes 2011). The introduction of radio and television in some parts of the British and French controlled territories in Africa was to provide information and entertainment to the British and French protectorates.

CONTENTS IN THE EARLY DAYS OF NIGERIAN MEDIA

Government control of radio and television in Nigeria, the Sub-Saharan, and Francophone Africa from inception was regimented and had some characteristic of an eagle eye on the media by the government (Bourgault 1995; Ba 1996; Hydén, Leslie, and Ogundimu 2002; Chalaby 2005; Uche, Nwosu, Okezie, Nwabueze 2020; Nyiam 2020). And as a result, media contents were tailored to suit and please the government of the day. Media contents had to be censored and must carry the bidding of the government because it was the government then who was empowered by the law to own broadcast stations. This is understandable because governments around the world always dread the power the broadcast media wields in terms of immediacy and mileage. Nyamnjoh (2005) points to the fact that France, Britain, and the US were the standard-setters and brand-bearers of the rest of the world's media, including Africa. Therefore, media content then had a foreign outlook and twist in terms of structure and layout. According to Akindes (2011); Omoera, and Ryanga (2017); and Effiong (2018), African media inherited characteristics from colonial media, such as language and organization. Moreover, as it is chronicled about many other countries, Francophone countries' first television broadcasters were controlled and directed by governments, hence their content (Akindes 2011; Ziegler and Asante 1992). No wonder Ba (1996) asserts that all Francophone televisions were regulated by structure and laws that were copied from France. Therefore, at the inception of the African media, government control was a common feature throughout Sub-Saharan and Francophone Africa and Nigeria was not left out, and as a result, content was structured and tailored to sing the praise of the government of the day.

TRANS-NATIONALISM AND MEDIA CONTENT

In many African countries such as Nigeria, the broadcast media contents were controlled and directed by governments (Ziegler and Asante 1992; Uche 1989). Government control over these media houses was unapologetically displayed in the news content and structure. Akindes (2011) citing Bourgault (1995) posits that African television in the 1970s served as the president's (or ruling party's) "personal address system" or as an inexpensive entertainment-provider. Tight government control of media structure and content in Sub-Saharan Francophone Africa lingered up to the late 1980s and early 1990s (Uche 1989). There was a sudden turn of events in the African media landscape in the early 1990s. There were several factors that necessitated the transformation of the African media landscape. The dynamics that changed the African media cloud from the authoritarian nature to the libertarian nature included the deployment of satellite broadcasting, changes in media regulation and laws, and the political democratization of Sub-Saharan Africa (Bourgault 1995; Ba 1996; Eribo and Jong-Ebot 1997; Hydén et al. 2002; Chalaby 2005). Myton, Teer-Tomaselli, and Tudesq (2005); Akindes (2011), "note that African space for transnational television broadcasters became open due to television technology, telecommunications, and information technology, coupled with the liberalization of media." When media laws in some parts of Africa were changed allowing private individuals to own radio and television stations, media contents changed. Though Akindes (2011) acknowledges that "new technologies' role in the change in the Sub-Saharan African media landscape is acknowledged, political democratization in the early 1990s is seen as the most influential." But it should be noted that people were no longer interested in the frequent lies that they were fed with in the states' owned media. This increased their taste and hunger for objective, unbiased and independent media content.

Major changes in media landscape across the African continent are often viewed from the angle of democratization perspective, but looking at it critically, the changes in media landscape in Sub-Saharan Africa were sparked up by technological changes in television broadcasting and the transformation of international media strategies. The satellite dishes were very common in most privileged homes in Africa. Ba (1996) confirmed that after the adoption of satellite television Africa grew exponentially media wise, just a few years after the technology's introduction. No wonder Paterson (1998, p. 547) mention that the merging of the French conglomerate Canal+ with South African Multichoice, and in partnership with Nethold, placed the group in a dominant position in Africa satellite broadcasting; and this further exposed the viewers to quality and the balanced media content they had been yearning for. South Africa's Multichoice and Africa TV are the two main suppliers of television packages to Anglophone Africa (Akindes 2011). Myton and Teer-Tomasell (2005) note that most of Multichoice and TV Africa program providers are outside Africa. Akindes (2011) in his narrative believes "since the time of Paterson's study of satellite television, broadcasting in Africa has continuously evolved over the years." Lenoble-Bart and Tudesq (2008) have pointed out the frequent changes taking place in the African media landscape due to Information and Communication Technology (ICT). In fact, the penetration of African television airwaves by foreign satellite television broadcasters such as Canal+, Multichoice, DSTV, and a host of local private television broadcasters emerged as a result of political democratization and broadcasting deregulation (Akindes 2011); and this changed the coloration of African media content.

MY THEORIZATION AND CONCEPTUALIZATION OF MEDIA CONTENTS

Prior to this time, the different segments of the African media were more analog in nature than digital. The operators in these sectors (broadcast, advertising, public relations, print, etc.) were mechanical in their day-to-day operations. But with the introduction of the internet in the African media space, it shaped and redefined the operations in these sectors; by that I mean the way things are done operationally. We were met with what I call "Media Fraternity," where a forum of the emerging media forced themselves into the sphere where the traditional media operate. In fact, the new and emerging media romance or fraternity with the traditional media brought some form of swiftness, speed, and ease to content gathering, packaging, and dissemination. When the old and the new media all digitally converged at one arena, media scholars call it Media Convergence (Hydén, Leslie, and Ogundimu 2002; Stöber 2004; Merlo 2008; Akindes 2011), which is the capacity to churn out shades of media channels via one digital platform. Therefore, this in turn technically creates a new media age where information is digitally gathered, packaged, and disseminated. However, what we must understand is that when all these shades of media channels (both traditional and new media) all converge via one digital platform for the purpose of sending out a message through any program genre (be it drama, magazine, documentary, feature, special package, montage, testimony, etc.), it has metamorphosed from Media Convergence to Media Fraternity because of the concept of "Program Specific." These channels can only converge, coexist, and remain in a state of inactivity, but when a producer or a presenter begins to deploy these various media channels for the production and dissemination of his message for a "Specific Program" concept, these channels move from the state of inactivity to a state of activity, and immediately the various media become active and there is a "fraternity" ongoing; all deployed for just one purpose, and that is for the success of the program. This entails that this program on the traditional media channel would be made available via all the social media platforms. For example, if there is a documentary program going on air, the social media handle of the station airing the documentary would be used to promote the program and as well receive feedback. At this level, they do not only coexist, they have consummated this coexistence. That is when messages start coming in via various social media handles, and the various social media handles begin to project and feature the station's ongoing documentary program via their handles. In other words, fraternity happens when broadcast channels such as radio, television and the internet all come together to distribute contents via different platforms for the purpose of the singularity of program concept reaching everyone on these platforms. This is the obvious reason media content is becoming and would continue to become increasingly digitalized. Regardless of whatever the nature of the signal, it can all become undifferentiated bits of data converged onto the same platform for media fraternity. When Nigeria finally migrates to the digital space, no major player in the various media industries would escape it, as this digital trend is bringing sweeping changes and unprecedented levels of complexity and technicalities to the current media business and operation across Africa.

EXPLORING THE TRADITIONAL
MEDIA CONTENT MODEL

The traditional media content has, over the years in Africa, been hinged on media owners acting as a middleman or conduit providing the information needs of content consumers via their traditional medium, which is the TV or radio. Second, consumers stay glued to these contents with no option or alternative. But presently, all that has changed because content consumers can generate their contents, upload it online, gather huge followers that can translate into commercial attention for companies to approach these content providers for access to advertise their goods and services. So, the tide has changed, and media owners need to sit up in order not to go out of business. This has helped in political and social activism. A classic example is the EndSars protest that greeted the streets of Nigeria where the youths took to the streets to demand reforms in policing due to police brutality. These events were streamed live on several social media platforms and everyone around the world watched it live. There was no more waiting for the traditional media like the television and radio to capture the moments.

THE DECLINE OF THE TRADITIONAL CONTENT MODEL

Before media convergence or my "media fraternity theory" ever showed up at the media arena, the taste buds of content consumers had been developed to a high taste, and this brought about the slow decline of content interest because some African media consumers who have access to the Western media or once lived in the West were constantly yearning for a different dose of what is offered them down here in Africa. A critical review and analysis of the factors leading to this decline points to two key factors, which include an oversupply and commoditization, politicization, and commercialization of flagship media content such as major news bulletins, and a decline of advertising effectiveness. In Nigeria, especially in the 1960s and 1970s, consumers had typically between one and six television channels which were state owned that carried out government propaganda; today, the average Nigerian household has over four hundred TV channels (both cable, satellite, and terrestrial), numerous radio channels, and several internet domains (NBC 2022). As a result, competition for the attention of the content consumer is fierce, margins are getting increasingly squeezed, and it is more difficult to secure a sizable number of audience base looking at the fierceness of the present media battleground. The internet has further accelerated the commoditization of media content, by granting consumers 24/7 free access to up-to-date online media content. This clearly undermines part of the revenue drive of business owners, also disrupts the flow chart of media content models, and as a result, many media channels are struggling to discover new viable revenue streams so as to continue to remain in business.

TRADITIONAL ADVERTISING HEADING DOWN SOUTH

In those days, traditional media channel owners were those who owned the audience (I mean media content consumers) and sold the same to advertisers. Media owners in those days boasted to advertisers their mileage and the vastness of their audience base. In this case, boasting of owning such a magnitude of advertising audience would be obviously doubtful because the audiences have been segmented and shared among the social media audiences who stay glued to it 24/7. When full digital migration is achieved in Africa, media owners must watch out for two dominant trends that would affect their advertising effectiveness and drive. The first trend that would affect advertising effectiveness and flow would be audience sharing and fragmentation. The traditional media owners can creatively hunt back and gather their audience by launching their platform online via the various social media platforms. The more gigantic the audience base and mileage, the more exorbitant the premium paid for the media space. For instance, prime-time spots on television typically would cost so much more than daytime or nighttime spots. As online media gets attractive and more participatory, it would create new media opportunities that would result in a large audience size declining, and flipping through the grip of the traditional media, because the taste buds of content consumers are becoming digitized, and this would pose a challenge for media owners. For the advertiser, this means that it would be more difficult to reach a specific audience, especially in the traditional media. For the media owner, it would pose a challenge for advertising revenue, and prime-time or premium charges might be affected as well, which in turn reduces the volume of revenues for these stations. The second factor that would affect advertisers is that they would tend to patronize social media advertising massively through different media vehicles, such as smartphones, digital street billboards among others because a vast chunk of the audience live online these days. The purpose of all of these is so they can massively reach out to different audiences via different social media platforms.

THE CONVERGENCE PART OF THE MEDIA: HAS IT TRULY COME TO STAY?

Looking at Marshall Mcluhan's assertion that the world would one day become a global village in the manner messages are sent, distributed, and consumed, (Mcluhan 1964), Thorstein Veblen's (1898) postulation of technology determinism, and Stöber's (2004) theory of media evolution, one may safely say that technological innovation would continue to drive media evolution such as we have seen in Media Convergence and Media Fraternity. Stöber theorizes three cycles of development in media: invention, innovation, and institutionalization. Also, Wilde (2019) is of the view that the media would continue to evolve as long as there is innovation in digital conception. In fact, media contents and media operations would continually witness unfathomable evolution as long as there is room for improvement, and as long as humans can think.

INVENTION

In the case of media convergence and media fraternity, the invention is the ability to convert differentiated bits of analog data (such as voice, text, audio or visual) to undifferentiated bits of digital data for either a singularity or plurality of media purposes. In applying invention to media convergence or media fraternity, it is evident that this phase is complete, as it has been possible to digitalize voice, text, audio, or visual data, and even move social media platforms into traditional media sets such as the television and smartphones.

INNOVATION

The innovation phase helps the digital platforms to fit into traditional media, maybe for family relaxation. Today, you can watch Netflix on your television set if it is a smart TV. In the case of media convergence or media fraternity, this is the ability to distribute and consume different media types, whether radio, TV, or internet through the same platform. This is a phase that makes it possible for media consumers to receive digitized media data from platforms such as cable or the internet.

INSTITUTIONALIZATION

The Nigerian media industry is now moving towards the institutionalization phase, which is defined as the adaptation to the emerging media environment and realities, so as to create a new media system, atmosphere and autonomy. Stöber (2004) spells out the four factors of change that occur simultaneously to shape a new system entity or atmosphere: technology, cultural, legal/political, and economic. Recently, the Nigerian government banned the use of Twitter when it suspected that it could be used against the government. Though the suspension has been lifted; however, an institutionalized statement was made as a result of the ban. That is why Stöber suggests that it is the culmination of these factors that will shape the media model. These four institutionalization factors may be applied to the media industry to identify the degree of change. The Nigerian media industries are undergoing an institutionalization phase, with technological, cultural, and political factors already in motion, the culmination of these will in turn shape the media terrain in Nigeria and Africa.

OPPORTUNITIES FOR MEDIA CONTENT CREATORS

Media convergence, media fraternity, and the changes affecting media content have quite a number of significant strategic implications especially for media owners. These strategic implications are wrapped up in globalization, and are media industry-inspired trends, consumer-inspired trends, and advertiser-inspired trends, and the unfolding opportunities and potentials that are enveloped in each of them for media content creators.

GLOBALIZATION

Cosenza, Gavidia and González-Avella (2020) posit that "in a social context, globalization implies increasing interconnectivity among people: any agent may interact with any other in a social system" (p. 4). It is media convergence that births globalization and the convergence of these media contents depends heavily on the internet to spread these messages via the different digital channels. It is the internet that drives the digital media. In fact, the soul of digital media is the internet. As the internet is globally opened and offers enormous open access and opportunities to most continental markets such as in Africa, media convergence will predictably become a global phenomenon. Globalization brings a wealth of exciting opportunities. The internet gets people excited as they surf the net, as a result, new markets can be found, firms can get closer to customers and have direct contact with them, unlike then where the traditional media owner was the middleman that connects the consumers with firms, and with this new turn of event, trade can be executed electronically in an instant digital arena. Nevertheless, there are some limitations to the impact of globalization. Although the internet overcomes most barriers to entry, inevitably there will be issues of cultural, economic, technical, and political barriers. For example, internet penetration might face some strong opposition in some African communities such as Nigeria where cultural and religious practices are quite vocal.

CONSUMER TRENDS AND NEW VISTAS

As the digital space is poised to usher in new dimensions of opportunities for media owners, it would equally foil layers of opportunities for media content consumers. Empirically, during the new media age that would sweep across Africa, consumers would be empowered to choose their own content as it is currently happening in the developed world, and decide when and where they want it, often free of charge and free of advertising, except for the data. This development would mean that some contents can teach consumers how to source, develop, package, and air their content to the outside world, thereby promoting globalization.

This reveals that the current customer trends and needs would be fundamentally and digitally shifted or evolved. There are five important trends in this respect as it affects content: the democratization of content, user-generated content, personalization of schedules, social networking, and divergence of consumer groups.

DEMOCRATIZATION OF CONTENT

Nowadays, media convergence has empowered content consumers to upload the contents of their choice, of whatever form or taste on the internet by a click of the button for public access and consumption. But the big question facing the industry today is whether the sharing of content is done professionally and ethically. This is arguably the single largest threat to the media industry world over. These days people depend on bloggers for breaking news in Africa, and this trend would further become a challenge for traditional media owners in Africa. According to a 2006 survey, 100 million video clips are viewed daily on YouTube, with an additional 65,000 new videos being uploaded every 24 hours (USA Today 2006). The site has hosted almost over 20 million visitors each month. In the UK, it already had a 64 percent share of the online video market. This should give traditional media owners something to think about in Nigeria.

CONSUMER-GENERATED CONTENT

Obviously, media convergence has massively equipped content consumers to produce and disseminate their own created contents via the new various channels of communication which are participatory in nature. These consumers have personal social media handles and they can upload whatever content (at any cost) they desire at no cost. Production costs are almost not there, and all thanks to digitalization, and the internet becomes a readily available source where these self-generated contents can be dumped. Overtime, user-generated content has attracted a lot of concern, with questions ranging from quality, standards, ethics, and so forth. Though there are fears that user-generated content in the form of citizen and parasitic journalism could render news sites useless. Although this may be overstating the matter, user-generated content does have a role to play in the new media landscape in Nigeria, which creates both challenges and opportunities because the audiences now have access to the digital space where before now, the traditional media could not avail these content users such opportunity. User-generated content gives mileage, scope, creativity, and option for co-creation in the form of blogging, and a lot of people now own a YouTube channel where they can generate and upload their self-generated contents for public consumption.

ACCESS AND STORAGE OF CONTENT

It is now possible for content consumers to access and store their desired contents in their gadgets in order to watch what they want and when they want it, via on-demand content or search content. Personal video recorders (PVRs) have further aided content consumers to personalize their schedules by recording large quantities of content and enabling consumers to skip over advertising. Therefore, traditional media owners in Africa must be consumer-centric.

SOCIAL NETWORKING AND VIRTUAL REALITY

In those days, traditional media outlets used to connect people socially through their programs, but these days, social media connects people more easily than you can imagine because media convergence aids participation. Attractive content can easily connect people, especially attractive pictures of people on Instagram.

OTHERNESS OF CONSUMER GROUPS

A new tribe of media consumers is emerging, composed of media literate and tech savvy consumers who can create and produce media contents competitively with the professional media man. This new tribe of media consumers can even train veteran journalists on digital gadget handling. Most times, we underestimate them. These dudes can help traditional media handlers enrich the quality of their programs digitally.

WHERE CONTENT IS FOUND THESE DAYS

It is obvious that contents now live online. Most pictures, images, videos, and other documents are now downloaded online via web cloud and other applications for safe storage. Members of the public can now access these materials. Producers can obtain these media contents online for their production; whereas in those days producers were traveling thousands of miles to access materials for their production.

WHERE MEDIA CONTENT CONSUMERS LIVE THESE DAYS

They don't live in houses anymore; they live on the internet, buy on the internet, and depend online for information. Therefore, Nigerian media owners must make up their minds for the digital shift in order to meet their audience at that level. That is the reason television and radio programs should be downloaded online as a form of podcast. These audience members can take their programs and share it on their social media handles for wider reach.

HOW MEDIA CONTENTS ARE CONSUMED THESE DAYS

Media contents are consumed digitally online. These days, we read newspapers online and watch our favorite ad online too. One can as well stay in the comfort of his home in Washington, DC, and watch a television station in Africa. Contents have squeezed into our smartphones. It can also be stored, retrieved, and viewed digitally with convenience at any given time.

HOW MEDIA CONTENT CONSUMERS PREFER THEIR CONTENT

Media content consumers now prefer their contents to be smart, sassy, and swift, and these qualities can only be gotten when contents go through digital production. That is why digital media contents are sharp, clear, smarty, and sassy these days compared to the analog contents.

CONCLUSION

Very soon, a digital tsunami is sweeping through the African media landscape and Nigeria will not escape it. The old would soon give way to new. It is a new dawn in the media world globally. It is a new dawn of media complexities, uncertainties, and opportunities, especially for traditional media owners in

Nigeria who have made up their mind to remain in business. The convergent nature of today's media is steering the technological change and growth in the industry, and the change will prove tremendous, gratifying, and irreversible. The invention and innovation phases of the transition are complete in other parts of the world, but just trickling into Africa. In other climes, the digital space is in the institutionalization phase. Growth along cultural, political, and technological lines are happening gradually, thereby creating lasting changes. Media owners should accept these technological changes, for there is a massive wealth of new vistas that would be thrown up from the new digital space. The traditional media model is almost gone and forgotten. Media owners in Nigeria need to fashion out a relevant strategy that would enhance their capabilities and capacity to cope in the digital environment. This would help them still retain their audiences who have migrated to the digital space. However, the environment is changing. The taxonomy of the traditional media globally is changing, its boundaries are being redefined, and the value chain is declining. Media owners will need to embrace and adapt to the change by designing relevant and effective strategies that can make them stand the taste of time in the digital era; because media convergence has equipped content consumers, who now can upload content, make money from it, generate followership from the content, and can select what to access online.

REFERENCES

Ademola, G. O. and Okumola, R. A. 2013. "People, Culture and Mass Media of Agents of Cultural Imperiation." *Covenant University Journals of Politics and International Affairs* (CUJPA), 1, 2.

Akindes, G. 2011. "Football bars: Urban sub-Saharan Africa's trans-local 'stadiums.'" *The International Journal of the History of Sport,* 28 (15): 2176–2190.

Aririguzoh, S. 2013. "Human integration in globalization: The communication imperative." *Nigerian Journal of Social Sciences.* (9): 118–141.

Ba, A. 1996. *Télévisions, paraboles et démocratiesen Afrique noire.* Paris: L'Harmattan.

Bourgault, L. M. 1995. *Mass media in Sub-Saharan Africa.* Bloomington, IN: Indiana University Press.

Chalaby, J. K. 2005. *Transnational television worldwide: Towards a new media order.* London; New York: I. B. Tauris; Palgrave Macmillan.

Cosenza, M., Gavidia, M., and González-Avella, J. 2020. "Against mass media trends: Minority growth in cultural globalization." *Plos Digital Health.* Accessed January 23, 2022. https://doi.org/10.1371/journal.pone.0230923.

Eastman, S. T. and Ferguson, D. A. 2009. *Media Programming, Strategies and Practice.* USA: Thomson Wadsworth.

Effiong, C. 2018. "Globilization, social media and imperatives in the promotion of Nigerian cultural values." *Journal of New Media and Mass Communication* (5): 1.

Ekeanyanwu, N. 2009. "Cultural implications of ICTs and globalization in the Nigerian society." *Journal of Communication and Media Research* (1): 14–29

Eribo, F., and Jong-Ebot, W. 1997. *Press freedom and communication in Africa.* Trenton, NJ: Africa World Press.

Flew, T. and Iosifidis, P. 2020. "Populism, globalisation and social media." *International Communication Gazette.* 82 (1): 7–25. Accessed January 23, 2022. DOI: https://doi.org/10.1177/1748048519880721.

Gaëtan T. 2012. "From Marshall McLuhan to Harold Innis, or from the global village to the world empire." *Canadian Journal of Communication* (37) 4.

Hydén, G., Leslie, M., and Ogundimu, F. F. 2002. *Media and democracy in Africa.* New Brunswick, NJ: Transaction Publishers.

Kelvin, W. 2003. *Understanding Media Theory.* London: Hodder Arnold Publications, 256.

Knut, A. and Jacobsson, S. 2002. "Political media contests and confirmatory bias." Research Papers in Economics, Department of Economics, Stockholm University.

Lenoble-Bart, A. and Tudesq, A. 2008. *Connaître les médiasd'Afriquesubsaharienne - problématiques, sources et resources.* Paris: Karthala.

Maldonado, M. A. 2017. *Rethinking populism in the digital age: Social networks, political affects and post-truth democracies.* Congreso AECPA, Santiago de Compostela.

McCavit, W. E. and Pringle, P. K. 1986. *Electronic media management.* USA: Butterworth Publishers.

Mcluhan, Marshall. 1964. *Understanding media: The extensions of man.* New York: McGraw-Hill.

Mcluhan, Marshall. 1969. *The mechanical bride: Folklore of industrial man.* Boston: Beacon Press (originally published in 1951).

Mcluhan, Marshall, and Fiore, Quentin. 1967. *The medium is the massage: An inventory of effects.* New York: Bantam Books.

Mcluhan, Marshall and Fiore, Quentin. 1968. *War and peace in the global village.* New York: Bantam Books.

McQuail, D. 2010. *McQuail's communication theory.* London: Sage Publications Ltd.

Merlo, O. 2008. "Media convergence and the evolving media business model: an overview and strategic opportunities." *The Marketing Review* 8 (3): 237–254. Accessed January 23, 2022. DOI: 10.1362/146934708X337663, https://www.researchgate.net/publication/233514874.

Merril, J. 2006. "Global Elite: A newspaper community reason in world media," Special. *Gunnet Centre Journal* 4 (4): 93.

Myton, G., Teer-Tomaselli, R., and Tudesq, A. 2005. "Transnational television in sub-Saharan Africa." In Chalaby, J. (ed.), *Transnational Television Worldwide: Towards a New Media Order*, 96–127. London: I. B. Tauris.

NBC. 2022. National Broadcasting Commission Newsletter.

Neto, B., Ishikawa, E., Groenli, T., and Ghinea, G. 2019. "Newsroom 3.0: Managing Technological and Media Convergence in Contemporary Newsrooms." A paper presented at the Proceedings of the 52nd Hawaii International Conference on System Sciences.

Nyamnjoh, F. B. 2005. *Africa's media, democracy, and the politics of belonging.* London; New York: Zed Books; Pretoria; New York: Unisa Press; Palgrave Macmillan.

Nyamnjoh, J. 2004. "Children: Media and globalization. A Research Agenda for Africa." In UNESCO Youth Media and Globalization.

Nyiam, D. 2020. "Globalization and the Media." *An Interdisciplinary Journal of Human Theory and Praxis* (3): 1.

Omoera, O. and Ryanga, H. 2017. "Social media and the propagation of violence against women." *Nigerian Theatre Journal* 17 (1): 38–49.

Orsgerby, B. 2020. *Youth culture and the media: Global perspective.* London: Routledge.

Paterson, C. A. 1998. "Reform or re-colonisation? The overhaul of African television." *Social Scientist* 17 (11/12): 99–109.

Scholte, J. 2005. *Globalization: A critical Introduction,* Basingstoke: Palgrave Macmillan.

Schramm, W. and Porters, E. 1982. *Men, women, messages and media: Understanding human communication.* New York: Harper and Row Publishers, 278.

Sparks, C. 2007. *Globalization, development and the mass media.* London: SAGE, 264.

Sterin, J. C. 2012. *Mass media evolution.* Boston: Allyn and Bacon.

Stöber, R. 2004. "What media evolution is: A theoretical approach to the history of new media." *European Journal of Communication* 19 (4): 483–505.

Tremblay, G. 2012. "From Marshall McLuhan to Harold Innis, or From the Global Village to the World Empire." *Canadian Journal of Communication* (37): 4.

Uche, L. 1989. *Mass media, people, and politics in Nigeria.* Accessed January 23, 2022. Books.google.com.

Uche, U., Nwosu, C., Okezie, V., Nwabueze, U. 2020. "Digital Media, Globalization and Impact on Indigenous Values and Communication." *Research Journal of Mass Communication and Information Technology,* (6), 2.

Udoakah, N. 2014. *Government and the media in Nigeria* (3rd. ed.). Ibadan: Stirling–Horden Publisher, Ltd., p. 125.

Udoette, D., 2004. *Globalization and the mission of the Church. Globalization: Implications for Africa* (NS), edited by Kekong Bisong, pp: 1–34. Enugu: SNAAP Press.

USA Today. 2006. YouTube serves up 100 million videos a day online. USA Today, July 16. Accessed July 5, 2021. http://www.usatoday.com/tech/new/2006-07-16 -youtube-views_x.htm.

Veblen, T. 1898. "Why is economics not an evolutionary science?" *The Quarterly Oxford Journal of Economics* 12 (4): 373–97.

Vivian, J. 2009. *The media of mass communication, Ninth Edition.* Boston (USA): Pearson Education Inc.

Von, Feltizena. 2004. "Children, Young people and Media Globalization." Science, Coordinator of UNESCO International Clearing House on children Youth and Media.

Wilde, Lukas R. A. 2019. "Recontextualizing Characters. Media Convergence and Pre-/Meta-Narrative Character Circulation." In: IMAGE. *Zeitschrift für interdisziplinäre Bildwissenschaft. Special Issue* 29 (15): 1, 3–21. Accessed July 5, 2021. DOI: https://doi.org/10.25969/mediarep/16391.

Wright, C. 1986. *Mass communication: A sociological perspective.* New York: Random House, p. 236.

Ziegler, D. and Asante, M. K. 1992. *Thunder and silence: The mass media in Africa.* Trenton, NJ: Africa World Press.

Chapter 2

The Structure and Nature of the Nigerian Media Industry

Ngozi Okpara

Media in traditional African society predates most modern African states. Apart from Liberia, most African states gained their independence after World War II (WWII) with Libya, Sudan, Morocco, Tunisia, Ghana, Cameroon, Senegal, Togo, Mali, Madagascar, Congo (Kinshasa), and Nigeria among the earliest to be free from colonialism. This marked their formal beginning as independent countries. In Nigeria for instance, the first newspaper, *Iwe Irohin Fun Awon Ara Egba ati Yoruba*, was published by Rev. Henry Townsend in 1859, over a century before Nigeria gained her independence in 1960. From the proper conceptualization of a newspaper which is a publication published either daily or weekly, *Kano Chronicle* has no record of being published as a daily or weekly publication and so cannot be said to be the first newspaper in Nigeria. Specifically, *Kano Chronicle* details the account of emirs that have governed the city of Kano since inception. Based on this, I do not think both pieces of writing can be compared. In Ghana, the first newspaper, *The Gold Coast Gazette*, was published by Sir Charles McCarthy, the governor of the British Gold Coast settlements in 1822, 135 years before Ghana's independence in 1957 (Davor 2015). In Morocco, the first newspaper, *African Liberal*, was published in 1820, 136 years before the country gained independence in 1956 (Zaghlami 2016). This shows that across the African continent, media existed before the emergence of many nations. It must also be noted that the earliest newspapers were used to propagate religious agendas (Nyamnjoh 2005).

In the mid-twentieth century, politically conscious media emerged with the aim of putting an end to colonialism. The print media was instrumental in this era because of the development of the printing press on the continent.

Print medium such as Herbert Macaulay's *Lagos Daily* Newspaper, Nnamdi Azikiwe's *West African Pilot*, Kwame Nkrumah's *Ashanti Pioneer*, among others, across the continent were at the forefront of the struggle against colonialism in their respective countries (Davor 2015). According to Gadzekpo (2008), the colonial media was majorly geared to achieve political ends. For instance, *West African Pilot*, *Lagos Daily News*, and Western Nigerian Television (WNTV) in Nigeria were used by Nnamdi Azikiwe, Herbert Macaulay, and Obafemi Awolowo, respectively, to propagate their political interests, forging a union between politics and the press (Omoera 2014; Ikiebe 2015).

A significant characteristic of the media environment under this era is the repressive policies enacted by the colonial administrators to curb the spread of indigenous media and control public access to information. Nyamnjoh (2005) revealed that media in both French and British colonies suffered restrictive laws that prevented the publication and distribution of newspapers in any parts of the colonies. Further, it was disclosed that "economic regulations were imposed that made it very difficult for Africans to import newsprint and other technological and/or structural necessities for building an indigenous mass media that challenged the rule of major colonial powers" (Nyamnjoh 2005: online). As a result, Africans were made to depend on foreign media who used the platform to propagate the interest of their national governments.

Following the independence of African states after WWII, it is ironic to realize that leaders of African states adopted the oppressive style of the colonial powers in their relationship with the media. Okwuchukwu (2014) averred that successive governments in Nigeria, having the full knowledge of the power of the media, chose to adopt the repressive colonial style in their relationship with the media. Kintz (2007) compared the structure of the colonial and postcolonial media in West African countries and found that there was no difference as both media environments operated under a centralized structure. It was revealed that new African governments, like their colonial predecessors, operate a centralized media structure in order to maintain a grip on the media. In Nigeria, the governments—through regulatory agencies and decrees—gagged the media and restricted its freedom. In South Africa, it was reported that the African National Congress (ANC), following the transition to democratic government in 1994, retained the apartheid media laws which placed restrictions on media reportage of issues, on grounds of national interest (Atal 2017).

Some media scholars have argued that the tight-fisted nature of African governments on the media in Africa is a result of over-reliance on government subvention and funding (Ikiebe 2015; Okwuchukwu 2014; Prat and Strömberg 2013). It is understandable that the media industry in Africa as well as around the world is capital-driven. It is an industry with low capital investment and unattractive to investors (Ikiebe 2015). Even government-controlled media outlets are not absolved from the malaise of poor funding. Financial inadequacy of the media forged an unwanted dependence on government and business owners for advertisement and funding. Agbaje (1992) cited in Oso (2012) stated that:

> Apart from the struggle for political power among the political elite, elements in the civil society are easily prone to incorporation because of their dependence on the state for contracts, appointments or in popular parlance "connection" which may include offer of political covering or protection for businesses and investments. Such dependence readily makes the press penetrable to state interference which may compromise its autonomy and freedom. (p. 34)

Omu (2000) noted that governments deliberately withhold their advertisements from media outlets that fail to promote their interests. On the other hand, Okwuchukwu (2014) revealed that private businesspersons would prefer to advertise on private media outlets with nationalistic outlooks. This form of media dependence on government and business owners has threatened media autonomy on the African continent. It is simply a case of *"He, who plays the piper, dictates the tune."* In Ikiebe's (2015) thesis, it was revealed that lack of sound business models and the inability to appropriately adapt technology are responsible for the perennial clinging by the media to the government.

The evolution of media technology has further put a rest to the debate concerning government control on the media. The proliferation of mobile communication devices, social media platforms, and the rapid penetration of internet technology on the African continent have further democratized access and ownership of media platforms. Realizing the impact of technology-aided media platforms and the speed at which information is disseminated, governments in various African countries are moving towards regulating the social media space.

In view of the aforementioned, it is evident that the media systems across the African continent share similar patterns associated with the colonial media. As a result, this chapter will use the Nigerian media industry as a reference for the media industry across the African continent. It will also discuss the general structure and nature of the media industry in Nigeria, highlighting funding, federal and state government-controlled media, liberalism as well as digitalization and globalization.

GENERAL STRUCTURE AND NATURE OF
THE MEDIA INDUSTRY IN NIGERIA

In discussing the structure of the media industry in Nigeria, emphasis will be placed on ownership and control of the media. The ownership structure in the Nigerian media can be categorized into government ownership and private ownership structures (Okoro 2012). Government-owned media structures are often under the control of the government and protect the interest of the government in power. Under this ownership structure, the laws that apply to the civil service regulate the conduct of practitioners. Furthermore, Iredia (2016) identified the uncontrolled power of the office of the Minister of Information, citing the example of the Nigerian Television Authority (NTA), as a negative influence because the medium is funded by public tax. Iredia stated that:

> Not many are aware that the Information Minister is empowered by law to give directives to the NTA to which it must comply. As a result, some ministers give directives that suit their political parties notwithstanding that the directives are not in the interest of the public (Iredia 2016: Vanguard online published March 27, 2016).

Government-owned media outlets are bedeviled by the perennial problem of favoritism and nepotism that characterize civil service. These falter its ability to fulfill its public mandate of promoting ethical reportage on the job. Chukwu (2015) revealed that in government-owned media, professionalism is relegated and sacrificed for sycophancy in the appointment of persons to positions of authority. According to Tony Iredia, former director general of NTA, a government-owned television channel in Nigeria is handicapped by unprofessional and unqualified personnel recommended by figures in both executive and legislative arms of government (Iredia 2016).

In the private ownership structure, indigenous entrepreneurs are the financiers of media business. Unlike government-owned media characterized by gross inefficiencies, Azubuike and Ikiriko (2019) averred that privately owned media is built for efficiency and modeled to achieve the objectives of its proprietors. In view of this, the proprietor's motive might be for profit like other entrepreneurs or a higher purpose.

Private ownership of the broadcast media in Nigeria increased sporadically following the enactment of the deregulation policy in 1992. The deregulation policy de-monopolized government ownership of the media and allowed private involvement in broadcast media (Kawonise 2012). As a result, between 1992 and 1997, broadcast stations such as African Independent Television (AIT), Channels Television, Minaj Broadcast International (MBI), DBN, Clapperboard, and Muri International Television (MITV) were licensed to broadcast. Prior to this era, ownership and control of broadcast media in Nigeria were vested in the federal and state governments (Chukwu 2015). For a while, the seeming marriage between media and politics was disbanded as private business-minded entrepreneurs approached media as a profit-making venture.

Following the transition to democratic practice in 1999, private media ownership in Nigeria returned to its early days as political actors took turns in establishing media outlets that pursued their political ideologies. The proprietors of popular media outlets are big wigs of both the ruling and opposition parties in Nigeria respectively. Table 1 shows the known political affiliations of media proprietors in the current democratic dispensation.

In view of the rekindled partisan structure of the Nigerian media, Oso (2012) averred that ownership of media outlets is a strategic pursuit by politicians to promote and articulate political concepts and ideologies. Oso further noted that the control for state power under the present democratic structure has been so intense that it calls for the "control of the means of shaping popular consciousness, social reality, primarily the mass media becomes crucial under this situation" (Oso 2012, p. 34).

Table 2.1. Political affiliations of media proprietors in the current democratic dispensation. *Source*: Author, 2020.

Proprietors	Media organizations	Political party affiliations
Raymond Dokpesi	Raypower and Africa Independent Television (AIT)	People's Democratic Party (PDP)
Ben Murray Bruce	Silverbird TV and Rythm FM	People's Democratic Party (PDP)
Mike Ajegbo	Minaj TV and Radio	People's Democratic Party (PDP)
Bola Tinubu	*The Nation* Newspaper, Max FM, Adaba FM, and TVC	All Progressives' Congress (APC)
Gbenga Daniel	*Compass* Newspaper	All Progressives' Congress (APC)
Orji UzorKalu	*The Sun* and *New Telegraph* Newspapers	All Progressives' Congress (APC)
James Ibori	*Independent* Newspaper	People's Democratic Party (PDP)
Jimoh Ibrahim	*News Watch* and *National Mirror*	All Progressives' Congress (APC)
Sam Nda-Isaiah (late)	*Leadership* Newspaper	All Progressives' Congress (APC)
Mr. Nduka Obaigbena	*This Day Newspaper, Arise TV*	People's Democratic Party (PDP)

FUNDING OF MEDIA INDUSTRY AND EFFECTS

Funding is an important matter upon which the sustainability and development of the media industry depends. Therefore, sufficient funding and access to resources should be the central goal of the regulatory framework for media. A number of media houses depend primarily on the goodwill of host communities or civil society organizations in order to establish, run, and sustain their media stations. It has, however, been discovered over time that the sustainability of the media industry is a function of the availability of diverse sources of funding for media companies and personnel (UNESCO 2017). In order to ensure that media companies in Africa serve their communities and audience effectively, the allocation of public funds to them must be non-discriminatory, clear, and impartial. This type of funding will go a long way in ensuring the growth and development of the media industry instead of trying to influence its operations. This reflects the need of the media industry for an independent body that can oversee its funding to prevent political pressure and arm-twisting, as it is in its license-allocation process.

According to Padania (2018), there are two approaches to the funding of the media industry. The first is the intrinsic approach which views that media are a public good, an end in themselves and as such requires support, funding, or investment. This approach is justified on the premise of the gains the media brings to the society at large. In this approach, supporters tend to give unrestricted funding to companies in sectors that they believe will contribute to the society's infrastructure and enabling environment such as the media. This category of funders respect editorial independence and do not require special access. The second approach is an instrumental approach in which the media is viewed as a means to an end. This perspective portrays the media as an important and trusted vehicle for thematic messages like the investigation and exposure of corruption in the society. This approach is mostly used by funders who have ulterior goals to which the media can contribute. They tend to use the media as a tool to foster and improve their mission. Such funders include civil society organizations. For them, the media is a tool for development.

TYPES OF PUBLIC FUNDING

According to Schweizer, Puppis, Künzler, and Studer (2014), there are different types of funding for the media industry such as direct public funding, direct government grant, funding from foreign sources, indirect funding, and fee waivers. However, the types of funding for the media industry are usually described as direct or indirect and at other times described as general or selective. The direct funding includes payments to the media companies while the indirect includes measures that create a satisfactory economic situation for media companies. Monetary funding for the media industry raises the fear of political or government influence. However, it is also important to note that government support for the media does not automatically mean there would be or not be government interference.

DIRECT PUBLIC FUNDING

It is expedient for media companies to have access to private sources of funding from commercial and voluntary contributions. It is utterly difficult for media companies to only survive on these sources of funding. Public funding must be done in a fair and impartial manner that must be supervised by an independent body which is able to make decisions in a totally impartial manner that accounts for editorial independence that is void of political influences. The application process for funding must be properly crafted to consider the developmental state of the media industry. The funding should be allocated on the premise of clear, preestablished public interest. The criteria must be chosen based on the existing situation and priority needs of the sector.

DIRECT GOVERNMENT GRANT

In countries that have dedicated funds to support the media industry, funding can be provided via a direct government grant, but they usually carry an attachment of ongoing political support. Funding can also come as cross-subsidies from commercial broadcasters. This can be worked by using levies paid by commercial broadcasters. This sort of direct funding is better and not directly dependent on political influence like government grants.

FUNDING FROM FOREIGN SOURCES

Another type of income channel for the media industry is foreign funding from both mutual and multifaceted sources. Such sources include bodies like UNESCO and the World Bank; it is important for media companies to have access to these sources. Consequently, media industry funding is supposed to be within the confines of a national space, this thus means there is a need to place some limits or conditions on foreign funding. These kinds of limits are deemed necessary to protect independence from cultural and religious biases.

INDIRECT FUNDING AND FEE WAIVERS

A no-waiver fee free pass for media houses can be an indirect fund source. In many African countries, the several fees imposed on media companies for license application, annual spectrum usage, among others, can be waived or significantly reduced. Another way of reducing expenditures of media houses is to either waive or reduce taxes on equipment procurement. Indirect subsidies for the media industry are widespread. The most frequent and, from a financial point of view, most important media support instruments are tax breaks. Other instruments used to indirectly support the media industry are subsidized tariffs for telecommunications, electricity, paper, or transport. Some other ways to indirectly fund the media industry include subsidies for news agencies, journalism schools, journalism research, reading promotion, or professional associations.

ERA OF FEDERAL GOVERNMENT-CONTROLLED MEDIA

Shortly after independence, Nigeria experienced intense tribal tensions and violence. This led to the invasion of the political space by the military. Subsequently, the nation experienced the first military coup which also led to a three-year civil war with the eastern region attempting to secede from the country. At the end of the war, the military government headed by General Yakubu Gowon launched a national reunification program called "Go on with One Nigeria" (Tar Tsaaior 2015, p. 15). The program was aimed at promoting national unity and identity through the media. This placed a ban on the regional entities from owning media broadcast stations. In its stead, the government established the Nigerian Television Authority (NTA), Federal Radio Corporation of Nigeria (FRCN), and the News Agency of Nigeria (NAN)—a news wire service with an editorial mandate to defend the honor of the federal government of Nigeria as well as promoting harmony among the tribes and ethnic groups through information and education (Kur and Nyekwere 2015). In a nutshell, the federal government became the sole transmitter of what goes on air.

The Nigerian media space experienced the worst of intimidation and oppression during the early years that followed independence. As a result of the devastation that characterized the 1962 federal elections, the federal government saw the dangers of allowing the power of the media to reside in the hands of individuals. As a result, the military government regulated the print media, through decrees such as the Newspaper Prohibition of

Circulation Decree of 1967, which illegalized publications that present the military in a bad light and threaten the stability of the federation. Newspaper houses—their owners and employees—that contravened this promulgation were incarcerated and others killed (Daramola 2006). Thus, this laid the historical foundation for the normative rationalization of Nigeria's media role in society. A major argument confirmed by Chukwu (2015) is that the military governments are of the opinion that when media ownership is left in the hands of private individuals, it could breed sectional inclinations and thus lead to another season of violence.

It must be noted that from 1962 until the implementation of the 1979 constitution, the federal government had absolute control over the media landscape, with the NTA enjoying a broadcast monopoly. The introduction of the 1979 constitution broke the monopoly of the Federal Government of Nigeria. The provisions of Section 36, subsection (2) of the constitution provides that:

> every person shall be entitled to own, establish and operate any medium for the dissemination of information, ideas and opinions; provided that no person, other than the Government of the Federation or of a state or any other person or body authorized by the president, shall own, establish or operate a television or wireless broadcasting station for any purpose whatsoever. (Federal Government of Nigeria [FGN], 1979)

This section did not abolish NTA; it gave the opportunity for state governments to establish and control the broadcast airwaves.

It must be stated that during the years the federal government controlled the media, different measures and obnoxious laws and decrees were used to prevent the media from fully expressing its mandate. For instance, Decree No. 4 of 1984 criminalized press reports and proscribed written statements that exposed an officer of the military government to ridicule. Also, Offensive Publications (Proscription) Decree 35 1993, gave the government the impetus to shut down six media houses across the nation (Okwuchukwu 2014). The decree in July 1993 empowered the military government of Gen. Ibrahim Babangida to close down seventeen newspapers and magazines and one broadcasting station in a day (Ojo 2001). Notable also is the assassination of Dele Giwa, the then editor of *Newswatch*, by the Babangida-led military government in 1986.

The era of the military-led federal government in Nigeria had the worst forms of media repression in the historical journey of the Nigerian media. Joseph (1997) cited in Okwuchukwu (2014) revealed that the military era in Nigeria was characterized by arbitral arrests and detention of journalists, extrajudicial killings, excessive use of force, torture of detainees, harassment of journalists and democratic activists as well as incendiary attacks on media houses. It was noted that, often, these attacks extended to family members of targeted journalists who refused to acquiesce to their demands.

ERA OF STATE-CONTROLLED MEDIA

The effective operation of the 1979 constitution broke the monopoly of the federal government as the sole controller of broadcast media. With it, other broadcast stations were allowed to coexist with NTA. This window was maximally utilized by state governments to establish television and radio stations during the Shehu Shagari administration. Between 1979 and 1983, Lagos, Ondo, Ogun, Oyo, Bendel, Imo, Anambra, Plateau, and Kano states had their radio and television stations broadcasting to their people (Chukwu 2015).

A critical feature during this era was that the state broadcast stations became the mouthpieces of the state government and by extension a political tool to fight opposition parties. Chukwu (2015) noted that the 1979 presidential election saw the National Party of Nigeria (NPN) control the center with other political parties in control of the governments at the state levels. State-owned broadcast stations acted as countering tools to the propaganda of the federal government–controlled NTA. This led to a media war which threatened the security of the Nigerian state and also undermined the ethics of journalism. The situation turned government-owned media to party organs financed by the public.

ERA OF MEDIA LIBERALIZATION

The agenda to liberalize the broadcast media began with the provisions of Section 36, subsection 2, of the constitution providing that

> every person shall be entitled to own, establish and operate any medium for the dissemination of information, ideas and opinions; provided that no person, other than the Government of the Federation or of a state or any other person or body authorized by the president, shall own, establish or operate a television or wireless broadcasting station for any purpose whatsoever. (Federal Government of Nigeria [FGN], 1979)

This provision was not fully actualized until 1992 when General Ibrahim Babangida initiated National Broadcasting Commission Decree 38 of 1992. Section 22 of the decree abolished the monopoly of the ownership of any form of media by the government and legalized ownership of electronic media by private individuals (Abubakar and Hassan 2017). In addition, the decree charged with the supervision of the broadcast industry marked the beginning of a new phase in the media system (Chukwu 2015). Though the broadcast media was deregulated in 1992, the first private broadcast station, Africa Independent Television (AIT), began operation in 1994.

One of the arguments presented by Babangida was the need to make the broadcast media lucrative to allow foreign investment (Chukwu 2015). In addition, it was revealed by Azubike and Ikiriko (2019) that the liberalization of the broadcast media created opportunities for indigenous entrepreneurs to invest in the broadcast media industry. As a result, Chukwu (2015) noted that between 1993 and 1997, NBC licensed eleven private radio stations, thirty television stations and eighteen satellite retransmission stations. This further birthed healthy competition as government-owned broadcast media were forced to upgrade their production to remain in the market. Rodney (2004) supports this claim as it was recorded that the Nigerian government increased its investment in the sponsorship of Federal Radio Corporation of Nigeria (FRCN) and NTA from ₦4.5billion in 1999 to ₦20 billion in the 2001 budget.

It is expected that the 1992 deregulation of the broadcast media, characterized by the increase in private ownership of broadcast media, will support free press and reduce the degree of government interference with the media. The extent at which the media is free in Nigeria is debatable. Oberiri (2017) averred that the presence of restrictive and repressive laws and intolerance of the government towards media criticism threatens media freedom in Nigeria. In spite of the huge presence of private owners in the broadcast media industry, repressive laws, decrees, and censorship still gags the media in Nigeria's modern democracy (Oberiri 2017).

ERA OF DIGITIZATION AND GLOBALIZATION

The wake of the new millennium ushered an advancement in media and communication technologies. These technologies have transformed the scope of media and broadcast operations in Nigeria and around the world. These technologies have further enhanced and improved the way media professionals disseminate information in a more efficient manner to a highly dispersed audience. According to Olorede and Oyewole (2013, p. 3):

> The catalyst for the transformation of media newsrooms is modern technology. These technologies have further enhanced media credibility, reliability and even affordability and accessibility, as events can be reported as simultaneously as they unfold, with little or no interference and audience's access at a relatively affordable cost. These technologies have also refurbished the obsolete face of

media newsrooms; the new sophisticated computers have replaced the old, time-consuming and outdated typewriters, and so on.

Earlier, Deuze and Dimoudi (2002, p. 97) averred that:

> The new media technologies are perceived to empower people and democratize the relationships between consumers and producers of content (which could be news or information). It also connects to online media logic as a concept which includes the notions of the audience as an active agent in redefining the work-ings of journalism.

From both comments, it is evident that with the emergence of new technolo-gies propelled by the internet and social media, the sphere of influence of media practitioners is no longer localized. They have the entire globe as a potential audience and as a result they have the responsibility of disseminat-ing only factual and truthful reportage. In this regard, social media has been a veritable and handy medium for such expressions. It has allowed media professionals to engage millions of audiences across the world. According to Asekun-Olarinmoye, Sanusi, Johnson, and Oloyede (2014), it is exciting how social media is connecting audiences to the newsroom in terms of news and event coverage. Social media has also included the audience across the world as active participants in the creation, sourcing, and dissemination processes of the news.

In Nigeria, the advent of digital media—promoted by the increase in online newspapers—has changed the face of media practice (Hassan, Nazri, and Nasidi 2018). Nigerian media platforms have been able to adapt conve-niently with digitization (Aliagan 2015). More media stations have an online presence which has facilitated more engagements with their audience. For instance, it is known that radio, as the most popular media channel in third world countries, has issues with connecting effectively with the audience because of its nonvisual features (Hassan et al. 2018). With digitization, radio stations have incorporated the visual features supported by social media plat-forms such as Facebook, Twitter, and Instagram to run online transmissions. This has driven more engagements and increased followership.

Media digitization came with numerous challenges ranging from the dis-semination of fake news, misinformation, and the spread of violent content that could stir panic (Ladan, Haruna, and Madu 2020). As a result, Nigerian governments at all levels are particular about measures to regulate social media, considering the harmful effect its misuse could spell for a nation. A vivid instance is the role social media played in the dissemination of fake news during the #EndSARS protest in the year 2020. This further opened the eyes of the government to the absolute freedom enjoyed by citizens in the use of social media. It has been argued in other quarters that the use of social media has increased participation and civic engagements among citizens (Natividad 2020).

Media Structure in the Digital Era

The introduction of modern technology has resulted in public engagement in the media and communication space. With the advent of smart and internet-enabled phones, there is a whole new era in communication forums. The use of emails and mailing lists to online discussion forums has also increased digital communication (Etika 2019). With the internet, people are able to communicate across continents for professional and social purposes. Digital media has changed the mode of communication, making the flow of news dynamic with significant changes to its manner of production, dissemination, and consumption by the public.

One of such dynamic changes stirred by technology and the proliferation of smart and internet-enabled devices is the rise of citizen journalism. According to Sunday (2011), citizen journalism grows on the fact that individuals with little or no journalism skill are involved in the production and distribution of news contents across social media. Oftentimes, they work as independent freelancers or in conjunction with established media houses. Banda (2010, p. 6) stated that citizen journalism is a "rapidly evolving form of journalism where common citizens take the initiative to report news or express views about happenings within their community." It was further described that these individuals who often are freelancers are not bound by conventional journalism ethics or code of conduct.

The rise of citizen journalism has generated mixed reactions including beneficial and consequential perspectives of this form of journalism. The advent of citizen journalism has significantly afforded both the professional and the nonprofessional similar opportunities to be actively involved in news content creation. Citizen journalism has broken the previously existing domination of the mainstream media giving rise to a more democratic and participatory journalism. In line with the Educause Learning Initiative (2014), citizen journalism grants anyone and everyone access to cover news by presenting a more personal view of events and has the potential to create and nurture communities of people with similar interests.

However, the notable consequences of citizen journalism to the newsroom cannot be overlooked. Some have argued that citizen journalism is a new way of spreading falsehood and other unethical practices under the guise of journalism (Apeh and Didiugwu 2017). The concept of false news is a concern that becomes inevitable when news is obtained from diverse anonymous sources. In the real sense of it, the news may be factual, but it has flaws such as ethical disregard, lack of objectivity, detachment, and balance (Apeh and Didiugwu 2017). There is also the possibility of a hidden agenda that is presented as fact or defamatory to portray subjects in bad light. The gatekeeping verification process in the mainstream media that helps to curb such practices is absent in citizen journalism (Odii 2013).

Citizen journalism is also said to have given rise to a concept referred to as the journalism of assertion (Noor 2017). This depicts that unverified and unsubstantiated opinions are disseminated, calling to question the credibility of journalism. There is also the issue of nonregulation among writers. Citizen journalists are known to sensationalize stories in the absence of ethical standards and gatekeeping. The public are confused on which to regard as a journalist since just about anyone can publish news. Citizen journalists exhibit little or no knowledge of journalism framework and since they do not have to follow specific journalism framework, their works lack credibility most of the time (Apeh and Didiugwu 2017). The inclusion of the element of sensation in content creation in citizen journalism is the basis to argue that most stories are imbalanced since they are told from the journalist's perspective.

Furthermore, digitization will further push the boundaries in media business as the emergence of online newspapers will further affect the circulation of physical newspapers as well as reduce the profit margins of publishers. According to Fortunati and Sarrica (2010), the emergence of online newspapers will have a great impact on the circulation and sales of physical newspaper copies. This will further affect the rate of profitability. Reduced profit margin to publishers also means that some other aspects of the production line will be downsized. For instance, in 2012, there was a massive purge of workers at Tribune, one of the foremost print media in Nigeria, over increasing operating cost and the company's inability to pay shareholder dividends (Adesina 2012).

A contemporary trend in the digital media landscape is the growth of fake news, misinformation, and disinformation. The concept of fake news has gained more popularity due to digital and social media interactions (Apuke and Omar, 2020). Social media is regarded as the lifeblood of fake news since anyone can share a story on it without verification and has the potential of going viral. There is a concern that fake news will continue to spread due to the ease of circulation on social media. The United Nations Education, Scientific and Cultural Organization (UNESCO) (2020) disseminated the results of a study by Bruno Kessler Foundation that in the hit of the first wave of the COVID-19, there were about 112 million social media posts on COVID-19 pandemic and 40 percent of the post can be linked to suspicious sources.

In addition to fake news, social media has been found to spread misinformation in public spaces. According to the BBC (2020), it was disclosed that the cost of misinformation on public health is huge and devastating. Waldrop, Alsup, and McLaughlin (2020) disclosed that some of the casualties of the COVID-19 were those exposed to the misinformation on the use of chloroquine in combating the virus. Obi-Ani, Anikwenze, and Isiani (2020) reported that social media platforms such as WhatsApp and Facebook are notable platforms for the dissemination of misleading contents. Russonello (2020) revealed that the continued spread of misleading information on digital platforms poses an ethical challenge to the sanity and safety of the public space.

As a way of combating the poisonous impact of misinformation and fake news on the human society, state and non-state stakeholders are in the process of instituting policies that would identify, and guard against the dissemination of fake and misleading information on social media. For instance, Facebook, Twitter, and Instagram have algorithms developed to identify and handle malicious contents on their platforms. These platforms also have privacy policies that empower other users to report posts with the tendency to incite violence. In addition, governments at all levels in Nigeria are working out policies to curb the indiscriminate use of social media to incite violence. Experiences with the #EndSARS protest of 2020 in Nigeria shows how dangerous social media could be if left unregulated.

CONCLUSION

The chapter discussed the historical antecedents of media structure in Nigeria. It assumes that media systems across the African continent share similar patterns that can be associated with the colonial media. As a result, it concludes that contemporary African media is a reflection of the colonial postures inherited by past leaders at independence. A major trend that was noticed is the unbroken cord between political actors and the media. This has been identified as the reason for the stronghold African governments have over the media. The game-changer is digitization with which there seems to be no regulation yet in some countries as to what is permissible for dissemination on the internet. Though digitization brought with it identified challenges such as source credibility, misinformation, and fake news, which could have disastrous impacts on the stability of African societies, it has necessitated policy makers on the continent to ponder on how the social media space could be regulated to protect the sanctity of African society.

RECOMMENDATION

In view of the above, the following recommendations are urgent:

1. For African media to be completely free from the aprons of the government, its management must think outside the box to implement sustainable business models that do not depend on advertisement as the sole source of revenue.
2. Restrictions on the media do not portray the government as credible in the international community; as a result, there is the need for leaders of governments in Africa to reduce their control and influence on the media. This will allow the media to perform its statutory role of information dissemination and surveillance.
3. It has been identified that the misuse of media by powerful individuals for ethnic, political, and personal interests is responsible for government control of the media. Therefore, media practitioners need to justify their calling by upholding the ethics of the profession regardless of ownership interest. The extent to which media practitioners can adhere and forgo sectional interest is of major concern considering the rate of poverty and poor condition of service to which they are subjected.

REFERENCES

Abubakar, U. and Hassan, I. 2017. "Regulatory and Political Influence on Mass Media Operation in Nigeria." *Scholars Journal of Arts, Humanities and Social Sciences* 5 (12C): 1935–1941.

Adesina, G. (2012). "Tribune Sacks 160 Workers." PM News. Accessed November 27, 2021. https://pmnewsnigeria.com/2012/11/01/tribune-sacks-160-workers/.

Agbaje, A. (1992). *The Nigerian Press, Hegemony, and the Social Construction of Legitimacy, 1960–1983*. Lewiston: E. Mellen Press.

Aliagan, I. 2015. "Examining survival strategies employed by Nigerian newspapers against loss of readership and revenues." *New Media and Mass Communication* 35: 9–16.

Apeh, A. C. and Didiugwu, I. F. 2017. "Implications of Citizen Journalism on the MainStream." Journalism. *International Journal of Academic Research in Business and Social Sciences* 7 (12): 1349–1362.

Apuke, O. B and Omar, B. 2020. "Fake news proliferation in Nigeria: Consequences, motivations, and prevention through awareness strategies." *Humanities and Social Sciences Reviews* 8 (2), 318–327.

Asekun-Olarinmoye, B., Sanusi, J., Johnson, D., and Oloyede, G. 2014. "Imperatives of internet and social media on broadcast journalism in Nigeria." *IISTE Journal* 23: 8–15.

Atal, M. R. 2017. "Competing forms of media capture in developing democracies." In *The Service of Power: Media Capture and the Threat to Democracy*, edited by Anya Schiffrin. Washington, DC: Centre for International Media Assistance.

Azubuike, C. and Ikiriko, S. 2019. "Challenges and Prospects of Private Broadcast Media Ownership in Nigeria: A Study of Stations in Port Harcourt." *Mediterranean Journal of Social Sciences* 10 (5).

Banda, F. 2010. "Citizen Journalism and Democracy in Africa: An Exploratory Study." Accessed January 11, 2020. http://milcon.org.ng/wp-content/uploads/2014 /08/Citizen-Journalism-and-Democracy-in-Africa.pdf.

BBC. 2020. "Social Media Firms Fail to Act on COVID-19 Fake News." BBC News. Accessed January 11, 2020. www.bbc.com/news/technology-52903680.

Chukwu, C. O. 2015. "Government Broadcast Media Ownership Pattern and Media Content in Nigeria—Its Threats to Democracy." *Research on Humanities and Social Sciences* 5 (16).

Daramola, I. 2006. *History and Development of Mass Media in Nigeria*. Lagos: Rothan Press, Ltd.

Davor, K. D. (2015). "The Changing Role of Christian Newspapers in Ghana: A Case Study of the Catholic Standard." School of Communication Studies, University of Ghana.

Deuze, M., and Dimoudi, C. 2002. "Online journalists in the Netherlands: Towards a profile of a new profession." *Journalism* 3 (1): 85–100.

Educause Learning Initiative 2014. "7 things you should know about Citizen Journalism." Accessed January 11, 2020. http://net.educause.edu/ir/library/pdf /eli7031.pdf.

Etika, D. N. 2019. "Citizen journalism and its impacts on professional journalism in progressive society: A study of 2019 governorship election in Cross River state." *International Journal of Recent Advances in Psychology and Psychotherapy* 3 (1): 13–24.

Fortunati, L. and Sarrica, M. 2010. "The future of press: Insights from the sociotechnical approach." *The Information Society* (26): 247–255.

Gadzekpo, A. (2008). "Guardians of Democracy: The Media," *in Ghana: Governance in the Fourth Republic*. Accra: Digibooks, 195–215.

Hassan, I., Nazri, N. L. and Nasidi, Q. Y. 2018. "The Survival of Nigerian Newspapers in Digital Age of Communication." *International Journal of Asian Social Science, Asian Economic and Social Society* 8 (9): 631–637.

Ikiebe, R. (2015). "The press national election and the politics of becoming in Nigeria." An unpublished doctoral thesis from the University of Westminster, London.

Iredia, T. 2016. "NTA's problem is not structure but government control." Vanguard. Accessed December 20, 2020. https://www.vanguardngr.com/2016/03/ntas -problem-not-structure-govt-control/.

Kawonise, S. 2012. "The Watchdog: Compromised ButBitting Still." Keynote address delivered at the 17th Annual Conference of the National Anthropological and Sociological Association, held at NnamdiAzikiwe University, Awka, Anambra State, on November 5, 2012.

Kintz, L. 2007. "Overview of Current Media Practices and Trends in West Africa." *Global Media Journal* 6.

Kur, J. T. and Nyekwere, E. O. 2015. "Television Broadcasting and the Democratisation Process in Nigeria: The Successful and Unsuccessful Story." *Online Journal of Communication and Media Technologies* 5 (4): 116–146.

Ladan, A., Haruna, B., and Madu, A. 2020. "COVID-19 Pandemic and Social Media News in Nigeria: The Role of Libraries and Library Associations in Information Dissemination." *International Journal of Innovation and Research in Educational Sciences* 7 (2): 2349–5219.

Natividad, I. 2020. "COVID-19 and the Media: The Role of Journalism in a Global Pandemic." Berkeley News. Accessed 25 July 2020. www.news.berkeley.edu/2020 /05/06/covid-19-and-the-media-role-of-jornalism-in-a-global-pandemic/.

Noor, R. 2017. "Citizen Journalism vs. Mainstream Journalism: A Study on Challenges Posed by Amateurs." *Athens Journal of Mass Media and Communications* 3 (1): 55–76.

Nyamnjoh, F. B. 2005. *Africa's media: Democracy and the politics of belonging.* New York: Zed Books.

Oberiri, A. D. 2017. "Exploring the extent of press freedom in Nigeria." *International Journal of International Relations, Media and Mass Communication Studies* 3 (2): 28–31.

Obi-Ani, N. A., Anikwenze, C., and Isiani, M. C. 2020. "Social media and the Covid-19 pandemic: Observations from Nigeria." *Cogent Arts and Humanities* 7 (1): 1799483.

Odii, C. 2013. "Public Perception of the Implications of Citizen Journalism for Nigeria's Democracy." Accessed January 11, 2020. https://academicexcellencesociety.com /public_perception_of_the_implications_of_citizen_journalism.pdf.

Ojo, E. O. 2001. "The Phenomenon of Corruption and the Challenges of Democratic Consolidation in Nigeria: A Prognosis." A paper presented at an international conference: "Towards a Corruption-free Sustainable Development: Challenges for Good Governance and Prosperity in the 21st Century." Sponsored by International Political Science Association (IPSA), Abuja, Nigeria, October 15–17.

Okoro, N. 2012. "Mass media in Nigeria: An exploratory analysis." *New Media and Mass Communication* (7): 6–12.

Okwuchukwu, O. 2014. "The Influence of Media Ownership and Control on Media Agenda Setting in Nigeria." *International Journal of Humanities Social Sciences and Education (IJHSSE)* 1 (7): 36–45.

Olorede, J. and Oyewole, A. 2013. "Level of Internet Compliance and Usage in the Newsrooms of Broadcast Media in Nigeria." *New Media and Mass Communication* (9): 2224–3267.

Omoera, O. 2014. "Towards Redefining the News Agenda in Nigerian Media for National Development." *Austral: Brazilian Journal of Strategy and International Relations* 3(5): 117–135.

Omu, F. 2000. "The Nigerian Press: Milestones in Service." In *Hosting the 140th Anniversary of the Nigerian Press, edited by* Oseni, T. and Idowu, L. Lagos: Solasprint (Nigeria) Ltd.

Oso, L. 2012. "The Burden of History: The Press and the 2003 General Elections in Nigeria." In *Perspectives in Language, Literature and Communication Studies,* edited by Babalola, S. T. and Azeez, T. Ile-Ife: Obafemi Awolowo University Press.

Padania, M. 2018. *An Introduction to Funding Journalism and Media.* Netherlands: European Funders for Social Change and Human Rights.

Prat, A., and Strömberg, D. 2013. *The Political Economy of Mass Media. Advances in Economics and Econometrics.* Volume 2, Applied Economics. Daron Acemoglu, Manuel Arellano, Eddie Dekel (eds.). Cambridge: Cambridge University Press.

Rodney, C. 2004. "Private broadcasting and the challenges of democratization of electronic media in Nigeria." *An Interdisciplinary Journal of Communication Studies* 3 (3): 23–31.

Russonello, G. 2020. "Afraid of coronavirus? That might say something about your politics." *New York Times*, March 13. Accessed January 11, 2020. www.nytimes .com/2020/03/13/us/politics/coronavirus-trump-polling.html.

Schweizer, C., Puppis, M., Künzler, M., and Studer, S. 2014. *Public Funding of Private Media.* LSE Media Policy Project. Accessed December 23, 2020. https:// blogs.lse.ac.uk/medialse/.

Sunday, D. 2011. "The Rise of Citizen Journalism in Nigeria—A Case Study of Sahara Reporters." *Reuters Institute Fellowship Paper Sciences* (5): 435–448.

Tar-Tsaaior, J. 2015. "Imagining Nationhood, Framing Post-coloniality: Narrativising Nigeria through the Kinesis of Hi(her)story." *SMC Journal of Cultural and Media Studies* 2 (2).

The United Nations Educational, Scientific and Cultural Organization (UNESCO). 2017. "Community Media Sustainability Policy Series." Accessed 23 December, 2020. www.unesco_cmedia_sustainability_policy_5_public_funding.

United Nations Education, Scientific and Cultural Organization (UNESCO). 2020. "COVID-19 Educational Disruption and Response." Accessed January 11, 2020. https://en.unesco.org/news/covid-19-educational-disruption-and-response.

Waldrop, T., Alsup, D., and McLaughlin, E. 2020. "Fearing coronavirus, Arizona man dies after taking a form of chloroquine used to treat aquariums." CNN. Accessed January 11, 2020. www.cnn.com/2020/03/23/health/arizona-coronavirus -chloroquine-death.html.

Zaghlami, L. 2016. "Colonial Media and Post-independence Experience in North Africa." *Journal of African Media Studies* 3 (15): 159–168.

Chapter 3

Media Law, Regulation, and Digital Space

Nasir Danladi Bako

The media all over the world situates its relevance, functionality, and inevitability within the general spectrum and the firmament of communication as an important vehicular platform for one of the most essential components of the ideal communication process. The media here typifies the instruments available and exploitable for the purposes of communication within the society. For the utilization of the media as a major catalyst for growth and development in any society, the culture of the society as well as the desirability of functionality of such media must operate in synergy and harmony with the content and context of ideas and messages directed at the community involved. Within the context of the developed industrialized societies, the media performs the roles as prescribed by early scholars, to primarily "inform, educate and entertain." But Akinfeleye (2008) states further that in relation to developing societies the basic philosophical foundations of the media go beyond the dictum to "inform, educate, and entertain," but should as a tool for good governance set the agenda for the people, monitor governance, and make the government accountable to the people (p. 19).

Siebert, Peterson, and Schramm (1969) assert that the mass media encapsulating radio, television, newspapers, billboards, as well as the new media and internet-driven technological implements like telephones, digital platforms and satellite receiving platforms, have reconfigured the entire communication chain and process almost relegating the traditional mass media to second place. This is also acknowledged by MacQuail (2000) who emphasizes that:

> The media have undergone dramatic transformations which have since the latter half of the 20th century impact on their capacities to deliver services to the

public. The 21st century further threw up new media that hold out possibilities of on-demand access to content anytime and anywhere on digital devices such as I-phones, Android and IOS tools. They facilitate interactive user feedback as well as user generated content in great detail. (p. 353)

Being a major communication component, the media's role in society can be contextualized by analyzing society as a people-populated body and the media as its tool for expressing and exchanging ideas as well as relating to each component of that unit. Merrill states that "mass media can contribute to the people's awareness of potentialities, dissatisfaction and desire to change a heightened sense of collective power among the people creating either stability or disruption and also creating realistic goals or extravagant exceptions" (Akinfeleye 2008, p. 21).

Within every society and conglomeration of humans, their rights and privileges, customs and traditions, beliefs and religion, limitations and boundaries become all embedded in their way of life generically referred to by both scholars and researchers as their culture. According to Iji and Betiang (2017), "culture is fundamental to human existence and human civilization, embodying in its dynamism, the totality of a people's response to the challenges of life, and living, culture offers meaning, purpose and value to the socio-economic, political and aesthetic ethos of society."

It is the interplay of these fine boundaries of human interaction within society and how the utilization of the media—traditional radio and television as well as the new digital media driven by the superhighway called internet—that defines the subject of this paper.

CONCEPTUAL FRAMEWORK

The predisposition of the media to perform its earlier enumerated roles cannot be discountenanced; indeed, it is well articulated in most constitutions all over the world, in which the freedom of the press is guaranteed and well defined. In the United States of America, the first amendment guarantees the freedom of the press when it states that congress shall make no laws binding the freedom of the press. The Nigerian constitution in chapter 2, section 22, states that "the press, radio, television and other agencies of the mass media shall at all times be free to uphold the fundamental objectives contained in this chapter and uphold the responsibility and accountability of the government to the people" (Akinfeleye 2008, p. 22).

This provision establishing the media role and importance in Nigeria situates this paper within the "Social Responsibility" framework of the Libertarian Press theory and philosophy. According to McQuail (2000, p. 15) the First World War saw the mobilization of press and film in most of Europe and the United States for nationalistic war aims of contending states, the results of which left little doubt about the potency of media influence on the masses, when effectively deployed. The mass media even before the advent of the social media and the internet had always been instruments of propagation of governmental policy issues, social harmony and national unity, as well as being a vehicle for propaganda at crisis times.

MEDIA LAWS IN FOCUS

Okpoko (2010, p. 161), situates the relevance and efficacy of the media as an institution for development and governance. According to him, "many scholars believe that the media are also instrumental in the dissemination of power, influence and conferment of status in society and that in some cases they serve as instruments of ideology and advocacy."

With the foregoing, it is an undisputed function of the media to provide the memory, protection of rights of individuals, disseminate views vertically and horizontally, and also hold the government accountable for its policies as well as activities. It is this imperative that necessitates the legislation of laws and corresponding sanctions in furtherance of societal harmony and curtailment of breaches by individuals, media organs as well as government functionaries. Criminologists and anthropologists will always vary in human deviant tendencies and propensity for greed and individualism as responsible for crossing of boundaries set by government rules and regulations. Crime and breaches are a fundamental product of our individualism within the context of self-definition, societal exigencies, as well as the power dynamics of such societies (Deridda 2011; Foucault 2011).

Therefore, the enactment of laws to guide and regulate the rights of all persons, bodies, and government is basically a given and its desirability within the Nigerian media industry is not in question. Over the years, especially in the last century, the following laws have been enacted either in form of decrees during the military regimes or enacted through the civil dispensation organs such as the National Assembly of the Federal Republic of Nigeria. They include:

a. The Nigerian Press Council Act, Cap N128 of the Laws of the Federal Republic of Nigeria which is set up "to promote high professional standards for the Nigerian Press and deal with complaints emanating from members of the public about the conduct of journalists in the professional capacity or complaints against organizations connected therewith. It is the regulatory body for the print media."

b. The National Broadcasting Commission Act, Cap N11 Laws of the Federation of Nigeria 2004. The Commission is the regulatory body established to, among other functions; "recommend applications through the Minister to the President for the grant of radio and television licenses as well as regulate and control the broadcasting industry." It also has the function to establish and disseminate a national broadcasting code to set standards with regard to the content and quality of materials for broadcast, as well as determining and applying sanctions including revocation of licenses of defaulting stations which do not operate in accordance with the code, and in the public interest.

There are other media laws establishing such media organs and also defining their functions:

- The National Film and Video Censors Board Act empowers the board to regulate the film and video industry in Nigeria.
- The Advertising Practitioner's Council Act defines its function as regulating standards in the advertising industry.
- The National Institute of Public Relations Act permits it to superintend over the practice of Public Relations in the country.
- The Nigerian Film Corporation is set up to promote the production of Nigerian films while the News Agency of Nigeria (NAN), the Nigerian Television Authority (NTA), and the Federal Radio Corporation of Nigeria (FRCN) are all saddled with the responsibility of passing government information to the governed as well as gathering feedback and reverting same to the authorities. Recently the Cyber Crime Act came into existence to check the dissemination of seditious and fraudulent materials on the internet. Similarly, the process of legislating a social media bill is ongoing at the national legislature in Nigeria, although it is facing stiff resistance from media practitioners and civil societies.

REGULATION OF THE MEDIA

Most challenging to the practice of journalism, especially in the past, was the Official Secrets Act enacted by the colonial masters at the height of the anticolonial struggle for Nigeria's independence. Strikingly, the frontliners in the struggle at that time in the 1940s and 1950s were journalist-turned politicians like Nnamdi Azikwe who was to later emerge as president; Obafemi Awolowo, Ernest Ikoli, and Increase Coker. Postcolonial administrations were also caught in the quagmire of how to handle what some hardliners termed "the excesses of the press." It was therefore not surprising that successive military regimes doubled their efforts to silence the press. Quite a few of them shut down media houses, shaved the heads of journalists, incarcerated some others, and enacted decrees to that effect with Degree 4 of 1984 being the most draconian. Not a few journalists spent time in jail for doing their constitutional duty. Suffice it to say that the return of civil rule and democracy saw the abrogation of most such laws.

Sequel to intense lobbying and advocacy by civil society organizations, driven by a virulent congregation of media houses and public-spirited professionals, the government within the last decade enacted the Freedom of Information Act further guaranteeing access to otherwise earlier classified information. This is a boost to holding the government accountable.

The mass media is not of course the only institution that performs the communication function in the Nigerian political system. According to Okpoko (2010) the media, as with human activity, subjects itself to various interpretations that abound with each law and with the context of the power dynamics or political struggles for supremacy or struggle for self-determination within that society. Nor is it the only instrument facilitating political, economic, social considerations and accommodation. These factors generate some tension and create platforms for the violation of the laws, willfully or otherwise. For instance, headlines of newspapers or their cover stories sometimes become not only sensational but also amount to blackmail and provocative reporting based on speculation. In the 1980s, a magazine publication was cited as the source of information that sparked off riots in Nigeria during the military regime of President Ibrahim Babangida. The story turned out to be a hoax. Even today many others are subject to the libel and slander laws in the courts due to the indiscretion and poor professional judgment of some of the media houses. However, it must be said that the Nigerian press was highly instrumental in the pursuit of self-government, independence, and championed the fight against colonialism, neocolonialism, as well as propagating the return of democracy in Nigeria. Therefore, essentially, its primary constitutional roles have been adhered to substantially.

The press in Nigeria has a huge amount of private entrepreneurial investors and businessmen whose acumen and diligence have today literally outlasted the government owned printing press and publications which are literally comatose—the likes of *Daily Sketch, Daily Times,* and *New Nigerian* newspapers. The broadcast industry today in Nigeria has at least eight hundred radios and televisions outlets covering federal, national, state, and private FM and television stations and regulating it has become a major challenge because of the sheer number of staff, equipment, and other production necessities. Therefore, a major philosophy of the regulatory body of the National Broadcasting Commission is to encourage self-regulation within the confines of the individual broadcast station where desirable, after which sanctions are applied in the case of breaches.

DIGITAL MEDIA SPACE

The advent of convergence of broadcast media, print media, and telephony content of voice and data has further challenged the regulators. According to Akinfeleye (2008):

> traditional print media operations in the country are branching out into internet publishing while newspapers have versions of their daily publications online. This makes them available not only to their local audiences in Nigeria but also to others all over the world particularly Nigerians in the Diaspora.

The migration of signals of broadcast stations is presently being progressively activated across the country and despite the slow protracted pace of the digitization and switchover process, it is expected that the whole of Nigeria's over 900,000 square kilometers landmass will be covered digitally within the next few years. One major challenge, however, is the difficulty of legislation and protocols. Most threatening is the poor enforcement of laws to regulate the internet or better still the enforcement of the available laws such as the Cybercrime Act of Nigeria. The internet is such a gargantuan platform that regulating it has become a challenge even for Facebook and Twitter. Only recently, despite all the media laws in the United States of America, Twitter had to resort to flagging a particular tweet of President Trump's referred to as "unacceptable." They insinuated that he overstepped the boundaries of decency and good conduct.

Despite the Nigeria Broadcasting Code's regulation that "broadcast stations shall not use foul or blasphemous language" (p. 70), some stations lift materials of User Generated Content (UGC) "straight from a website or blog and transmit as fact without verifying the authenticity of the material which negates the tenets of journalism *ab initio*." Indeed chapter 5:13 states that "Fake news is prohibited." Quite clearly enforcing this regulation along with that of prohibition of hate speech has been on the front burner in recent times all over the world. Certainly, with the endless stream of information on voice and data platforms, the world is at crossroads in enforcing regulation on the internet, also known as social media. Taylor, Nwosu, and Mutua-Kombo (2004, p. 274) opines that "statistics from Brain and DMR Digital Marketing Rumblings websites show that social media have become so popular that there are well over 500 different sites around the world with several billions of people as users. Facebook had 1.23 billion active users as at December

2013, Twitter had 645 million, YouTube 1 billion as at March 2013." Therefore, the regulation of such global community and public spheres has become a major challenge for regulators.

CHALLENGES

The redefinition of borderlessness of the internet has complicated law enforcement and its execution of the regulatory statutes, both of individual countries and the world at large, despite the domestication of cyber laws in individual countries and also the monitoring of seditious as well as incendiary materials. As with the case of some Nigerian self-determination protagonists who broadcast illegally, even locating them and their media has become a problem because of the capability of media organs to transmit from various locations all over the world using new technologies. The Nigerian government, over a long time, had problems locating such radio stations such as *Radio Kudirat* operated by democracy movements during the late Nigerian military dictator General Sani Abacha's military regime of the 1990s in Nigeria. The same situation applies to the current *Radio Biafra* which operates from offshore locations outside Nigeria.

The provisions of the Nigerian Broadcast Code make the licensee liable when its contents are in breach of the code, but in this case, the licensees Facebook and Google are not registered in Nigeria as broadcasters. However, the options of following the Chinese, Iranian, and North Korean regulation by blackout of such outlets seem very undesirable or unappealing in a country dithering to promote its democratic credentials.

Expensive cost of monitoring social media, which requires huge data costs for each network and for continuous monitoring, are a major challenge as well. Besides the cost of such monitoring equipment and blockage as well as power supply consistency, the personnel and data costs are humongous if proper monitoring and enforcement is to be achieved. The access to information from government functionaries as well as certain private sector organizations using the Freedom of Information Act 2011 has also been slow and not encouraging both on the part of journalists as well as the public and civil service operatives.

CONCLUSION

As the mantra of journalism stipulates that one of the functions of the media remains that of a gatekeeper, the present ubiquitous and omnipresent nature of numerous 24-hour broadcast stations make monitoring and regulation a tedious and near impossible challenge bedeviled by a neck and neck race with the social media platform over control of the public sphere of about three billion individuals as participants. Therefore, shall we say this marks the death of the gatekeeper? Maybe not yet, Foucault (2011) posits that "we cannot take concepts that we use in our present context and assume that they are somehow eternal and that all we have now is a history of ideals." Essentially the way the media has functioned in the past and how it was regulated have been overtaken by new technology and consequently new legislation.

The vicissitudes of change and evolution of media technologies and media regulation is a function of every civilization and era. It is the era of digitization, horizontal communication and democratization of the public sphere that evokes the feeling of oneness at one level and yet individuality and regional differences at another level.

It is therefore incumbent on all media regulators to engender the necessary regulation of the media platforms both on the traditional media (print and broadcast) along with the creative global synergy of collectively enforcing media regulation and hygiene on the internet. In Nigeria, there has to be a more conscious effort through advocacy to further enlighten citizens of their rights within the broadcast, print, and social media platforms. There has to be more professional commitment on the part of media operatives in both adhering to the laws as well as their desire to work for public good and national interest.

REFERENCES

Akinfeleye, R. 2008. *Health and Behavior Change Communication for Development*. Ibadan. Spectrum Books Ltd.

Deridda, F. 2011. *The Philosophy Book.* London: DI and H Books, p. 302.

Federation Radio Corporation of Nigeria Act.

Foucault, M. 2011. *The Philosophy Book.* London: DI and H Books. p. 302.

Freedom of Information Act 2011.

Iji, E. and Betiang, L. 2017. *Theatre and Media in the Third Millennium.* Ibadan: Kraft Books.

McQuail, D. C. 2000. *Mass Communication Theory.* London: Sage Publications.

National Broadcasting Commission Act 1999 (as amended).

National Film and Video Censors Board Act.

The Nigerian Cybercrime Act 2015.

Nigerian Press Council Act 1992.

Okpoko, J. 2010. *Understanding Development Communication.* Zaria ABU Press.

Siebert, Fred S., Peterson, Theodore, and Schramm, Wilburn. 1969. *Four Theories of The Press: The Authoritarian, Libertarian, Social Responsibility and Soviet*

Communist Concepts of What the Press Should Be and Do. Urbana, Chicago, London: University of Illinois.

Taylor, Donald S., Nwosu, Peter Ogom, and Mutua-Kombo, Eddah. 2004. "Communication Studies in Africa: The Case for a Paradigm Shift for the 21st Century." *Africa Media Review* 12 (4).

Chapter 4

Nigerian Media Industry Business Imperatives in a Hyper-Connected Ecology

Abigail Odozi Ogwezzy-Ndisika, Kelechi Okechukwu Amakoh, Olubunmi Ajibade, Teslim Olusegun Lawal, and Babatunde Adeshina Faustino

In today's hyper-connected ecology, many are always caught in the web of looking down at their gadgets, gleaning numerous tons of information rather than even paying attention to the neighbor sitting next to them. Digital natives are upwardly mobile and can only be targeted with the digital mind-set. Hence, journalists must leave the filter bubble they have built around themselves and be willing to evolve. As such, there is a need to understand the operation of these platform capitalists, who have become digital intermediaries between publishers and their target audience.

So, the era of living in self-denial is over and media stakeholders must begin to embrace the realities on ground as well as brace up to make the best out of it, by understanding business dynamics of today's journalism in an increasingly competitive business environment of media convergence. Media convergence will not only keep the media surviving; it also has the potential to make the media industry thrive beyond all reasonable doubts. This is against the backdrop that media houses still striving today are those who found a way of ensuring that they get acquainted with the latest trends and remodeled their strategy towards making the best out of these trends (Ogwezzy-Ndisika 2019). Thus, we argue that in Nigeria, most media houses are yet to understand this truth, hence, the retrenchment of staff, poor remuneration, shallow content production as well as failure to perform its watchdog function. Ipso facto, the Nigerian media industry has come of age for a new course to be set. Hence, this chapter stirs conversation in this area, as well as turns the searchlight media establishments as well as the industry in this direction.

CONCEPTUAL CLARIFICATIONS

Media convergence is not a buzzword, but our present-day reality. The word convergence is synonymous with words such as: intersectional, interplay, and hybridity. We conceptually mean that through convergence, the media space with the advancement in technology, culture, and economy continually alters the relationship between media consumers and producers. In this day and age, former consumers (fan community, readership base, followers of news) have become powerful to the extent that they are fellow purveyors of information. Much more, these fellow producers have become participants in this media space. This practice is what Yochai Benkler, a professor of entrepreneurial studies at Harvard Law School defines as a "hybrid of media ecology" in his 2006 seminal work titled *The Wealth of Networks.*

To help us unpack this term better, two reputable scholars in media con-vergence culture field: Henry Jenkins, a professor at the Annenberg School of Communication, University of Pennsylvania, USA; and Mark Deuze, a professor at the University of Amsterdam, The Netherlands, in an editorial written in the 2008 edition of *Convergence Culture Journal* defines conver-gence as a:

> top-down corporate-driven process and a bottom-up consumer-driven process. Media companies are learning how to accelerate the flow of media content across delivery channels to expand revenue opportunities, broaden markets and reinforce consumer loyalties and commitments. Users are learning how to master these different media technologies to bring the flow of media more fully under their control and to interact (and co-create) with other users. (Jenkins and Deuze 2008, p. 6)

From Jenkins and Deuze's explanation, the convergence culture puts media companies in the position to continually learn and update their capacity to navigate this large body of delivery channels provided by advancement of technology in order to reach its audience, make money, and retain market leadership.

On the other hand, the media consumers (now producers and participants), are as well trying to understand the intricacies of being bombarded with several alluring media technologies all fighting for attention. This continuous battle is all thanks to the activities of platform capitalists such as Facebook,

Twitter, Google, Netflix, YouTube, LinkedIn, Amazon, and the likes. These companies are altering the journalism business. In fact, they continue to reposition to ensure that every member of its community need not leave its platform to do anything. From reading books to consuming news to even purchasing household appliances, these platform capitalists are taking up the attention of the media industry's target audience. Much more, digital advertising is the order of the day. Google alone accounts for 31.1 percent of the total global advertising spending followed by Facebook, Alibaba, and Amazon, respectively (eMarketer 2019). In terms of engagement as of April 27, 2019, *alexa.com* stated that "The Top 500 sites on the web" ranked Google as the first website globally. Following closely are YouTube, Facebook, Baidu, Wikipedia, Yahoo (9th), Amazon (10th), and Twitter (11th).

In Nigeria, Google ranks number one (*The Guardian* 2022). The others among the top five include Bet9ja, YouTube, Facebook, and Yahoo. In fact, Nairaland (11th), a discussion forum where Nigerians converge, debate, and share content, ranks higher than any media company platform in the country (Punch Online ranks 12th on the ranking). This day's technology continues to dwarf the practice of inflation of circulation figures to attract advertising. The advertisers now know the way, and will continually go through a route proven with real numbers.

In other words, the rise of emergent new media should be a reason for media practitioners to strategize on how to be relevant. The world is digital. According to the 10th edition of *Measuring the Information Society Report,* published by International Telecommunications Union in December 2018, it was noted that 51 percent of the world's population (3.9 billion) are using the internet. Of all the continents, Africa recorded the largest growth rate. From 2.1 percent of internet users in 2005, ITU, a United Nations ICT agency based in Geneva, Switzerland, noted that Africa has 24.4 percent of internet users as of 2018. Indeed, this shows the import of internet access and usage. With this increase, there is no gainsaying that the practice of journalism has evolved, is evolving and will continue to evolve. With this surge, African media companies have no excuse not to be intentional about ensuring optimum use of this advantage in repositioning their editorial and business models to remain relevant and profitable.

JOURNALISM IN THE ERA OF
DIGITAL INTERMEDIARIES

The truth be told, the sea of companies camping at Silicon Valley are gaining mastery of the audience we once had at our fingertips. They have unique audience profiles and can alter algorithms for their own specific needs. As a profession believed to be Anglo-American, this is an ongoing concern for media industries across the globe. As such, there is a need for media houses to be circumspect of the workings of these technologies as well as be proactive to seek for new ways to create tools to engage the audience.

In a study conducted in 2017 on *Dealing with Digital Intermediaries* by Rasmus Kleis Nielsen and Sarah Anne Ganter of the University of Oxford, United Kingdom, it was observed that media houses were reactionary in their approach to the rising dominance of digital intermediaries. Hence, there is a need for media houses to take the initiative, be proactive, collaborate and develop media products. There is also the need for newsrooms to gravitate towards improving its technology base for times ahead. Some argue that, with the interplay between journalism and technology, it is likely that a computer will win the Pulitzer Award very soon.

Big media corporations like the *New York Times*, the *Washington Post*, and CNN are continually strategizing and repositioning for the next level in journalism practice. In a report in the *New York Times*, released by its president and chief executive officer Mark Thompson in March, *New York Times*' digital revenue currently stands at $709 million (about ₦256 billion) (*New York Times* 2019). This implies that within three years of its five-year digital revenue target of $800 million by 2020, it has grossed 87 percent of its target. Apparently, they are bound to surpass their target before its expiration next year. This is impressive and they are not resting on their oars. Furthermore, within 2018, they added 716,000 new digital subscriptions, taking their total paid digital subscriptions to 4.3 million (*New York Times* 2019). Additionally, the company launched *The Daily*, a news and opinion podcast in 2017 and broadcasts twenty minutes a day and five days a week. In 2018, its "smash-hit podcast" episode on the "Blasey-Kavanaugh Hearing" (a hearing which saw the accusation of Judge Brett Kavanaugh for "grave sexual misconduct" by Christine Blasey Ford) became Apple's most downloaded podcast. To sum up, *NYT*'s convergence culture is summed up by Thompson as thus:

> we're not letting up on exploring new ways of telling the most important stories of the day and meeting the needs of our audience in every form, from the written word to visual to audio to television to streaming. (Thompson in *New York Times* 2019, p. 8)

With its progressive nature, Thompson also announced *NYT*'s commencement of a new television program by next month (June 2019) known as *The Weekly.* Hence, the media company has resisted the notion that journalism must be statistical and maintain the status quo.

At this junction, it is also important to draw from lessons of the convergence culture in European newsrooms. From studies conducted recently, it is observed that newsrooms in Europe are embracing the convergence culture. Most especially, Scandinavia and the United Kingdom are at the forefront of convergence culture. In other parts of Europe, the convergence culture is growing. In a study conducted by a team of researchers in 2018 within newsrooms across Germany, the Netherlands, Switzerland, Austria, Spain, and Portugal, it was observed that:

> a shift from print to convergence culture is occurring . . . a hybrid newsroom culture is developing that increasingly incorporates convergence; that said, newsrooms have to be able to translate convergence from the strategic level to applicable procedures and policies within their editorial departments. (Menke et al. 2018)

Aside from the digital wave hitting the newsrooms in US and Europe, worthy of note are the remarkable strides recorded by *De Correspondent* of The Netherlands led by Rob Wijinberg and Ernst Pfauth. Through a crowdfunding business model, it raised $2.6 million from 45,888 founding members from 130 countries (including Nigeria) by December 15, 2018, in order to kick- start its English version (Menke et al. 2018). This success was achieved through the pooling of resources from across the globe. Now, with the funds realized, they are set to begin publishing what they call "unbreaking news" by September 2019. This model is also recommendable. With this model, *The Correspondent* intends to run an ad-free kind of journalism, no to click-bait and targeting, fighting stereotypes, solution journalism, and collaborating with its "knowledgeable" members.

In fact, with this advancement in models and designs, new titles are emerging in the newsrooms. This shows how creativity brings about new dimensions to the profession, new job portfolios, and leads to a robust and sustainable business model. In the digital news project conducted by Nic Newman titled: *Journalism, Media, and Technology Trends and Predictions 2019*, the two hundred journalists interviewed across twenty-nine countries (including Kenya) had titles such as: chief data officer; chief marketing officer; head, audience engagement; head of development/innovation; director of strategy; head of multimedia; director of product, among others.

It is important to highlight here that despite the innovations and tweaking of practice to fit the digital age, traditional journalistic values must be upheld. Value must not be sacrificed on the altar of innovation and search for new and sustainable business models. According to Thompson of *NYT*:

> the Company's commitment to investing in journalism and upholding traditional journalistic values and our continuing focus on sweeping digital innovation has helped us create a sustainable business model for news. Today, the *New York*

Times is a leading global news provider and among the world's most successful news subscription businesses. (Thompson in *New York Times* 2019, p. 8)

THEORETICAL FRAMEWORK

Understanding the media environment and the extent to which this evolution has impacted on it can best be seen from the prism of the technological determinism theory, which is a reductionist theory that believes that a civilization's technology determines the path and pace at which such civilization's social structures and cultural values develop. The term is believed to have been coined by Thorstein Veblen (1857–1929), an American sociologist. According to Lievrouw and Livingstone (2006), technological determinism is "the belief that technologies have an overwhelming power to drive human actions," which leads to social change. Technological determinism was propounded in 1962 by Marshall McLuhan and it states that media technology shapes how we as individuals in a society think, feel, act, and how society operates as we move from one technological age to another (Tribal-Literature-Print-Electronics).

From the business angle, Gabberty (2011) also points out that new age businesses' recognition of how technology can change how they do business is a strong argument for technological determinism. He argues that technologies can be used strategically to fashion out and exploit opportunities to provide additional marketing- value offering while maintaining efficacy in their operations. Several technologies provide the backbone for various expressions of convergence; however, as Krotoski (2011) points out, the internet is a major platform, whose spinoffs have fostered more channel fragmentation than any other technologies; and created a strong case for convergence as an operational strategy, not just affecting which technologies to pander towards, but also to determine how content is developed and managed to cater to the needs of an already "converged" audience, which is the key to achieving business objectives. Thus, the view of Thompson of *NYT*, who posited that the company's commitment to investing in journalism and upholding traditional journalistic values and their continuing focus on sweeping digital innovation has helped create a sustainable business model for news is the assumption guiding our position. Therefore, we argue that latching on and maximizing hyper-connected ecology opportunities is a business imperative for Nigeria's media industry in order for it to remain afloat and sustainable in an increasingly competitive business environment.

THE NIGERIAN MEDIA AND THE
CONVERGENCE CULTURE

While the developed nations continue to shift from the previous mode of practicing journalism to a flexible, upwardly mobile and innovative mode, we must not be left behind. With the in- reach, in terms of digital penetration in Sub-Saharan Africa, in general and Nigeria in particular, media convergence remains a viable option in remaining relevant and we commend the efforts of newsrooms in Nigeria already going digital and embracing the convergence culture. Also, we commend the efforts of Channels Television in engaging a multi-dimensional technology known as the *Channels Visual Interface* in the reportage of the just concluded 2019 general elections in the country. Through this technology, reporters were beamed live from different studios in real time to discuss issues relating to the election. This is a welcome development. Another example of innovation we noticed during the election coverage was the opening of the Vanguard LIVE hub in Lagos by Vanguard Media in collaboration with Journalism Clinic.

Much more, some newspaper companies like *The Punch, The Nation, The Guardian, and Vanguard* among others are beginning to make some entry into online broadcasting. This is a welcome idea and there is always room for improvement. Like Henry Jenkins mentioned in his seminal work on *Convergence Culture* in 2006, media companies must"renegotiate their relationship with their consumers" in order to come out of the quagmire of surviving the onslaught of dwindling revenue and activities of the digital intermediaries. So, it is imperative for more newsrooms to gravitate towards embracing technology. It is a sure tool in restructuring and meeting with current trends and realities worldwide. Therefore, a media outfit, an editor or a journalist unwilling to move with the current dispensation of the convergence culture train, is only bidding time before journalism waves them off the coach.

In a 2017 article titled: "What Newspapers Must do to Survive the New Media *O*nslaught" by Lekan Otufodunrin, former managing editor, Online and Special Publications, *The Nation* newspaper, it was put succinctly that "days of old-school editors are numbered." It cannot be said better than by a former editor of a national newspaper, who led a newspaper digital team. The earlier editors begin to understand the current realities and step up their game, the better. There are still some media practitioners that wave this trend and continue to rely on traditional means of news collection, production, and dissemination. Anyone still in the cadre can only be living in a filter bubble waiting to burst.

Much more, there is a need for media houses to focus on instituting policies to guide the usage of these platforms. Drawing from big media corporations, social media policies play a major role for every journalist working under its fold. In 2017, *NYT* staff received a memol from Executive Editor Dean Baquet stating the following:

> We believe that to remain the world's best news organization, we have to maintain a vibrant presence on social media. But we also need to make sure that we are engaging responsibly on social media, in line with the values of our newsroom. That's why we're using updated and expanded social media guidelines. . . . Please read them closely and take them to heart. (*The New York Times* 2017)

In as much as there is need for remodeling of newsroom practice, there is also the need to consider the policy aspect to ensure every journalist upholds brand integrity and dignity even on the digital street. The call to go digital is also a call to maintain couth, respect, and integrity. The social media policy of the British Broadcasting Corporation (BBC) is striking. Its policy addresses three core areas of social media engagement. In Nigeria, we doubt if most media houses have instituted such policies. This is a call to consider instituting such policies to strengthen the media's integrity. Beyond having the policy, there is a need to put it to effective work. Taking a cursory look at how some Nigerian journalists engage on these digital platforms, there is a need to ensure the defining of boundaries. These boundaries also have a power to influence the survival strategy of the media industry.

No one envisaged that a time will come when a president of the free world can speak to the world through a touch of the button on his phone while using the popular microblogging website Twitter. Indeed, this was never predicted. Hence, the need for editors to be innovative, proactive, and dynamic in their approach.

There is no end to learning. As such, there is room for learning of these tools as well as the inclusion of technology-savvy digital natives in handling how the Nigerian media works.

So, drawing from *NYT*'s model, there is always the need for Nigeria's media industry to uphold traditional news values without compromise as it has always done, because it distinguishes the professionals from nonprofessionals marauding within the journalism field in Nigeria. Notwithstanding, it is imperative that the Nigerian media industry repositions and embraces the convergence culture with both arms to remain sustainable by opening the vista of new ideas and refreshing strategies to take the media industry to the next height it deserves in a hyper-connected ecology. The examples examined in this subsection show that it is achievable.

CONCLUSION AND RECOMMENDATION

With the world now digital, any journalism model that seeks to strive and excel beyond bounds sustainably, must consider the right way to harness digital elements for a greater good. So, we conclude that Nigeria's media industry embraces technologies and use them strategically to fashion out and exploit opportunities to provide additional marketing value offering, while maintaining efficacy in operations; not discounting profitability and business sustainability in an increasingly competitive world. Therefore, we recommend a more holistic approach towards retooling strategies and being innovative in order to remain relevant in this technologically defined age.

REFERENCES

Adepetun, A. 2022. "Nigeria's Internet speed ranks 16th in Africa as Airtel emerges fastest operator." *The Guardian*, February 21. Accessed January 15, 2020. https://guardian.ng/news/nigerias-internet-speed-ranks-16th-in-africa-as-airtel-emerges-fastest-operator/.

Benkler, Y. 2006. *The wealth of networks: How social production transforms markets and freedom*. New Haven, CT: Yale University Press.

Enberg, J. (2019). "Global Digital Ad Spending 2019." Insider Intelligence. Accessed October 31, 2022. https://www.insiderintelligence.com/content/global-digital-ad-spending-2019.

Gabberty, J. 2011. "Information and Communications Technology: A Comparative View of Technological Determinism." *The Journal of Applied Business Research* 23 (3): 11–22.

ITU. 2018. "Measuring the Information Society Report." Accessed March 6, 2018. https://www.itu.int/en/ITU-D/Statistics/Documents/publications/misr2018/MISR-2018-Vol-1-E.pdf.

Jenkins, H., and Deuze, M. 2008. "Editorial." *Convergence: The International Journal of Research into New Media Technologies* 14 (1): 5–12. Accessed March 6, 2018. DOI: 10.1177/1354856507084415.

Krotoski, A. (2011). "What effect has the internet had on journalism?" *The Guardian*, Februrary 20.. Accessed January 30, 2021. https://www.theguardian.com/technology/2011/feb/20/what-effect-internet-on-journalism

Lievrouw, L. A. and Livingstone, S. 2009. Introduction in *New media: Sage benchmarks in communication*, edited by Lievrouw, L. A. and Livingstone, Sonia. London: SAGE.

Menke, Manuel, Kinnebrock, Susanne, Kretzschmar, Sonja, Aichberger, Ingrid, Broersma, Marcel, Hummel, Roman, Kirchhoff, Susanne, Prandner, Dimitri, Ribeiro, Nelson, and Salaverría, Ramón. (2018). "Convergence Culture in European Newsrooms," *Journalism Studies* 19 (6), 881–904. Accessed July 2022.

DOI: 10.1080/1461670X.2016.1232175. https://pure.rug.nl/ws/portalfiles/portal /76276787/Convergence_Culture_in_European_Newsrooms.pdf.

Newman, N. 2019. "Journalism, Media, and Technology Trends and Predictions 2019." "Digital News Project." Reuters Institute for the Study of Journalism, Department of Politics and International Relations, University of Oxford.

New York Times. 2017. "The *Times* Issues Social Media Guidelines for the Newsroom." *New York Times*, October 13. Accessed June 24, 2021. https://www .nytimes.com/2017/10/13/reader-center/social-media-guidelines.html

New York Times. 2018. "The New York Times Company 2018 Annual Report." Accessed August 15, 2021. https://s1.q4cdn.com/156149269/files/doc_financials /annual/2018/updated/2018-Annual-Report-(1).pdf.

Nielsen, R., and Ganter, S. A. 2018. "Dealing with digital intermediaries: A case study of the relations between publishers and platforms." *New Media and Society* 20 (4): 1600–1617. Accessed September 23, 2019. DOI: 10.1177/1461444817701318.

Ogwezzy-Ndisika, A. O. 2019. "Understanding business dynamics of today's journalism." Keynote address delivered at the opening ceremony of the biennial convention of the Nigerian Guild of Editors held on May 4, 2019, at Lagos Airport Hotel, Ikeja, Lagos.

Otufodunrin, L. 2017. "What newspapers must do to survive the new media onslaught." Media Career Development Network, August 20. Accessed January 15, 2020. https://mediacareerng.org/2017/08/20/what-newspapers-must-do-to-survive -the-new-media-onslaught/.

Peiser, J. 2019. "The New York Times Co. Reports $709 Million in Digital Revenue for 2018." *New York Times*, February 6. Accessed July 1, 2022. https: //www.nytimes.com/2019/02/06/business/media/new-york-times-earnings-digital -subscriptions.html.

Chapter 5

Fake News and General Elections in Nigeria

Fighting the Canary in the Digital Coal Mine

Abigail Odozi Ogwezzy-Ndisika, Kelechi Okechukwu Amakoh, Olubunmi Ajibade, Teslim Olusegun Lawal, and Babatunde Adeshina Faustino

In this post-truth era, issues surrounding fake news, disinformation, and misinformation are very important to discuss and proffer solutions. In 2017, Charlie Beckett defined fake news as "the canary in the digital coal mine," (p. 34). He further noted that fake news is "a symptom of a much wider systemic challenge around the value and credibility of information and the way that we—socially, politically, economically—are going to handle the threats and opportunities of new communication technologies." For Allcott and Gentzkow (2017), fake news is regarded to be news items that are intentionally planted in the media with the aim of confusing or misleading the news consumers. Thus, we argue that fake news is a threat to our cyberspace. As such, stakeholders in the media industry must stop at nothing to ensure that truth prevails. For the purpose of this paper, we shall stick with the use of "fakes" to imply: fake news, misinformation, disinformation, and hate speech.

During the week of October 7, 2018, another set of fakes hit Facebook. Many messages were circulated saying: "I have only one Facebook account. Please ignore any friend request supposedly from me." Another read like this: "Heads-up!! Accounts are being cloned. Your picture and your name are used to create a new Facebook account (they don't need your password to do this). They want your friends to add them to their Facebook account. Your friends will think that it's you and accept your request. From that point on they can write what they want under your name. I have NO plans to open a new account. Please DO NOT accept a 2nd friend request from 'me.' Please forward to all your contacts." The third variant of the hoax messages disseminated read like this: "Hi. . . . I actually got another friend request from you which I ignored so you may want to check your account. Hold your finger on the message until the forward button appears . . . then hit forward and all the people you want to forward too. . . . I had to do the people individually. PLEASE DO NOT ACCEPT A NEW friendship FROM ME AT THIS TIME." All these messages turned out to be false after a terse statement from Facebook headquarters. This is not the first time Facebook users will receive hoax messages.

Again, many of us are familiar with Donald Trump, the former president of the United States of America and his constant "war" on fakes. In a 2017 study carried out in the country, it was found that only 6 percent of the population trust online news sources all of the time (Statista 2017). In another survey in March 2018, 52 percent participants stated that they believe online news sources constantly publish fake news stories (Statista 2018).

For us in Nigeria, we have had our own tale of fake news, and during general elections, discourse around the influence of fakes heightens. It is a discourse that every stakeholder partakes in order to fight fakes headlong. Thus, during the last two general elections in Nigeria (2015 and 2019) stakeholders in government, media, political parties, academia, and the corporate world of Nigeria at various times discuss the issue of fakes, which this chapter sheds light on and distills in this era where fakes travel faster than the truth.

THE MEDIA AND FAKES

We live in an era where fakes travel faster than the truth, and it has become an international phenomenon as there is an increase in the sponsoring of untrue stories, distortion of the coverage of a specific topic, propaganda, half-truths, and conjectures in the media, especially the online media. First, let us refresh our minds with the submission of a one-time president of the United States of America, Thomas Jefferson, in 1787 on the importance of the media. He said, "The basis of our governments being the opinion of the people, the very first object should be to keep that right; and were it left to me to decide whether we should have a government without newspapers, or newspapers without a government, I should not hesitate a moment to prefer the latter. But I should mean that every man should receive those papers and be capable of reading them" (Ogwezzy-Ndisika 2018a, p. 2).

Therefore, the media is an important part of any society. If you underrate the media, you do it at your own peril. The power of the media is potent to influence any narrative as created by its owners. This is done with an expected outcome in mind. As a result of its importance, stakeholders in the industry must uphold the ethics of the profession. The fourth and fifth estates of the realm must never relent in its quest of being the watchdog of the society. This duty of the media is one that cannot be underestimated. In this era of social media, it behooves on the media to ensure that their platforms are not compromised, no matter the cost involved. Journalists, bloggers, content creators, and social media managers must begin to work together to ensure the fight against fakes is won ultimately.

This is against the backdrop that many are turning to social media for several reasons. A group of people utilizing social media are politicians. Some argue that a political process in any given society is not complete without activities on social media. In Nigeria, during the past few general elections, most of the presidential aspirants declared their intentions on social media. They have constantly used the media as a platform to advance their visions for the country.

In terms of history, the era of social media and elections can be traced to the 1990s when the former vice president of the United States of America, Al Gore, engaged in online conversations for his presidential campaign. Also, in 2008, the then US president, Barack Obama, also massively used social media for his presidential campaign (Green 2015). His successful use of social media in 2008 and 2012 influenced other politicians.

On the other hand, the 2016 US presidential election took another turn. It is believed that the election that brought in President Donald Trump was influenced by Russia. According to a 2017 report by the director of national intelligence, United States of America, the government of Russia influenced the US elections in a bid to support the candidacy of Donald Trump over the then secretary of state, Hilary Clinton. This was made possible through the cyber attacks launched by the Russian government. As of June, eleven officials of the Trump administration had admitted the interference of Russia in the elections.

Similarly, in 2017, the French presidential elections had 60 million Twitter exchanges between 2.4 million users. However, it was observed that 72.9 percent of all fake news during the election analyzed was produced and disseminated by only two political communities (Gaumont *et al.* 2018).

Nigeria, on the other hand, is not immune to these interferences. Earlier 2019, there were allegations of interference by Cambridge Analytica in Nigeria's 2015 presidential elections. According to the *Guardian* (2018), there was a video portraying one of the presidential candidates as a supporter of Sharia law. "The video was distributed in Nigeria with the sole intent of intimidating voters. It included content where people were being dismembered, where people were having their throats cut and bled to death in a ditch. They were being burned alive. There were incredibly anti-Islamic, threatening messages portraying Muslims as violent" (Cadwalladr, 2018). In sum, the video was created to influence the voting pattern of Nigerians. So, it is obvious that the era of fakes is here with us.

Apart from the influence of fakes during elections, its impact has been felt in other aspects of Nigeria's existence. In July 2018, Honorable Minister of Communication and Culture Lai Mohammed, while launching Nigeria's campaign against fake news, noted that:

> In a multi-ethnic and multi-religious country like ours, fake news is a time bomb. And in recent weeks, many anarchists have been doing everything possible to detonate the bomb. But for the prudence and vigilance of Nigerians, they—the religious and ethnic bigots among us—would have set the nation on fire, especially over the farmers-herders clashes as well as communal clashes. There is an epidemic sweeping the world. If left unchecked, it could be worse than all the plagues that the world has recorded put together. It is a clear and present danger to global peace and security. It is a threat to democracy. It is the epidemic of fake news. Mixed with hate speech, it is a disaster waiting to happen. For the media, the epidemic is even worse. This is because fake news, in most cases, is designed to misinform, undermines confidence in the media. And once the people lose confidence in the media, the society is in trouble. (Nwafor 2018)

The above is against the journalism code of ethics, which states in part: "Truth is the cornerstone of journalism and every journalist [mainstream or citizen journalist] should strive diligently to ascertain the truth of every event. [Again, it states that] Journalism entails a high degree of public trust. To earn and maintain this trust, it is morally imperative for every journalist and every news medium to observe the highest professional and ethical standards. In the exercise of these duties, a journalist should always have a healthy regard for the public interest" (Nigerian Press Council, 2009, p. 10). Thus, in this era of media convergence, it may be argued that media industries (both the fourth and the fifth estates of the realm), can fight fakes, a canary in the digital coal mine in this era of media convergence by adopting self-regulation; and this will only be effective when there is a clear collective and individual self-interest to make it work.

THEORETICAL FRAMEWORK

The issue of media ethics has been on since the twentieth century. The book *Four Theories of the Press* by Wilbur Schramm, Fred Siebert, and Theodore Peterson—written in 1963—presented four different theories popularly referred to as press theories. Although the four theories explain the operations of the press, one of them is very relevant to the issue being examined, that is, the social responsibility theory. It has its roots in mid-twentieth- century society and revolves around ethics in the media but has always existed as an ideal.

According to Folarin (1998, p. 28), the theory postulated the specific functions of the media to include serving "the political system by making information, discussion and consideration of public affairs generally accessible; to inform the public to enable it to take self-determined action [and] to serve the economic system." This view was also vividly recaptured by McQuail (2013), Baran and Davis (2012), as well as Aneato, Onabajo, and Osifeson (2008). For instance, McQuail (2013, p. 45) argued that media, irrespective of its owners, has an ethical obligation to society without any discrimination on the basis of *sex* orientation and they should discharge their duties in a truthful, fair, and objective manner in order to make it relevant to all members of the wider society. McQuail (2010, p. 171) further argued that "the media should be free, but self-regulated . . . [and] follow agreed codes of ethics and professional conduct."

This theory brings to the fore that the media should be responsible in the performance of its functions: provision of information, discussion and debate on political issues, enlightening the public for self-government, safeguarding the rights of individuals by acting as watchdog to the government, servicing the political system through advertisement of candidates and parties, providing entertainment and maintaining its own self sufficiency, and be free from the pressures of special interests.

Using this theory as a framework for discussing fakes and general elections in Nigeria, this chapter opines that media industries (both the fourth and the fifth estates of the realm), can fight fakes, a canary in the digital coal mine, particularly during elections by adhering to the media code of ethics, which, among others, states that the media must be fair, unbiased, and accurate, completely factual and professional in their reporting and information sharing, which is the tandem with social responsibility media theory, hence the theory formed the framework for analysis.

NIGERIA, FAKES, AND GENERAL ELECTIONS

In 2014, Nigeria battled the Ebola scourge. This period caused a whole lot of panic among Nigerians. One event that took place was the spread of fake news on social media. The Attah of Igalaland, Idakwo Michael Ameh Oboni, had prescribed bathing with salt as the solution to the Ebola crisis. To this effect, many began to send this information. This led to some dying and many being hospitalized.

Similarly, since the outbreak of COVID-19 in Wuhan, a city in the Hubei Province of China in December 2019, inaccurate information has been spreading widely and at speed, making it more difficult for the public to identify verified facts and advice from trusted sources, such as their local health authority or WHO. Thus, as the world responds to the COVID-19 pandemic, we are faced with the challenge of an overabundance of information related to the virus, some of which may be false and potentially harmful (World Health Organization 2021). This is partly responsible for the difficulty in flattening the curve, globally.

Specifically, on Nigeria, Sulaiman et al. (2020), in a study that examined information sharing and evaluation as determinants of the spread of fake news among Nigerian youths on social media using experience from COVID-19 pandemic, found that most Nigerian youths used Facebook, Twitter, WhatsApp, and Instagram to spread fake news on COVID-19, especially on treatment, vaccines, numbers of cases, and symptoms. This may be partly accountable for the plateauing in the number of COVID-19 cases and the spiking death rate from the disease in the country. In addition, even the blind can see that the hospitals are overwhelmed, not discounting the fact that tests and treatment are expensive, leaving the risk of death on the prowl. Indeed, the curve is rising, and the federal government has threatened a second lockdown!

Also, at other times, fakes have caused unnecessary damage to the reputation of individuals. This trend has taken a new turn with the improvement of technology. In August 2018, Honorable Minister of Information and Culture Alhaji Lai Mohammed recounted the fake news on social media about his driver abandoning him on the road and decamping to the opposition party, Peoples Democratic Party. Mohammed termed the news as "ridiculous." He further explained that his "driver is a civil servant, who I inherited and even if he has political leaning, he should let me know. Why would he now be so irrational to drop me in the middle of the road just because he wants to defect to PDP?" (Nwafor 2018).

In 2015, the use of hate speech took the center stage. Several hate speeches and fake news were spread by leaders, candidates, and citizens through the use of the media. There was the use of "acerbic words, half-truths and outright lies in their electioneering campaigns. The election was seen as a 'do-or-die' affair by the politicians. These activities were alarming, and apprehensions were rife about the success of the election and peaceful transition of power" (Ogwezzy-Ndisika 2018b). Also, the election was a "show unguarded, offensive, uncouth, uncultured and absolutely damning inexcusable statements emanating from the two major parties during Nigeria's 2015 presidential election campaigns" (Ogwezzy-Ndisika 2015, p. 7). "Hence, the two major contestants, Goodluck Jonathan and Muhammadu Buhari along with nine other party leaders first signed the 'Abuja Accord' on January 14, 2015. The peace pact was witnessed by former United Nations Secretary-General, Kofi Annan and former Secretary-General of the Commonwealth, Emeka Anyaoku. The substance of that accord was their commitment to free, fair and credible elections in Nigeria" (Ogwezzy-Ndisika 2015).

Although at the expiration of the period for the conduct of party primaries on Sunday, October 7, 2018, in Nigeria, preparatory to the 2019 general elections, about twenty presidential candidates emerged. The candidates included: the incumbent president Muhammadu Buhari, former vice president and serial presidential aspirant Atiku Abubakar, former governor of Cross River state Donald Duke, and former minister of education and activist Obiageli Ezekwesili, Kingsley Mogahlu, and a former deputy governor of Central Bank of Nigeria, among others. Albeit this, there were two major candidates. Thus, when Nigeria was preparing for the 2019 general elections, two presidential candidates—the then incumbent president Muhammadu Buhari and former vice president and serial presidential aspirant Atiku Abubakar—signed the "Abuja Accord" under the auspices of the National Peace Committee (NPC) in December 2018, and again on 13 February 2019, enhancing confidence in the 2019 electoral process. The National Peace Committee, led by former head of state, General Abdulsalami Abubakar, and composed of, among others, both Christian and Muslim religious leaders, was formed after the signing of the Abuja Accord to oversee implementation of the agreement. Similar non-violence agreements were subsequently signed by political party representatives in most Nigerian states on March 26, two days before the presidential election (European Union Election Observation Mission 2019, pp. 8–9).

Notwithstanding, again, looking at the new media, European Union Election Observation Mission (2019, p. 30–33) observed that for the growing population of internet users, 111 million in December 2018, online media and social networks were important platforms to impart and access information; this was demonstrated in vigorous political discussions and online space, giving an alternative platform for political parties to campaign, at times in a distorting and acerbic manner. EU EOM analyses found that multiple

Twitter accounts, which are relatively easy to establish, appear to have been strategically used in a coordinated way to amplify partisan messages. The EU EOM also found that "social influencers" (with a substantial number of followers) were sometimes synchronized in promoting contestants. Party affiliates informed the mission that these strategies were used in the campaign and that various groups of social network users were employed by parties to promote contestants or attack opponents. Comment sections were found to include some inflammatory language along party lines, as well as regional and ethnic lines.

These may account for why Pate (2011) and Ogwezzy-Ndisika et al. (2019, p. 16) decried the high degree of professional breaches in communication during elections as manifested through "character assassination, false accusations, blackmail and misrepresentation of facts . . . to the extent that the unity of this country was shaken to its very foundation." Also, capturing it, Kukah (2015) asserted that the media has become a vehicle for negative political messages that has defied logic, an action that is in clear violation of a provision in the Nigerian Amended Electoral Act, 2011, which requires that "abusive, intemperate, slanderous or base language or insinuations or innuendoes designed or likely to provoke violent reactions or emotions shall not be employed or used in political campaign."

Furthermore, the European Union Election Observation Mission Report stated that parties used online platforms to campaign, at times distorting the information environment and spreading false news. There was vigorous political discussion online and several fact-checking initiatives countered frequent disinformation messages. This, the report attributes to Nigeria lacking specific data protection laws, leaving personal data, collected by several state institutions including the Nigerian Communications Commission and INEC, potentially vulnerable to potential abuse.

However, in a positive development, on 25 January 2019, Nigeria's National Information Technology Development Agency issued the Nigeria Data Protection Regulation 2019, which includes several concepts included in the EU General Data Protection Regulation (GDPR). To date, local institutions are not familiar with this regulation, and it is not yet possible to assess its reach and implementation. A Digital Rights and Freedom Bill was promoted by civil society to fill the legislative gap. It passed the National Assembly but has not been assented to by the president and its future status is unclear. The 2015 Cybercrime (Prohibition, Prevention, etc.) The Act, in section 24, penalizes cyberstalking with up to three years in prison, a fine, or both. This includes broad prohibitions on messages that are "false, for the purpose of causing annoyance, inconvenience, danger, obstruction, insult, injury, criminal intimidation, enmity, hatred, ill will or needless anxiety to another." This section of the Act has been used on several occasions in recent years to arrest bloggers as well as journalists, including over the election period. Civil society organizations are currently challenging this section of the act at the Supreme Court (European Union Election Observation Mission [2019, pp. 3, 30–33]).

Again, Friedrich-Ebert-Stiftung (FES) (2019, p. 17–18) stated that, in terms of the use of new media for election campaigns, website, blogs, and other digital platforms are not required to register with or obtain permissions from state authorities; [and] Nigerian authorities have not yet blocked or filtered websites and internet content. Authorities can only monitor but they cannot block or filter the internet. Notwithstanding, authorities have resorted to more classical means of silencing the online public, such as the harassment of citizens based on their communication via the internet and social media. Cybercrime policing has sometimes been misdirected towards online communities critical of the authorities, adding that security officials have openly stated they would clamp down on social media communications that breach public peace.

CONCLUSION

In this era of post-truth, the fight against fakes must be done holistically and collectively. Thus, the collective efforts of the government, media professionals, politicians and citizens at large are required to find lasting solutions to the spread of fakes. As such, election periods call for due diligence by government, media practitioners, politicians, and citizens in order to combat the menace of fakes.

COMBATING FAKES: THE WAY FORWARD

The fight against fakes is a fight to ensure the spread of truth and absence of undue influence in cyberspace. Nations are rising up to combat against fakes. In September, the Danish government revealed an action plan of eleven initiatives to counter any form of influence that might occur as they prepared to vote in the 2019 parliamentary elections (Ministry of Foreign Affairs of Denmark 2018). It is believed that there are planned influence campaigns by Russia within the Nordic-Baltic region (the region of Denmark).

In Denmark's neighboring country, Sweden, the authorities worked assiduously to avoid interference in the elections that were held on September 9, 2018. Speaking before the election, Swedish prime minister Stefan Löfven noted: "It has become increasingly obvious that foreign powers are trying to influence an election and its outcome. Obviously Russia was active in the US election. We cannot assume that we are immune."

Asides the fight by nations, several international organizations are combating the spread of fakes through their platforms. In March 2018, Google announced an investment of $300 million to fight fake news in the next three years. In addition, it launched two initiatives: Google News Initiative and Digital News Initiative. In the same vein, Facebook has begun the fight against fakes on all its platforms: Facebook, WhatsApp, and Instagram. This fight was a fallout of its link to the interference of Russia in the US elections four years ago. About 600 million fake accounts have been deleted on Facebook. On Twitter, 70 million fake accounts were deleted recently.

In July 2018, the Nigerian government launched a campaign against fake news. The campaign is believed to be a collaboration between National Orientation Agency and the media in order to educate the citizens on fakes and its adverse effect on the nation. This is a welcome development. Media and information literacy is a sure way to go. Citizens must be equipped with the right mentality on how to communicate online, access and analyze information disseminated through the media. A media literate citizen will be equipped to critically interpret, create, and act on media messages.

Furthermore, online media professionals must practice journalism from an informed perspective. The power to create and disseminate information without any holds barred is not a license to peddle falsehood. The basic tenets of the profession must be upheld. This distinguishes and gives the online brand prestige. Due to the activities of some online media platforms, their brands have failed the integrity test. Thus, subsequent updates on their websites are never trusted.

For citizens, the craze behind the share button online must be curtailed. Before sharing that information, it is important to confirm it rather than send a piece of information with words like "copied," "passed as received," "I don't know how true." These days of instant messaging platforms like WhatsApp, Messenger, and the like, it is important to discern what message is right from the other to fight the canary of fakes in the digital coal mine.

Essentially, the media must avoid being the pawn during election seasons. All said on elections, while social responsibility on the part of the fourth and fifth estates of the realm will combat fakes, an issue-based campaign, which will rise above an individualistic approach to campaign to a robust and articulate debate among politicians, will help fight fake news during elections. In amplifying the voices of politicians, cyberspace must be a platform to encourage issue-based debates and action plans for those vying for different elective positions.

REFERENCES

Allcott, H. and Gentzkow, M. 2017. "Social media and fake news in the 2016 election." *Journal of Economic Perspectives* 31 (2): 211–236.

Aneato, S., Onabajo, O. S., and Osifeson, J. B. 2008. *Models and theories of communication*. Maryland: African Renaissance Books Inc.

Baran, S. J. and Davis, D. K. 2012. *Mass communication theory: Foundation, ferment and future*. Boston: Wadsworth.

Cadwalladr, C. 2018. "Revealed: graphic video used by Cambridge Analytica to influence Nigerian election." *The Guardian*, April 24. Accessed October 31, 2022. https://www.theguardian.com/uk-news/2018/apr/04/cambridge-analytica-used-violent-video-to-try-to-influence-nigerian-election.

Electoral Act as Amended. 2010. Abuja: Independent National Electoral Commission (INEC).

European Union Election Observation Mission. 2019. "Nigeria general elections 2019 final report." Accessed May 22, 2021. https://eeas.europa.eu/election-observation-missions/eom-nigeria-2019_en.

Folarin, A. B. 1998. *Theories of mass communication: An introductory text*. Ibadan: Stirling–Horden Publishers (Nig.) Ltd.

Friedrich-Ebert-Stiftung (FES). 2019. *African media barometer (AMB) Nigeria 2019*. Friedrich-Ebert-Stiftung (FES) *fesmedia*Africa: Windhoek, Namibia.

Gaumont, N., Panahi, M., Chavalarias, D. 2018. "Reconstruction of the socio-semantic dynamics of political activist Twitter networks—Method and application to the 2017 French presidential election." *PLoS ONE* 13 (9): e0201879.

Green, R. K. 2015. "The game changer: Social media and the 2016 presidential election." *Huffington Post*, November 16. Accessed February 3, 2021. http://www.huffingtonpost.com/r-kay-green/the-game-changer-socialm_b_8568432.html.

Kukah, H., 2015. "Hate speech, social media and the 2015 Election." Pointblank News, January 27. Accessed June 10, 2021. pointblanknews.com/pbn/ . . . /hate-speech-social-media-2015-election/.

McQuail, D. 2010. *McQuail's mass communication theory* (6th edition). Thousand Oaks, CA: Sage.

McQuail, D. 2013. *Journalism and society*. London: Sage Publications, Ltd.

Ministry of Foreign Affairs of Denmark. 2018. "Strengthened safeguards against foreign influence on Danish elections and democracy." Accessed April 5, 2021. https://um.dk/en/news/newsdisplaypage/?newsid=1df5adbb-d1df-402b-b9ac-57fd4485ffa4.

Nigerian Press Council. 2009. *The Handbook of the Nigerian Press Council*.

Nwafor, Polycarp. 2018. "Fake news, hate speech threat to national security—Lai Mohammed." Vanguard, July 13. Accessed May 8, 2020. https://www.vanguardngr.com/2018/07/fake-news-hate-speech-threat-to-national-security-lai-mohammed.

Ogwezzy-Ndisika, A. 2015. "Hate speech, media ethics and 2015 electioneering campaign: Insights from relevant codes and the electoral act." A paper delivered at the United States Consulate on May 5, 2015.

Ogwezzy-Ndisika, A. 2018a. "Let's fight fakes together." A paper delivered at Guild of Professional Bloggers of Nigeria (GPBN) Inaugural Lecture held on Saturday, October 13, 2018, at the Radisson Hotel, Ikeja, Lagos.

Ogwezzy-Ndisika, A. 2018b. "Towards a peaceful 2019 Nigeria general election." A paper delivered at the official launch of the Nigerian Verification Project, *CrossCheck Nigeria,* on Wednesday, November 28, 2018, in Lagos.

Ogwezzy-Ndisika, A. O., Faustino, B. A., and Amakoh, K. O. 2019. "Curbing hatred: The ethnic diehards' agitations and 2015 presidential election campaign in Nigeria." *Journal of Hate Studies* 15 (1): 233–253. DOI: http://doi.org/10.33972/jhs.169.

Pate, U. A. 2011. "Media and the process of democratization in Nigeria." A paper presented at a workshop on the media and democracy in Nigeria. Organized by the INEC Press Corps holding at Kaduna, December 15–17.

Statista. 2017. "Level of trust in selected online news sources in the United States as of June 2017." Accessed June 28, 2020. https://www.statista.com/statistics/620130/online-news-sources-trustworthiness/.

Statista. 2018. "Perceived frequency of online news websites reporting fake news stories in the United States as of March 2018." Accessed July 10, 2020. https://www.statista.com/statistics/649234/fake-news-exposure-usa/.

Sulaiman, K. A., Adeyemi, I., and Ayegun, I. 2020. "Information sharing and evaluation as determinants of spread of fake news on social media among Nigerian youths: Experience from COVID-19 pandemic." *International Journal of Knowledge Content Development and Technology* 10 (4): 65–82, December 2020. Accessed May 22, 2021. DOI: 10.5865/IJKCT.2020.10.4.065.

World Health Organization. 2021. "How to report misinformation online." Accessed January 14, 2022. https://www.who.int/campaigns/connecting-the-world-to-combat-coronavirus/how-to-report-misinformation-online?gclid=EAIaIQobChMIsJH3j-bF7gIVk7PtCh0mDgy2EAAYASAAEgIxHvD_BwE).

SECTION II

Journalism

Chapter 6

Nigerian Journalism

*Metamorphosing from the Traditional
Media Realm into the Digital
Space, Challenges and Prospects*

Ray Ekpu, Shamusi Olarenwaju
Tiamiyu, and Azuh Arinze

In the contemporary media environment, digitization and globalization have
become buzzwords that provide a veritable anchor for robust intellectual discourse and commercial examination of their effects (positive and negative)
on the existing business model in the journalism industry. It must be stated
upfront that there is no way one can carry out an effective examination of the
journalism practice in Nigeria without taking a study journey, even if not in
a comprehensive manner (because that would form the basis of another book
in itself), into the beginning of the evolution of journalism in the country—its
growth and development and its future prospects.

HISTORICAL PERSPECTIVE OF THE PRESS IN NIGERIA

Historically, journalism is older than Nigeria—indeed there are few social
institutions in the country today that can lay hold to greater antiquity than
Nigerian journalism. Whereas journalism was birthed in the country in
1859, the geographical space now known as Nigeria came into being in
1914 through the instrumentality of amalgamation which saw the merging of
Northern and Southern Protectorates by the British colonial administration.
Again, at the time Nigeria gained her political independence from Britain in

October 1960, Nigerian journalism had thrived for over a century. Needless to say that in the last 161 years of its existence (1859 to 2020), journalism as a profession has faced a lot of daunting challenges which sometimes threatens its very foundation. But in all, it has been able to weather the strongest storms as it were, and is today standing shoulder to shoulder with other professions in the country.

According to Fred Omu, from a place of refuge for a variety of frustrated and distressed people in the nineteenth century (Omu 1980, p. 38), and "an unprofitable, frustrating and soul-depressing career" (Awolowo 1960, p. 80), journalism has today become in the first two decades of the twenty-first century, an attractive, dignifying and much-sought-after profession.

THE ADVENT OF PRINT JOURNALISM IN NIGERIA

Print journalism started in Nigeria through the pioneering efforts of the Reverend Henry Townsend of the CMS persuasion who established the first newspaper in the country in 1859. The fortnightly publication entitled *IweIrohin* was domiciled in Abeokuta, a rolling mountain city in the then Western Region of Nigeria. The stated primary objective of the bilingual paper was to develop and encourage the reading culture among the indigenous people of the region. But according to Omu (1967, p. 80) the *IweIrohin* did pursue other campaigns of a purely political nature which aroused hostile reactions from the colonial administration in Lagos and foreshadowed the endemic confrontation between the press and government in the country.

After the debut of *IweIrohin*, other publications of the humanitarian hue emerged on the fledgling newspaper landscape of Nigeria. Notable among these was the *Anglo-African* which was established in Lagos on June 6, 1863, by Robert Campbell, an American immigrant activist of Jamaican origin. The mission of the weekly newspaper was to serve as a platform for interaction between Britain and Africa (Omu 1996, pp. 206–212). Living out its mission statement, the *Anglo-African* focused its attention exclusively on literary matters which were aimed at encouraging the growth of literacy in the country. For this reason, personal disputes or differences among individuals were uncompromisingly excluded from the pages of the publication. But the paper could only last for about two years because by December 1865, it had ceased to exist. The main cause of the early demise of *Anglo-African* had been blamed on its elitist stance which made it impossible for it to attract large patronage from the mainstream of the society.

THE ROLE OF NIGERIAN NATIONALISM
AND IDEOLOGICAL PRINT MEDIA

Although the Nigerian journalists who succeeded their missionary counterparts also encouraged the promotion of education because they belonged to the pioneer intellectual elite of Lagos, which owed its emergence to missionary effort (Omu 1996), their focus was different. For one thing, Nigerians as the colonial subjects were excluded from effective participation in matters that affected them. So the new crops of journalists and the educated elite were not merely concerned with people being able to read and write, but that the knowledge they had acquired should enable them to form and express strong opinions that the colonial administration could not ignore. Inevitably, the press took the role of opposition to the government (Omu 1996). The press thus became a rallying point for the articulation of nationalist views and opinions, which propelled the agitations for a greater say by Nigerians in how the country was being run. They engendered a sense of political and nationalist awareness and active engagement by providing a platform for the criticism of the government, spreading disaffection with some aspects of official policies and programs which were considered inimical to the well-being of Nigerians.

This was the beginning of what was later to be known as "adversary journalism," which became an ideological weapon to wage a literary war against the occupation of the country by foreign power and eventually led to political independence in October 1960 without firing a bullet. This scenario gave birth to the sobriquet "the pen is mightier than the sword."

THE GENESIS OF BROADCASTING IN NIGERIA

For almost four decades, Nigerian journalism operated on one leg—the print media. But by 1933, the story changed with the advent of radio broadcasting. Radio broadcasting as a genre of journalism made its debut in the country that year via the Radio Diffusion System (RDS)—that was seventy-four years after the publication of the first newspaper—*IweIrohin* in 1859 as earlier mentioned. Although radio broadcasting came to Nigeria in 1932, it was not until 1950 that broadcasting could be said to have really taken root in the country. In that year the RDS metamorphosed into the Nigerian Broadcasting Service (NBS), with radio stations in five centers in the country, namely: Lagos, Ibadan, Enugu, Kaduna, and Kano. Largely due to political exigencies of the time, the NBS was chartered in 1956 by an act of parliament and became the Nigerian Broadcasting Corporation (NBC)—on April 1, 1957. The birth of radio broadcasting in Nigeria was a reaction of the colonial government to the activities of newspapers, especially the nationalist newspapers and their proprietors whose primary aim was to ensure that Nigerians were given the opportunity to participate in governance and eventually oust the colonial overlords.

GROWTH OF BROADCASTING IN NIGERIA

One notable feature of the development of electronic media in Nigeria is that right from its inception it has been a monopolistic enterprise of the ruling class, especially at the central government level (Tiamiyu 2018). Before October 1959, when the Western Region launched its radio and television services, radio was exclusively controlled by the British colonial administration. From 1959, however, it became a concurrent item in the country's constitution making the regions (later states) and the central (federal) government the only two authorities that could establish radio and television stations in the country. This was the situation until 1992 when the military government of General Ibrahim Badamasi Babangida took the bull by the horns as it were and liberalized the ownership structure of the electronic media. The liberalization paved the way for private ownership of radio and television stations.

The first person to take advantage of this opportunity was Dr. Raymond Dokpesi, a businessman who established DAAR Communication, Plc. By September 1994, the company's first radio station with the call sign of Ray Power 100.5 FM established its presence on the nation's broadcast space. Its television arm, Africa Independence Television (AIT), came upstream not long after. Other businessmen followed the footsteps of Dr. Dokpesi in quick succession and currently there are over one hundred private radio stations in the country and an almost equal number of television outlets. Many of the nation's high institutions of learning have also been licensed to establish radio and television stations as part of the training tools for their students.

TRADITIONAL PRINT MEDIA: METAMORPHOSING INTO THE DIGITAL REALM

We are informed that the newspaper as we know it today is a dinosaur that is heading for the museum. Is that a fabulous doomsday prediction or a statement of fact? Shall we wake up tomorrow to find out that our favorite newspaper, tabloid, or broadsheet is gone, never to be back? The unvarnished truth is that there is an information explosion; there is an increase in the ways in which we receive information today. Before now we received our news and other pieces of information largely from radio, television, newspapers, and magazines, all of which are classified as traditional or mainstream media. Today, technology has opened up the information space, increased the sources and methods of giving and receiving information. Communication has been democratized even in societies that are or used to be authoritarian. People can get their content from laptop computers, tablets, and smartphones. The internet has become the new hunting ground for content. Social media has become a force for good or ill. A new lexicon has developed that encapsulates the language of the digital era. Such words as "platforms," "websites," "blogs," "online," "social networking," on "air personality (OAP)," and "social media influencers (SMI)" have crept into our daily vocabulary. The internet has changed the face of communications the way we receive our information. You can receive the news in your living room or your office or your car or on the road as you go on your normal business. You can get your news on the go conveniently. This has made life easier, more exciting, and information very accessible. Of course, this comes, like all new technologies, with its downside, which we will treat later.

INTERNET'S THREAT TO PROFESSIONAL PRINT JOURNALISM

While the internet has improved considerably the journalist's ability to report and process his stories, do online interviews, and take photographs, it seems to be the biggest threat to the survival of newspapers and magazines, not only in Nigeria or in Africa but around the world. That is why many analysts think that the newspapers are on their way to the grave. Nonprofessionals have now invaded the media space hitherto controlled by traditional journalists, set up blogs and websites, and are busy churning out content, verified or largely unverified. They use such social media outlets as Facebook and Twitter to communicate news and opinion content to consumers. For them there are no deadline barriers which the traditional print media face. They simply publish the news as it breaks at any time of the day. They also update the news and get instant feedback. This is a major threat to newspapers which now also have their websites and permit the content consumers to access their content for free. They simply type the web addresses of their choice and read the newspapers for free. Today, all editions of Nigerian newspapers are served free on the websites. This has affected hard copy sales negatively. Competition faced by newspapers today comes from various sources: radio, television, outdoor advertising, and new publications, but the internet is the most potent threat because of its versatility. It has the capacity to carry text, photos, audio, videos, and graphs. The website is the engine room of the internet. It offers a bigger audience, a bigger community of content consumers; it also offers interaction between consumers and producers or their consumers and advertisers, and provides information to a wider audience at a low cost with adequate and timely updating and feedback. Most newspapers in Nigeria now have their own websites to take advantage of the immense possibilities offered by the internet. This media convergence ensures that they do not lose out in the scramble for the consumer's attention as the news breaks and gets updated frequently by active social media operators. Newspaper proprietors now know that readers may not want from newspapers what they have already got on radio or television or on Facebook.

The advantage of websites established by newspapers is that they have more credibility because they are owned by reputable news organizations that cannot afford to gamble with their credibility. Also newspapers are structured to ensure that stories for publication are channeled through several editorial staff who have the responsibility of ensuring that they meet the professional requirements of fairness, objectivity, balance, and accuracy (FOBA). Since newspapers operate under a code of ethics it can be assumed, all things being equal, that their stories meet journalism's gold standard. But how tough is the challenge that newspapers in Africa and the rest of the world face from the digitalization of the news? In the first quarter of 2014 the *Sunday Times* of Johannesburg reported a hard copy circulation of 405,458. In the first quarter of 2018 the circulation had come down to 260,132. The *City Press* newspaper sold 118,676 copies in the first quarter of 2014 but in the same quarter in 2018 its circulation was down to 58,566. From the above statistics it is clear that both papers had lost about 50 percent of their circulation within four years. A 2015 study by Kenya National Bureau of Statistics showed that the daily English and Kiswahili newspapers in the country have continued to decline due to the growth of online readership of news content. In 2014 the circulation figure was 102,000. By 2015 it had nose-dived to 98,548. In 2015 newspaper figures in the United States fell by 7 percent, Germany and France by 3 percent, and the United Kingdom by 12 percent. Surprisingly, the figures went up in India. The Audit Bureau of Circulation (ABG) figures released in May 2017 showed that over the last ten years its newspaper circulation figures had grown from 39.1 million in 2006 to 62.8 million in 2016, a 60 percent increase. The speculation is that the increase may have been due to the improvement in education and in the disposable income of its urban elite. Even then it is doubtful if those two factors can truly and fully explain the Indian exceptional situation.

THE NIGERIAN EXPERIENCE

In Nigeria the circulation figures of both local and national newspapers are treated as trade secrets since no functioning Audit Bureau of Circulation (ABC) is in operation. But it is obvious that the figures have plummeted since the arrival of the internet. It is estimated that about 120 million Nigerians out of a population of 206 million people are active users of the internet. Social media platforms such as Facebook, Twitter, Instagram, and WhatsApp are greedily patronized by Nigeria's young and upwardly mobile professionals and students (Bahia et al. 2020). Bahia et al. (2020) also added that Nigeria's economy has been severely affected by the COVID-19 pandemic for several months. The lack of vibrancy in the economy translated into low disposable income, irregular salary payment, high unemployment, and general poverty. In such a situation the newspaper industry is often one of the sectors affected from budget cuts, both by the public and private sector operators. This often affects not only hard copy sales but also advertising revenue. The 2016 Media Facts report published by Media Reach OMD stated that Nigeria's total advertising expenditure in 2015 was ₦97.9 billion. In 2016 it fell to ₦81 billion. The bulk of this was shared by outdoor, broadcast, and online media. In 2015 print advertising was ₦24.5 billion, while the figure dropped to ₦18 billion in 2015 and ₦9 billion in 2016. Radio received ₦15 billion in 2015 and ₦13 billion in 2016. Media Facts (2016) also reports that television received the largest share of ₦39 billion in 2015 and ₦31 billion in 2016. These dwindling figures are a reflection of the state of the Nigerian economy which fell into recession three years ago. It is difficult to know the number of visitors that Nigerian newspapers receive on their websites because they are not always given full disclosure due to competition between them. The United Kingdom's *Guardian* revealed some time ago that it receives 38 million unique visitors per day on its website, whereas its print circulation is only 200,000 copies. Nigerian newspapers have to work on improving access to their websites, making their content desirable so that they can have more visitors and adverts (Media Facts 2016). They must pay more attention to investigative and exclusive news, good design, and visuals. They must train their staff to provide depth, color, and good analysis in more visibly creative packages that can keep and grow readership especially among the young. Getting the young is very important because the youths constitute about 67 percent of Nigeria's population. Many young readers today did not grow up reading a newspaper, so they may not miss a newspaper. They want their news on small screens, a PC or tablet, or a mobile phone. Newspapers can maintain Facebook and Twitter accounts for breaking news alerts and snippets of the newspaper content. They can also do live streaming videos on their news websites. To cope with the shift in the readership they can monetize the traffic of the websites and earn some income. But overall, many newspapers must think outside the box and find multiple revenue streams for survival since there is the view that the reading habit of young Nigerians is poor. If that is so, newspapers must find ways of enticing them to their online platforms and keeping them there. Newspaper proprietors must understand that youths want instant messages and also, sometimes, instant feedback. The news destinations today are dispersed and not supplied only from the traditional media. This makes it difficult to target the consumers. To fill the gap many newspapers are printed and published from two or three points in the country. They now transmit Portable Document Format (PDF) pages to printing plants outside their headquarters where their staff produce an appropriate edition for that territory. The advantage of this is that the news can be published fresh to take care of both local and national interests wherever the consumers may be in the country. It also reduces the cost of transporting the newspapers every day from the printing plant in the newspaper's headquarters to far flung places in the hinterland. This approach makes for diversity and inclusivity, two issues that are favorite buzzwords in Nigeria today. It does appear that newspaper proprietors in Nigeria are flying blind. There is no evidence that they have done any research to identify who their present consumers are, what they want to consume, and in what format. Or should they target a new set of consumers that might be interested in what they are offering? Do newspapers offer something of relevance to the new generation of consumers in order to satisfy their craving? Or do the newspapers just offer what they think the new generation of content consumers need? The relevance of content to consumers is the determinant of patronage. Relevance is what would make a consumer want to part with his or her money. It is also what will make the consumer come back and ask for more. The reader is the equivalent of a beautiful bride. The newspaper must court her and seek to win her love and keep her for good. It must be borne in mind that consumers can evolve, become better educated, earn a better income, and search for items of comfort and relevance that meet their new status. A man who was reading a foul-mouthed tabloid may grow out of it and seek to read the *Economist* or *Time* or *Esquire*.

THE EDITOR'S CHALLENGE

But the greater problem with content selection today is actually the choice between what the content consumer wants and what he needs. It is an age-old problem. It has always been there in the decision-making process. If the reader wants a lot of stories on sex or crime in a general interest newspaper does the editor give him that in order to gain his favor and keep him glued to his newspaper? But a newspaper is not like any other item of consumption such as rice or clothes. It really does not matter if a consumer eats either Uncle Ben's rice, which is foreign, or Abakaliki rice, which is native to the Nigerian environment. It does not matter if a man wears designer clothes or clothes pieced together by a local tailor. But the content of a newspaper must matter not only to the consumer but also to the society. The regular and intensive publication of crime stories may lead to the view that crime is being glamorized. The regular and intensive publication of sex stories may elicit the view that pornography is being patronized. These views exist in a country like Nigeria where some of the states wear the sharia law like a badge of chastity, punish their citizens for drinking alcohol or for doing other things that other members of the community consider normal. So, today the craze for high traffic on stories published puts the editor on the horns of a dilemma even more than it did yesterday. He has to decide whether to give the reader what he wants or what he needs, or a combination of the two. The pressure for high traffic may push the vote in favor of what the consumer wants, but the consideration for a sane society may tell him to offer more of what he needs. Each decision has marketing consequences as well as consequences for the well-being of society. These are not new issues, but they have been magnified by the presence of social media in the communications mix and the absence of a stable readership demography for the print media today.

PROFESSIONAL AND ETHICAL CONSEQUENCES

These pressures to publish sensationally or die have had adverse consequences on the professional and ethical practice of journalism today. This is because social media has given the mainstream media a run for their money. The social media operators believe in the arcane philosophy of publish first and verify later because many of those who operate these media platforms are untrained in journalism. They call themselves on-air personalities (OAPs) and social media influencers (SMIs). Their fare is sensational, true or false; their target is high traffic, fair or foul; their target is cash, quick cash, raked in. For them, there is no correction of mistakes. They only do updates. There is no apology for errors. They only do updates. There is no verification of information or sources. Their ambition is to be the first to break the news. This culture of sensationalism or even fictionalization of the news by the one-man blogger is called Citizen Journalism or Personal Publishing. In Nigeria they have declared some well-known persons such as Professor Wole Soyinka, a Nobel laureate, and General Yakubu Gowon dead. Both men are still alive today. The more bizarre one was the declaration that Nigeria's president,

Muhammadu Buhari, had died in April 2018 and the power elite at the presidential villa recruited one Jubril Sudani from Sudan to pretend to be Nigeria's president. Nothing can be more bizarre. But it lacks the rigor of journalism. Journalists are trained to write stories to meet the professional canons of fairness, objectivity, balance, and accuracy (FOBA). Journalists operate under a code of ethics that supports those professional principles. There are in many countries professional bodies that stand guard over ethics and punish ethical infractions accordingly. In spite of these, we must admit that the boundaries of journalism are no longer secure and impenetrable. They have been invaded by charlatans and interlopers with laptop computers but absolutely no experience in professional news collection, processing, and dissemination. They are now in serious competition with professionally trained journalists. They are here with us, practicing their own brand of journalism, and many journalists have been tempted to copy them, cut corners, and publish unverified stories with anonymous sources. This is a devaluation of journalism as we know it. When they get the facts wrong, they refuse to make corrections or even to admit their errors. This behavior is said to be anchored on the desire for a free press, but it does not lead to a fair press. Journalism is a fact-based profession, which, if practiced rigorously, can lead to truth-telling. Truth-telling is a virtue for all seasons. Without truth-telling the society would be going in the wrong direction. Some publications go to great lengths to verify the information at their disposal so as to ensure their correctness and reliability. The *Reader's Digest* (2020), for example, employs twenty checkers who consult reference books, make phone calls, and even visit locations to confirm tiny details. A checker at the *New Yorker*, according to Michael Ryan and James W. Tankard Jr., author of *Basic News Reporting*, once called the duke of Windsor to verify a description of the garden around his country home. *Reader's Digest* on another occasion reported that the *New Yorker* checkers spent five weeks in a Washington hotel examining five hundred documents to verify an article by Seymour Hersch. That is how far some mainstream media go in setting high standards for the achievement of their truth-telling objective (*Reader's Digest* 2020). In Nigeria there have been several cases of positive performance by social media. One example was the case of a senator, Elisha Abbo, who slapped a woman in a sex toy shop. The episode went viral, and the police were compelled by public pressure to investigate the matter. There was also the case of a minister of finance, Ms. Kemi Adeosun, who was caught with a fake National Youth Service Corps exemption certificate. The online media that uncovered the case, *Premium Times*, followed it meticulously to the end. The minister had to resign. One of the online news media, *The Cable*, was very efficient in doing fact-checking during the 2019 presidential campaign. However, the attempt to divert journalism from the path of rectitude is not the only problem faced by the press in Nigeria today.

The political elite who rode on the back of the press to power are now putting pressure on the legislature at the national level to put chains on the press. Since the return to democracy in Nigeria in 1999 the political elite have been trying to padlock the media by introducing several obnoxious bills. We have had several acts that regulate media practice even before social media appeared on the scene. These acts are still alive today but there seems to be an inexplicable fear of social media today. There have been several episodic attempts to regulate, or more appropriately censor, social media through punitive legislation. A few years ago, there was the frivolous petition bill which prescribed jail terms and a $10,000 fine for offensive social media posts. The bill was only withdrawn when there was widespread public criticism of it. Two other oppressive bills have also been introduced in the last five years aimed at social media and online communication. They are the Protection from Internet Falsehood and Manipulation Bill and the National Commission for the Prohibition of Hate Speech Bill. These two obnoxious bills were shot down with the lethal bullets of public disapproval. But those who are scared of the enormous reach of social media are not giving up. They have reviewed the regulatory powers of the National Broadcasting Commission (NBC), giving it the teeth of a lion in the control of the electronic media. In October 2020, four of Nigeria's television stations, namely: AIT, Channels Television, Arise Television, and Television Continental were slammed with hefty fines by the NBC for alleged infractions. Interested parties, including civil society organizations and lawyers, are lining up in court in defense of the four media outfits affected. So the battle for freedom of expression remains a current issue in Nigeria. The obsession with control of the media by government and security agencies has heightened after a successful public protest by youths in Nigeria in October 2020. These protests were conducted with the enormous aid of social media and officialdom feels threatened by the awesomeness of that power. There are fresh moves to censor the social media, but the public mood does not favor it because, despite its excesses, the social media are a great force in citizen communication. It has led to the exposure of malfeasance, corruption, and other forms of misconduct in the public arena. Some of the officials are still pushing for more curbs on social media even though there exists the Cybercrime Act of 2015. This Act provides jail terms, stiff fines, or both, for purveyors of fake news and libelous information.

FITTING THE SENSATIONAL INTO THE DIGITAL SPACE

In Africa, human stories give hope. These unique narratives also guarantee continuity and preservation of culture, developments, trends, and identity.

That is why Africans value literature and storytelling because stories outlast war drums and the exploits of fighters on the battlefield. Nigerians are celebratory in nature and love to display their achievements in the media. This has often been the tradition of Nigerians historically. That is why you see the ancient "Ewee" among the Yoruba people of the southern part of Nigeria where they use it in praise singing the successful people in the society. This similar culture is also seen among the Igbo speaking people of Eastern Nigeria. Therefore, the desire and the quest to display one's wealth, splendor, grandeur, and political and military might is historical among the several cultures in Nigeria. That is the spirit behind why Husspupi, the notorious Nigerian cyber money launderer and fraudster, could not hide his ill-gotten wealth but flaunt it on Instagram for all to see. And a lot of bloggers and journalists interviewed him and gave him publicity.

As society advances, better, faster, formal forms of displaying these achievements moved to the media channels such as the radio, television, magazines, and newspapers, hence the birth of soft sale magazines such as *Ovation*, *Fame*, *City People*, and *Yes*. All these magazines came out to tell stories that the hard news would ordinarily ignore. Today, interestingly, a lot is happening with Africa's human angle stories due to the global technology revolution. Like other continents of the world, Africa is also reaping the benefits of this digital age with regard to human angle stories. Daily, we are inundated at the speed of sound with developments in Nigeria, Africa, and even beyond. This, indeed, is one of the wonders of this age.

CLASSIC EXAMPLES

For instance, without technology, the alleged bribery scandal involving Governor Abdullahi Ganduje of Kano State would not have resonated as much as it did. The outrage that followed the footage from that development in Kano placed other politicians, particularly governors, on notice. Though not much has changed despite the damaging publicity, the good thing is that some public officers are now conscious of the fact that, with technology, nothing is hidden any longer—and especially after making their way to the digital space.

For the first time, we are seeing state actors and other public officers at a very close range because of science and technology. Before now, leaders in Africa operated on a different wavelength. In fact, they paid little or no attention to quality representation and accountability because there were hardly consequences for actions. Now, the leaders are at a touching distance in a new age that challenges, engages, and exposes every action and inaction to a critical audience.

This digital age is also helping in putting the searchlight on the reprehensible activities of members of Boko Haram, herdsmen, kidnappers, armed robbers, and other bandits that terrorize communities across Nigeria. The ignoble actions of soldiers in Niger Delta, the mass resignation of soldiers in different theaters of war, the soldiers' disquieting accounts from the war fronts, the ongoing war in Southern Kaduna, the public hearings at the National Assembly, and other developments would not have reverberated without technology. No doubt, this has changed our story in many ways. And unlike what hitherto obtained.

Sometime in July 2020, the digital space brought the interesting life and times of flying officer Tolulope Arotile, Nigeria's first female combat helicopter pilot, through the eyes of her family, friends, and admirers. The young lady's life was tragically cut short in an eccentric accident mistakenly ignited by a former classmate.

Prior to the governorship election in Edo State, we were constantly reminded by those in Peoples' Democratic Party (PDP) and other sympathizers of the current governor, Godwin Obaseki, of Adams Oshiomhole's brash leadership style and political doublespeak which are now major issues and talking points in the politics of Edo State and also Nigeria. These accounts, of course, are fresh and possible because we are in a digital age. Outside the drama and political show in Edo and other states waiting to elect their representatives, technology is also helping in creating political awareness and voter education for citizens. In the case of Edo, for instance, videos of Oshiomhole's doublespeak haven't stopped trending, even after the election has come and gone. Of course, thanks to technology and digital space.

About a year ago also, the world heard the pathetic story of Success Adegor, a seven-year-old pupil of Okotie-Eboh Primary School, Sapele, Delta State, on social media. Adegor, a primary three pupil who was sent out of school for nonpayment of examination fee, grabbed the attention of public-spirited Nigerians who came to her rescue. That intervention by a young lady who recorded and shared the little girl's moving story on social media eventually changed the life of Adegor forever.

Again, in August 2019, officers of the Lagos State Police Command arrested a woman (Onyinye Mbadike) who detained a boy (Chibuike Eziamaka, ten) in a dog cage. The officers actually acted on information and a shocking viral video. Many people expressed outrage and called for the prosecution of the woman and every person involved in the obnoxious act. She was eventually arrested and charged for assault and child abuse, thanks to social media.

A few months later, the police in Enugu State arrested a couple (Jude and Ifeoma Ozougwu) for allegedly torturing and drilling nails into the head of a ten-year-old house maid (Nneoma Nnadi). It was later gathered that the victim was at different times abused with objects like a pressing iron, iron rods, and household metals. Nigeria is also witnessing an upsurge in the number of abusive marriages where people in relationships abuse each other to gain power and control. Without the social media, many of these developments would have remained unreported or even underreported.

Recently too, a little boy (Oreofeoluwa Lawal) was caught on camera negotiating his punishment with his mother (Tolu Lawal) who was bent on disciplining him despite the boy's entreaties. The video (Mummy Calm Down) did not only go viral but attracted the attention of Lagos State governor, Babajide Sanwo-Olu, who eventually met the lad and his parents.

REBRANDING NIGERIA IN THE DIGITAL SPACE USING HER SOFT STORIES

Notwithstanding all that, the big question remains: How does one rebrand Africa given the continent's unenviable status as the most underdeveloped continent in the world? How about issues of deliberate distortion of facts, prejudices, ignorance, presuppositions, and other obstacles on the way to understanding Africa and her people?

Well, to rebrand Africa by any means possible is not only legitimate but also necessary for a continent with multifarious realities and challenges. So, in the interest of this generation and the coming ones, Nigeria, and Africa at large, must change the narrative urgently too. After all, there is more to Africa than wars, famine, natural disasters, purposeless leadership, illiteracy, anarchy, coup d'état, dictators, and sit-tight leaders. These are what we do in *YES* magazine. We look away from the woes and the dark side of our environment to beam, project, and portray that which is positive, beautiful, and lovely about Nigeria and Africa as a whole. This is what chief Dele Momodu did using his *OVATION* magazine during the military dictator days of General Sanni Abacha. All the media houses were reporting how the military is hunting and gunning down virtually everyone in the country, whereas OVATION was celebrating Nigerian and African successes and wealth in and outside the continent of Africa. For those who care to know, Africa is reputed for being communal with a spirit of cooperation and belonging that is second to none. Apart from being the cradle of civilization, it is also a preferred tourism destination, a place of knowledge with rich cultural heritage and clement weather conditions. It equally has a welcoming people. Africa is waiting to be discovered by everyone, including those in the diaspora and with roots in the continent. That is the only way to erase the fears and falsehood about this part of the world. And that is what we must project more.

POSITIVE AND NEGATIVE EFFECTS OF DIGITIZATION

The future of the Nigerian mass media as a whole, not only broadcasting, is inextricably tied with technology. Of course, throughout the ages, technology, or the new method of doing things, has always played a pivotal role in man's developmental effort. For example, the paradigm shift in transportation brought about by technology relieved man of the drudgery of horse riding through the introduction of cars, railway, airplanes, and so forth. However, in the twenty-first century, it is going to be the main determining factor between success and failure in every aspect of human endeavors as has been seen in the last few decades of the twentieth century.

Nevertheless, it has been said and perhaps, rightly too, that the greatest challenge staring the Nigerian journalism in the face today—both the print and electronic media—is modern technology. Not only has the revolution in telecommunication technology ushered in the era of digitization which has changed the character of information gathering and dissemination, it has also brought with it the need for a complete reappraisal of the training and role of the journalist. And according to Michael Schudson, professor at the Columbia University Graduate School of Journalism, what we thought we once knew about journalism needs to be rethought in the digital age.

Technology, like any good medicine, always has positive and negative side effects. But the reality is that a medicine's side effects will not prevent the doctor from prescribing it for his patient, since the positive side is what is focused on. Digital technology has a lot of benefits that commend its application to several aspects of daily life and living, including the operation of the media. No doubt it has its downsides, but the benefits outweighed its negativity. The question is what is digitization?

According to McQuail (2000), digitization is the process of converting information into a digital format. In other words, turn it into a form that can be read easily by a computer. In simple terms, digitizing means the conversion of analog source materials into a numerical format known as binary digits or bits for short. The allure of digitization is its versatility—it allows information of all kinds in all formats (be it in text, picture, graphics, or sound)—to be carried with the same efficiency and also intermingled. It also makes it a lot easier for data to be shared and accessed and can, in theory, "be propagated indefinitely without generation loss (loss of fidelity) provided it is migrated to a new stable format as needed." This is a big benefit for broadcasters because digitization allows them to squeeze more information into a small space without loss of fidelity, thereby freeing scarce spectrum space for other uses.

Digitization of broadcasting also engenders better signal quality, which increases its robustness and makes it less prone to atmospheric interference. It must be stated that both television and radio signals are susceptible to atmospheric conditions, making them lose fidelity at the receiving end. For radio, the transition from amplitude modulation (AM) to Frequency Modulation (FM) has not completely solved the problem of interference challenge. However, with the digitization, static noise and other atmosphere-induced noises are almost 100 percent eliminated, resulting in near CD quality sound output. However, there are gloomy sides to digital technology. One of them according to experts is data security. With digital technology a vast amount of data can be collected and stored—this can be private information concerning individuals or organizations, and because of the difficulty in keeping data secured, hackers, including ordinary criminals, terrorists, and business rivals, can breach them with catastrophic consequences for their owners.

CRIME AND TERRORISM

The internet as an offshoot of digitization is a fertile ground for malevolent forces to operate. Because of its global availability and relative anonymity that users can enjoy, criminally minded individuals, including terrorists, use social media to promote themselves and encourage others; drug dealers also use dark web to trade while pedophiles employ chat rooms and other places to groom potential victims. Kidnappers also use them to negotiate ransoms on their victims.

LOSS OF PRIVACY

In the digital world, many people have been stripped naked in a manner of speaking. In other words, they have been robbed of their personal privacy. This is on top of the danger of their personal data being stolen or sold.

RAPID TURNOVER OF MODELS

Another concern about digitization is that digital gadgets typically have a short life span and become archaic relatively within a short space of time necessitating their replacement as the technology advances. The cost implications of this can be high for the media industry, especially radio and television organizations which may be faced with having to replace their equipment at regular intervals amid dwindling resources.

GLOBALIZATION: ADVANTAGES AND DOWNSIDES

Nothing in the world exists in a vacuum—in most cases, one thing acts as a catalyst for the evolution of another. Following this train of thought, it can be said that globalization is the driver of digitization. Through it, digital technology has transverse boundaries and penetrates international frontiers with all of its benefits and downsides. In fact, it can be argued that without globalization technological transfer of any kind will be difficult if not totally impossible.

To start with, what is globalization and what are its advantages and disadvantages?

Arising from its root word, "globe," which means the world, especially when emphasizing how big it is or that something happens in many diverse parts of it, globalization points to the whole effort towards making the world a global community in the sense of one village. In practical terms, globalization means interconnectivity of global businesses and processes into one business pool affording participants the opportunity to take advantage of economies of scale in their operations due to reduction of cost in the management.

Globalization is in fact the expansion of the old international trade in which one country exports its product to another and at the same time, imports what it needs from such other countries. However, in the practice of globalization, a country does not just export and import from another, transfer of technologies also take place through the establishment of offshore business sites and factories by one foreign company in another. Today, many American companies and other Western nations have factories in China taking advantage of availability of cheap labor and large markets in that country. This has engendered the transfer of American and Western technologies to China.

Globalization also enables foreign capital to flow into another country, especially Western capital into developing countries. This has provided the much-needed capital resource for developmental efforts in the less prosperous economies of the world. For instance, the Nigerian Stock Exchange, like any other in the world, is being actively driven on a daily basis by the infusion of foreign capital portfolios into the market. Another advantage of globalization is that it fostered the quality standard of goods as a result of competition. It goes without saying that any business that wants to succeed in the international marketplace must aim at high standards in order to be able to compete favorably with other players in that market.

SIDE EFFECTS OF GLOBALIZATION AS THEY
AFFECT DEVELOPING COUNTRIES

As good as globalization is, it is germane to highlight some of the negative effects of this global business philosophy on the way of life of people in developing nations such as Nigeria. In the first instance, globalization has made it possible for skilled manpower in the developing countries to migrate to the developed nations of the West and some rich ones in the Middle East. For example, in the last three decades, thousands of experienced medical doctors and other health workers have left Nigeria (most of them to the rich Arab nations, especially Saudi Arabia) in search of the proverbial green pastures leading to the phenomenon of brain drain in the country. In the area of culture, globalization has facilitated the spread of negative Western culture and influence in the country at the expense of local culture. This is particularly worrisome because the demographics that are usually caught in the web of this culture transfer are the youths who copied hook, line, and sinker everything glamorous from the West, especially the liberal American culture. It is common sight to see young Nigerian boys and girls as well as the not too young attired in tattered and faded jeans already perforated all over, making them look like a man in the early stages of mental derangement. Tattooing and sagging are also common fads among these young people.

Trade policy has also continued to be an important component of globalization, especially in some low-income economies. For instance, the widespread application of social media including computers, faxes, and mobile phones, the advent of the internet and e-commerce as well as quicker and cheaper means of transportation in some cases, offer opportunities to developing countries but in many cases aggravate the gap between transnational firms and traditional industries.

Dumping of foreign goods in developing countries is another major shortcoming of globalization. This is a situation whereby most industrialized nations dumped their goods in the developing countries as a result of relaxed tariffs and less tight border controls. One of the ripple effects of dumping is the stunting of local industrial concerns which cannot cope with the stiff competition of the foreign goods, some of which are heavily subsidized by their home governments to make them cheaper than local products. Indirect loss of jobs resulting from dumping is also a socioeconomic problem for the developing countries. However, like Kulkam (2009) posits, although globalization has created many negative effects, it is always better to look to the future with optimism and hope.

CHALLENGES AND FUTURE PROSPECTS
OF JOURNALISM IN NIGERIA

One trait inherent in Nigerian journalism is its stamina and ruggedness to withstand and survive seemingly indomitable challenges. Over the many decades of its existence, journalism in Nigeria and its practitioners have passed through a lot of faith-testing problems as mentioned somewhere before, but it always bounced back even stronger. However, while its challenges in the past were majorly politically induced, journalism problems today center around survival in the face of technical innovations brought about by digitization driven by globalization.

One of the fallouts of the advent of digitization was the birth of digital journalism or citizen journalism or better still, online journalism. Several people have offered diverse definitions of what online journalism is. According to Radsch (2013, p. 45), "Citizen journalism is an alternative and activist form of news gathering and reporting that functions outside mainstream media institutions." On the other hand, Rosen (2011) says "Citizen Journalism takes place when the people formerly known as the audience employs the press tools they have in their possession to inform one another." In her own contribution, Baase (2008) posits that citizen journalism is citizens playing an active role in the process of collecting, reporting, analyzing, and disseminating news and information. No matter the definition it is given, the introduction of citizen journalism into the journalism industry and its meteoric rise to prominence within a short space of time not only in Nigeria but also in other parts of Africa, has created some uneasiness within the legacy or traditional media and among their practitioners.

To some people, citizen journalism poses serious threats to the survival of traditional journalism and portends its ultimate demise. On the flip side of the coin are people who see the phenomenon as a welcome development since, according to them, it will complement traditional journalism. And this is the crux of the matter. Whichever side one belongs to in the intellectual discussion about the pros and cons of citizen journalism or online journalism, the truth is that the journalism landscape has changed and with it comes the challenge that tests the resilience of the traditional Nigerian media industry. Stuart Allan, one of the repertoires of the fifth Future of Journalism Conference held in Cardiff in September 2015, submits that "journalism as an industry and a profession is today faced with profound transformations which affect every aspect of the institution including the economic health of journalism as well as the condition and self-understandings of its practitioners" (Allan 2019).

Also in one of the papers presented at the conference, Bakker (2012) points out that as a result of these transformations, "commercial newspapers and

broadcasters have been losing audiences and advertising revenues and making cutbacks across the board, often leaving journalists at national, regional
and local publications stretched thin." This scenario is no less true in Nigeria
as many newspapers have, over the last couple of years, recorded significant
loss in revenue partly as a result of dwindling patronage by readers, many of
whom now source information online, and partly because advertisers are also
having better alternatives on the internet.

STRATEGIES FOR SURVIVAL FOR THE LEGACY MEDIA

Change in ownership structure: journalism practice in Nigeria in the
twenty-first century will no longer be business as usual to borrow that old
maxim. At its inception, journalism, especially the print sequence, was a
privately owned endeavor—first with a lone man (the Reverend Henry
Townsend) operating in the firmament of the journalism universe. Later, a
succession of several individuals appeared on the scene and set up their own
newspapers and had control over them. Much later, there was government
involvement in newspaper ownership and joint ownership (government/
private, as was the case in the later life of the *Daily Times*). Before the 1992
liberalization of the electronic media, the government at both central and
regional levels had total control of radio and television media. That ended
with the 1992 decree that deregulated the electronic media.

But in practice, the ownership pattern which has been the bane of the media
development in the country has not changed significantly—it is still who
"pays the Piper dictates the tune." For instance, the government has undiluted
ownership of its media outlets creating problems of funding for them and
stunting their growth. In the private sector media, their sole ownership is the
proprietors (with the exception of Daar Communication Company which has
gone public and has its shares quoted on the Stock Exchange). Again, this
constitutes a great impediment to the development of these privately owned
electronic media houses because they lack the necessary funds to embark on
innovative expansion that should enhance their competitiveness and revenue
intake in the long run.

Aside from government media establishments whose philosophy of existence is not primarily for profit making, all private radio and television as
well as newspapers houses are established and are run on business models
with the ultimate goal of making a profit. But in the last couple of years,
the financial fortunes of these private media establishments have witnessed
a steady downward trend, first as a result of a bad economic situation of the
country compounded by the shock of the advent of the new media. Therefore,
it is imperative for these private media houses to reappraise their ownership

structures (as difficult as this might be) to enable their operators to think outside the box and collaborate among themselves, especially in the areas of technological acquisition and research—market, readership, audience preferences, and so forth. This is necessary because none of them can go it alone and hope to survive under the present circumstance—they need to pool their resources to achieve a common goal of survival; united they stand, divided they fall.

The operative word in a developing economy like that of Nigeria is collaborative competition. This is because it does not make sense to adhere religiously to the theory of survival of the fittest in an industry devoid of logistic and adequate financial backing. In the words of Stanley Egbochuku, speaking from the point of view of a newspaperman, "There is need for cooperative research to identify the common problems of the industry in the areas of readership profile, behavior and data study, editorial content analysis and readership interest and attitude" (Egbochuku 2020). For radio and television, the need for research is no less important. These stations, through collaborative effort, need to know what their audiences' needs and tastes are in the face of competition from online media platforms. Such audience research will enable them to find programs to invest on that will interest their audience members. Right now, there is too much complacency among these radio and television media outlets that amounts to taking their audiences for granted—no longer do they produce informative and educative programs. In fact, producers and presenters on these stations now rely almost 100 percent on the audience to supply content for their broadcasts through phone-in. Gone were the days when people rushed home so as not to miss the latest episode of *Village Headmaster*, *Samnja*, *New Masquerade*, *Cockcrow at Dawn*, *Mirror in the Sun*, and so forth. It is pertinent to warn that if these stations want to survive the current onslaught of the online media, they must be ready to take a critical look at their program contents which must now be driven by audience preferences.

MEDIA CONVERGENCE

Another strategy for survival is media convergence. This is a buzz term in the media universe of today. Essentially, convergence can be examined under two perspectives. The first one is what I call "converged operations," while the second is "multimedia convergence." Under the first concept, newsroom operations are converged. For instance, a media outfit owning both radio and television (which is the current norm in Nigeria today) which hitherto had operated as if they were owned by different proprietors, will now pool their resources—equipment and personnel—for effective utilization thereby saving cost and maximizing available resources. In practical terms a reporter going out on assignment will see himself first as a staff of the broadcasting organization not as a radio and television reporter. With that mind-set, he will cover the assignment with a clear view that he will be writing for both radio and television arms of the organization. Of course, such a reporter will go out with a television camera and other apparatus pertaining to their medium to be able to report effectively for it. Already some multimedia broadcasting organizations in the country are doing this on a trial basis but it should be the norm now.

MULTIMEDIA CONVERGENCE

This is the practice whereby there is a collaborative effort across media genres—print, radio/television, and social media. According to Deuze (2004), "Fully integrated multimedia newsroom is where teams of news workers from print, broadcast and online jointly gather information, mine databases and plan story packages intended for distribution across all media." Verweij (2009), as cited by Amobi (2014), opined that "Converged newsrooms offer more opportunities for the public to be informed and involved in a story and offer the reporter and editor more integrated tools to tell the story."

TRAINING

The importance of training and retraining for media practitioners cannot be overemphasized. Even though many of the pioneers of the profession were not formally trained as journalists in any institution of higher learning, they had vibrant and intimidating writing skills while a few of them like Herbert Macaulay had professional training in other fields. Much later on, most of the practitioners received on-the-job training and for a long time; federal government broadcast media placed more premium on in-house training whereby new entrants were tutored in the various aspects of broadcasting by their senior colleagues. The success of this in-house training was what informed the establishment of the Radio Nigeria Training School (now Broadcast Academy) in 1957, which became the first professional training institution for broadcasters outside of the university in the country. The NTA Television College in Jos came on much later.

Although on-the-job training is still a key to proficiency in any journalistic endeavor, old journalists who are still in service are now being encouraged to acquire university education. Of course, it must be noted that many of the new entrants into the profession are graduates of tertiary institutions—university and polytechnic. Therefore, it goes without saying that for journalism in the country to survive the challenges posed by the technical innovations of the twenty-first century, its practitioners must be ready to acquire new skills through training and retraining. According to Pini Jason, "the journalist of the future will be a technician whose usefulness will depend on his competence and efficiency on the computer, and whose attention will increasingly be focused on the information superhighway" (Jason 2000). Because multimedia is the way to go now, news reporters in advanced countries are being trained to handle video cameras and write in a style appropriate to internet news pages. It must also be stated that for the training and retraining of journalists to be beneficial, the curricula of institutions offering mass communication studies and journalism in the country must be restructured to meet the current needs of the profession.

ONLINE PRESENCE

The shift to digitization in the contemporary media world has created implications for traditional mass media products—news, programs, advertisements, and so forth. As has been observed by some experts, the more technology advances, the more converged the realm of mass media will become with less need for traditional communication technologies. What this means is that within the next one decade or so, the old ways of carrying out media chores would have been achieved leaving anyone that fails to embrace the new technologies in the unenviable state of regrets. The import of this for the Nigerian media industry is that it cannot afford to be an onlooker in the face of the rapid transformation in telecommunications technology if it hopes to be relevant in the twenty-first century and beyond. So it is in its best interest to join the bandwagon and appropriate the opportunities presented by digitization and globalization facilities to guarantee its future.

Although nearly all the media houses in the country—newspapers, magazines, radio, and television—are already online, the majority of them merely provide avenues for people online to read their publications, listen and watch their productions free; this must change if they are going to take full advantage of that veritable platform. Therefore, they must explore ways and means to make people pay for their online products. In order to achieve this goal, they must speak the language of the net which means that all the media must not just upload their hard copies or texts online, they must repackage them in conformity with online rules.

Again, they must do something about their websites to make them visitor-friendly. Right now, while it takes a visitor a few seconds to access Aljazeera television live streaming on the net for instance, it is a painful experience trying to access the website of any Nigerian television on the web. However, it has been pointed out that the ease with which one can access internet television is predicated on internet streaming speeds which are linked to broadband penetration in any given country—the higher the broadband penetration, the easier it is for people to have a seamless access to internet television. This is where the government comes in because as of February 2020, broadband penetration in Nigeria stood at less than 40 percent. The government must, therefore, take necessary steps to boost the country's broadband penetration even as it plans to embark on digital switchover.

Also in terms of cost of delivery per household, internet television is very expensive compared to open broadcast television or cable television. This is because the content production for internet television does not come cheap given its multimedia and interactive aspects. Perhaps that is why Noan (2003) has suggested that internet television should be used for only specialized programs with a narrow or dispersed base of users. This again brings us to the issue of collaboration as several stations can team together to produce content for their online presentations. This, apart from cutting down cost per participant, would also increase the number and quality of programs they can jointly produce.

CONCLUSION

For the print media in Nigeria today, the pressures are coming from various sources, ancient and modern. These pressures are affecting the way journalism is practiced today: the drift towards sensationalism, the decline of investigative journalism, the increase in crime coverage and exhibition of pornography. These issues are not entirely new, but they have become some of the defining features of the practice of mainstream journalism. With the rapid advances in technology which have transformed people's lives in many ways, journalism could not possibly be an exception. We are therefore compelled to accept this sea change as part of the territory, the new normal in journalism today.

Life is a continuum, and in the existential journey through life there are pathos and ethos that help to shape our resolve either to continue to remain rooted in the tradition of known experiences or to move with the tide of change where lies the elixir for our individual and collective survival.

As has been explained in the previous pages, technological innovation is one of the greatest challenges confronting journalism practice today, not only in Nigeria but also in other parts of Africa. But the reality is that it is not all bad news because there are many positive sides to digitization and its hand-maiden, globalization. All the media industry needs to do is to acknowledge and adapt the good aspects of the new technology to its operations in order to survive. Attempts have been made previously to suggest pathways to survival for the media practice in Nigeria. To recapitulate, these include embarking meaningful collaboration among the various arms of the industry to achieve a common goal. This may mean tinkering with the ownership structures, especially of the private media to enable their operators to think outside of the box. Training and retraining of media practitioners are also a must to equip them with the necessary operational tools to fit into the new technology. Mention was also made of media and multimedia convergence, which are buzz terms in the media universe of today.

The bottom line is that it is wishful thinking for any individual or corporate entity to believe that he/it can survive the present strong wind of change without being broken—he must bend with it. For one thing, technology, especially telecommunication, is not going to slow down, instead, it is going to gather more speed as we climax in age, and this is biblical. For the Good Book says in the later days, knowledge shall increase, and men shall run to and fro.

RECOMMENDATIONS

In telling their stories, Africans must be frank, unpretentious and detailed about themselves. They must also draw attention to the many years of misrepresentations, stereotypes, and biased writing which do not say exactly who they are. Over the years, we have cases of young Nigerians who are still in secondary and elementary schools building innovative machines and the world is not aware of them. They can be encouraged and showcased to the world on the pages of our soft sales. The onus, however, is now on the continent and its people to correct all the lies and propaganda using human angle stories in this age of information and technology. This is the only way to go because in the final analysis, that will be the ultimate rebranding experience for a highly misunderstood continent.

So, for the discerning, the future is already here. That hope we anxiously await will be driven by this digital age. What becomes of our lives individually or collectively will equally depend largely on how we make the most of the information age. But the time is now as there could not have been a better time to tell our human angle stories to a skeptical world. Everyone is waiting to see and hear from these highly misconstrued people where everything, including civilization, began. And the earlier we start the better for us. So, my dear Africans, let's tell our stories, let's rebrand Africa!

REFERENCES

Adefela, V. O. and Lalekan, O. 1979. *History of the Nigerian Broadcasting Corporation*. Ibadan: University of Ibadan Press.

Allan, S. 2019. *Innovations, Transitions and Transformations*. The seventh biennial Future of Journalism Conference. The School of Journalism, Media and Culture (JOMEC) at Cardiff University, UK.

Amobi, T. 2014. *Issues and Techniques in Multimedia and Online Journalism*. Lagos: Concept Publication.

Awolowo, O. 1960. *Awo: The Autobiography of Chief Obafemi Awolowo*. Cambridge University Press, London p. 80.

Baase, S. 2008. *A Gift of Fire: Social, Legal and Ethical Issues for Computing and the Internet* (3rd ed.). Prentice Hall, ISBN 9780136008484.

Bahia, K., Castells, P., Cruz, G., Masaki, T., Pedrós, X., Pfutze, T., Rodríguez-Castelán, C., and Winkler, H. (2020). World Bank Group Report on Policy Research Working Paper on "The Welfare Effects of Mobile Broadband Internet Evidence from Nigeria." https://papers.ssrn.com/sol3/papers.cfm?abstract_id=3593892

Bakker, P. 2012. "Aggregation, Content Farms and Huffinization: The Rise of Low-Pay and No-Journalism," *Journalism Practice* 6 (5–6): 627–637. Accessed June 16, 2022.

Deuze, M. 2004. "What Is Multimedia Journalism?" *Journalism Studies* 5 (2): 139–152.

Egbochuku, S. 2020. "Marketing and Marketers." Marketers Conference of Nigeria. Ikoyi, Lagos.

Jason, P. 2000. "The Journalist of the future." A speech delivered at the Nigerian Guild of Editors Conference. Lagos.

Kulkam, T. 2009. *Globalization and Media Consumption*. Hong Kong: Pricey Books.

McQuail. D. 2000. *McQuail's Mass Communication Theory* (4th ed.). Sage, London, pp.16–34.

Media Fact. (2016). http://www.mediafactbook.ro/. Accessed June, 16, 2022.

Nnamidi, A .1970. *My Odyssey: An Autobiography*. New York/London: Pracger, p. 300.

Noam, E. 2003. "Will Internet TV be American?" In *Trends in Communication*, special isssue, "Impact of New Technology on the Traditional Media," edited by David Ward. Routledge: London.

Omu, F. 1967. "The Iwe Irohin, 1859–1867." *Journal of the Historical Society of Nigeria* 4 (1): 35–44.

Omu, F. 1980. *Press and Politics in Nigeria, 1880–1937*. London: Cambridge University Press, 38.

Omu, I. A. 1996. *Journalism in Nigeria: Issues and Perspectives.* Nigeria Union of Journalists, Lagos State Council, Cargo Compass Nigeria.

Radsch, Courtney C. 2013. *"The Revolution Will Be Blogged: Cyberactionism and the 4th Estate in Egypt."* Doctorate Dissertation, American University. Definition of digitization at Whatis.com.

Reader's Digest. (2020). https://www.readersdigest.co.uk/ Accessed June, 16, 2022.

Rosen, J. 2011. *JFK assassination.* Accessed February 18, 2012. http//jfk50d
.blogspot. C['om/2011/11/national.geographic-to-air-jfk.lost.htmlThree.

Schudson, M. 1978. *Discovering the News: A Social History of American Newspapers.*
New York: Basic Books, Inc., Ipp 36–37. "A Most Useful Definition of Citizen
Journalism," Press Think.

Schudson, M. 1986. "Why? Deadlines, Datelines and History." In *Reading The News,*
edited by Manoff Schudson, pp. 81–82.

Tiamiyu, S. 2018. *Radio News Editing and Production.* South Africa: Reach
Publishers Services.

SECTION III

Production and Presentation

Chapter 7

Broadcast Media Content Packaging in the Era of Digitization and Globalization

Unwana Samuel Akpan

The mass media as an institution is as old as humanity, because man has always yearned for information either for health, commercial, security, entertainment, or educational reasons. Institutionalized media in the society had started even in the stone age (Uche 1989; Curran and Park 2000; Nightingale 2011; Haggerty and McGarry 2015; Hall, Evans, and Nixon 2013; Hill Collins and Bilge 2016; Dwyer 2019), and this aided in information credibility and believability because they were processed and packaged from trusted sources. This explains why Cosenza, Gavidia, and González-Avella (2020, p. 31), while citing Mccombs and Shaw (1972), posit that "the interaction with mass media have experienced important changes: in on one hand people get informed by the media, while on the other hand the information is influenced by the evolution of people's preferences." Other studies have also shown how media content consumption by members of the public have equally evolved (Crane, Kawashima, and Kawasaki 2002; James and Tulloch 2010). Consumable media contents fit for public consumption have always been conceptualized, commissioned, gathered, packaged, censored, and disseminated. Creatively packaged media content is capable of causing major changes in the society, either positively or negatively (Teun 1991; Kelvin 2003; Twenge, Martin, and Spitzberg 2019; Chaume 2019). That is why some media contents serve a variety of purposes including socialization, advocacy (propaganda), political communication, public relations and advertisement, entertainment, and public service. Cosenza, Gavidia, and González-Avella (2020) aver that "with the advent of globalization, broadcasting, telecommunication, and internet-based companies have also become global; mass media messages can practically reach all individuals and groups in the society" (p. 2).

The mass media form an important sociological institution, playing an increasingly important role in the shaping of the society and formation of opinions and lifestyles because of how its messages are packaged. According to Sparks (2007), from inception, the mass media has used its contents to affect the way people think, behave, respond, or postulate. According to Udoakah (2014, p. 2), "It is a channel for social communication and for publishing information which affects the life and future of citizens." That is why another communication researcher, Merill (2006, p. 93), postulates that:

> Mass media contents can contribute to the people's awareness of potentialities, dissatisfactions and desire to change (positively or negatively) a heightened sense of collective power among the people either stability or disruption of the society, either instilling in the people realistic goals, behaviors or creating the people realistic goals or creating extravagant exceptions. (p. 93)

Media contents are purveyors of information, and entertainment, and the way and the channels these messages are packaged and conveyed to contemporary audiences have evolved. The fact that media contents are indispensable to the process of social change is no more debatable, and this was demonstrated during the Black Life Matters uprising across the world and of course the EndSars protest in Nigeria. Media contents have been involved in significant social change since they came into existence and have also contributed to the growth of some societies (Schramm and Porter 1982; Wright 1986; Curran and Park 2000; Hall, Evans, and Nixon 2013; Hill Collins and Bilge 2016; Dwyer 2019). In fact, Thomas Jefferson, one of the great men who ruled the United States of America, before he became the president, did not really see the importance of the media. But when Jefferson became the president of America, he said if he left to choose between government and mass media, he would prefer the latter. Jefferson's aphorism not only brought to reckoning the fact that the mass media and social change are inseparable, but it also calls to memory the fact that the mass media contents are capable of metamorphosing to fit into the everyday or present day unavoidable global innovativeness and technological realities sweeping across all the industries across the world.

There are a good number of literature (McCavit and Pringle 1986; Vivian 2009; Eastman and Ferguson 2009; McQuail 2010; Sterin 2012; Nightingale 2011; Hall, Evans, and Nixon 2013; Haggerty and McGarry 2015; Hill Collins and Bilge 2016; Dwyer 2019) wrestling with the issue of media content, but none is addressing the issue of aesthetically framing these contents for meaning and smartness in the era of digitalization and globalization.

GENERATING BROADCAST MEDIA CONTENT

Generating content for any broadcast format is always a nightmare for a young producer or an upcoming content provider. The art of generating and gathering broadcast content is imperative to the success of any program format. The question whether a program succeeds or fails can be answered during this process. Content can mar or make a program. It is the duty of the producer to generate content and in order to do this, he needs to be intelligent, smart, see beyond the audience, and should have the ability to create, generate, and unfold silences teeming in every sector of our society. Content defines your program and gives your program a good command of respect. It stands out from others. It is what enables you to win an award as a producer.

Media contents are raw audio/visual elements obtained from the field, when put together during program packaging to give a program direction, meaning, and excellence. These elements can be captured in the form of pictures, sound, interviews, statements of experts, eyewitness accounts, statistical figures, and projections. These are what we call contents in production that are broken into logical pieces or sound bites and when inserted in between lines or script paragraphs for chronological flow of the producer's line of thought and idea. That's why technically, most of these media messages are called "inserts," because they are inserted in between scripts to give a voice and image to a reporter's or the producer's claims. Media contents help give credibility to both a program and the media organization.

THE TAXONOMY OF CONTENT

The layers of contents in a program are what lures the audience, therefore its taxonomic display is very key to any program's success. Broadcast audience members are discriminatory, restless, migratory, and selective in their consumption of broadcast programs. In order to prevent a scenario whereby the producer's effort and resources are useless, the broadcast program producer needs to chronologically weave his or her contents in a pattern that would draw and sustain attention. He or she can achieve this by making sure that the content regions are placed in the chronological order. Good media content must be aesthetically structured and laid in a manner that can chronologically create and attract attention of the audience; and the chronological content layout must create meaning and understanding in order for the attention to be sustained. Therefore, the taxonomical layout of content most times goes in this dimension.

Intro Region

This is a section of the intro that is very key and important because it deter-mines whether people would listen or watch the program. At this point, the producer must give a creative and a luring start. He must be able to rearrange the inserts that should easily and immediately get the attention of the audi-ence without the listener thinking whether to listen or not. For instance, using a voice or video clip of Hilary Clinton saying, "I am contesting." You can be sure that it will get a lot of attention. And then the presenter would add, "that was Hilary Clinton making a declaration of her interest in running for the office of the president of the United States of America in 2016, and with the recent happenings in America today, we went to the streets to sample the views of a cross section of the society whether they would love Hilary Clinton to re-contest for the office of the president of the United States of America." This is an attention-getter be it in America, Europe, Russia, or Africa. This sort of content creates, attracts, and sustains attention because it is a subject of general interest.

Analytics Region

This is a section of the content that offers explanation, purpose, logic, and rationale. Using Hilary Clinton's insert, it is from the producer's script voiced by the presenter that would do the explanation; the purpose behind the vox-pop is to find out the audiences' perception of her re-contesting the presidential election.

Digestion Region

This is the part of the content that allows the audience to soak in and mentally process the information, thematic, concepts, and ideologies inherent in the media content. And after the audience members have analyzed the content, an impression is made whether to accept the media content or not.

Impression Region

This is a section where an impression is created or made in the subconscious-ness of the audience. When an impression is created, it can trigger a reaction or an action from the audience. This is the point of indoctrination.

Indoctrination Region

This is a point in the section designed to get the audience indoctrinated after being exposed to the media. This is the point of making the audience a believer of that content. When an audience is indoctrinated, that is when the audience marks the day of the week and the time the program is aired.

Takeaway Region

This is the section in the content where something is learned from the media content in terms of ideologies, information, tips, and so forth, of which this can become a habit or help the audience to form a new habit. A very good example is religious broadcasts.

Action Region

This is a section in the body of the content that compels, encourages, motivates, or elicits an action from the audience. This is a point where an action or a reaction is made as a result of the content. Contents with lines like, "Arise, Arise, Arise Oh ye people, let's match as one, one indivisible people" can easily stir up action. Contents with lines like, "The Federal Ministry of Health warns that smokers are liable to die young" can elicit behavioral change that could be sudden.

SHADES/CHARACTERISTICS OF BROADCAST CONTENT

- Contents teemed with legal implications.
- Contents laced with professional/technical jargons.
- Undiluted content: These are contents unfit for conventional broadcasting but can go for Guerrilla Broadcasting, like Guerrilla Radio, etc. For instance, a statement like, "Buhari is stupid" from a source; or you bring the religious/ethnic side into the herdsmen killings is a good example of an undiluted content.
- Diluted Content: These are contents that are censored, edited to give us what we want. This is what we do most times as content providers so that we would not enter into any trouble with our paymasters or the government of the day or insult the sensibilities of the public.
- Rich Content: These are contents rich in facts, figures, dates, etc.
- Shallow Content: Either the source is not an authority in it, or he lacks communication skills, or the content provider could not ask intelligent

questions that can elicit intelligent responses or answers. As a result, this will obviously show when putting lines of thoughts together in order for it to be a program.

CONTENT STRATIFICATION

Two Basic/Major Forms of Content:

- Local content: These contents are mainly generated within the geographical location of the media house or the host community. Any content obtained within the operational base of a station is local content.
- Foreign content: These are contents generated outside the shores of a station base and this must be done with utmost carefulness and attention to exactness of information and given credit to the source. This will save your station from unnecessary lawsuits.

There are the basic forms of contents. Contents come in these two basic forms. They are either local or foreign.

QUALITIES/SKILLS NEEDED TO GENERATE CONTENT IN THE ERA OF DIGITALIZATION AND GLOBALIZATION

The content provider must:

- Have a "Blank Mind"—Pretend you don't know anything in order to learn. Keep what you know to yourself in order to explore.
- Develop an appetite for digital-based gadgets such as iPad, smartphones, if you must be a successful content producer in the digital age.
- Get used to audio and visual editing software such as Adobe, Nero, etc.
- Do not be ashamed to ask for assistance on how to operate IT-based gadgets.
- Have the ability and the courage to discover, explore, and explain silences and areas where you have untapped potential and go for the content lurking there.
- Have interest in thorough research. Research helps a producer or content provider discover facts and figures that might proffer solutions to societal issues.
- Have the ability to ask intelligent questions from sources because intelligent questions give birth to intelligent answers.

- Be a keen observer of events, phenomenon, trend, statistical trend (whether it is increasing or decreasing).
- Be ready to respect the laws and culture of your host.
- Be versatile with indigenous languages, this is because language can pave the way for acceptability.
- Be a friendly person with a charming smile.
- Have a diary where phone numbers of respondents or sources are kept.
- Be a good listener. Don't interrupt your sources; just allow them to flow because you might make them forget a very important point by your frequent interruptions.
- Be creative in your thinking.
- Be able to see what others cannot see.
- Be able to see beyond the impossible.
- Be able to use digital gadgets for information sourcing and packaging.

CONTENT RICHNESS

Broadcast media scholars have argued that the effectiveness of any content depends on the elements in the content and how these elements are packaged to become a content in order to persuade or inform (Hill Collins and Bilge 2016; Dwyer 2019; Cosenza, Gavidia, and González-Avella 2020). Media contents are a product of a creative mind geared towards informing, educating, and entertaining. Theoretically and practically, for any media content to be considered rich it has to have the following "content abilities and capacities," which are interactivity, flexibility, clarity, simplicity, globalized, elasticity, competitive, compatibility, convertibility, transactional, catchy, punchy, smarty, acceptability, sustainability, curiosity, and agenda-setting. These are contents rich in facts, figures, dates, and so forth. It also should generate and sustain interest, create change, foster behavioral change and should serve as pointers to subtle phenomena and projectors of concepts and outcomes.

When contents are rich, they can sell goods and services, attract sponsorship, change and direct national and global attention, cause behavioral change, evoke emotions, and create trends. This is the kind of content that provokes public interest and interactivity and can birth social, economic, and political movements.

MEDIA CONTENT RICHNESS THEORIES (MCRT)

Content is what lures the audience both on new media and the traditional mainframe media. Content aids in weaving arts together so as to produce suspense. That is why those who use words as a tool to address the mind to either laugh, cry, or for behavioral change pay attention to concise words and their richness (Mccombs and Shaw 1972; Dwyer 2019; Nixon 2020). An aesthetically rich content provides or evokes interest, pity, awareness, humor, stirs to action and changes behavior or behavioral pattern; therefore, there should be theoretical explanations that could offer better understanding of the power of media contents. Any media content that is rich is teemed with persuasive, flowery words, up to date data, statistics, facts, and subtle appeal. That is why any artistically packaged and aesthetically weaved media content can elicit shades of actions and reactions. These are rich contents! I mean media contents teemed with clarity of historical background, dates, numerical concepts and figures, projections, projection reminders, neutrality, and all-sides balance. Therefore, theoretically speaking, there are personally conceived intellectual explanations the author has theorized that can give some insights into the concept of media content.

SELF-MARKETABILITY THEORY

If you ask broadcast station managers, there are programs that basically attract sponsors and advertisers simply because the content is laced with aesthetic elements that are capable of creating, attracting, and sustaining attention. Such programs enjoy mass viewership and listenership. Corporate organizations only go for programs and broadcast stations with huge followership. They approach producers of such programs for advert placement without the stations' marketers approaching them for sponsorship or advert placement (Nunes and Stroebel 2004; Mulder 2004; Van der Waldt 2005; Nixon 2020). All agree in their submission that good broadcast programs can attract a large audience and market interests. If content is not fantastic, it cannot draw listenership, let alone self-marketing itself. A fantastic content will draw the best and good audience and use this huge audience base to market itself. There are marketable programs and there are self-marketable programs.

The difference is that a good program is marketable, but a rich, fantastic, responsible, and creative content makes your program enterprising; what you would ordinarily call, *marketable.* Fantastic content attracts advertisers. Note that it is a good program that is *marketable*; or better put, it is theorized that a program that is not "all that good" that is marketable. But "a fantastic content/ program" markets itself. Advertisers come begging for a slot within such a program, simply because it is fantastic. Therefore, the theoretical angle to this is the fact that a "fantastic content markets itself," while a "good program" is just ordinarily any kind of program.

CONTENT CAPSULATION THEORY

The aesthetic injection of different shades of ideas, concepts, and meaning into a single line of media message that the audience might deduce different shades of meaning from is called "content capsulation." This theory is used when a producer does not want the audience to figure out what the message is all about at the beginning or from the face value, but with time, in the middle or the end of the message, the listener can say, "oh, I now understand, so this is what this message actually conveys or says." Just like in medicine, when a medication is encapsulated in order to shield the bitter part of it; media contents can be equally capsulated; and when consumed can spark different shades of perception and meaning. Most commercials use such messages, as well as political rhetoric.

CONTENT CONTAINERIZATION THEORY

Maritime ships convey different commercial cargoes to different parts of the world, and when these containers arrive, you will find all manner of items inside it. Equally, media contents and formats can be containerized. A very good example is a magazine program where it is a potpourri of different program formats converging. Inside it could be an interview, drama, sports, news, and so forth. A containerized message is the kind of message, when churned out, is laced with shades of insights that touch and illuminate other areas.

ELECTRONIC ICONOGRAPHIC
COLONIZATION THEORY

This is a "media role model" theory that explains the conscious simultaneous creation of false heroic activities so the audience members can be "wowed'"; that is mesmerizing, so they can desire to yearn to be like the portrayed hero or heroine. These media super icons are consciously created to promote a terrestrial ideology, concept, or product so you consider your local content as inferior or not-up-to-standard with the media icon you have been exposed to. The Western media are masters of this elusive artistic creation so as to further colonize the creative minds of the rest of the world. This is done to cripple the creative minds of those who may be capable of creating their own media icons or promoting indigenous heroes. Good enough the "Black Panther" as a "media iconographic creation" is beginning to show the world that Africans can create their own brand, icon, and role model worthy of identifying with, that is superior to or compared to the Western over-popularized and overhyped Superman, Spiderman, Voltron, or James Bond. This justifies the clarion call by contemporary African scholars who are very vocal in promoting Afrocentric ideology that the African media and communication are still colonized, hence the need for decolonization and de-Westernization of African media and communication processes (Doob 1985; Mazrui 1986; Moemeka 1998; Ansu-Kyeremeh 2005; Waisbord and Mellado 2014; Mawere and Mubaya 2016; Langmia 2018; Asante 2018; Milton and Mano 2021; Mano and Milton 2021).

AESTHETIC ELEMENTS IN DIGITAL MEDIA CONTENT

There are some broadcast aesthetic elements that can be fused into a content to attract, lure, and sustain the attention of the audience for a desired and expected outcome. Media aesthetics is simply using media content to achieve the goal of a particular published or broadcast message. Therefore, there are certain artistic digital elements that the producer can inject to achieve this goal, such as lighting, sound, animation, image, and so forth.

THE METAMORPHOSIS OF CONTENT

Metamorphosis is a major and constant phenomenon in life. Just like a caterpillar can metamorphose into a butterfly, so are some works of arts and technological inventions. A lot of inventions have metamorphosed over time to fit into the everyday realities. For instance, the analog telephone used in those days has metamorphosed into a GSM phone today, and virtually most gadgets (camera, calculator, watch, alarm clock, notepad, and the rest) that used to function independently now take residence in the GSM phone. Also, producers can take a portion of audio or visual clip from a sea of activities and trim it, then use that portion to create media messages; or insert the audio/visual clip in his or her script to support, strengthen, and embolden the idea, concept, or claim projected in the program. When this is done, a portion of that happening carefully trimmed by the producer has metamorphosed into something useful in the form of experts' views and a short scene of the event. In this regard, something has metamorphosed. Most scholars and media professionals do not have the slightest idea that media contents can metamorphose into something else. For instance, a talk show can generate content that can be used for educational programming, news content, and empirical data for researchers, exhibits, evidence, or proof for police or judicial investigations. Moreover, a copy of a newspaper publication or a clip from a radio/television documentary could be used as evidence for a libel suit in the court of law. For example, in the heat of the 2015 presidential election in Nigeria, African Independent Television (AIT) aired a documentary called "The Lion of Bourdillon," targeted at former Lagos State governor and the national leader of the All Progressive Congress senator Bola Ahmed Tinubu. In a swift response, the senator sued AIT for damage to his personality. In another development, for instance, Esson (2015), while trying to justify his postulation in an article journal where he investigated footballers' migration from Africa to Europe, took a CNN media content and translated it into an empirical data in order to further strengthen his research argument. In this regard, the CNN media content has metamorphosed from a media content into empirical data. He penned:

> In May 2008, a fish trawler abandoned by its captain was found off the shore of Tenerife. Regrettably, the contents were not of the aquatic variety. The cargo consisted of approximately 130 West African males suffering hypothermia and dehydration (McDougall 2008). The last decade has witnessed increasing numbers of African migrants attempting to enter Europe via unauthorized journeys across the Mediterranean Sea and the Atlantic Ocean. Yet what made the above incident particularly newsworthy was the discovery that several of the survivors found onboard were teenagers erroneously embarking on a journey they believed would lead to football contracts with Real Madrid or Marseille.

In a similar development, Onwumechili and Akpan (2020) also took media content and converted it to academic empirical data in their study of "Footballers' Wives and Communication Pattern." Here is how they did it:

> In early 2010, *The Guardian* newspaper in the United Kingdom published an article asking: why do women want to be Wags (Women and Girlfriends) of footballers? The article wrote: "many young women still dream of marrying a footballer and living the life of perma tanned luxury. But is life as a Wag all it is cracked up to be?

CONTENT CONVERSION

While discussing Content Metamorphosis, I did mention that media contents can metamorphose into several things such as empirical data, exhibits, artifacts, and all of that. Also note that media content can be "converted from," "converted to," and "converted into." If an American comes to Nigeria for a summer holiday, for him to be able to buy anything, he would have to change his currency, which is dollar to naira, otherwise, he would not be able to purchase anything. As attractive as the dollar, the local crayfish seller would not accept it from him unless he changed it, which is a form of conversion to naira. This is because dollars are alien to the everyday economic transaction of the populace. In this instance, the dollar becomes irrelevant within the Nigerian system. That is what happens to a media content that is not properly converted from its original state or the program format it was lifted from to fit into the terrain of a particular program format the producer intends to use. Mostly, it is the members of the public and content provider/producers who can convert any media content to fit their purpose. After any content has been gathered, trimmed, and fit into a media content for broadcast, members of the public, when exposed to such media programs, use such to meet the needs of either their information, education, or entertainment needs. On the other hand, when a reporter or a producer gathers information from "a body of happenings" or events in the society, regardless of the scenario, he or she would have to systematically, intelligently, and carefully select the portions in the happenings that make a meaning when weaving them together. In this sense, the producer is converting the raw materials or data that was gathered into what I postulate as "straight-aligned-information flow" for attention getting and meaning to the audience. Therefore, contents can be "converted From" the seas and level of raw data into "straight-aligned-information flow" of broadcast messages for attention getting and meaning to the audience. Also media contents can be "converted to" empirical data, artifacts, exhibits, and so on, just as in the case of Content Metamorphosis. Also, media contents can be "converted into" a need. You probably would ask why and how? Why? Because humans have biological and sociological needs. The sociological needs of any human include information, education, and entertainment. Humans want to stay informed and aware of their environment, they want to be enlightened about certain phenomena and also entertained as a form of relaxation and unwinding. When you dance after listening to a piece of music on the radio, your senses have automatically converted the message of the music media into satisfying your entertainment needs at that point in time (Akpan 2019). When you obey the stay-at-home order of your government due to the COVID-19 pandemic, your senses have responded to your information needs. And when you suddenly adapt and adjust to the new normal by learning to wear a face mask as a result of media awareness messages, you have converted the media content into your education needs.

CONTENT MODIFICATION

Content modification is a situation when a documentary insert can be used in a news program. Where a clip for an interview program or phone-in program can be taken and modified to fit into a talk show, sports program, or maga-zine program. In this instance, it is the script that does the modification to fit into the programs format the content provider/producer intends to use. The producer has to script the program in a way that would introduce the media content or insert to fit the genre of the program he is producing. He has to also technically trim and cut the media content taken from another media format to fit the program format he or she wants to produce. This is important. For instance, an insert gotten from a personality interview program should be cut and trimmed to fit into the traditionally thirty-seconds insert for a news bulletin, which is a program on its own. The news bulletin producer or the news editor does not have such a luxury for time in his news bulletin as the producer of a personality interview. Don't forget that interview programs are always long; this is because you have to give the interviewee the time and space to talk. In fact, the anchor is not permitted to interject while the person-ality is talking because he might cut short an important point the interviewee wants to make. The interviewee might even forget what he wanted to say if the anchor cuts in abruptly. If a news producer or editor finds a portion of the personality interview educative, informative, or entertaining, for his or her news bulletin, he or she would have to locate a punchy and a direct line of the personality's comment that would directly support the claim of that particular bulletin and give credibility and "ownership to the news report." By owner-ship, I mean the news producer or editor making the source to own up to what he said on tape or camera. The news producer or editor can only achieve this by attaching the original video of the source in the form of an insert.

HANDLING OF CONTENT IN THE DIGITAL ERA

When most African countries finally switch from analog to digital broadcast-ing, most producers or content providers who cannot make their content fit in digitally might lose their jobs. This is because any employer of media labor would readily go for a digitally skilled producer who can trim the script and inserts to fit into the digital space or social media handles of their organization for easier accessibility by members of the public. These days, virtually all the radio and television stations have social media handles such as Facebook, Twitter, WhatsApp, Instagram, SnapChat, YouTube, and all of that. Before a program goes on air, producers are to produce a one-minute thriller and place them on the station's social media handles so people can see it online and hook onto the program. This is also called "program promo." One of the broadcast aesthetics or features on the promo that can attract large viewership or listenership is extracting a controversial insert (a comment from your source or resource person) from the body of the program and using the same to promote your program.

Promos are always voiced by a presenter, asking listeners/viewers to listen or watch a program. It tells the topic that would be treated, the resource people who would be on the program, time and date of the program. After a program's broadcast, what obtains now is that the producer of that program is mandated to upload the program into the station's various social media handles. This is the process known as media convergence, where various arms of media (mainstream media and social media) converge to churn out or air a particular message. Therefore, it is at the interest of the producer to be able to script and produce for both the mainstream media and social media.

The producer should be able in the era of digitization and globalization to know how to mechanize the script or production to fit into the mainstream media and social media. At this level, media contents are crisp, smarty, punchy, intelligent, aesthetically crafted, and timely. Contents fit for the digital space should be able to get peoples' attention very easily, create interest and curiosity, sustain interest, and set an agenda. Contents at this level should be expository and controversial. When media contents are teemed with these characteristics, they can attract, lure, and sustain the interest of a global audience. It is at this stage local media contents and local talents can be projected to become international brands.

CONTENT DEPLOYMENT

Before any media content is deployed from one "Media Domain" to another, the producer has to ask himself or herself what result do I want to get, what impact do I want to create, what do I want to stir up, and what changes do I seek to create? Answering these questions is germane because it will help the producer to know the right and the size of the insert or content fit for any media domain. This is because there are still a considerable number of people who do not use or visit a particular media domain. Media domains are the terrain various media genres beam their signals to. I call it "Broadcast Media Tracks." Just as the train and the plane have their tracks, so are the various media, be it the mainstream media or social media. The electromagnetic waves or signals of radio are different from that of television. The same goes for the internet broadband that the social media streams from.

Therefore, a radio or television content can be deployed to social media, but first, the producer would have to convert it as we have discussed here to fit into the digital space. Social media audiences do not have the time to listen to or watch very long media content, they are always impatient, so the producer would need to do a lot of content trimming, getting only the exciting part of the program and placing it online for the online audience

DIGITIZED CONTENT SPECIFICATION

Contents for the digital space are specified, otherwise they would not fit into the digital space. The digital space is a very competitive market square where digital touts aggressively draw the attention of the online audience. By touts, I mean aggressive marketers who would employ every means (pictures, animation, graphics, sound, and videos) to draw, get, and sustain online audience attention. Therefore, the producer who is providing content in the digital space must provide content that would specifically fit the digital space; order wise, the possibility of losing the global audience the digital space provides is eminent. Therefore, digitized specifications for content should be: short in size (length and duration), sharp picture, crisp and luring video, punchy start, catchy introduction, simple but luring headline, provocative ending, need satisfying, inviting, traffic accumulator, sustaining, engaging, novel, and daring.

WHERE TO OBTAIN CONTENT

- Primary Source
- Secondary source
- Traditional Source
- Technological Source
- Online Sources (with utmost caution and fact-checking)
- Mortuaries
- Cemetery
- University Faculties/Departments

CONCLUSION

Scientifically and technically, there is a Siamese-twins cum symbiotic subtle and an unobserved relationship that exists between the broadcast message consumers audience and the electronic media. The reason broadcast media exist today and would continue to exist is because audience members are desirous of their content. Looking through this relationship, audience members would continue to dictate the direction of content, and this makes the audience the king. The broadcast audience members have migrated over time to the digital arena, therefore, irrespective of whether the broadcast station is a public or commercial station, such station will not survive in the digital era or become relevant if its operations are not digitally in tune with program concept, audience size, or lack the understanding of the type of media consumers it serves or seeks to serve.

RECOMMENDATION

In the digital space, broadcast stations, regardless of ownership or market drive, would not escape engaging in digital research-based programming and not think that the audience would just sit and wait for the usual. Nowadays, audience members understand the dynamics and the mechanics of digital media production, so they would desire something topnotch from program producers to wet their program appetite. Therefore, there is need to broadcast talents to befriend technology in carrying out their broadcast chores. This is because media owners would want to hire talents who can operate digital gadgets in carrying out their on-air chores.

REFERENCES

Akindes, G. 2011. "Football bars: Urban sub-Saharan Africa's trans-local 'stadiums.'" *The International Journal of the History of Sport* 28 (15): 2176–2190.

Akpan, U. 2019. *"Hip Hop Music on Radio and the Lifestyle of Students in Select Tertiary Institutions in Lagos, Nigeria."* Published PhD Thesis. Lambert Publishers.

Ansu-Kyeremeh, K., ed. 2005. "Indigenous Communication in Africa: A Conceptual Framework." In *Indigenous Communication in Africa: Concept, Application, and Prospects*. Accra: Ghana Universities Press.

Asante, M. 2018. "The Classical African Concept of Maat and Human Communication." In *Black/Africana Communication Theory*, edited by Kehbuma Langmia. Cham, Switzerland: Palgrave Macmillan, 11–23.

Ba, A. 1996. *Télévisions, paraboles et démocraties en Afrique noire*. Paris: L'Harmattan.

Bourgault, L. M. 1995. *Mass media in Sub-Saharan Africa*. Bloomington: Indiana University Press.

Chalaby, J. K. 2005. *Transnational television worldwide: Towards a new media order*. London; New York: I. B. Tauris; Palgrave Macmillan.

Chaume, F. 2019. *Localizing media contents: Technological shifts, global and social differences and activism in audiovisual translation*. London: Routledge.

Cosenza, M., Gavidia, M., and González-Avella, J. 2020. "Against mass media trends: Minority growth in cultural globalization." *Plos Digital Health*. Accessed May 22, 2021. DOI: https://doi.org/10.1371/journal.pone.0230923.

Crane, D., Kawashima, N., and Kawasaki, K., eds. 2002. *Global Culture: Media, Arts, Policy, and Globalization*. New York: Routledge (Taylor and Francis).

Curran, J., and Park, M. J., eds. 2000. *De-Westernizing media studies.* London, UK: Routledge.

van Dijik, Teun A. 1991. *Media contents: the interdisciplinary study of news as discourse.* London: Routledge.

Doob, B. 1985. *Communication in Africa*; "Oramedia in Africa." In *Mass Communication, Culture and Society in West Africa*, edited by Frank Okwo Ugboajah. London: Hans Zell, 165–186.

Dwyer, P. 2019. *Understanding media production.* London, UK: Routledge.

Eastman, S. T. and Ferguson, D. A. 2009. *Media Programming, Strategies and Practice.* Boston (USA): Thomson Wadsworth.

Eribo, F. and Jong-Ebot, W. 1997. *Press freedom and communication in Africa.* Trenton, NJ: Africa World Press.

Esson, J. 2015. "Better Off at Home? Rethinking Responses to Trafficked West African Footballers in Europe." *Journal of Ethnic and Migration Studies* 41 (3): 512–530. Accessed May 22, 2021. DOI: 10.1080/1369183X.2014.927733.

Haggerty, G. E., and McGarry, M., eds. 2015. *A companion to lesbian, gay, bisexual, transgender, and queer studies. Chichester,* UK: Wiley-Blackwell.

Hall, S., Evans, J., and Nixon, S. 2013. *Representation: Cultural representations and signifying practices* (2nd ed.). London, UK: Sage.

Hill Collins, P., and Bilge, S. 2016. *Intersectionality.* Cambridge, UK: Polity Press.

Hydén, G., Leslie, M., and Ogundimu, F. F. 2002. *Media and democracy in Africa.* New Brunswick, NJ: Transaction Publishers.

James, P. and Tulloch, J. 2010. *Globalization and Culture*, vol. 1, Globalizing Communications. New York: Sage Publications, Ltd.

Kelvin, W. 2003. *Understanding Media Theory.* London: Hodder Arnold Publications, p. 256.

Langmia, K., ed. 2018. *Black/Africana Communication Theory.* Cham, Switzerland: Palgrave Macmillan.

Lenoble-Bart, A., and Tudesq, A. 2008. *Connaître les médiasd'Afriquesubsaharienne - problématiques, sources et resources.* Paris: Karthala.

Mano, W., and Milton, V., eds. 2021. *Routledge Handbook of African Media and Communication Studies.* London: Routledge.

Mawere, M., and Mubaya, T. 2016. *African Philosophy and Thought Systems: A Search for a Culture and Philosophy of Belonging.* Bamenda, Cameroon: Langaa RPCIG.

Mazrui, A. 1986. *The Africans: A Triple Heritage.* London: BBC Publications.

McCavit, W. E., and Pringle, P. K. 1986. *Electronic media management.* USA: Butterworth Publishers.

Mccombs, M. E., and Shaw, D. L. 1972. "The Agenda-Setting Function of Mass Media." *Public Opinion Quarterly* 36: 176–187.

McQuail, D. 2010. *McQuail's communication theory.* London: Sage Publications, Ltd.

Merril, J. 2006. "Global Elite: A newspaper community reason in world media." Special issue of *Gunnet Centre Journal* 4 (4): 93.

Milton, Viola C. and Mano, Winston. 2021. "Afrokology as a Transdisciplinary Approach to Media and Communication Studies." In *Routledge Handbook of*

African Media and Communication Studies, edited by Winston Mano and Viola C. Milton. London: Routledge, 270, 257.

Moemeka, A. 1998. "Socio-Cultural Environment of Communication in Traditional/ Rural Nigeria: An Ethnographic Exploration." *Communicatio Socialis Yearbook, vol 3.* (1984): 41–56; "Communalism as a Fundamental Dimension of Culture." *Journal of Communication* (48) 4: 118–41.

Mulder, D. 2004. "The evolution of marketing communication: from selling to integration." *Communicare* 23 (1): 220–237.

Nightingale, V., ed. 2011. *The handbook of media audiences*. Chichester, UK: Wiley Blackwell.

Nixon, L. 2020. "Predicting your future audience's popular topics to optimize TV content marketing success." In *Proceedings of the 2nd International Workshop on AI for Smart TV Content Production*. Access and Delivery, pp. 5–10.

Nunes, V., and Stroebel, J. 2004. "The effectiveness of product placement in films as a promotional tool: A survey investigating students' attitude, recall and specific behaviour at the University of Pretoria." Pretoria: University of Pretoria. Unpublished postgraduate research report.

Nyamnjoh, F. B. 2005. *Africa's media, democracy, and the politics of belonging.* London; New York: Zed Books and Pretoria: Unisa Press.

Onwumechili, C., and Akpan, U. 2020. "African footballers' wives: 'Those paid dollars and pounds, their heads are not five!'" *International Review for the Sociology of Sport* 56 (5): 641–57.

Schramm, W., and Porters, E. 1982. *Men, women, messages and media: Understanding human communication.* New York: Harper and Row Publishers, p. 278.

Sparks, C. 2007. *Globalization, development and the mass media.* London: SAGE, p. 264.

Sterin, J. C. 2012. *Mass media evolution.* Boston: Allyn and Bacon.

Twenge, J. M., Martin, G. N., and Spitzberg, B. H. 2019. "Trends in U.S. Adolescents' media use, 1976–2016: The rise of digital media, the decline of TV, and the (near) demise of print." *Psychology of Popular Media Culture 8* (4): 329–345.

Uche, L. 1989. *Mass media, people, and politics in Nigeria.* New Delhi: Concept Publishing Company.

Udoakah, N. 2014. *Government and the media in Nigeria.* (3rd.). Ibadan: Stirling–Horden Publisher Ltd., p. 125.

Van der Waldt, De la Rey. 2005. "The role of product placement in feature films and broadcast television programs: an IMC perspective." *Communicare Journal for Communication Sciences in South Africa* (24), 4.

Vivian, J. 2009. *The media of mass communication (9th ed).* Boston (USA): Pearson Education, Inc.

Waisbord, S. and Mellado, C. 2014. "De-Westernizing Communication Studies: A Reassessment." *Communication Theory* 24 (4): 362.

Wright, C. 1986. *Mass communication: A sociological perspective*. New York: Random House, p. 236.

Ziegler, D., and Asante, M. K. 1992. *Thunder and silence: The mass media in Africa*. Trenton, NJ: Africa World Press.

Chapter 8

From Analog to Digital

What Would Change in Broadcast Management in the Era of Globalization

Kingsley Datubor Uranta, Chukwudi Ogbuaja, and Abiola Ajibola

It is important to state from the onset that migrating from analog to digital will not only change a lot of things and stop there, but it will keep on changing rapidly as we have been recording in recent times. The advent of digital technology has brought about a new era of rapid dynamism in the Broadcast industry. In other words, what changed yesterday may change tomorrow as technology keeps evolving. In fact, the rapidity of change has kept everyone on their toes, not only in the media industry but in all facets of life.

Someone might want to ask: What isthe trigger for all these changes? One of the principal triggers of change in life is efficiency. Efficiency is the measure of how time, energy, and space are saved for a particular purpose. In the case of the broadcast industry, digital technology has the capacity to offer efficiency in the areas of transmission spectrum (or space), content clarity, media production, and distribution processes. For transmission spectrum, a lot of space could be conserved for other communication systems to be accommodated within the transmission spectrum as a lot of radio stations can be multiplexed within a small bandwidth. This conserved space can be converted to money when deployed for other applications.

For content clarity, video and audio information could be made of much cleaner quality with higher fidelity resulting in a better user's experience. For example, the analog films that we used to watch in the olden days now come with crisp clean pictures and sharper sound with progressive technology advancement from 3D to 4D and lately to 5D.

Also, volumes of analog materials used in the radio and TV stations in those days have become drastically reduced in sizes and weight (thus conserving space), all courtesy of digitization (Chukwu 2015).

For media production and distribution, the time, cost, and energy deployed in carrying out these processes have become considerably lower as digital facilities have made this possible. For instance, music lovers need not go to stores to procure physical copies of albums as it was in the past. They could easily access the musical tracks on the internet, an innovative product of digitization.

No doubt, the advent of digital technology in a globalized world has turned the media industry into a phenomenal environment. Today, news moves at the speed of light with tweeting, blogging, and citizens' journalism everywhere all being the fallout of digital technology. Fiber optics, which is one of the engines of digital technology, has made the internet relatively cheap, fast, and accessible to a large number of subscribers even in remote locations, courtesy of the transition from 2G to 3G to 4G. With this, more people have been able to log into a host of digital services with the use of smart phones to receive digital contents.

WHAT IS DIGITIZATION

Digitization is an electronic process. It helps convert information that is analog in form, and of whatever size into digital format. The information may be text, images, videos, and so forth. To do the conversion, the analog signal is organized into discrete units (called bits) that can be separately addressed, usually in multiple bits called bytes or binary data (i.e., 0 or 1). The binary data are what computers and many digital devices with computing capacity (e.g., camera, biometric machine, etc.) recognize and process.

For example, when a scanner which is an analog device captures an image, it converts it to a digital image file such as bitmap. In the case of an Optical character Recognition (OCR) device, it analyzes the text or message for light and dark areas in order to identify each alphabetic letter or numeric digit and converts each character into an ASCII (American Standard Code for Information Intelligence) code. ASCII is the most common digital format for text files in computers and on the internet. In an ASCII file, each alphabetic, numeric or special character is represented with a seven (7) bit binary number (i.e., a string of seven 0s or 1s).

In the case of audio and video analog information or signal, the digitization process is completed by making the continuously varying signal to be changed without altering its essential content. The process is done by sampling the amplitude of the signal at evenly spaced markers which then becomes the numerical values for input as digital data. Generally, the digitized signals are easy to preserve, access, and share. For example, an original historical document usually in an analog format may only be accessible to people who visit its physical location. But if the document is digitized, it can be made available to all people worldwide online. Essentially, while globalization can be said to be an agelong phenomenon, digitization is a recent development whose impact on the broadcast industry has been awesome and is still ongoing. Of course, it can also be said that digitization has been a good catalyst for rapid globalization.

BROADCAST TECHNOLOGY

Broadcast technology is the art or technique of converting audio/video materials into electronic signals in such a way as to make it suitable for transmission through a medium to a wider audience. This can be regarded as sending messages from one source to many people or a point to multipoint. This model of broadcasting started globally on a commercial scale in 1920 with AM/SW radio, which was an improvement over the point-to-point model of communication that worked through a distributive radio telegraphy method (Daramola 2006).

Telegraphy radio broadcasting was introduced to Nigeria on December 10, 1932, basically as an extension of the Empire service of the BBC implemented with a relay station and a wired system connected to loudspeakers.

The AM/SW radio, which was already working in some countries, was later introduced to Nigeria some few years after. It was coordinated by Nigeria Broadcasting Services (NBS) and later NBC in 1957, when full broadcasting operations started nationwide by an Act of Parliament.

Broadcast technology continued to develop worldwide with the advent of the Frequency Modulated FM Radio System that brought about more clarity in reception of radio information. And as expected, the infrastructure was acquired by the federal government and of course various state governments, an action that started the proliferation of the broadcast industry in the country.

In the case of television, it was introduced to Nigeria in 1959 with the western regional government of the country blazing the trail. It was regarded as the very first in Africa. Other regions also followed suit thereafter, including the federal government.

The entire broadcast landscape took a new dimension when the sector was deregulated in 1992. This obviously brought a new vista into the industry because it broke the monopoly of government ownership and control of the industry. The competition that came into the industry no doubt accelerated development in the sector with all manner of frequency modulated equipment being acquired. However, while this lasted, all the entire broadcast equipment and infrastructure remained analog up until today.

DIGITIZING BROADCASTING

Broadcasting in Nigeria started its digitization journey in 2008 when an advisory committee on Digital Switch over DSO was set up and driven by the International Telecoms Union. Of course, being the largest country and an economic giant in Africa, it quickly accepted the technology switchover system as it was feared that the race to digitization might affect the people and government of the country if not well managed. The committee pursued every effort to make sure Nigeria joined the train by fixing the DSO date for June 17, 2012, three years ahead of the ITU global deadline of 2015. In spite of the laudable recommendations of the committee, the deadline could not be met for certain undisclosed reasons. Having kept the document for three years without any action, the federal government was moved to inaugurate another fourteen-man team tagged "Digiteam" to drive the process towards actualizing the dream.

Although the Digiteam in collaboration with NBC could have been able to conclude the migration by June 2015, financial constraints were a major issue they battled with.

According to the white paper released by the government, three broadcast signal distribution licenses were to be issued to the following:

1. The infrastructure organization to be carved out of NTA.
2. To a private firm based on competitive bidding.
3. To another firm based on future market demand.

However, for lack of funds this could not be implemented at that time. But while the financial delay continued, NBC/NTA decided to partner with digital television service provider StarTimes so as to give Nigeria the feel of what digital television broadcasting on a subscription basis entails. With other pay TV schemes on board for the same purpose, eight years after the initial deadline, nothing much was put on ground as regards the official switchover except for the Jos pilot scheme of DSO that was launched in April 2016 putting Nigeria's digitization process back on stream. Of course, in 2018 another scheme was launched in Abuja but whether the schemes were able to produce the expected result is a different ball game altogether.

HOW THE TECHNOLOGY OF DIGITIZATION
WOULD AFFECT BROADCAST SOFTWARE,
EQUIPMENT, AND BROADBAND

Digitization has not only affected broadcast software, equipment, and broadband, but has been having tremendous impact on them despite the fact that Nigeria and many African countries have not officially switched over. While the coast for digitization is not very clear, most equipment manufacturers invaded the Nigerian market with fully digitalized infrastructures. These of course come along with the required strings of software which are like the drivers of the digital devices.

There are three main types of software, namely, system software, application software, and network software. The system software controls the equipment's internal functions and the connected peripheral devices. Many digital broadcast equipment function along this pattern ranging from television studio equipment to the transmission devices. The application software directs the broadcast equipment to execute certain commands given to it by the user, which may include programs to carry out certain processes in the studio. For instance, an audio playback application software can be installed in a live studio base station. This will allow the system to play back selected and programmed musical tracks without any human interference.

The third type of software, namely, network software, coordinates communication between equipment within a network. For example, a studio camera can communicate with the video console to bring about a balanced output. All of these are the current scenario in a typical modern and digital TV station. A very striking observation in the digital era is that most of the equipment comes in small and lightweighted versions.

Another important area that the technology of digitization has impacted is the Broadband. For the digitization process to work effectively in some digital equipment, a-high speed internet connection is required. As the process of digitization is evolving in the broadcast sector, so is the broadband infrastructure also expanding, culminating in efficient and effective digital broadcast services. In the immediate past, internet services were by dial-up connection which is very slow but cheap. However, the evolution in the telecoms sector has brought four different techniques of delivering efficient broadband services, namely, digital subscriber line (DSL), cable, fiber optics, and satellite with the fiber optic having the upper edge because of its capacity to deliver very fast and reliable internet services.

HOW TECHNOLOGY OF DIGITIZATION
WOULD AFFECT CONTENT

There is no way we can have diverse and multiple platforms which digitization offers that we will not have bloated content components, and of course we have been experiencing this. Africa, and particularly Nigeria, have diverse urban and rural settings filled with potential content materials. The country's diversity, evolution as a nation, languages, music, folktales, food, economy, education, and many others make a variety of contents possible.

With over 250 radio stations and 145 TV stations, the media space is filled with all manner of contents, each of them in different niche areas, all courtesy broadcast digitization. This no doubt is a positive development as every community feels heard and represented in the scheme of things.

HOW THE TECHNOLOGY IS AFFECTING
PERSONNEL AND OPERATIONS

Digitization, while having its positive effects, has its negative effects also, principal among which is the reduction in the number of personnel required to handle various broadcast operations. Many of the job schedules previously handled by humans have now been programmed into the broadcast equipment, making some operations run on autopilot.

By the time the digitization process gets to another level of development as expected in a couple of years, a lot of personnel will also be displaced. Obviously, with the advent of the 5G network and development in the area of artificial intelligence, most camera work in both live and production studios will be handled by robots.

As expected, most other jobs in the broadcast chain process and operations will be taken over by anticipated results in augmented reality and virtual reality which will not only cause job displacement but will make television production to be faster and viewing more lively.

CHALLENGES AND PROSPECTS

The digitization of the broadcast sector has no doubt opened up a lot of opportunities, prospects, and of course challenges, especially in the African environment. As the journey progresses, so are new situations emerging. Even though Africa belongs to the third world, where used technology is usually dumped, globalization has made it possible for reigning technologies and innovations to get to the countries without much delay. Globalization has indeed broken every barrier while advancement in technology has further shrunk the global village. This in effect has made the broadcast industry respond quickly to technological developments and changes as they are unveiled.

CHALLENGES

The challenges of a digitized broadcast environment like Nigeria include the following:

1. Unavailability of stable power supply: Digital equipment is prone to giving unreliable performance without a very stable power supply which is a serious challenge in Nigeria. Equipment failure may even result, and this may constitute a serious problem to time-bound programs.
2. Lack of manpower: Having qualified manpower to handle sensitive digital equipment is germane to smooth broadcast services. This therefore makes the training and retraining of existing staff very inevitable.
3. Financial challenge: The digitization of the broadcast industry obviously comes with attendant high cost of the equipment and facilities. The cost of sending staff on training is another area of challenge.
4. To a non-vibrant economy, all this may pose some critical problems to the industry.

PROSPECTS

Broadcast digitization offers a lot of prospects among which are:

1. Enhanced two-way communication between the broadcast organization and the listeners or viewers. This gives the listeners or viewers, as the case may be, a lot of confidence in the organization.
2. Improved media relations comes as a result of the communication established with the listeners and viewers.
3. Career development will also be enhanced as practitioners learn on the job.
4. Enhancement of organizational image will be achieved as digitization demands that the organizations have websites and social media pages to reach out to the people.
5. Digitization also offers very good and veritable marketing strategies that can be deployed for commercial advantage.

WHAT IS BROADCAST MANAGEMENT?

Let us face it squarely: the current era is the period at which humans are standing on the bilateral edge of super information highway industry and tradition. Long age corporate traditions would want most broadcast managers (BMs) to remain in their comfort zones, by this I mean what they are used to. Broadcasting management is a special endeavor because of its peculiar nature and ubiquitous power, popularity, and glamor. Its mere nature of housing a collection of creative minds requires extraordinary ability to manage, supervise, direct, cajole, and lead in the day-to-day running of the industry. The inner workings of the broadcast industry are enormous. This invariably means it requires a leadership and followership structure which ensures order, control, and discipline from the topmost management to the least staff. The industry is a web of chains of command, input and output, which makes it as strong as its weakest link because every department and unit depends on each other to perform. In other words, interdepartmental dependability and cooperation are the bedrock of a successful broadcast medium. For example, for a news program on a television station, news editors, reporters, cameramen, personnel of the electronic news gathering (ENG) unit, news casters, floor managers, drivers, and even cleaners are needed, and they cannot afford to fail in their assignment.

WHAT DOES A BROADCAST MANAGER MANAGE?

The underlying fact here is that the broadcast industry is a well-structured combination of men and material with the sole aim of affecting and influencing the society through programs that provide information, education, and entertainment from where the people gauge the society, organize, and express themselves. The management of the broadcasting industry has assumed a different coloration since the liberalization of the broadcast media landscape in the 1990s. Before then, only government media outlets known as public broadcasters were the primary sources of news and entertainment and were subjected to the whims and caprices of the government of the day in line with the civil service structure. The emergence of the "new minds" with private sector business mentality and creative freedom meant that all had to change. The audience now has a variety of options as news sources and entertainment. With the enormous capital outlay in running a television station in a competitive environment, and with no subvention from government, for example, managers would need to evolve business modules and strategies that would ensure better programming, consistency underpinned by professionalism that would attract and retain advertisers, eyeballs and eventual return on investment which is usually a long-term stretch. Managers of broadcast stations must by now be conversant with the creative latitude and freedom which young professionals in the industry possess. It therefore matters that managers must know how to mix and match freedom with the straight line required to instill discipline to meet deadlines and stay afloat. Fact is, the young crop of practitioners must be managed properly in an era when the media landscape has been permanently disrupted by technology and the new media. Nigerian broadcast managers, particularly those who run private stations are confronted by myriads of challenges. They have to deal with infrastructure—electricity, broadcast hardware, dwindling advertising earnings, staff remuneration, attitude, mental well-being, talent (only a handful of private media organizations in Nigeria pay salaries, and take staff welfare seriously, the rest owe up to two or three years in areas), ownership whims, and political pressure. It therefore goes without saying that broadcast managers must be under intense difficulties in running their outfits. However, the coast is always clear for those who like to make the first move and dare to take the risk to innovate and invest in infrastructure, technology, training, content development, and securing rewarding partnerships. Such stations will always enjoy the first mover advantage.

HOW BROADCAST MANAGERS RESPONDED TO GLOBALIZATION

Worldwide, with the coming of globalization, BMs in most competitive corporate organizations had to respond to increased competition for globally mobile talents, changes in both workforce attitudes and composition, shifts in the employer/worker relationship and rapid advances in BM technology. New kinds of technical knowledge, skills, and abilities would require BMs in the future to be flexible and willing to deal with the ever-accelerating pace and often unpredictable changes in the global workplace such as the broadcast sector. The broadcast manager needs to evaluate the implications of a movement into an era of decentralization, which, if used properly, can lead to emancipation. The era will require a new kind of organization, based on a different system that can bring together the contribution of autonomous individuals in a socially sustainable way. It is thus clear that a new way to manage broadcast talents as a system is emerging, as well as how well new broadcast managers should manage themselves.

WHAT SHOULD BROADCAST MANAGERS
IN NIGERIA BE CONCERNED WITH?

Using Nigeria as a case study, Africa's population is young. Broadcast managers should be thinking of content to satisfy the young, discerning, and critical mass of content consumers, while still meeting the needs of the aging and older audience. Akin to this, is the need for a visible and result-oriented policy framework and activation of a modern broadcasting space. The digitization and digitalization of Nigeria's broadcast space should be the next big thing in the industry, and broadcast managers should be up to the challenge and opportunities that come with the innovation. The threat of the new media is a source of concern to broadcast media managers across the world. The emergence of "unschooled" self-appointed "journalists" who I have decided to call "rumor merchants" means that real trained broadcast journalists and their managers must up the ante to counterbalance the misinformation, disinformation, and mal-information which have polluted the information dissemination space. Fake news, unverified information rules the space. To worsen the malady, consumers of such information have become so gullible to the extent that everything is consumed, retweeted, forwarded, rebroadcast. News can be sourced from the palms of the hand and at will. The undiscerning public is always excited at such quality of information. It becomes worse in a country like Nigeria where the malady of ethnicity and religion are ready tools at the disposal of the untrained hands to cause disaffection in the polity. Broadcast media managers and journalists at large can continue to bemoan the development; but there are great opportunities to counter the challenges. As mentioned earlier, managers of broadcasting organizations will have to retool their strategies by identifying and segmenting their target audience and combine the social media and traditional platforms as conduits for reaching such publics. It is important to note that modern consumers, especially the young population, have a very short attention span. Therefore, using social media as one of the channels to reach this segment must be produced in short, innovative and interesting formats. The place of training and retraining of broadcast personnel in all the departments to equip them for the demands of modern-day broadcasting cannot be overstated. Oftentimes, however, attention is beamed to practitioners in the field—reporters, editors, cameramen and engineers. Broadcast managers and media owners need to be trained in the management of modern-day broadcast stations. This is quite true because a station can hardly grow beyond the vision of its owner or manager. In Africa, more than ever before, positive reportage and programming should not suffer relegation even as the media, the broadcast media in particular, continue to help the people hold the government to account, stimulate openness, and deepen democracy. Managers must rise to the occasion, especially at times like this when doubts about Nigeria's ability to sustain its unity and leapfrog into prosperity have come under intense questioning.

MANAGING THE TALENTS IN THE DIGITAL SPACE

Managing broadcast talents presently that the industry is still at the analog stage in Nigeria is a bit easy because broadcast managers are used to it. But managing these talents under a fully digitalized broadcast environment would be a different ball game entirely. Speaking professionally, the present crop of broadcast talents is more of millennials who are very conversant with technology from infancy, therefore, their mind-set, orientation, and skill set is different from the generation I started broadcasting with. Globalization with the revolution of information technology has dramatically changed human behavior, management of corporations, and governance of states much more than the industrial revolution transformation of those days. The present crop of presenters and producers are at home with digital gadgets, want to work virtually, want to explore beyond their office space to showcase their talent in the digital space. Some of them own blogs, personal websites, YouTube channels, and so forth. These might go against or run contrary to the traditional policies of their respective employers, and as a result, this explains the frequent movements you see in the broadcast sector where talents work in five different stations within a space of one year. This is because he is looking for a station that can allow him to express and showcase his artistic prowess in the digital space without any fear of intimidation from his bosses. The talents in the digital age want to be heard, seen, and felt globally; they want a global acceptance of their broadcast skills, and most stations feel this might come in the way of their chores. Some feel that the broadcast talent might soon become more popular than the station itself owing to the fans the talent might gather in the global space. But some broadcast managers should learn to know that their talents' global fan base can equally bring popularity and commercial interest to their stations. Most broadcast managers get intimidated when the talents under them get a massive online following. But let us look at it this way; these massive mixed audiences can be used for the benefit of the station, especially in the area of building the station's online community. Broadcast managers need to understand that the tide has changed, and they need to flow with the digital tide.

HOW COVID-19 CHANGED BROADCAST
PRESENTATION MATRIX

Surely COVID-19 has dealt the entire world one big blow, the effect of which will linger for quite some time. It has been an ill wind that has blown no one any good. But then, it is clear to observers that the pandemic has expanded the scope of digital activity in the world, profoundly. Individuals, who live in countries which are still lagging behind in terms of advancement in broadband connectivity, might not appreciate what is being talked about here. However, the inescapable fact is that the world is digitizing and globalizing. Africa has its technological inhibitions; still, it cannot ignore the bandwagon. The worst that can happen for now is for it to tag along!

The other day, we watched for perhaps the fifth time, how the Nigerian president Mohammadu Buhari had taken to virtual meetings like a duck to water. Without doubt, if the leader of Africa's biggest economy and most populous nation had been told toward the end of 2019 that national executive committee meetings would from February 2020 (or thereabout), hold in Aso Rock without physical interaction by ministers and other public functionaries, he would have virtually scoffed at the suggestion.

But then, something called COVID-19 came calling and the world shuddered to the fatal influence of its dreaded presence and, thereafter, picked up a new-found need for reinforcing or increasing the intensity of the virtual life. Most of us are a "voracious consumer" of news. When we watch the major networks in the world interview resource persons who speak almost from their kitchen these days, you marvel at the new normal which internet-based communication has assumed. Whether it is a satellite link-up, a Skype, Zoom, or WhatsApp meeting, the effects of COVID-19 have brushed aside studio aesthetics to accommodate functional but somewhat bland audio-visual backdrops just to keep the news going. And just as well! What the news broadcaster cannot do is concoct news situations in the face of what was a telling lockdown or seeming international "standstill" as coronavirus was being battled. But as sure as eggs are eggs, those who can afford it have latched onto the internet as an alternative to life profoundly changed by the virus. Whether COVID-19 is tamed by a vaccine (hopefully by the end of the year) or not, one thing is certain: some of the current platforms of interaction will not be retired or given up for a complete return to old habits which demanded journeys by air to major capitals so that meetings could hold! Such is the compulsion accompanying the world's march towards more digitization and globalization.

AFRICA MEDIA INDUSTRIES: WHAT'S THEIR CURRENT STATE?

For purposes of streamlining this discussion, Africa media industries will refer to any activity that educates, entertains, or informs and how such activities are affected by access to good data. Taking Nigeria as a test case, chief engineer and ICT supervisor at foremost private radio and TV broadcaster, Africa Independent Television (AIT) and Raypower, Tony Uyah gave us a clear picture of attempts to digitize broadcasting in Nigeria since 2008. Mr. Uyah is a pioneer staffer of AIT/Raypower and the size of the broadcast outfit he works for, necessitates a watchful eye on Nigeria's moves at modernizing radio and TV signals distribution to bring it in line with what obtains in major economies in the world.

According to Mr. Uyah, who was a member of the presidential advisory committee on digitization, "Nigeria initiated the idea of transition from analog to digital terrestrial television transmission in 2008 with the setting up of the Presidential Advisory Committee on Transition from Analogue to Digital Transmission." It had all stemmed from an agreement under the auspices of the International Telecommunication Union (ITU). Clearly ambitious to beat the June 17, 2015, deadline set by ITU for it to digitize its media operations, Nigeria decided that June 17, 2012, would be her target. By the arrangement, broadcast content providers would no longer be responsible for transmission of signals via their existing terrestrial broadcast infrastructure, but rather, will become content providers who push out such content to a third party for transmission. Set-top boxes would be commissioned for distribution of signals while satellite transmission would fill in the gaps in areas where terrestrial transmission would face huge challenges. Subscription to the set-top boxes would make available to the consumer a bouquet of programs which would be suited for the needs of particular communities of consumers/viewers. It would all result in licensees going out to city, regional, and national television stations. Two distribution entities, ITS Limited, which represents the Nigerian government and private communications outfit, and Pinnacle Communications, which won licenses for the distribution of signals. ITS rolled out its first digital signals in Jos, Plateau State, in the North Central region in Nigeria in 2016 (Azubuike and Ikiriko 2019). There have been attempts to replicate the effort in cities such as Abuja, Kaduna, Ilorin, Enugu, and a few other places. So, What has been the major hindrance to a smooth roll out of these well-sought-after signals?

1. Set-top boxes are not readily available while the platform is plagued with too few channels.

2. There are issues with the conditional access systems, and billing while determining charges for carriage of the channels is a problem besides license fees.

So, a project dreamed for a 2012 switch-on, is in 2020, still mired in operational incoherence. Mr. Uyah further observes (and this is very important) that, "A laudable process of migration which would have expanded the variety of content available to the Nigerian audience has practically stalled owing largely to too much government involvement in the processes." From Uyah's summation, the road to Nigeria's digital poverty is largely paved with lofty government intentions—the people are not getting what they want (the poverty), while the government still believes it has the people's best intentions at heart and won't let go of its hamstring-inducing control! Uyah relishes in his mind, the better sound and picture quality, possible interactivity with the audience which a seamless switch-over to digital broadcasting would have translated into. Content specialization would by now have become a strong contender for channels which are desirous of it.

But the head of Channels Television's (another Nigerian private TV station) IT unit, Abraham Eguare, is not particularly saddened by the limited or inhibited growth of digitization in Africa. He points out that the growth in the media industry across the globe has continued to improve the way people interact and source for information in both print and broadcast media. This has now been further enhanced with the coming of the new media where electronic transmitting and receiving of information is made possible through the use of social media and streaming services. The newspaper, as we knew it, is no longer a format held constant by agelong print practices. These days, a newspaper can break its news online almost as fast as radio or television.

Digitization has truly reshaped the speed of audio-visual communication. According to Eguare:

> Before digitization, newspapers could only be accessed from local vendors, but today, almost all print media in Africa now have a website where readers can access their news updates and publications. These websites also provide a platform for the users to subscribe so they could receive electronic editions of the newspaper. The reign of the hard copy is taking the backseat. With digitization, they are able to use relevant technology to reach the global audience. Most Print media also have software applications (apps) which enable anyone with a smartphone to get news updates. Before digitization, these newspapers were restricted to their immediate locality and not-too-far-away parts of the country. (Eguare 2021)

Eguare observes that there was a time when some states in Northern Nigeria had to wait until the next day to procure a newspaper due to transportation constraints. Digitization has changed it all and Africa, not just Nigeria, has joined a global audience that has a newspaper served hot, fresh, and juicy to readers, almost in real time! Looking at this with the broadcast media lens in Africa, digitization, according to Eguare, has tremendously improved the way news content, programs, motion pictures (film or movies), and other media content are transmitted across the globe.

THE MAGIC ABOUT DIGITIZATION

In radio or television stations across Africa, digitization has helped the media houses to store, process, and transmit information to the public via various streaming platforms and social media. One can now watch live programs and video on demand via apps created by these media outfits. For example, in Nigeria, Channels Television, African Independent Television (AIT), and Nigerian Television Authority (NTA) can be watched on their apps, on social media, websites, and satellite parameters. But there are some local media outfits which still operate on the terrestrial platform, reaching limited viewers or listeners. With digitization, African media outfits have been able to conduct interviews over the internet via video conferencing applications such as Skype, Cisco, Webex, Zoom, Google Hangouts, and others. Just as we earlier indicated, Eguare affirms that this has been of immense benefit since the advent of COVID-19 due to restriction of movements. Utilizing these technologies has helped to cut cost and increase the speed of production. Also, the media industries in Africa have been able to utilize cloud storage to store and share footage and other media content. Some of these are Google cloud technology, FileFactory, 4shared, and WeTransfer. Files are shared almost seamlessly where broadband inhibitions are surmounted. Before digitization, media outfits in Africa used available airlines or road transportation to send footage stored in video home system (VHS) cassettes, DVDs, or flash drives from the field to the studio. News reports suffered delays in that practically manual arrangement.

But in spite of huge inhibitions, digitization has influenced the way African media industries use technologies to change business models, provide new revenue streams, value-producing opportunities, and reach global audiences. At the individual level, many smartphone owners can now access applications that give them the ability to engage an interesting level of clip editing and sharing. About a year ago, we were at Afe Babalola University, Ado Ekiti, ABUAD, in Western Nigeria alongside three other journalism trainers who had visited the Mass Communications Department of the university to address the needs of third and final year students. The video and graphics editor who accompanied us also doubled as our cameraman. He made clips of the students interviewing potential resource persons for two news stories which two groups of students had been instructed to produce and present. I was surprised when after the trip to get shots, some of the students told me that they had no issues with getting a montage to launch the "mock newscast" required of them. Their phones were just good enough to download the apps necessary for cutting montages and transporting their final work to whichever destination they wanted it sent to! This labels the huge empowerment that digitization has afforded the Nigerian youngster with a mind on producing and streaming video at will. These are all possible because of growing digital realities which keep collapsing activities in the world into the palm of the hand, so to speak. Not only can individuals now record video; they can stream the same and send it to any part of the world due to digitization and globalization.

Still recalling my experience at ABUAD, the students ended up convinced that there was a lot they could achieve if they pursued employment after university, sticking to the direction to which mass communications was leading them. It was quite a relief to hear them say this, because out of a class of twenty-four students, only about six had spared a thought for mass communications as a possible job provider after school. At the end of the course, the number had climbed to fourteen! It had all resulted from getting them to discover "extra functions" for their digital phones and how audio-visually creative they could become. This takes us to another very important inquiry which Africa has to build into efforts to maximize gains from rising digitization and globalization.

WHAT IS THE LEVEL OF AWARENESS ABOUT OPPORTUNITIES?

In one of our COVID-19 imposed home teaching rounds on the outskirts of the Nigerian capital where I live, a parent got excited when in her presence, I asked her daughter how much she was using her phone to help the mother's agro-business. The young lady obviously had never contemplated such support for her mother's agricultural venture even when she was in a pole position to use her smart phone to attract customers to the business. As we gauge Africa media industries in an era of digitization and globalization, a little shift of focus to what the individual can and is actually doing with their laptop or cell phone is very relevant. It turns out that not much of Africa's youthful population is aware of the immense benefits their devices can bring into life and living and indeed provide a solid platform for further self-empowerment.

The young lady we mentioned earlier could easily have put her mother's business on a wider market by giving social media publicity to the business. It just happened that she was not "thinking like that." And many of her colleagues are just like her—they hold the ultimate gateway to favorable exposure to life's breadwinning endeavors but fail to utilize the opportunity. Surely some of her friends make more productive use of the cell phone. What is in contention is the percentage of those who are taking such an advantage. And this brings us to the question of what amount of awareness the individual young man or woman has, concerning the immense possibilities on the internet. Obviously, more seminars and workshops are needed to re-announce the huge gains that are still largely untapped by Africa's internet users.

Connectivity to broadband seamlessness remains as elusive as ever to mainstream Africa. If the continent's media outfits are struggling for access to data that simply moves content on the touch of a button, the lot of the individual isn't in any way better. They are all working in the same prism of inadequate broadband infrastructure. Ironically, COVID-19, which is opening up more awareness of, and a resolve to engage a digital life more, is also the stumbling block to funds that would facilitate the world bank–assisted broadband infrastructure which is likely to break the jinx confronting Africa in terms of digitization. The funds needed would be delayed by the struggling economies of Africa which are more focused on feeding communities in dire straits than committing to funding easy connectivity.

Against all the odds, effective digitization and globalization of African media industries have taken an impatient refuge on the corridor. It is unarguably needed by all for a well-connected and interactive world, but yet in clear need of the right circumstance to happen! As Uyah toned in the opening of this piece using Nigeria as an example, there will be continuing attempts to fully digitize African media industries, but those efforts which would naturally lead to better international cooperation and development will for sometime be inhibited by a lack of solid infrastructure and in the case of Nigeria, needless government control!

GLOBALIZATION: THE LANGUAGE IMPLICATION

In our sojourns in the English phonetics class, we have always harped on the need for the regular Nigerian using English on the internet to remember that communication that crosses its channel only to hit a dead end at its destination (in the form of lack of understanding of what is said or delivered) is as good as not having happened at all!

What we learned in the linguistics class is that, sitting at the base of human communication is the imperative of mutual intelligibility. It is nonnegotiable and is the matador whose absence "kills off" any effort at verbal, print, or sign language interaction.

In the realm of spoken English for instance, "I live here," delivered in a manner that doesn't help the other person understand what vowel is being pronounced in "live" could lead to confusion. In Nigeria, the vowel which speakers are more conversant with is /i/. Nigerian languages do not have the English long /i/, distinct from the short /ɪ/ still in the same English. The dilemma this leads to, is that a British man for instance would more likely understand "I live here" from the lips of a Nigerian as "I leave here" because the pronunciation would have moved more towards /i/ than /ɪ/.

So, the Nigerian, if they are not well-versed in what meaning difference /i/ and /ɪ/ bring about in minimal pairs in English, sticks to one form, /i/ to the detriment of meaning differentiation. Anyone caught in such a web, however pedestrian it may sound, might bump into quite a number of failed attempts at communication that they prefer silence at a point to expressing themselves at all.

This reminds us of the experience of a lady we worked with at a television station in Lagos, Nigeria. The woman, Victoria, undertook a trip to her cousin's in London but had to relocate to the home of another relative after three days. Her cousin's children drove her away with an embarrassing string of "What did you say?" and "I don't understand you"!

What the above scenario is all about is the need for whoever is delivering content to so many people in the world to learn and use forms that can be understood by the widest audience possible. First language influences are inevitable, but this is an aspect of globalization that cannot be taken for granted.

Let's take it a bit outside our scope here in Nigeria. At the Channels TV academy in Abuja, Nigeria, where we had the privilege of coaching journalists in "Election Reporting" in 2019. One of our facilitators, an American, eased so many minds when he said: "Please I have an awful American accent. If you do not understand anything I say, just stop me so I can go more slowly!" He surely put many souls in that room at ease because of his humble admission.

To finally drive it all home, where African languages contain an average of ten vowels as against twenty-five in British English (please refer to the International Phonetic Alphabet), those vowels of English missing from many African languages must be learned by the Nigerian who is keen on delivering English content to an audience in England for instance!

It is clear therefore that part of what is needed from the individual sending content to other parts of the world is to engage forms that will be more readily understood by the target audience, especially in the use of the spoken word. The African presenter or producer can only ignore this to the detriment of effective communication. At the level of grammar, the issue is not too different. We will quickly illustrate this with a question; How would the American or British person understand that "talkless of" used by so many Nigerians is actually a corruption of "not to talk of," "not to mention" or the more regular "let alone"? Globalization carries the onus of broadening the communication ability. Anything short of this cannot lead to effective communication!

SUMMARY

We strongly recommend that broadcast managers need to be retrained, relearn, unlearn, reskill if they must effectively manage millennial broadcast talents. In fact, I recommend that stations should hire more broadcast managers who are millennials or understand how millennial talents think and work. Every broadcast manager should be aware that the license to operate the station is held in trust for the people. After all said and done, managers of broadcast media have enormous powers to either keep afloat or sink through their programming due to lack of it, poor vision, paucity of trained manpower, and failure to innovate. They must run their stations with the utmost sense of responsibility, integrity, independence, fairness, and balance in this era of distortion in the broadcast media landscape. And above all, have it at the back of their mind that if broadcast talents must produce the required results and measure up with the rest of the world, attention must be paid to creating digital space and allowance for these broadcast talents to function freely wherever they are without any geographical restrictions. Remember, in the digital space, there are no limits!

The advent of digital media has no doubt turned the media landscape into a phenomenal space creating fundamental shifts from what was acknowledged to be better sometime ago. With the revolution taking place in the telecoms industry, today especially, in the area of broadband, 5G technology, augmented reality, and the internet of things, a lot of dramatic shifts are being expected in a couple of years. With the convergence of telecommunication and broadcasting, there is no doubt that a new era of broadcasting will eventually emerge, and this will change the world as we know it. Of course, it has been speculated that 5G technology will not only revolutionize the broadcast sector but all other areas of human endeavor like medicine, transport, commerce, agriculture, and so forth. We perceive that the initial concept of digitization may be overtaken by new development in technology, and this might essentially affect the traditional method of broadcasting as the changes continue. Already, there is a high-level competition between the traditional and the new media as we write. On our final note, broadcast organizations in Africa cannot afford to sit on the fence if they must remain relevant.

They have to come along with the trends in the global village to which they also belong.

REFERENCES

Azubuike, C., and Ikiriko, S. I. G. 2019. "Challenges and Prospects of Private Broadcast Media Ownership in Nigeria: A Study of Stations in Port Harcourt." *Mediterranean Journal of Social Sciences* 10 (5).

Chukwu, C. O. 2015. "Government Broadcast Media Ownership Pattern and Media Content in Nigeria—Its Threats to Democracy." *Research on Humanities and Social Sciences* 5 (16).

Daramola, I. 2006. *History and Development of Mass Media in Nigeria.* Lagos: Rothan Press, Ltd.

Eguare, A., 2021. A personal interview on broadcast digitization.

Chapter 9

The Place of Presentation Training for Broadcast Quality in the Era of Digitization and Globalization

Bimbo Oloyede

If broadcasting must regain its pride of place as the premium mode of communication in Nigeria, those of us who have spent decades operating as professionals within this noble profession should speak now or forever hold our peace, especially in the place of content and presentation. Broadcast media content scholars believe that a good presenter makes any content come alive in the manner of his or her presentation (Eastman and Ferguson 2009; Akpan 2019). It is clear to me that posterity will be deservedly unkind to us if we continue to gloss over the obvious cracks; ignore the gaping potholes and cover up the ever-increasing number of anomalies that currently bedevil broadcasting and broadcasters.

I make no apologies about being "old school." Indeed, I am at an age where I qualify as being an old school adherent. In fact, some of my colleagues and I, who are in the same age bracket have been described as "ancestors," which again is quite amusing, but I must say that I wonder what word today's broadcasters would come up with, for the generation of broadcasters and presenters who preceded my group of practitioners. According to Akpan (2019) and Uche (1989), a good number of the pioneer broadcast presenters in Nigeria learned on the job as some of them did not have any formal presentation training. Some of these pioneers, who are thankfully still guiding those who care to listen, are Dr. Christopher Kolade, CON, Mrs. Stella Awani, and Dr. Vincent Maduka. They presided in the 1970s, or set standards for my colleagues and I, when we began our careers as radio and television presenters and producers. The late Mrs. Enoh Irukwu and Ambassador Segun

Olusola (Member Nautical Institute, MNI), were also very vibrant members of this group.

My seniors included Femi Adeniyi-Williams, Anike Agbaje-Williams, Julie Coker, Tom Adaba, and those of blessed memory are Buki Ajayi, Mike Enahoro, Ikenna Ndaguba, Bode Alalade, James Audu, Kere Ahmed, Joe Ebuwa, Art Alade, and Earnest Okonkwo.

Between the mid-seventies and the early eighties, some notable present-ers included Dele Adetiba, Ron Mbatogu, Sienne Allwell-Brown, Rosaline Ogunro, Sadiq Daba, Lola Alakija, Ronke Ayuba, Soni Irabor, Bisi Olatilo, John Momoh, Sade Marquis, Timaus Matthias, Funmi Odubekun, Ruth Benammissia, Emmanuel Onumonu—popularly called by radio name Mani, Danladi Bako, Femi Sowoolu, Sola Momoh, Marius Ugada, Sola Omole, Cyril Stober, Eugenia Abu, Patrick Oke, Jones Usen, and Yori Folarin. We can never forget Joan O'dwyer, Tokunbo Ajayi, Yinka Craig, Halifa Baba-Ahmed, and Ibrahim Abba-Gana, who have passed on.

I do not intend to play the blame game. It would be ridiculous. How does one write one chapter about a situation which requires an entire book and has been caused, knowingly or unknowingly, by every so-called stakeholder in the broadcast industry? How can any contributor to our present crisis be exonerated when we are all culpable? Rather, my task is to consider the place of presentation training and broadcast quality in the era of digitization and globalization. It seems to me that although we can look at this from three different perspectives—presentation training, broadcast quality and digitiza-tion/globalization—the reality of the situation is that they are intertwined and inseparable. I believe that it is because of the current disconnect between these three broadcast elements that broadcasting has sunk to an all-time low, when by all accounts, digitally and globally, broadcast professionals should be enjoying an all-time high.

PRESENTATION: THE HEART OF BROADCASTING

Professionals have lost sight of the fact that presentation is the heart of broadcasting. It is an all-encompassing offering for public consumption, created to educate, inform, entertain, and engage viewers and listeners in a tactful, tasteful, imaginative, and memorable manner. It is an entire purpose-driven entity that should provoke participation, provide knowledge, and offer style and content, in a creative way. If we are to provide an acceptable array of programs, within a given number of hours, the bouquet on offer requires subtlety in planning, management, and output. It is a blend of voices, faces, sequences, and schedules that suit audiences, time frames, program objectives, and station visions. It is the totality of deliberate teamwork, based on strategies, preparation, and the organized use of talent and human capital.

Unless and until we return to these foundational principles, broadcasting and broadcasters will continue to be used for suspicious rather than altruistic purposes. It is crunch time and we must decide where we stand. This decision cannot be based on assumptions or guesswork or imagination, there is only one place where the solution can be found—and that is in the training room. I have already stated that I see a program as a presentation. In my view, if a station is broadcasting for twelve hours, then the entirety of that twelve hours is one unique presentation which offers several components. Clearly this cannot be an ad-hoc or haphazard arrangement, it must be planned, and planning does not take place in a vacuum—it must be learned. Of course, even without me mentioning it, you know where it must be learned.

THE PLACE OF PRESENTATION TRAINING

As with many other professions, I do believe that it is possible to learn practically how to be a broadcaster, so on the job training is definitely to be encouraged. My grouse, however, is that even before broadcasters are allowed to handle the microphone, they should undergo mandatory training in basic broadcast ethics, presentation techniques, basic production principles, basic journalism tenets, reporting techniques, and of course, pronunciation. Then, as happened in the past, trainees should go through a period of internship, understudying their seniors, as it were, experiencing studio operations on a daily basis, until such a time as they are allowed to voice scripts, and eventually, assigned specific on-air duties to build their confidence and competence. Once they are on air, they need close monitoring, and naturally, training should be continuous, even if it takes different forms.

The question is who is going to teach today's practitioners the art of presentation, many of whom believe that recognition is tantamount to competence and ability? Presentation is key to any program (Vivian 2009). In those days, a new entrant into broadcasting would just "sit-in" to watch the older hand display the skills of presentation, imbibing over time the ethics, techniques, and tenets of this prestigious career. When we were employed, we discovered that every presenter, irrespective of grade or position, was subjected to a weekly presentation meeting. It took place every Thursday at Broadcasting House, in Ikoyi, Lagos, although after the advent of the Network News on television, sometimes the meetings were held at Television House on Victoria Island. Wherever it was held, we all knew that our superiors would choose one of our broadcasts for assessment. We called these sessions "Post Mortems," because, truth be told, the entire presentation was thoroughly dissected and every mispronounced word pointed out. It was sometimes humiliating, always embarrassing but believe you me, nothing kept us on our toes like the knowledge of exposure before our peers and bosses. No one was spared. In fact, the fear of the presentation meeting was the beginning of wisdom for every radio and television presenter.

Looking back, I can say it was a veritable, continuous training ground. Everyone learned from everyone else's mistakes, and it was clear that no one was above making a mistake. Whether you liked it or not, we were openly reprimanded. If our competence was in question, there were no qualms about suspension. We would be sanctioned and considered as "off-air," until we had received more training and had been certified "fit for broadcast." It was as simple as that. There was no hiding place and no one to cover for us. We were on our own and we sank or swam by the level of our commitment and competence.

Presentation training, both theoretical and practical, should involve acquiring several critical skills which have become more important today than ever, because in the real world employers are keeping red eyes on the bottom-line by ensuring that their stations can boast of multitalented staff with several skills. Presentation skills are developed with time (Vivian 2009). The same cannot be said of many of our station owners, who for reasons best known to them, do not provide training opportunities for their staff. Granted it does come at a cost, but even when such training is offered free of charge, because some broadcast organizations have not fulfilled their obligations to various statutory bodies, their staff are not eligible, and the opportunity is lost.

I have often wondered if this is because many of today's industry employers are not professionals, and as such do not realize that there is a purpose and process to professional presentation. Consequently, they are not in a position to insist that their operatives abide by what we know to be fundamental tenets. It is a case of the one-eyed man being king in the country of the blind. This regrettable situation perpetuates the falling standards we are currently witnessing and exposes our noble profession to avoidable ridicule and disdain. Sadly, decades of nepotism, godfather-ism, political largesse, territorial abuse (under the guise of Federal Character), and personal rewards, have frustrated true talent and edged out deserving voices and faces from giving stellar performances. The nation loses, the station loses, the public loses, the talent loses and ultimately the biggest loser is the broadcasting profession itself. Sadly, too, a beleaguered and fatigued body politic is not in a collective frame of mind to hold practitioners accountable, and the general malady of accepting mediocrity in all spheres is perpetuated. For the discernible few, they are simply aware that once upon a time things were different.

DIGITIZATION AND PRESENTATION

Digitization and globalization appear to offer many more opportunities for broadcasting in the twenty-first century and I dare say they do. However, there are emerging issues that have become somewhat worrisome. In an age when everybody is a journalist because everybody has a device that can record news and events as they are happening and send them to any international or national broadcaster, how do we hold such citizen journalists accountable for their contributions? How do we limit the perimeters of social media influencers, whose penchant for fake news and sensationalism is becoming a global irritant? I have no quarrel with information being made available to all, as long as it is accurate and objective, but I am aware that objectivity is subject to interpretation and I also appreciate that there is much entertainment value in being sarcastic and melodramatic. Style is a matter of preference. It seems to me, however, that if social media brands are here to stay (indeed, they are likely to increase), then broadcasters must work harder to show the difference between social media "stars" and broadcast professionals. Broadcasters should not be lured into thinking that being a brand is more important than having an enviable reputation. I believe that if we execute our jobs properly, we will inevitably become brands. My younger colleagues have often told me that mine is a generational point of view, which may very well be true, but when I ask them to give me names of present-day broadcasters who are worthy of emulation, after mentioning a few popular presenters, they have to think quite deeply before they continue. Conversely, when discussions arise about broadcasters of yesteryear, be it in the areas of sports, news, entertainment, and so forth, names are easily listed by those who were greatly impacted by the performances of such practitioners.

Performance is a keyword in our current reality. Digitization offers us a plethora of "presenters" who daily assail us on various social media platforms. It is clear that the majority have little knowledge of professional presentation. We thus find ourselves in a situation where impact is momentary because performance benchmarks are not being met. However, because these materials are easily accessible, they can be revisited a number of times. I make bold to say that online presenters need to not only be trained but also produced, if they aim to be more effective and make a lasting impression. Content is not the issue; rather, the presentation of the material leaves quite a lot to be desired. It is ironic that as young broadcasters, we operated in a place and time when equipment was seriously insufficient, the environment was much less conducive, the existence of the military often restricted content, remuneration was always inadequate and often broadcasters spent their own money to ensure that their programs did not fail. Yet, the quality of our broadcasts was never in doubt.

BROADCAST QUALITY ISSUES

Quality! The content! The presentation! The impact! Quality is a key pre-requisite for broadcasters, and we cannot ignore its importance. I have often asked broadcasters a simple question: Do they want to be Nigerian broadcast-ers, or do they want to be broadcasters who work in Nigeria? It's a straight choice and clearly a decision has to be made either way, because everything about their professional lives depends on their conclusion. I maintain that broadcast quality in this digital and global dispensation can only be guaran-teed if practitioners are exposed to presentation training at the right time and in the right way.

The first step has been taken by the unbundling of the curriculum for mass communication undergraduates. Now that subjects taught to students of broadcasting will be streamlined to specifically address relevant core skills and disciplines, it is also necessary to go back to the drawing board to look closely at the current teaching and learning processes that are available to would-be broadcasters. A situation where students are only taught by academ-ics, who have never practiced professionally, cannot be allowed to continue. We understand the need-to-know theories, philosophical perspectives, prin-ciples, communication models, et al., but these do not open doors in the job market. No matter how prestigious the institution, if graduates cannot prove their competence practically, only back-door tactics will work for them. In as much as I have already indicated that these days, favoritism and partiality is the name of the game, but eventually, businessmen will expect a return on their investment, and we all know that broadcasting is not cheap. It should also be noted that professionals in the field have neither time nor inclination to teach or put their junior colleagues through their paces.

It seems to me that at the point where the academics hold sway, the input of practitioners is equally essential, if quality is to be assured in the future. Since I have also established that station owners are training-shy, let us get it right by building a solid foundation so that the building blocks do not falter and crack at a later date. Educational and training institutions must now offer stu-dents the opportunity to practice their craft under the guidance of a combined faculty of academicians and seasoned professionals. Going forward, this is the only way to improve broadcast quality in these times. From past training experiences in tertiary institutions, students found themselves in a different world, when professionals moved in to give them practical training. It turned out to be a far cry from classroom theory.

MEDIA OWNERS AND THE ADVANTAGES
OF TRAINING PRESENTERS

You may ask why presentation training is so important. The answer is simple. Presentation training is rigorous and detailed and prepares the broadcaster for holistic performance. By the time trainees are able to identify the qualities they need and their roles and responsibilities to various constituencies, such orientation gives them a different perspective. They also learn about program types and applications, script interpretation, phonetics, reading for meaning, and different interview techniques. They come to terms with the nitty gritty of practice as reporters, news anchors, producers, and editorial assistants. All these contributors to the communication and broadcast process need to appreciate and imbibe basic presentation skills to perform their related roles effectively.

I have come to realize that producers get better results from presenters when they have an understanding of what the presentation is about. Not only do they appreciate some of the challenges inherent in presentation but they are also better placed to pay attention to details that they might otherwise have ignored. There is equally no doubt that since they have imbibed the benefits of diction training, the language of their scripts is more fluent and easier to speak. Back in the day, presenters knew that producers had the last word, unlike the current trend for presenters to assume a superior position because their names, voices, and faces are easily recognizable. Teamwork is obviously the ideal situation but at the end of the day all roles should be properly defined and established; with appropriate training putting an end to these irregularities. Ultimately, practitioners are not the only beneficiaries.

POOR PRESENTATION IN THE DIGITAL ERA AND
DECLINING PROFILES OF BROADCAST STATIONS

Media owners should create a situation where they have knowledgeable, flexible, and adaptable staff who can operate in multiple spaces. Trained staff will of necessity become more discerning, and work more diligently towards upholding standards and media owners will be able to reduce the cost of talent, while freeing up resources for producing better content. However, these benefits are only possible when qualitative output is sustained.

Media owners should expect the opposite if they do not invest in their human resources. Unfortunately, they can only expect a situation where their revenue from advertisers nosedives, resources for production shrinks, the payment of salaries becomes irregular, and staff morale falls. Once the station's ambassadors lose enthusiasm, no matter the quality of content, voices become dreary, and faces lose their sparkle. The personal profiles of broadcasters become questionable and predictably eyeballs and eardrums will divert their attention elsewhere.

The digital era has opened up the space in such a way that elsewhere offers a huge array of choices for a more discerning public, whose age range is not only expanding by the day but who also have increased access to digital devices at cheaper and cheaper prices. Let alone growing competition from community broadcasters, who equally compete for dwindling advert revenue to sustain operations.

Is it not worth it for media owners to forestall this inevitable outcome by investing in creating an enabling environment, which of course, includes training? After all, is it not said that "If a thing is worth doing, it is worth doing well"?

ESSENTIAL ELEMENTS OF A GOOD PRESENTATION

So let us consider the vital components of a good presentation. Professional broadcast content needs to fulfill four key aspects to qualify as quality presentations. The presenter needs to be heard, understood, respected, and remembered. Without paying attention to these elements, presentations are unlikely to serve a useful purpose. If presenters are to be heard, it is important that all efforts are made to protect the voice, which is the main instrument of communication. Presenters should not abuse their vocal cords, nor should they take their voices for granted by exposing their throats to harsh extremes. Presentation cannot be professional when throats are sore or voices croak. Presenters should be aiming for a smooth, melodious output that arrests the attention of the listener. When listeners or viewers can hear clearly, their next hurdle is understanding.

Presenters are expected to pronounce words, names, and places correctly. It is vital for presenters to appreciate that anyone in the world has access to broadcasts on various electronic devices, irrespective of their being on terrestrial or digital platforms, on radio or television, through podcasts or live streaming. Whatever the language of communication, vocal drills should be an important feature for professional presenters. Consistency is a necessary characteristic for presenters and practice is the only way to sustain standards. Knowing the right way to use words and phrases is also a useful skill. Good diction also promotes understanding as does the use of intonation, which adds variety to the way content is delivered. Being a presenter is a privilege and it is just as important to be respected by viewers and listeners as it is to have self-respect. That entails being of good character and behaving appropriately in public. That way, the presenter ensures that they present the news rather than becoming the object of the news. It does not speak to credibility.

Credibility is actually the watchword when it comes to content because respect is equally attained when information is unfailingly correct. It should be well researched, so that the information is not only complete but well balanced. A presentation is not professional if all angles are not covered and the time of broadcast should also be taken into consideration, so that the targeted audience receives the full benefit from viewing or listening at the right time.

These elements all help to make the presentation memorable. There is really not much point in going the extra mile to present a program if it makes no impact. Something should resonate about a presentation. Something should make viewers and listeners remember it. It could be style, or courteous manners, or relevant, insightful questions, or excellent guests, or even an unusual topic. There are many ways to make a presentation stand out, and as long as it is remembered for good reasons it can be concluded that the presenter aimed for quality and achieved it.

GLOBAL EXPECTATIONS

Audiences are universal in their expectations of professional presenters. It is understood that subject matter and timing will determine the type of audience listening or watching at any given time, however, the guidelines and principles remain the same for achieving an excellent program. No matter where anyone is situated, we all know first rate production when we see and hear it. There is actually no excuse for producing a substandard program. The buck stops in front of the presenter, who, regardless of scripts and backgrounds offered by the producer, should have his or her own arsenal of facts, comments, and questions. These all provide backup to fill in the gaps and deliver a memorable presentation.

Although global audiences are consistent in their expectations, it is fair to say that perceptions differ. This is where African presenters have a responsibility to create and sustain a positive media image that commands respect. African broadcasters are duty-bound to change the current negative narrative being perpetuated globally about the African story. A very high percentage of audio/visual materials focus on undesirable aspects of the African experience, giving the impression that the continent has no redeeming factors. It has become necessary to address this bias and the most strategically placed personnel to do this are African broadcasters. A deliberate effort must be made to present positive aspects about the continent to the rest of the world. Digitization will no doubt produce brighter visuals and cleaner sound, however, it will be most unfortunate if this enhanced technology only serves to exaggerate Africa's damaged image, instead of boosting it. The continent's producers and presenters need to come to an unspoken agreement that at least 70 percent of their content, commentary, and comments must present African countries in a positive light. It is not possible for Africa not to have its fair share of inventors, initiators, artistes, medical marvels, sports wonders, heroes, heroines, explorers, leaders, entrepreneurs, young maestros, and so forth. When will global audiences hear about them, and who will tell their stories if not their compatriots (broadcasters) who are in a position to do so? What images do we want to portray on our digital spaces? Do we continually wish to portray want and degradation or do we think we should encourage ourselves, our people, and our diaspora citizens by also revealing hope and possibilities? Is it not time for us to create an African digital image that commands respect globally and whose accessibility is available to all, defying time and geographical boundaries?

THE DANGER OF POOR PRESENTATION
IN THE ERA OF GLOBALIZATION

Finally, we have all witnessed the exponential boom in do-it-yourself videos during the global pandemic that began in 2020. Everybody has become a trainer, a marketer, a salesperson, a motivational speaker, a self-help guru, a trendsetter, an influencer, an anything to anyone who has a device and is willing to click, scroll, post, cut, paste, or do whatever one does to manipulate, operate, or activate a digital device.

The big question is, Is everyone making an impact? How much of what you see do you remember? If everyone is relying on their sixty- second teaser or promo to get everybody else's attention, whose introduction will gain traction? What will they do to capture your initial interest and lure you back again and again? They may get away with poor presentation if their knowledge is exclusive or their topic is such that it piques curiosity.

However, I submit that such people will need to be trained on how to become professional presenters. How to select the appropriate words and phrases. How to work with the camera. How to engage. It is not an all-comers' affair and eventually they will realize that whatever natural talent they have and however well they can communicate, there is a technique which has to be learned and a skill which needs to be transferred.

Let us not forget that when materials, audio or visual, have been broadcast, some people will definitely listen or view them. Unfortunately, mistakes make the loudest noise. In fact, they scream and leave the longest impressions. Imagine that such materials are uploaded for the world to view at its leisure. Imagine the damage done to the presenter, when the world hears or watches and then imagine the conclusion reached by the viewer or listener, who may be a first-time observer. Then consider the fate of the presenter who is being assessed for the first time. Even if the material is deleted, the deed has been done, the dye has been cast and the impression becomes cast in stone!

What happens to the efforts made by the rest of the team that produced the program? Would their names be rubbished because of poor presentation? Would we blame observers for criticizing not only the presenter but also the entire production? After all, that presenter is supposed to be a professional and should have known what we have all been taught over the years. "A presenter is as good as his or her last presentation."

REFERENCES

Akpan, U. 2019. *Hip Hop Music on Radio and the Lifestyle of Students in Select Tertiary Institutions in Lagos, Nigeria.* Published PhD Thesis. Lambert Publishers.

Eastman, S. T. and Ferguson, D. A. 2009. *Media Programming: Strategies and Practice.* Boston (USA): Thomson Wadsworth.

Eguare, A. 2021. A personal interview on broadcast digitization.

Uche, L. 1989. *Mass Media, People, and Politics in Nigeria.* New Dehli: Concept Publishing Company.

Vivian, J. 2009. *The Media of Mass Communication, 9th Edition.* Boston (USA): Pearson Education, Inc.

Chapter 10

Nigerian Voiceover Artistes in the Market Place of Digital Media

Challenges and Prospects

Femi Sowoolu

The above subheading and quote serve as my formal introduction typical of a book chapter.[1] The seed of my radio broadcasting career started at Ogun State Broadcasting Corporation (OGBC), Nigeria. I have also worked with Voice of Nigeria, Ikoyi-Lagos, Radio Nigeria 2 (RN-2)—renamed Metro FM, Rhythm FM, Lagos, Radio Continental, Lagos, and JAMZ FM, Ibadan, Nigeria. I have always wanted to be a broadcaster. From early childhood, I had been fascinated by the emerging technologies. By the time I was born, the world had finally shaken off the deliberating effects of Hitler's war, which had ended over a decade before. My love for radio was nurtured in Ibadan. Although born in the UK, I spent my secondary education in Ibadan at Loyola College. Just across the gates of the school compound lived a certain George Jobarteh. Jobarteh was a top radio star at the popular WNBC, the regional state radio station up until the creation of more states in Nigeria in 1967; still in operation and now called Radio OYO. Because of the aura around this person, who was one of the more prominent radio personalities at the time, as students we often snuck into his pad to listen to the music of the popular artistes of the time, basically soul music then—James Brown, Tamla-Motown and Stax label artistes, Santana, Sly and the Family Stone, and so forth. I had a number of transistor radio sets during my secondary school years; often seized by prefects and housemasters, but undeterred, my love for radio grew.

A BIT OF HISTORY

The history is important to show the relevance of Ibadan to the broadcasting industry in Nigeria, but even more important, to explain the advantages of employing media in development, particularly the electronic arms of media, even more essentially the unique position of radio in integral development of society, as utilized by Awolowo in 1959 (Kintz 2007). The question begs asking: Why Ibadan?

Ibadan was the melting pot of broadcasting in the 1960s (Okoro 2012). There's no need to take you into the full history of broadcasting in Nigeria, it would be suffice to just mention that prior to independence in 1960, radio broadcasting had started in Nigeria in 1932 (Uche, L. 1989), heralded by the installation of a Radio Distribution System in Lagos by the colonial administration, which was supervised and controlled by the Department of Post and Telegraphs, on behalf of the British government. At that time, its major goal was to serve as the reception base of the British Broadcasting Corporation (BBC). Then in 1935, there was a name change from Radio Distribution System to Radio Diffusion System by the British Colonial Government to serve and project Britain and its allies' interests during World War Two (Uche 1989). This further led, in 1939, to the establishment and commissioning of the Ibadan Station. That introduced the popular "Rediffusion boxes" found in most households around Ibadan, pre-independence. However, it is apt to say that television broadcasting started in Nigeria in 1959 when the Western Region of Nigeria pioneered television broadcasting in Nigeria with the establishment of the Western Nigeria Television (WNTV), established by the then premier of Western Region, Chief Obafemi Awolowo. It was established mainly to propagate formal and nonformal education in the region (Uche 1989).

In the 1960s, arguably, Ibadan was the most cosmopolitan city in Nigeria. It was the site of the University of Ibadan; it was the hubris of burgeoning political thought. Leading academia, the most petulant ideological thought emanated out of the campus grounds. Also, the Western Regional government was also, without political bias, the most effective government of the era; the entire region itself became the bedrock of development and the example of good, people-oriented governance that many developing countries around the world sought to seek. Political awareness unfortunately also often leads to uprisings and upheavals against the status quo. One resultant effect was the adage that emerged out of the region, "The Wild, Wild West," and the bigger affectation that had on Nigeria's emerging politics in general. There was one fallout of this investment in political endeavor—the development of an elite social class—and affluent, cosmopolitan, yet middle-class society that defined the Ibadan community: educated, politically conscious, and intelligent. This is evidenced sublimely in the number of Government Reservation Areas (GRAs) that exist within the Ibadan metropolis, arguably more than in any other region within Nigeria. These were the impressions I had of Ibadan when we decided to set up a radio station there in October 2016.

MY INTEREST IN BROADCASTING DEVELOPS

Prior to setting up, I spent a month in Ibadan doing a "recce" of existing radio stations in the city. I spent most of the time tuned in and monitoring all the stations within the axis. I was surprised that they were all, save one particular station, doing the same localized programming. English broadcast programming was limited, and the themes and concepts were similar. It was as if the same station was replicated on various different dials. It was local, even primitive at times. It got me wondering about broadcast standards. The Ibadan radio stations seemed to disobey every single rule of the game. Sadly, they seemed to be flourishing. Though a bit disappointed, it reaffirmed to me perhaps the most important thing about setting up a new radio station—Be Relevant to Your Environment. So, we decided to set up a sort of hybrid station, a mix of sorts—music based, with information as prime in both English and Yoruba presentation, but with high quality productions as the running theme.

VENTURING INTO VOICEOVER INDUSTRY

My production company, FM Productions, was set up in the months following my exit from Grant. It wasn't much, initially. My credentials were based more on my broadcast and advertising background and experience and ability to perform exceedingly well in these two areas than on an exotic office, or flashy official vehicle, or any of the other perks that advertising agencies and production houses employ to dazzle their clients. I actually operated out of my briefcase, though I could boast of a couple mean suits! While at Grant I had become rather well known in the industry, and only one or two close associates knew that I regularly voiced commercials produced by rival agencies. Many of these rival agency producers knew of my radio background and the quality I could deliver beforehand. To them, competitiveness or rivalry was not enough reason to ignore the quality advantage I offered as a credible option. So if I wasn't at the agency, I was obviously at one studio or the other, busy doing one voiceover or another. There was a pitch we once made for the Central Bank of Nigeria account—I produced my own agency's presentations, but what nobody knew was that my voice was used by three other agencies on their various presentations. Grant didn't win, but one of my other "presentations" did!

Breaking into the exclusive field of the "voiceover artiste" is often an uphill task. Earlier I have explained how I was introduced to this "most lucrative aspect of broadcasting." The terminology, "voiceover" means "the art of using your voice to bring life to written words." The voiceover artiste becomes an actor using his voice as his major resource. There are many rewards gained from being a voiceover actor, or artiste, as we refer to them in Nigeria. Besides the love for the art and the ability to use one's voice in a constructive and creative manner, the more obvious benefits are those of time and money. Voiceover artistes are paid generously for the short period of time required in the recording studio. More generously elsewhere in the world than in Nigeria, but that is only reflective of the general lazy nature of the earnings and rewards structure, and our unenlightened penchant for downgrading artistic endeavor. The astute voiceover person is always in demand and could easily take home a large pay packet daily. Very little time is wasted during a voice session, the routine is simple—you get to the studio, receive your script from the producer, spend a couple of minutes rehearsing the script and practicing the various stresses in sound and characterization, reflect on the production preferences, you record the material and voila! Payday! The voice "specialist" at the head of the class can easily do many of these "zaps" between various recording sessions, earning him a sizable amount. Also the audio only attribute of not being seen, offers advantages over real acting, television, or stage work. No time is wasted on "makeup," a fashionable wardrobe, or fussing over oneself. But, to excel as a voiceover artiste requires exceptionally hard work, dedication, and the will to succeed, because there will be many frustrating moments. Brilliance never appears overnight. Perseverance is often the key to success, as well as talent, of course. But know this: if your primary aim of wanting to do voiceovers is to make money, you cannot succeed. Don't get me wrong—you may make the money, eventually, but you'll never ever get to be as good as you really can. You must love this work to stay at it. But then also, voiceovers are not only an art; they are also a business—and there's a scientific method to that business. Behind every good voice actor is a hard- working businessperson who must toil, sweat, and study to get to the top.

THE INDUSTRY IS MAFIA-LIKE

The field of voiceovers is extremely specialized and because of this, outsiders and newcomers often describe it as a "mafia." The truth is, it is extremely hard to break into, but not impenetrable. Friendships created between voice talents and producers over time involve trust and loyalty and are hard to break down. Producers prefer to stay with what they know rather than seek out the unknown talent or untested new voice. But if a new voice talent enters the market with something unique, special, and bankable, the talent agent or producer would be shortsighted in not signing such a person. Most often the new talents' breakthrough into the business comes out of sheer desperation when the producer's first choice is unavailable. That's all the chance you need to prove you can be a member of the mafia!

MY OUTSTANDING PRODUCTIONS AND
COLLABORATIONS IN THE INDUSTRY

Aside from voiceover responsibilities, FM Productions was also involved in production of radio and television commercials as well as documentaries and programs. Within a short time, the production of sponsored syndicated radio programming soon became our forte. One of the first independent radio productions I handled was a one-hour jazz program called *Calypso Jazz*. Sponsored by Nigerian Distilleries, makers of Calypso Coconut Liquor, an account then owned by LTC Advertising (Lawson, Thomas & Colleagues), Apapa. It was an extremely popular show, especially for jazz aficionados. Most jazz music presentations don't really understand the true format of the genre, or the particular hype required and style of script and presentation that would appeal to the jazz listening audience. Jazz is master's music, music that can last forever, like classical repertoire. The first production task I had was to do the required research and to find a source for acquiring the music. I knew quite a lot about jazz music ever since my "Brother Jazz" days at OGBC, alongside Deji Lewis, (who was "Uncle Jazz"), and forward to my association with "Freaky" Fred Oshodi, when fusion was the in-thing. I first updated my library with the purchase of new compact discs from Kunle Tejuoso's Jazzhole, which easily had the largest stock of jazz and Afrocentric music, magazines, collectibles, and trivia in Nigeria. Jazzhole was an offshoot of the bigger superstore, Quintessence. I made friends with Kunle along the line, and he often lent me a massive ledger—it was more than just a book, called *S Complete History of Jazz*, I think. I also signed up for monthly subscriptions of *Bluebeat* and *Blues and Soul* magazines.

To create a good jazz program, you have to delve deep into the history behind the music that you play. The origins of jazz go to the very beginnings of slavery in America, and even beyond, into its African roots; the history is rich and meshed in folklore. These historical perspectives make a colorful background for the music of the plantation workers and freed slaves, through the Deep South, and meandering northwards by route through the Underground Railroad's secret pathway to the backstreets of Watts in Chicago and Harlem in New York City. The music called jazz was a special kind of music. In preparing your presentation script, you can add to these historical perspectives a little insight about the origins of the varying terminologies that differentiate one aspect of the art form from another, and then pick up on the instruments. What can they do? How are they used? Who uses them? In what formats do they realize their potential? Next, you create awareness of the musicians, their early beginnings, previous associations, influences, instrumental capabilities, eccentricities—oh, they all had them, and other profiles. The true lover of jazz already knows these details, but he gets more excited if you offer him extra updates with newer details. There is so much to talk about when the topic is jazz; such that you could run a jazz program for a hundred years without repetition! Calypso Jazz put all this together. The program was scripted, produced, and presented by me. It featured all shades of jazz, from the traditional to fusion, from the contemporary to the eclectic, from New Orleans to Canada, Germany, South Africa, and Japan, anywhere jazz was exported, from Gillespie to Fela Anikulapo-Kuti! There were stories with every episode, and both client and agency loved it. Calypso Jazz ran for three great quarters. It would be the first of many sponsored musical shows that I produced.

I was also contracted to produce a program, by Sesan Ogunro's Eminent Advertising, for Wonder Foods, which had introduced Top Tea to the Nigerian market. It was a five-minute daily series called *Moments of Pleasure*, mostly a mix of motivation and inspiration, followed by a featured song and a little discography from a selected artiste with some informative value on the Top Tea brand. This allowed me to review music over an expansive period and through varying genres. It went on to be broadcast over stations spread nationwide and was always looked forward to, whichever part of the country it was aired on.

There was also a program called *Fine Tunes*, which was used as a launch pad for the introduction of Fine King-Size Filter cigarettes into Nigeria. This was under the auspices of the agency MC&A, which was affiliated with the Saatchi & Saatchi Group, and which had been earlier set up by its mother company, Insight Communications.

Of all these independent broadcast productions however, perhaps the one that made the most impact was *Benson & Hedges Golden Tones*, a ground-breaking program idea first mooted by Funmi Onabolu, then outgoing general manager at Insight, and on the verge of setting up a marketing services agency, called Cosse. Funmi was an old friend from my Abeokuta days. He was Uncle Yom's nephew. We had both earlier sat for auditions and had both been employed, on the same day, as announcers at OGBC. He also had a stint later, at the Lagos State Broadcasting Corporation, Radio Lagos, before deciding to devote the rest of his professional career to marketing communications. Funmi had asked me to produce a pilot that was to be presented to the British American Tobacco board of directors in London. This was done, and the program was approved. The next task was to search for a presenter because although I had voiced the pilot, the *Fine Tunes* show was still running, so until that was shelved, I was counted out. I had to think up a few suggestions. First name on my list of possible presenters was Patrick Oke, who I don't think had done any radio work since the heady RN-2 days. Patrick ran a few editions of *Golden Tones* but couldn't continue after a handful of episodes. Again, I was called upon to tinker a solution. It dawned on me that I could create the scripts and handle production, leaving the presentation to someone else. "Great idea," Funmi agrees, "but then, who?" We couldn't think of anyone, but just then Bola Makinde walks up and offers his services. Without him having the pedigree of being a particularly experienced music show host at the time, we mull over it, eventually deciding to give the idea a try. He managed to present one rather lackluster episode, which led us to put on our thinking caps again. I offered to co-present, alongside Makinde, the *Fine Tunes* program by that time, having ended its final season. We did the first episode, which was rather exciting. *Golden Tones* eventually became the most-listened to program within the radio-marketing industry. Later, a then budding back-up singer called Silo Udo-Afia joined the team, making it a compulsive threesome with a *helluva* knockout punch! And *B&H Golden Tones* became the yardstick by which standards were judged in the industry and remained so over the three seasons that I was in charge of production, and to some extent still provides the template for most entertainment show presentations in Nigeria to date, radio and TV alike! But like they say, nothing lasts forever. My father used to say, "If things seem to be going well for you over time, watch your back!" Cosse was able for long enough to convince the British American directors to renew, season after season, but all agencies know well to prepare towards the inevitability of losing choice accounts and learn strategies toward recovery. The strong agency learns how to build on such unexpected losses. The weak ones just die. When things are good for you, you should spread the goodness among your subordinates. Like leadership trainer Stephen Covey puts it in his 8th Habit: "Listen to your workers. Inspire them to find their strengths, their passions and their talents. Teach them to find their voices."

I had prepared a presentation to renegotiate production terms, harmlessly believing it would improve the quality of programming if presentation fees and other costs were reviewed across board, and I presented this request to the management at Cosse, citing the added costs in sourcing material, production, inflation, and a few other extras. We had discussed these issues at a pre-presentation meeting, and I had assumed I had the support of my co-presenters. I found out, however, that I was fighting a lone battle. What really hurt, at the time, were the scathing statements made afterwards, implying that I was selfishly asking for an increase only for myself! This was absolutely outrageous. In the aftermath of the unfortunate misadventure, there was very little I could do to defend my position, and I opted to not fuss too much about the issue back then because what's done *is* done and life has always got to move on! After my forced, sudden departure, the program also forced its existence on an unwary audience. It was a hard-listen, often stunted, noisy, and lacking in originality; the templates were there—my old scripts were rehashed and reworded, but if you don't have original ideas, you can only say the same things for so long before you become a bore. *B&H Golden Tones* bowed out a shadow of itself about a year after my departure. It should have been stopped long before. We must all understand that the first complement required to be successful in any chosen field should never be about financial reward. It must always be about service. Why are such simple lessons so hard to understand? However, it is commendable to the vision, adeptness, and creative largesse of Funmi Onabolu and Cosse that the agency has sustained and flourished to many other successes over the years, indeed!

PRODUCTION STRUCTURE IN VOICEOVER

The Association of Voice-Over Artistes (AVOA) has become well established over the years, thanks to the dedicated efforts of its executive leadership, however, it was not always so. Many former voice talents may have a thing or so to say, but I dare stick my neck out to state that I personally played an integral part in the establishment of this honorable body. When I became a bonafide voice actor around 1990, I was made to understand that many previous attempts had been made to set up an association that would protect the rights of members of this branch of the performing arts. All attempts failed, I was informed, due to bloated egos, petty rivalries, and disagreements over the most mundane issues. Whenever money is on the line, emotions and tensions are apt to run high. To fully appreciate this, you must first understand the structure of studio production.

Every production has a producer who is in charge of the production process. He prepares an estimate of the production which includes all the various costs that a production will entail; the cost of renting or using a studio, cost of hiring a voice artiste, costs of all materials needed including tapes, cassettes, compact discs, transfers, library music, and so forth. Costs of transportation and duplications are sometimes also included. This list has to pass through approval of the creative management and the client who owns and approves the job. After this is done production can proceed. It is at this stage that the producer can make contact with the artistes required. Since there is usually a large pool to choose from, such a producer must use fair judgment and discretion to decide which voice would give the product the best impact.

But sometimes, a producer may be stuck between many great options and may have to rely on dependability or easy accessibility to make a decision. Having made such a decision, the astute producer may decide to make up with the neglected artiste by choosing such artiste the next time the opportunity arises. Most artistes do not understand the politics involved in such decision making and therefore tend to personalize issues. This may lead to friction among artistes and between artiste and producer. It is therefore not uncommon to find rivalries among voiceover artistes, but these should never be allowed to develop into deep-rooted grudges. However, this was the environment we operated within in 1993, when Tony St. Iyke and I mooted the idea of setting up an association of voiceover artistes.

BIRTHING VOICEOVER ARTISTES ASSOCIATION

There were various camps within our membership. I didn't realize how deep these rivalries were until after we had gone ahead and created a logo, designed and printed letterheads, and chosen ad-hoc officials, all done at my personal expense! I had believed that to be able to fully represent the interests of artistes whose voices were the identity of most advertising agency products, but who had no "voice" within the agencies, it was important to establish a union, or a body like the American Screen Actors Guild (SAG) or the Radio and Television Theatre Workers Union (RATTAWU), which guided the interests of media practitioners on radio and television stations in Nigeria. I also knew that based on human nature, if we just kept on discussing and dithering on decision-taking, nothing would get done. Believing that the best option was to act, and not only that, to also let some money do the talking, by making the immediate financial commitments, we decided to take a position. Unfortunately, Tony St. Iyke didn't have many friends. I was surprised and disappointed to learn that among those who were most bitterly against the efforts we had made were his kinfolk! It was a lesson to me, although a rather disappointing one. Like the good old paladin would say, "Even though you champion noble causes, expect to have a few enemies." I never fully accepted membership of the association after that, preferring to remain on the fringe. Once, I was asked to contest for the presidency of the body. I gave it deep consideration before I opted out. I don't think I have ever explained my reasons for doing so.

Maybe now is the perfect time to state my position. I have told you about the Mafiosi nature of the voiceover merchant's trade. It was never designed to be an all-comer's affair. Sadly, during the tenure of Isaac Ijeoma, one of the finest pidgin and Igbo language linguists in Nigeria in his day, all kinds of new entrants were "permitted" to join the profession. Many did not have the basics required of even the most junior radio announcer, most had no media background whatsoever, and a good number had joined because of the money prospects they had heard it offered. A large number had no business being in the voice business. Ijeoma's rather relaxed laissez-faire style had been overtly complaisant, allowing all to come in who could pay the dues. I was not very impressed with the membership composition of AVOA at the time. Standards were not what they were—even only just a few years before. Many misfits had come to rub shoulders with star performers. If I were to become president of AVOA, my first task would have been to weed the stables and clean up the mulch and grime that had been allowed to permeate over the years of inertia. These untrained members would have misunderstood this, and I would have made more enemies than was necessary for anyone to have.

That was the situation at that time, and I thought it best not to fight a battle I would certainly lose. I did not envisage the possibility of a win-win situation emerging, and therefore saw no need to involve myself in a non-provident venture. Like American president Woodrow Wilson said, "I would rather fail in a cause that will ultimately triumph than to triumph in a cause that will ultimately fail." Although it is not absolutely necessary to join AVOA, my advice for any up-and-coming voiceover artiste is that it is highly recommended.

PRODUCER VOICEOVER ARTISTE RELATIONSHIP

It is great to have a good relationship with a producer, but this should not be done to the detriment of production quality. Having been an agency producer myself, and one still very involved with production, I strongly believe that to excel as a producer, you should have no favorites. You must endeavor to choose the best voice personality suited to the production requirements, no matter the temptation. I have met many agency producers in my time, not all of them have been excellent. Some were outright incompetent, others you had to teach and direct, but quite a handful, were brilliant. Top of the class has to be George Curtis Nkem Okoli (For the girls!) Or simply, Georgie P! (For the boys, only!) George was without doubt the best audio production man in advertising, and he was widely regarded as such, even by his contemporaries.

As production head at Insight Communications for many years, George added Promethean altruism to technical clout. His only mistake was never taking center-stage in matters of personal attainment. I always believed that with his experience and professional knowledge, George should have taken more of a determined centrist position in official affairs. At times he seemed too complacent, often showing a lack of interest in affecting managerial decisiveness, always willing others to claim his glory—a superb trait if your calling was in the church, but certainly not an ideal trait to have in the media, where you often had to fight for respect and position! George was efficient, but he was no politician, and his agency, as with all advertising agencies, was a den of *politricks!* Then again, after office hours, he was the consummate Biafran! We chided him often for that, claiming he was much too young to have fought in the Nigerian Civil War.

But you could never put down George's belief in the Biafran cause. He was always proud to be called Biafran. I first met George as a studio manager at RN-2 in 1978 and we've been the best of friends ever since—not that we haven't had our fallouts. He's a jolly good fellow, George. I was once opportune to join the elite membership of presenters of Masculine Line, an avant-garde RN-2 program that has been hosted by some of the finest Nigerian media personalities, including Willy Egbe, Emmanuel Onumonu (popularly known by his radio name, "Mani—the man with the honey"), Richard Ikiebe, OhiAlegbe, and dramatist, advertising guru, producer, writer, and broadcaster, Ihiria Enakhimio. I was invited to host the show by its then producer Ndidi Osaka, who had asked George to source for her, a presenter. Well, thanks, again, but I do believe I have paid the favor back fourfold, George!

TECHNOLOGY AND BROADCASTING

There is no doubt technology has enhanced radio broadcasting. In 2011, I wrote an article entitled, "The Death of Radio?" Allow a reprint, slightly edited for time relevance:

> Radio has always been a survivor. It survived the dawn of television, it meandered itself through the age of music recording techniques—cassettes, cartridges and compact discs; it is blending perfectly with the challenges of digitalization. Still everyone ponders, will it survive this new challenge that seems to be attacking it from a myriad of frontiers? Can radio outlast the novel, more domineering threats of the so-called new media?

The social networks have bludgeoned their dominance through with a relentless surge of revolutionary ethos in our global societies. Social media manifested in what became known as the Arab Spring, bringing down age-old governments, traditions, and institutions from Tunis to Damascus. It has gridlocked financial empires from Wall Street to the City of London, and it's already knocking on doors from Banjul to Blantyre, bringing with it, social change, revolution, and a new world order. Without a doubt we are firmly hedged within the social media age; and no matter what age you are, if you don't tweet, you're definitely beat!

But there's a disease that has propagated over the past dozen years, spreading more quickly as the internet penetrates deeply into society. Many within our media industry presently suffer from it. It sometimes invades an entire sector—as it has with the radio industry, and advertising agencies wanting to impress upon clients that all the client needs is the old media brilliance agencies possess. This disease dulls the senses. More appropriately, it dulls *common* sense. Newspapers are probably farthest along the path of being infected, although multiple other businesses are suffering similar fates (travel agencies are already feeling its symptoms and bookshops are not far behind). What is this disease? Complacency. Simply put, being stuck within a comfort zone, blinded to what surrounds. The motto of the afflicted: "What I don't understand can't hurt me!"

WEBCASTING: A CHALLENGE TO
RADIO BROADCASTING

With the growth in online radio stations and an explosion in internet music discovery services, you may appreciate why there should be concern for anyone who makes their living in the radio industry. The competition envisaged is not just in terms of advertising revenue. It spreads further into artists' involvement and, most importantly, in the time a listener has to listen. Remember that radio has always been a secondary medium—that is a medium that allows the listener the advantage of listening to radio while involved with another more primary assignment. As time goes by, with all these challenges put to consideration, will we still need radio? I wonder how many people are troubled by the industry's poor use of new media. Others might think that new media advances have little effect on what's happening with local radio stations today. Here's a checklist of some alternatives to traditional radio, many of which are challenging the continued existence of our much-loved channel: web/internet radio, podcasts, the social networks, Apple Music, YouTube, iTunes, Pandora, blogs, mobile applications, MP3s, and iPods. The list increases exponentially—Google Magnifier launched as a blog to accompany Google Music Beta. This giant company's move into allowing consumers to listen to their music collection via Android devices (and through computers), was another challenge to radio. (Add to this the newer emergent applications: TikTok, Spotify, Soundcloud, Deezer, Audiomack, Tidal, etc.) All these new entries into music discovery/consumption add to the growth in competitors of music radio. Musicians can find that using these services is much easier than pounding on the door of a radio station to try and get a little airplay.

These alternatives are drawing youth and, to a large degree, young adults away from turning on the local radio station in home, office, and car. Whether you believe they pose a threat to local broadcast is something I have no control over. I can, though, tell you that they are real and building audiences filled with people who used to spend all their radio-time listening to their favorite station(s). If you can't see what's in front of you by now, you won't be able to see how a continued morphing of listener's options has the potential to damage the broadcast radio industry. It's not that there hasn't been enough warning. It's ignoring the warnings that eventually will reduce, but not eliminate, broadcast radio. The marriage of music and technology has made it easier than ever before to find and keep track of the most exciting sounds of yesterday and today.

Despite the intimidating incursions, however, radio listening figures remain exceptionally high for the time being, while other media (TV and print) are falling and failing left, right, and center. (Think Netflix!) Radio is still popular because, as explained earlier, it is an ambient media—you don't have to pay attention. But the story isn't entirely rosy—younger people are moving away from the medium. Why is that, and how do radio companies innovate to meet the so-called generation Z? Think about what didn't exist just some years ago: no Facebook, no YouTube, no Twitter, no Instablogs. Many younger people are looking for something different and maybe something more interactive. Within the advertising industry, many view radio as some sort of boring old media that nobody cares about anymore, as radio advertising budgets shrink. So how does radio become hip? What does the industry need to do to enrich the radio experience? As many media owners have discovered, the advertising market is pretty fickle. Can digital iterations allow for better alternative revenue streams? Perhaps the solution lies in making ambient media more interactive. We listen to radio in the background, so is interactive a complete red herring? Most modern broadcasters would argue not. Yet, there's so little being done to exploit these new models of consumption.

ADVERTISING IN THE DIGITAL ARENA

One international agency ran an advertising campaign designed to see what media would send the most traffic to a client's website. It ran a three-month campaign on five radio stations and on a video network in six supermarkets covering approximately the same geographic area as the radio stations. The advertiser was a furniture store offering an online gift certificate whenever anyone visited the website and put in a key word unique to each medium. The objectives were to: determine if people respond to these media; how well the various radio stations and the video network performed; and the cost per response from each media and to get people to subscribe to their e-newsletter. The stations used were a pop music station, an adult contemporary (AC) station, a country station, a talk station, and a soft rock/easy listening station. On the first day, the country and soft rock stations each sent one person to the site. On the second day the pop music station sent 37 unique visitors, the AC sent four, the country sent two more, the soft rock sent one more and the talk station sent one more, and the video network sent one visitor.

The sudden appearance of 37 visitors from one station in a matter of hours attracted attention. Upon investigation, it was discovered that the pop station's morning personality did indeed tweet to his 133 followers at the time, to go to the client's site and put in the key word for his station. And when they checked Facebook, they also found the same personality sent the same message to his approximately 1,300 Facebook followers at the time, but this time included a direct link to the client's site. Further insight on Google's source tracking revealed that of the 37 visitors, 11 came directly from Facebook and three came directly from people at the station. It was interesting that the soft rock station and the talk station, which are sister stations to the pop station, only sent a total of three visitors the entire three months. By that research strategy, it was learned that the internet has the ability to get a quick response at no financial cost. But before we all get excited about this knowledge, consider how many hours it takes to get 1,300 friends on Facebook, and 133 followers on Twitter. Then, once you get the friends and followers, what does it take to get the credibility or popularity to get them to respond? While it appears the internet outperformed radio, radio can take credit for the large following and credibility of the pop station personality.

The challenge before the managers of the traditional electronic media is to work with/collaborate/utilize social media within the framework of improved performance, not fight or distance their organizations. Social networking and radio can work hand-in-hand: The modern media manager must think in terms of the numerous ways that social networks can enhance the listener base and profitability of the station by employing regular usage and daily air mention of Twitter feeds, Facebook pages, even LinkedIn and YouTube videos, as well as encourage the usage of blogs and podcasts by its air personalities to encourage interactivity between station and audience in these changing times. As a handful of Lagos area stations are already showing, it can be used to benefit the station. The only thing one needs to fear is fear itself.

Most of that article, if not all of it, is still today's reality. We created a modern station in Ibadan and went against the norm. We were a terrestrial station that utilized the whole hog of online interactivity—using both web and application live in-studio videos, employing Facebook, Twitter, Instagram, and WhatsApp to reach wider audiences. Our ratings did improve, no doubt. Even though we became the "fastest rising Urban radio station in the area," the process was lengthened by the lethargic attitudes of the majority of the Ibadan-based audience. Perhaps I was wrong in my earlier estimations of the Ibadan audience?

One cannot ignore the influence of policy. Nigerians often make that mistake. Politics should never be equated with policy. Political thought may be the foundation of wants and needs, but policy must be able to distance itself from politicking. The earlier broad developments made by the Western region leaders after independence were never replicated nor improved upon by those who held the helm of affairs upon the creation of states. As a personal view, in my estimation, after the administration of Bola Ige as governor of Oyo State (1979–1983), every single civilian administration has backstepped. Without mentioning names, each civilian administration has been worse than the one from which it took over from. The effect is a citizenry that has been deprived of any ability to reach towards excellence. Today's Oyo State is sadly a reflection of its most recent leadership. It is a sad, harsh reality. I do not think there's any need for further explanation.

THE VOICE ACTOR'S STAGE IN THE DIGITAL ARENA

Just in case I did not tell you this in my opening: first, let's understand who a voiceover artiste is and what he does in the broadcasting arena, especially in this digital era. A voiceover artiste is whose rich and performative voice you hear behind the radio and television commercials. They dramatize every advertising copy and give life to the script so as to be able to lift the product or goods out of the shelf. Not just goods, but services too. At Jamz100.1 FM,we were often described as, "a Lagos station." Others said we were far ahead of our time. I want to believe we were revolutionaries, ahead of the curve, as they say. This final bit is important: Change isn't just inevitable. It has happened. Tomorrow's change is coming. The wise person sees it, well before its time.

One particular area of performance art where change has very visibly affected operation is media production. Digitalization has allowed for ease in operation in many wide areas of production for radio, television, film production, and performance arts in general. As a broadcaster, at some stage of your career you will encounter voice acting and the challenge of becoming a "voice artiste," and getting involved in performing voiceover productions. In the 1990s, when I worked in one of the leading advertising agencies in Nigeria, I was in charge of the media department, which involved roles of producing radio and television advertising materials and also making place-ments on leading media organizations around Nigeria. In those days, my tech-nical gadgets filled up two huge office spaces, one for the radio production equipment—reel-to-reel machines, cassette tape recorders, boxes of 3-inch spools, recorders, and so forth—the other full of bulky U-Matic produc-tion gear for TV editing as well as cartridge decks, television monitors, TV production mixers, a production camera, and so forth. Over the last twenty years, and perhaps more intensely over the last decade, with the additional unique capacity of the internet, production has metamorphosed by renew-ing itself, over and over again. Where once you had to physically be inside a production studio to do a voice production, these days everything can be done in the comfort of your home with the right digital set up. There are many downloadable applications that one can pick up online to enhance production, from the basic amateur to the top-notch professional. All you really need is a computer, a microphone, audio interface software, and a recording app, for example, Audacity, which allows free downloads of its digital recording and editing facilities. This is the exact software used by voiceover artistes in the civilized world that makes voicing very sound and can be played or aired anywhere in the world.

In the old days, as an advertising executive, we once had a client in the neighboring Benin Republic, a bank called BiBe, that needed to engage some advertising material for its customers, based on both sides of the border. I had to physically spend a week in Benin, moving between Cotonou and the surrounding towns in an effort to get a template of campaign requirements. The eventual recording had to be produced at the state television station, in French, by two of the leading Beninoise presenters of the time. Engaged with the same challenge today, I daresay everything would've been completed online, in a matter of minutes!

That is the compelling reason a voiceover artiste in this era of digitization and globalization must as a matter of urgency befriend and embrace technol-ogy. He needs to own a mini studio in his house where he can record himself and do the production all by himself. A simple click on the Google Play store for recording software can do him a great favor. This is because he can stay in the comfort of his home and use digitized software to record himself; and if he is skilled, flesh it up with the right artificial ambience he can gather online and then produce his commercial and send it to his clients in any part of the world without leaving the comfort of his home. Now, for me that is a perfect digital voiceover production that can go global.

LEVELS OF EXPERTISE OF A VOICEOVER ARTISTE

Voiceover actor, casting director, producer, and copywriter Elaine Clark explains in her book, *There's Money Where Your Mouth Is: An Insider's Guide to a Career in Voice-Overs*, that there are four levels of learning:

Level 1 is the unconsciously incompetent stage. This is the point-of-entry level when you may assume that all you require to make money in the voiceover business is a good voice. At this level you are not cognizant of the technique, skill, and craft involved in delivering believable copy. By simply accepting the fact that learning how to do voiceovers requires time, commitment, understanding of copy, interpretation skills, breath-control, and voice techniques, you can progress quickly to the next level.

Level 2 is consciously incompetent. At this second stage, you may be able to hear your mistakes, but not know how to fix them. This is where practice comes in. If you can record your rehearsals, playback your recordings, analyze your delivery and attempt to fix the problem on subsequent recordings, you should be able to progress easily to level 3.

Level 3 is consciously competent. This third stage has the greatest learning curve. The brain does most of the work here. If you think about the copy and how you want to say the words, you can actually deliver the dialogue as you envisioned it in your mind. Also having a trained "second ear" will help you balance out what you think you are doing with how the performance really sounds. At this stage you may consider enrolling for professional voiceover training. Ultimately the goal all voice artistes want to attain is level 4.

Level 4 is unconsciously competent. Like the professional tennis player who no longer has to stop and think whether to swing forehand or backhand as the ball approaches, the unconsciously competent voiceover professional looks at a script and knows reflexively what to do. This actor trusts his or her skills and allows the words to flow from the lips effortlessly, without the brain calling signals.

Unfortunately, many voiceover artistes never reach this final stage of perfection. The financial and artistic rewards however are vastly more significant for artistes and actors who aspire to higher excellence. To get there you must be patient and not expect brilliance to happen overnight. Study hard and enjoy the work. The hard truth is that it's the unconsciously competent artistes who get most of the work. To get a better picture of this, turn on the radio or television for thirty minutes and keep track of the commercials you hear, you will probably get to hear some voices more often than others. The goal is to become the best, so you might have to work a little harder on your craft to secure a stronger voice-hold in the industry.

Over the ages, quite a few voices controlled this stronghold in the Nigerian advertising/marketing industry. Ray-Michael Nwachukwu is regarded as the ultimate master of the art. His Arr-ems Studio for years was the leading production outfit in Lagos. I actually came into the business trying to out-hype Uncle Ray-Mike. I have already earlier mentioned Mani Onumonu, who for many years was the in-demand English language voiceover artiste. He did this alongside his duties as a top-flight broadcaster with Radio Nigeria, perhaps the reason for his frequent spats with his superiors. Other names come to the fore—my friend Kunle Oladapo was the epitome of "unconscious competence." No matter the conditions, or his condition for that matter, you could be sure that "KOP" would belt out a good copy.

A more recent example of this stage of performance excellence is Frank Edoho who hosts the Nigerian version of the international franchise *Who Wants to Be a Millionaire?* Frank has a wonderful voice, and his delivery skills are even more exciting. That is one name destined for the top as a voiceover artiste and a presenter of repute. Mark my words!

The local languages have also had their prima donnas. For many years, Ali Usman stood tall over the Hausa language voiceover territory. He has no equal in that department. Even to date! Isaac Ijeoma and Tony St. Iyke ruled the Igbo and pidgin English terrains for many years, and it is only in their absence that other voices have been able to excel.

In most markets the world over, the percentage of work reflective of gender is 75–80 percent men to 20–25 percent women. So it is not a solely Nigerian trend to fashion out more jobs to men than women, but that doesn't take away the chauvinist nature of these statistics.

However, some brilliant female voiceover artistes have plied their trade in this industry. Veronica Osawere of blessed memory came with a rich broadcasting heritage. The consummate broadcast all-rounder, it's a pity that administrative duties prevented her from creating more time for a fuller career in voiceovers. Daphne Atere-Roberts came from a journalistic background to become the "queen" of voiceover artistes. Daphne is a wonderful person who perhaps contributed more toward the voice associations' sustenance and recognition than any other person. Utterly selfless to a fault, her major flaw was that she devoted too much time and energy to others, often neglecting her own needs, hardly ever getting a deserved "thank you" in return. And how could I ever forget that wonderful lady of the stage, Tosan Ederemoda-Ugbeye. An actress par excellence, she often brought her skills, and more, into the voiceover trade.

RECOMMENDATIONS

If you intend to stay within the voiceover angle of presentation duties let me leave you with a few tips to guide you along the way:

Pay attention to the industry trends. This requires regular viewing and switching between television and radio stations. Learn to adjust to these changes in voice and style demands as they occur. Try to remain flexible.

Never let ego interfere with your performance. Trust your ability to perform and forget about the need to stay on top. Learn from your mistakes as well as your successes. Personal growth comes through experience. Get to know and be friendly with as many agency producers as you can. This adds a comfort level to your performance and reduces stress.

Be professional in the studios. Try not to distract from the job at hand. Don't put on "noisy" attachments, like heavily starched clothing, bangles, and so forth. Switch off mobile phones and other gadgets. Performance quality and professional behavior determines whether or not you are hired again. "Read the room"; never overstay your welcome. As the day progresses, schedules get tighter.

Don't add to the problem by hanging around if you're no longer needed. Unless the signals are otherwise, thank the people in the control room and leave. Don't be self-conscious about your facial or body movements. No one is judging your dexterity. I've seen all kinds of comic and eccentric postures in the vocal booths while production is on. Every actor has his or her own characteristic stance, style, nuance, or emotion in the effort of achieving perfect delivery. Stand on your head if it helps you to give your best performance! Watch your voice; it's your major asset. Don't drink while there's work to be done, and never smoke. Don't give up. Ever! Voiceovers are a freelance profession. It takes time, commitment, and talent to succeed. You may be lucky to get work immediately, but it takes three years to become established. Expand your repertoire by studying, taking classes, and performing. By the time you have ten years behind you, you'll be amazed at the complexities of your voice and your understanding of subtle improvements, which eluded you in earlier years. Prepare yourself for lean days, for they will come! There will be times when you work a lot and other times when the work temporarily dries up. Stay focused, make phone calls to stir up more work, and, above all, don't get discouraged. Otherwise, choose another job! Strive for the ultimate goal—to execute wonderful voiceovers reflexively; to achieve the fourth level of learning where your verbal masterpieces are created effortlessly. Remember that practice, commitment, and trust are the keys to success. The real fun begins when you open up your imagination and let the words come alive.

MY LAST THOUGHT AND ADVICE

It is obvious that globalization has been engaged in the most positive attributes, but the real impressionable thought I should leave on your minds of how much improvement digitization has had on the media industry is reflected in the personal relationship I share with most of my clients and associates today. In a huge majority of my voice productions over the past three or so years, not once have I met any one of my clients, or partners physically. Everything has been done by using all the technological interactions achievable, from A–Z, from concept, to production, to delivery. So, live your dreams, be ready to explore the digital space and technology to add to your voicing expertise. Do not allow the advent of new technology to render you useless, irrelevant, or dislodge you from the voiceover industry. In the digital space, you can deliver. Seamlessly!

NOTE

1. Portions of this chapter were previously published in "The Voice Actor's Stage" in chapter 8 of my book *There Are No Heroes: An Autobiographical Instructive for the Modern Broadcaster*, Quramo Publishing, 2016.

REFERENCES

Kintz, L. F. 2007. "Overview of Current Media Practices and Trends in West Africa." *Global Media Journal* 6.

Okoro, N. 2012. "Mass Media in Nigeria: An Exploratory Analysis." *New Media and Mass Communication* (7): 6–12.

Sowoolu, F. 2011. "The Death of Radio?" A paper presentation at a media clinic in 2011 in Lagos.

Uche, L. 1989. *Mass media, People and Politics in Nigeria.* New Dehli: Concept Publishing Company.

Chapter 11

Broadcast News Production and Presentation Skills in the Digital Era

Challenges and Prospects

Ijeoma N. Onyeator

Newsrooms in Africa have changed irrevocably because the news industry has been digitally disrupted. Media houses have traded in typewriters for desk computers, and secretaries for electronic devices with multiple applications. As a result of this disruption, the newsrooms in Africa are both "paradoxically growing and shrinking." Growing in terms of visibility, real and potential reach, while simultaneously shrinking in terms of passive audiences, causing some mainstream media news organizations to draw heavily from what was once considered strictly alternative media. Previously, news production incorporated audience input in the form of letters-to-the-editor, where people would send in their comments via letters or email, and the editors would cherry-pick them, after verifying the sender. Today, editors find themselves sifting through the comment sections of non-mainstream sources like blog sites and websites to incorporate audience's accounts into their work.

For this reason, the production of news content on the African continent once distilled by professional journalists (gatekeepers) is now largely controlled by alternative intermediaries in the public space. This state of affairs is not specific to Africa alone. The Reuters Institute Digital News report (RDNR), arguably the most comprehensive study of news construction, production, and consumption in the world found that people prefer to source news through search engines, social media, news aggregators, and intermediaries, to listening to the accounts of human news editors (Newman et al.

2019). Therefore, while mainstream professionals once played the keepers' role, digitization and the affordances of new communication technologies defy the whole notion of a "gate" (Bruns 2005; 2011; Gans 2007; Bottcher 2014; Newman et al. 2019).

Nigeria's media ecology now comprises a web of actors and each plays a crucial role in the media ecology providing a range of services including the construction, production, and dissemination of news and other media offerings through unbridled access to the internet. A growing number of print and broadcast journalists now receive their "scoops" and "breaking" news from web sources. For the broadcast industry, trends suggest that mainstream television news workers are *changing channels* and increasingly gathering information using digital methods (Onyeator and Okpara 2019).

The empowering of non-mainstream actors into the news media ecology is largely made possible by media globalization and technological change. These twin concepts have caused mainstream professionals such as editors, reporters, presenters, news anchors, and producers to rethink the news construction process in terms of participation—first in terms of collaborative news gathering and then concerning the production of stories. The digital revolution has also enabled mainstream and non-mainstream news actors to acquire new skills and tricks of the trade from a presentation perspective. The former (media globalization) came about as a result of the flow of information and communication products within the global system. However, technological change and the digital age has been facilitated by the revolution in information and communication technology. The result of this change is that vast amounts of information are now transferred around the world via broadband, digitalization, cable, the internet, and its associated technologies (Schlosberg 2016).

This instantaneous transfer of information also includes greater opportunities not only to access but to speak to a global audience. As Obiaya (2010) suggests, the increased visibility of the audience on the iInternet also enables media producers to have access to them at any time to obtain instantaneous feedback. This foregrounds the prime position of the internet as an enabler of audience participation in contemporary communicative practice. Furthermore, the convergence of media forms has caused traditional mass media like radio, television, as well as audiovisual content (films, etc.) to fuse into handheld mobile phones, iPads, and laptops. Armed with these devices, everyday people stream live videos, pictures, and other content. This transformation is largely responsible for the shaping and reshaping of the media environment where everyday people operate as news workers. New media has changed the face and function of today's traditional newsroom where social media has sped up the news gathering process—altering the way editors and reporters report the news and influencing the way news anchors deliver the news.

News consumption patterns in Nigeria and by extension Africa have also changed. Audiences are now at the heart of everything a news provider does, and such audiences are more proactive than they used to be with many hunting for information themselves online. Broadcast houses have therefore been playing catchup and the challenge for news providers is therefore balancing changing audience demands while riding the digitization speed train. But there is another angle. Audience attention span is limited, and this is particularly true for news and current affairs programs aired on television and radio. For this reason, the presentation of news in terms of scripting and reading has changed along with them in the past twenty years. As a broadcast journalist, presenter, news anchor, or newsreader, the big question therefore is—in a digitized world where there is fierce competition for the attention of the viewer, why should anyone listen to you?

STORYTELLING SKILLS IN A DIGITAL AGE

The competition for the attention of audiences in the media business is fierce. To attract audiences, news producers often have to make their content available to search engines and social media, sometimes with little or no financial return. To satisfy the workings of digital platforms, news producers must now create content that is more emotive, animated, and shareable. The contemporary media environment has introduced new challenges to maintaining journalistic quality—the 24/7 news cycle; first to break the story, algorithms, and the participatory blogosphere. For news consumers and producers, this represents a new challenge of information delivery.

For broadcast journalists, information delivery or "talk" is important for two reasons. From the perspective of storytelling, the *talkability* of a story—that is, the extent to which it is being talked about—is now regarded as a measure of its importance and newsworthiness. While virality and user comments may seem like legitimate news values as they speak to the significance of a story to the audience, they may also be regarded as a feedback mechanism that loops the voice of the audience into news construction. On a critical note, however, they could also be regarded as a thinly disguised marketing effort to pander to the wishes of the audience to expand viewership. The challenge, however, is that mainstream media may, inadvertently, become purveyors of personal opinions of uninformed writers who pass off themselves as knowledgeable, shielded by the cloak of anonymity offered by cyberspace. Therefore, in line with the findings of Asekun-Olarinmoye et al. (2014), it can be argued that as far as the Nigerian media (and by extension the African media) is concerned, the aggregation, filtering, and distribution roles within the information network are a moving target.

Another concern regarding talkability is the sourcing of information for breaking news or developing stories. Information about scoops was once gleaned by journalists from professional news sources. Reporters would arrive at the scene of an occurrence to verify the scoop, gather additional information, and then construct their stories for broadcast or publishing. Today, contemporary editors and journalists frequently jump on the bandwagon of scoops from everyday voices online, without necessarily getting to the scene of the incident or carefully verifying if the information is true. These findings mirror a study on online news headlines in which Lombardi (2018) found that alternative media platforms such as social media are important drivers of what *breaks* and what does not. But it is insufficient to simply argue that news construction practices have changed as a result of the introduction of alternative sources. How should journalists respond?

From a production perspective, the outstanding presenter's goal is to satisfy the needs of the audience in line with contemporary news values. For instance, there is a deluge of stories trending on alternative platforms and these now form part of a whole new set of news values to consider in mainstream news production beyond the traditional newsworthiness markers—proximity, timeliness, relevance, impact and public interest. The comments of everyday people on alternative platforms are now key factors in the construction of news and contemporary broadcasters must take these alternative voices into consideration in the construction of their stories. How can this be done? Digital tools and non-mainstream entrants into the industry are here to stay. Rather than ignore, or cast aspersions on them, universities, schools of journalism and other institutions of higher learning should explore creative ways of establishing professionalism among non-mainstream journalists. Short basic I-writing, I-news reporting as well as I-ethics courses may help sensitize the new generation of journalists—especially those who regard what they do as a noble profession and civic duty—as their responsibility to society and bolster their sense of accountability to society. It is hoped that some non-mainstream journalists will welcome training opportunities that lend credence to their work.

Secondly, with the ubiquity of the media and the relentless crossflow of news from both mainstream and non-mainstream sources, society literally exists in a chamber of news voices. Thus, the media are a principal part of the social fabric and news from the media has become the inescapable reality of citizens, who serve not only as news consumers but also, increasingly, as news producers. It often becomes difficult to separate the wheat from the chaff, leading to cognitive dissonance as well as the moral fright about citizen journalism and its supposed corollary of fake news. But media literacy presents a more sustainable option for society. At no time in the annals of human history has media literacy become more critical for optimal functioning within society. In simple terms, media literacy refers to the ability to understand and use mediated communication effectively and efficiently. Although discourses on media literacy largely target students of media and communication, media literacy is critical to every consumer and producer of digital news.

Indeed, contemporary broadcasters need to understand not only the news they have been exposed to but also the source of the news, the values that drive the reporters, their approach to news gathering and construction and so on to evaluate the news from the media and make informed decisions about what to share, tweet, like, forward and disseminate. As information managers, journalists certainly need to understand the intricacies of digital communication channels and the language embodied in such media. In light of the above, there is no doubt that professional journalists also need to improve their media literacy skills. They need to understand what constitutes a credible and viable source. They need to be critical enough to discern when citizen journalists frame their personal opinions as news or when they have planted a story to push a specific agenda. That way, journalists are less likely to fall victim to fake news in their news construction. They also need to reconsider the extent to which they rely on anonymous sources in deference to the ethical demands of journalism practice.

SPEAKING SKILLS IN A DIGITAL AGE

From the perspective of speaking, the *talkability* of a story must come across in the newscast and the onus lies on the presenter. Good speech for broadcasters is often synonymous with the mastery of elocution. Budding broadcasters are often introduced to modules of the English language ranging from phonemes and pronunciation to the modification of indigenous accents to sound more Anglicized. Elocution classes broadly touch on speech clarity vocal impact and developing presence and confidence through the voice and typical areas of work in elocution training include:

- Pronunciation of vowels, consonants, phraseology, stress, inflections
- Clarity, articulation, definition, and fluency
- Authenticity, personal connection and rapport with listeners (eye contact, amiable personality, gesticulations)
- Overcoming phobias, nerves, fear, and anxiety
- Developing authority, confidence, range, and vocal stamina

This was the way to go two decades ago. However, the contemporary broadcast journalist must now be schooled in digital elocution—the language of the diginatives. The development of digital speaking skills is fundamental for broadcast journalists to communicate effectively with their contemporary audiences. With the myriad of web tools, software, and hardware available, media owners can choose the ones that are appealing to make a difference in the presentation of their newscasts and programs. Presenters must be able to interpret, manipulate, and speak to information generated on animated LED screens, tablets, magnetic boards, whiteboard animation tools, and touch screen monitors. It is no longer enough to speak well or enunciate phonemes perfectly.

Today's broadcasters are judged by their ability to *speak* to 3D images, effects, graphics, audio, and text that is arranged creatively for their presentations. They must also be able to interpret videos downloaded as mp4, wmw, mov, avi, or other information shared directly through YouTube, Facebook Live, and other related image sequence driven applications. Typical areas of work in digital elocution training should therefore include:

- Sight-reading and speaking from iPads, tablets, digital-cue cards, and autocue
- Speaking to electronically powered visual aids (LED screens, magic magnetic boards, whiteboard animation tools, and touch screen monitors)
- Body framing and positioning for green screens, body cameras, and robotic cameras
- Frequent digital training of production and presentation staff to improve intermediate or low proficiency levels

Furthermore, in the past, audience members were able to peer check and identify pronunciation errors made by presenters in their newscasts. Today's active audience, armed with technological tools, use automated fact-checking apps to fact-check every claim, statistic, and word spoken by broadcast journalists on air. Presenters must therefore understand how these tools work to avoid embarrassing situations. Since 2015, European countries have been developing technology to help increase the speed, scale, and rate of fact-checking.

Media outlets in Africa must therefore join the movement to bring the benefits of such tools to businesses. A broadcast journalist should therefore:

- Anticipate the most important thing to be fact-checked each day
- Know when someone repeats something they already know to be false
- Fact-check information in as close to real-time as possible
- Match claims with evidence

The metaphor of the maze best describes the broadcast journalist's *speaking* role in a digital era. The presenter is at the beginning of the maze and the task is to navigate the audience to the other side of the grid, using the most effective tools and route. There are many distractions along the way, but the presenter must ensure that they have a positive memorable experience while being led down the winding twists of the maze to emerge on the other side. If they enjoy the journey, they will go again! To navigate this digital maze successfully, the contemporary broadcaster must be able to answer these two key questions: What is the essence of the story I am trying to tell and how best can I convey that story using my digital voice?

CHALLENGES AND PROSPECTS

The conversion of contemporary broadcast content (including sound, images, and text) from analog to digital format and the acquisition of digital elocution is at the very heart of digital transformation. Unlike analog data, which suffers a loss of quality each time it is transmitted, digital data can be reproduced with absolutely no loss of quality or content. Content quality is improved, and for this reason broadcast stations constantly seek digital solutions to their problems. The unique challenge for news providers is therefore balancing changing audience and content demands while riding the digitization speed train. But there are even greater challenges on the African continent that make progress in this regard slow. Broadcast equipment is expensive and the infrastructure to support it is often lacking. In Nigeria, for instance, private broadcast houses are under financial strain as a result of rising overheads, heavy job losses owing to COVID-19, and the challenge of meeting the nation's digital conversion deadline. There are also challenges associated with oppressive legislative sections of the Broadcast Code and overbearing activities of industry regulators. How then can the African media tap into the digital future?

The answer lies in transforming creative indigenous ideas into globally acceptable innovative media products and leveraging on international partnerships for profitability. Therefore, the disruption discussed at the beginning of this chapter is not entirely frightening. It should inspire Africa's media enterprises and entrepreneurs to transform their business models and see digital competition from the West as opportunities to expand and collaborate. Professional collaborations and partnerships improve access to knowledge, they mitigate risk and provide the opportunity to tap into a wider pool of technical and practical expertise, skills, labor, and global networks.

In a world where multiple information gates now exist and the boundary between mainstream and non-mainstream media has blurred, media organizations have a responsibility to determine how best to practice their profession.

They need to determine their *glocal* response. They need to reevaluate their professional ethics, partnerships, and news processes. This involves considering how best to bridge the intellectual divide between mainstream and non-mainstream media and repositioning themselves for relevance in a new media world without compromising professional ethics. At the same time, mainstream media organizations may need to provide timely resources to their workers to limit their reliance on non-mainstream sources, especially those of doubtful credibility. On the other hand, non-mainstream organizations will need to professionalize their work—very few are doing this—to guarantee their place in the pantheon of credible news channels and voices. On the whole, the fact that the journalism profession has stretched, buckled, expanded, and has now become diverse and permeable, does not mean it will disintegrate. Contemporary journalism—and by extension, the treatment of its offerings like news and programs—will become more variegated and more multifaceted. Despite these changes, it will retain its preeminence in democratic societies.

REFERENCES

Asekun-Olarinmoye, O., Sanusi, B. O., Johnson, J., and Oloyede, D. B. 2014. "Imperatives of internet and social media on broadcast Journalism in Nigeria." *New Media and Mass Communication* 23: 8–15.

Böttcher, A. V. 2014. "Twitter, news aggregators and co: Journalistic gatekeeping in the age of digital media culture." Bachelor's thesis, Blekinge Institute of Technology. Accessed September 30, 2021. http://www.diva-portal.org/smash/get/diva2:833239/FULLTEXT01.PDF.

Bruns, A. 2005. *Gate watching: Collaborative online news production.* New York: Peter Lang.

Bruns, A. 2011. "Gatekeeping, gatewatching, real-time feedback: New challenges for journalism." *Brazilian Journalism Research* 7 (11): 117–135.

Gans, H. 2007. "Everyday news, news workers and professional journalism." *Political Communication 24* (2): 161–166.

Lombardi, D. 2018. "Critical discourse analysis of online news headlines: A case of the Stoneman Douglas high school shooting." Master's thesis, Malmö University. Accessed September 30, 2021. https://pdfs.semanticscholar.org/8e91/10d3c08bc4fd86705c9b9c96f5591edc4fb8.pdf.

Newman, N., Fletcher, R., Kalogeropoulos, A., Levy, D. A., and Kleis, N. R. 2019. "Reuters Institute Digital News Report 2019," *Reuters Institute for the Study of Journalism.* Oxford: University of Oxford.

Obiaya, I. 2010. "Nollywood on the Internet: A preliminary analysis of an online Nigerian video-film audience." *Journal of African Media Studies* 2 (3): 321–338.

Onyeator, I. and Okpara, N. 2019. "Human communication in a digital age: Perspectives on interpersonal communication in the family." *Journal of New Media and Mass Communication* (78): 35–45.

Schlosberg, J. 2016. *Media ownership and agenda control: The hidden limits of the information age*. New York; London: Routledge.

SECTION IV

Nigerianism in the Digital Space

Chapter 12

How Nigerian Media Contents Affect the Social Identity Formation and Information Sourcing of Second-Generation Nigerians in the United States of America

Unwana Samuel Akpan

This article sits and fits firmly within "a new field of study that is comparative, global, cross-disciplinary, and multi-paradigmatic, and that construes ethnicity, race, and nationhood as a single integrated family of forms of cultural understanding, social organization and political contestation" (Brubaker 2009, 22). Though diaspora communication is a nascent and an emerging field of inquiry in communication, studies in this infant field seek to expand and improve upon the parochialism, fragmentation, and non-interdisciplinary approaches taken by previous studies on diaspora communication, ethnicity, race, nations, and nationalism. No wonder a Finnish professor, Osmo Anterior Wiio (2009), while penning the general definition of communication, believes that one cannot not communicate. In essence, what he was trying to pass across is the fact that in whatever way, be it cultural or identity formation, the communicativeness of what is intended or not intended cannot be overlooked. That is why communication is a fundamental factor in any socioeconomic, sociopolitical, and sociocultural factor because diversity cum cultural communication is key to identity formation. The author is a Nigerian, he was born and bred in Nigeria where the natives show very strong cultural leaning to their ethnic inclination; and he is quite conversant with the average

189

Nigerian cultural attachments to his or her social identity. Nigerians who live in the diaspora are regarded as an under-researched group, and they are considered the most rapidly growing black immigrant group in the United States and the United Kingdom (Elam and Chinouya 2000; Logan and Deane 2003; Sharkdam, Akinkuotu, and Ibonye 2014; Alakija 2016).

Therefore, this work critically examines aspects of historical/cultural and media access available to second-generation Nigerians in the United States of America. Notably, these second-generation Nigerians are considered part of the Nigerian diaspora (Awokoya 2012). The logical starting point for this study must entail a clear understanding of the term, Nigerian diaspora. "Diaspora" refers to a group of people that have spread around the world from a common point of origin (Williams 2013, p. 113). Gilroy (1993) tells the story of the earliest African diaspora as slaves brought in from the continent of Africa to the New World and the descendants after them. As Paul Williams notes, "travelers and migrants brought different cultures into contact with each other, and new cultures were produced of this intermixture" (p. 114). The intermixture, identified by Williams, could be problematic. For instance, second-generation Nigerians faced by such intermixture in the United States of America, could possibly forget everything about the homeland.

In a study of African-Canadians, Codjoe et al. (2005) find that children born to first generation Africans are faced with the intermixture dilemma, but Codjoe et al. failed to explore whether those children use certain sources of information to keep in touch with the homeland. However, Bailey, Georgiou, and Springer (2007), analyze the consumption of media by diasporic communities, and the attitude of the diasporic community towards the host media. Though there have been significant studies trying to answer the question of the second-generation migrants' social identity globally (Jones 2008; Sabatier 2008; and Hume 2010) and as well as specific studies zeroing in on second-generation Africans and identity in the diaspora (Watson 2004; Cooper 2008; Akinrinade and Olukoya 2011; and Rivers 2012), researchers have not explored aspects of communication these second-generation Nigerians use in sourcing for their social identity in the homeland media, means of self-identification, and how these can impact on their social identity.

STATEMENT OF THE PROBLEM

The idea of exposure of media intermixture of homeland media and its possible impact on national identity, particularly among second-generation Nigerians in the United States, is a key reason for this chapter. Scholars have pointed out that Nigerians are one of the most successful immigrant communities in the USA (Onyejekwe 2018; and Rivers 2012). Roberts (2005) has also claimed that the number of Africans who arrived voluntarily to the United States, since 1990, has doubled the number that arrived as slaves. Other scholars claim that the African immigrant population has grown over 40-fold between 1960 and 2007, with much of the growth occurring since 1990 (USA Census Bureau 2002; Konadu-Agyemang and Takyi 2006; and Terrazas 2009). Going by the 2005–2009 United States Census American Community Survey, Nigerians constitute the largest community of immigrants to have emerged from Africa based on 191,203 foreign-born Nigerians in the United States of America. Also 42,216 persons born in the USA claim Nigerian ancestry and they constitute the second-generation (USA Census Bureau American Community Survey 2010a; USA Census Bureau American Community Survey 2010b). Balogun (2011) estimates the numbers may be as high as double the official count. According to the United States Census Bureau, 4 percent of Nigerians hold a PhD degree compared to 1 percent of the general US population, and 17 percent of Nigerians hold a master's degree while 37 percent have a bachelor's degree. The immense contributions of these appreciable dozens of highly educated youths to the United States of America and indeed global civilization cannot be easily quantified.

The figures above demonstrate Nigerian interest and desire to live outside their home country. Whether one calls it adventure, tourism, search for greener pasture or the Golden Fleece, what is clear is that there is hardly any country in the world where Nigerians do not form the majority of the African population (Agugua, personal interview).[1] It needs to be pointed out clearly that this situation existed long before the years of austerity, economic downturn at home as observed by Iwuagwu (personal interview). There is no doubt that the slide in the country's economy caused a certain acceleration in the pace of the migration of the youths, in particular, outside Nigeria.

In Nigeria, several sources of information are used in the teaching of history, civics, and current affairs in primary and secondary schools. This has helped to ensure that Nigerian children are fairly familiar with the events and affairs that shape their country and motivates national identity. The average Nigerian school child will tell you more about the past nationalists such as Dr. Nnamdi Azikiwe, Chief Obafemi Awolowo, and Sir Ahmadu Bello. In Nigeria, there are school songs in different dialects praising these nationalists for their role in Nigeria's independence. Perhaps, since this knowledge is part of the local school curriculum, the child learns about nationalists in order to pass the examinations. But the American school system, obviously, does not require second-generation Nigerians to know about Nigeria's cultural history.

Nevertheless, civilization entails the study and knowledge of one's origins in order to position the person to understand his or her present circumstances and prepares one to face the future (Elias 1998). This being the case, second-generation Nigerians have the responsibility to get fully acquainted with aspects of their family and national history. Nigerians are known to be quite ebullient, especially when they travel abroad (Agugua, personal interview 2018). They like to talk loudly about themselves, their nation and its affairs. Some Nigerians residing in the USA, particularly those who went there for further studies but decided to stay back, might want to keep a tab with developments at the home front. While several studies have explored this interest of first-generation Nigerians, not much has been done investigating if second-generation Nigerians develop such curiosity about the history of their parents' homeland via any information sources.

Obviously, Gilroy (1993) argues that the African diaspora cannot retrace its historical journey and make its way back to the point of origin. This is because "diasporic identity was irrevocably altered by the experience of slavery and has been transformed too extensively to be returned to a state of cultural purity" (p.115). Austin Anene (personal interview 2019), a Nigerian based in the United States of America, appears to affirm this in an interview: "it is not common knowledge that most Nigerian American parents in the USA do not attach much importance to this role (of teaching their children about the African homeland)." Many of them simply believe that their children are full-fledged American citizens and have no need to bother about goings-on in the homeland. In essence, second-generation Nigerians may well be faced by this problem of transformation which Williams (2013) had also described as "cultural intermixture." But the studies done by Chacko (2019), Heyd and Honkanen (2015), Nwabara (2017), and Ogunyemi (2018) all tend to disagree with Gilroy's assertion that Africans in diaspora cannot retrace their historical journey back to the African homeland. Those latter scholars demonstrate the quest of young second-generation Nigerians in the United States of America for identity with the homeland. Also, numerous studies have shown that diaspora, homeland transnational citizenship and transnationality history should be of concern to any first- and second-generation migrants (Halualani, Mendoza, and Drzewiecka 2009; Brubaker 2005; and Blunt 2007).

The literature above and those by Awokoya (2012), Clark (2008), and Curtis (2005) have focused on the identity question as well as relied on parents to obtain information about the second-generation Nigerian. Notably, none of them have investigated the communication aspects of the identity of these second-generation Nigerians. By communication, this article refers to sources of information important to developing identity with a nation or culture. Numerous studies have tried to investigate the media consumption of second-generation Africans in the diaspora, (Fortunati, Pertrera, and Vincent 2012; and Sanyu 2018), and the closest, being Mustapha and Wok (2015), who investigated the media consumption of Nigerian students in Malaysia. Nevertheless, researchers have neglected investigating what channels of communication second-generation Nigerians use in sourcing for as well as forming social identity, hence this article. This article looks at the plight of second-generation Nigerians in the diaspora, with special interest on Nigerians living in the United States of America in their quest to use the various channels of communication in the Nigerian media to explore the African homeland, amid the influence of Western culture, and how this impacts their contact with their homeland, if at all. To investigate the above, the article shall address the following research questions.

RESEARCH QUESTIONS

RQ1a. What communication sources do second-generation Nigerians in the USA use in obtaining information about Nigeria?

RQ1b. How do second-generation Nigerians use information about Nigeria?

RQ1c. Why do second-generation Nigerians seek information about Nigeria?

RQ2. Do demographic variables, including gender, play a role in the choice of communication sources of second-generation Nigerians in the USA?

RQ3. What level of the historical/political knowledge about Nigeria's nationalists do second-generation Nigerians have?

This research provides empirical data on the sources second-generation Nigerians use in gathering information about Nigeria that might shape their interest and identity. The research, apart from adding to the body of knowledge in the area of culture, history, and media in respect to the Nigerian diaspora, is also useful in identifying how these Nigerians use the Nigerian media to meet their interests. Rowley et al. (1998) carried out a study which showed the relationship between racial identity and personal self-esteem, hence, the need for this article since social identity has a way of boosting self-esteem, and in order to find out the modes of communication/information second-generation Nigerians in the diaspora use in sourcing for self-identification that might birth self-esteem.

LITERATURE REVIEW

Investigating how second-generation Nigerians use the media to seek information about Nigeria can be informed by Elihu Katz's (1974) uses and gratifications theory. The theory emerged in the early 1970s as Katz and his two colleagues, Jay Blumler and Michael Gurevitch, questioned the assumption that the audience passively consumed media content. According to Baran and Davis (2009), the uses and gratifications approach views the audience as active, meaning that they seek out specific media channels and content to achieve certain results or gratification that satisfy personal needs. Gratification theory tends to look into what people do with the media and what the media do to people. It stresses that the media have in one way or the other touched the lives of the audience and they have also derived pleasure from the media through the various functions of the mass media.

Baran and Davis (2009) and Spring (2002) further state that audience gratifications can be derived from at least three distinct sources: media content, "exposure to the media per se, and social context that typifies the situation of exposure to different media in various ways." According to Research Base (2022), "users take an active part in the communication process and are goal oriented in their media use." Therefore, the theory asserts that media users make media decisions concerning media consumptions in terms of the channel that he or she selectively chooses, attends to, perceives, and retains. This presumes that the second-generation Nigerian has alternate choices to satisfy needs for a cultural identity. For instance, recent studies, such as Korhan and Ersoy (2016, p. 1804), in their study of uses and gratifications theory, "showed that, younger and older generations have different taste of social network sites application use and different preference for the functionality and usability factors." This is the case of the second-generation African in the diaspora sourcing for cultural identity via the multi-available media platforms that are functional and available to him. That is why Jenkins' (2008) definition of identity is helpful. He defines social identity as:

> the human capacity—as rooted in language—to know "who's who" (and hence "what's what"). This involves knowing who we are, knowing who others are, them knowing who we are, us knowing who they think we are, and so on: a multi-dimensional classification or mapping of the human world and our places in it, as individuals and as members of collectivities. (Jenkins 2008, p. 5)

Ledbetter, Taylor, and Mazer (2016) in their study of communication medium effectiveness have revealed the fact that communicating via an unsatisfying medium may hamper continuous usage of such a medium of communication, especially by the youths. In a related study of uses and gratification and media use by young people, the cultural factor of individualism—collectivism had a positive impact on the pervasive adoption of social network sites, and this was evident in students from more individualistic cultures (Ifinedo 2016). This cultural factor of individualism-collectivism could be in terms of the social identity of the second-generation Nigerian in the diaspora as it relates to communication medium. Some recent studies have also pointed the fact that with the multiple sources of communication channels available these days as a result of advancement in social networks, source of communication choice and preference would be a function of what the young people want in a medium and the gratification which may be developing social identity using that medium (Sehee, Jinyoung, Heeseok 2015; and Dolan, Conduit, Fahy, and Goodman 2015).

THE BURDEN OF FIRST-GENERATION IMMIGRANTS

Beyond theorization, there are several studies of second-generation immigrants and their consumption of certain media for cultural identity. For instance, Balogun (2011) describes the chances of second-generation Nigerians learning the Nigerian culture via any channel of communication as very slim. In her words, "There are many children of Nigerian migrants who are married to citizens of the country they live in today. It will be much more difficult for kids produced from such marriages to learn of our culture because in such homes, Nigerian language will almost certainly not be spoken" (Balogun 2011, p. 437). Not surprising, a Nigerian newspaper, *Punch*, surveyed first-generation Nigerians in the United States and found that most of them do not bother to teach their children Nigerian culture and historical heritage (*Punch*, 2018). Hernandez (2015) posited that many Nigerians in the USA suffer great limitations that affect their ability to teach their children Nigerian history and nationalism. According to him, these limitations range from demanding work schedules, pressure to pay bills, and other social pressures. Therefore, it is imperative to learn the sources that second-generation Nigerians use in getting information about the homeland. The newspaper's submission drove the point home for this study. Separate research studies by Adeniyi (2007) and Suleiman (2016) also provide support for this research study. Adeniyi (2007) and Suleiman (2016) seem to hold a common view, as they focus squarely on the essence of Nigerian nationalism abroad. They state that some Nigerian American parents in the USA keep a large stock of Nigerian cultural movies, music, and literature in their homes as tools needed in getting their adolescent children to embrace Nigerian culture and history. They also believe that the rise of Nigerian religious houses, dance and drama groups in the USA, can contribute to promoting Nigerian history and culture across the Atlantic. How can we adjudge this to be true if the second-generation Nigerians (i.e., children born to these set of Nigerians abroad) are not personally interviewed?

Naturally, anyone who finds himself in a strange land and wishes to settle there might wish that children born to them in the diaspora learn and imbibe the cultural behaviors of their homeland, and they don't mind their children knowing the culture of the host country, but they would prefer the cultural identity of their homeland to be imbibed by their children for posterity's sake (Iwuagu, 2018 personal interview). In a study of new media, diasporic identity, and social exclusion of everyday practices of identity negotiation among second-generation Ghanaian women in Hamburg, Sanyu (2018) investigated how second-generation Ghanaian women living in Hamburg use new media to negotiate a diasporic identity in the face of social exclusion. One of the objectives in this study is to investigate whether gender as a demographic variable has a role to play in the choice of communication medium second-generation Nigerians in the diaspora use in molding their social identity. Nonetheless, this article is in no way seeking to provide answers to the second-generation Nigerian woman diasporic identity and which of the medium of communication she tilts to for social identity.

Newbold and Campos (2011) have noted that in the past few decades, electronic media have stepped to the forefront of communication, and diaspora communication has evolved to reflect this. Many channels of communication can be used in diaspora communication—newspapers, direct mail, booklets, television, and radio, internet, among others, especially with online newspapers, online radio and television, among others. Importantly, the reach and frequency of media exposure are predictive factors of message acceptability and a campaign's success (Noar 2006; and Hornik and Kelly 2007). As Harrison (2000) suggests, "media users may be affected by what they view, but they also selectively expose themselves to media content that is congruent with their existing worldview" (p. 138). Based on the above, this study seeks to explore the media that second-generation Nigerians in the diaspora use to construct social identity with their parents' homeland.

SECOND-GENERATION IMMIGRANTS
AND INTEREST IN THE HOMELAND

Nevertheless, development entails the study and knowledge of one's origins in order to position the person to understand his or her present circumstances and prepare one to face the future (Elias 1998). This being the case, it is expected that second-generation Nigerians would be acquainted with aspects of their family and national history. While several studies explore the interest of first-generation Nigerians in consuming news about their homeland, not much has been done investigating if second-generation Nigerians develop such curiosity about the history of their parent's homeland via any information sources.

Interestingly, Gilroy (1993) argues that the African diaspora cannot retrace its historical journey and make its way back to the point of origin. This is because "diasporic identity was irrevocably altered by the experience of slavery and has been transformed too extensively to be returned to a state of cultural purity" (p. 115). Austin Anene (personal interview 2019), a Nigerian based in the United States of America, affirms this in an interview: "it is not common knowledge that most Nigerian American parents in the USA do not attach much importance to this role (of teaching their children about the African homeland)." Many of them simply believe that their children are full-fledged American citizens and have no need to bother about goings-on in the homeland. In essence, second-generation Nigerians may well be faced by this problem of transformation which Williams (2013) had also described as "cultural intermixture."

But the studies done by Chacko (2019), Heyd and Honkanen (2015), Nwabara (2017), and Ogunyemi (2018) disagree with Gilroy's assertion that Africans in diaspora cannot retrace their historical journey back to the African homeland. Those latter scholars demonstrate the quest of young second-generation Nigerians in the United States of America for identity with the homeland. Also, numerous studies have shown that diaspora, homeland trans-national citizenship and transnationality history should be of concern to any first- and second-generation migrants (Halualani, Mendoza, and Drzewiecka 2009; Brubaker 2005; and Blunt 2007) for posterity sake.

INFLUENCE OF NEW MEDIA

There have been loads of academic studies on diaspora identity and focus on the impact of mass media channels, including new technologies of communication such as social media use among established diasporic groups. Some clear examples are, South Asians (Vertovec 1999), Filipinos (Ong 2009; Ong and Cabañes 2011), Greek Cypriots (Georgiou 2006, 2001), Punjabi South Asian youth (Gillespie 1995), Turks (Robins and Aksoy 2000), Iranians in London (Sreberny 2005), Greeks, Cypriots, and Turks (Madianou 2002, 2006), and other minority groups living in Britain and elsewhere. However, we find no study that measures consumption of Nigerian media content by second-generation Nigerians in the United States, such as music or movies, and how that consumption helps us to understand the role of class differences (Ong and Cabañes 2011). Hence this study is important in addressing such a gap.

Media and migration scholars reveal how media channels help migrants and their children to stay in touch with their homeland and help them build social identity in tandem with the native homeland (Johnson and McKay 2011; Ong 2009; Madianou 2005). Numerous studies such as Oh (2012), Christoph (2012), and Croucher et al. (2009) surveyed Korean American youths, second- and third-generation Turks in Germany, and first- and second-generation French Muslims, respectively, and find that the preference for ethnic media has a role in creating boundaries, resisting assimilationist policies and negative representation in mainstream media, and in fostering "a group identity if they are largely dissatisfied with their personal circumstances" (Christoph, citing Schneider and Arnold 2006). Karim (1998, 2003, 2006, and 2012) has researched various aspects of the use of communication technologies by members of the diaspora for news needs in the homeland. Their yearning for information and entertainment, he observes, has led to the proliferation of ethnic media, and therefore warrant exploration, particularly the effects of media on issues of citizenship and social cohesion as well as their relationship to mass media (Alakija, 2016).

Identity formation and the media have been extensively researched. Regarding identity, the influence of media on identity formation and nation building has been established by previous studies (Dayan 1999; Anderson 1993). Alonso and Oiarzabal (2010) believe that with the coming of social media, ethnic groups in the diaspora would lose touch with their native homeland. That is why Web (2012) researched how second-generation Portuguese residents in Port Elizabeth, South Africa, use the media, and the findings show that the new media helps them stay informed about their native homeland. The findings of both Abu-Lughod (1993, 1989) and Mitra (2001) are also instructive on how migrants use the media to negotiate social identity to their advantage. They notice that previous research neglects the nationalities and ethnicities of the participants and gives little attention to factors such as gender, age, class, and the text itself (Madianou 2002, pp. 80–81). They conclude that media usage by migrants depends on their cultural background and ethnic experiences (Morley 1980). Faist (2010) is of the belief that agelong generational media consumption habits and other social practices could inform the diasporic experiences. Studies such as Madianou (2005), Silverstone and Georgiou (2005), and Schlesinger (2000) also demonstrate how media provide symbolic space for articulating identity. According to Aksoy and Robins (2003), this contradicts the notion of "banal transnationalism" and the ordinariness of media consumption by migrants. Their findings from an examination of the second-generation's media consumption is similar to those of Adeniyi (2007).

METHODOLOGY

For this study, qualitative data are collected through focus group discussion with a semi-structured instrument. Focus groups come handy here as it is a "form of group interview that capitalizes on communication between research participants in order to generate data . . . focus groups explicitly use group interaction as part of the method" (Kitzinger 1995, p. 299). This will give participants room to express themselves, especially in the midst of their peers. Focus groups are helpful when investigating subjects like identity (Creese and Kambere 2003). The study uses three focus groups consisting of six people in each group, thereby involving a total of eighteen participants. For gender balance, there is an equal number of both sexes represented. The participants are selected using the purposive sampling method. These sets of participants were from the age of 18 years and above in The Redeemed Christian Church of God, 1515 Kenilworth Avenue, Southeast, Washington DC. Selection was done based on ethnicity, that is, to represent the three major ethnic groups in Nigeria, which are Igbo, Yoruba, and Hausa, as well as gender representation. (Please see the profile of the participants in Table 1 at the end of this chapter.) The focus group discussion took place in the youth auditorium of the Redeemed Christian Church of God, 1515 Kenilworth Avenue, Southeast, Washington, DC. Parts of the questions asked during the session bothered on what sources of communication used in obtaining information about Nigeria; how frequently do they use the medium; in what context do they use the medium; what and how do they use the information after obtaining it; and what motivates them to seek information about Nigeria?

Before each session begins, each participant completed the consent form as well as the demographic survey instrument. The researcher recorded the focus group session electronically with the use of the researcher's phone voice recorder for transcription. The researcher facilitated the discussion to be sure that one person does not dominate the entire discussion and the researcher was sensitive to follow-up questions.

Recorded discussions from each focus group session were fully transcribed. The researcher used an explanatory thematic qualitative media analysis approach that was done by Boyatzis (1998) and Mcnamara (2005), to analyze the audio recordings from the focus group discussions which are entirely media content in outlook. This investigative approach is suitable for analysis of media contents such as audio and video recordings (MacNamara 2005; and Altheide and Schneider 2013). Sociologist Max Weber posits that thematic analysis is crucial as it often pictures the sociocultural terrain of a society it operates from (Hansen et al. 1998; and Macnamara 2005). During the focus group discussions, participants were asked the same questions about going back to homeland, social identity formation, sources of communication they use in getting information about their homeland that might lead to their social identity formation with homeland, how frequently do they use it. The researcher then carefully transcribed the recordings and used it to find out how second-generation Nigerians in the USA obtain the information that help them to form social identity. More so, thematic analysis aided the researcher to understand broader cultural traits (Neuendorf 2002; Gerstl-Pepin 2015; and Smith 2019).

TESTING THE RESEARCH OBJECTIVES

Having established the issues of second-generation social identity in the United States of America and sources of information, now I will turn to examining their motivation of their social identity and sources of information by using the following research objectives: to (1a) find out communication sources second-generation Nigerians in the USA use in obtaining information about Nigeria, (1b) assess how second-generation Nigerians use information about Nigeria, (1c) examine why second-generation Nigerians seek information about Nigeria; (2) evaluate demographic variables, including gender, how they play a role in the choice of communication sources of second-generation Nigerian in the USA; (3) explore the level of the historical/political knowledge about Nigeria's nationalists second-generation Nigerians have. The findings from in-depth focus group sessions and observation were used to reveal key insights into second-generation Nigerian identity in the United States of America and sources of information. I conducted the focus group discussion sessions myself. The entire focus group sessions lasted between 45 to 75 minutes.

DISCUSSION OF FINDINGS

The first focus group session had six participants of four males and two females, and they were all students. Coincidentally, two groups of the participants were of similar ethnic roots being of Yoruba race, while the others were of other ethnic races in Nigeria. These respondents are identified as African-Nigerian-American because they were born and raised in the USA. These sets of second-generation migrants in the United States felt they could directly relate with the experiences of this racial group more than their African heritage. They insist that their social identity is more of what they describe in local Nigerian parlance as "Naija Identity." For example, some of the respondents felt less attached to their African ethnic roots. This being that they claim to have some level of comprehension of their homeland's local language. Some of them said they do not speak Yoruba, but agreed to the fact that they would want to learn their respective homeland's local languages at some point in their life. Most of them proudly told me that having an African last or first name gave them a sense of pride. All of them said that they would stay in the USA because they knew very little of Africa and could never live there but only visit.

For research RQ1a: What communication sources do second-generation Nigerians in the USA use in obtaining information about Nigeria? The researcher relied on the responses elicited from the answers supplied from the focus group discussion sessions of second-generation Nigerians living in the United States of America to answer this question. When this question was asked to the three sets of focus groups at different times, a good majority of them said they relied on Nigerian YouTube channels to gather information about Nigeria, just a few of them said they asked their parents. A majority of them said they don't really bother about news from Nigeria via online newspapers because they believe they are from the United States of America. One of them put it this way, "Why bother your head about a country you rarely visit?" When asked how often you use this/these sources of communication to obtain information about Nigeria, a great number of them said they use those sources too often, especially YouTube, to obtain information about Nigeria.

For RQ1b: How do second-generation Nigerians use information about Nigeria? The researcher asked these groups separately; in what context do they use this/these sources of communication to obtain information about Nigeria? A great number of them who said they go to YouTube to obtain information about Nigeria said they use that medium to check out new Nigerian music dance steps and new releases of Nigerian hip hop artistes on YouTube. When asked whether they believe that the cultural attributes linked to their ethnic background as portrayed in their source of information on Nigeria has in any way helped them to form their social identity, most of them started dancing, showing off their new dance steps from Nigeria they learn from You Tube. "Of course yes! This is because some of us now do the Naija swag, Naija songs, Naija praise and worship songs and we are beginning to appreciate our Naija names now," were their responses. Apart from being an African-American, do they identify as being black; one of them told me, "even my skin would tell you that I am a Nigerian, and if you miss my skin color, you cannot miss my Nigerian name, Adekunle. My bangle is the map of Africa and I am a proud African." The researcher further probed whether they speak any of the Nigerian native languages or pidgin English? "I don't speak Yoruba, but I understand it to some extent. I understand a bit of Pidgin, but cannot speak it," were most of their responses.

For RQ1c: Why do second-generation Nigerians seek information about Nigeria? The researcher asked them that, after they obtain the information about Nigeria, how do they use it? After learning new dance steps from Nigeria on YouTube, they said they would showcase the new dance steps to their American friends who would learn it from them. And they said they also use the dance steps learned from YouTube to do dance choreography in church. When asked, what purpose do they use the information they obtain about Nigeria for? They said basically for entertainment. They said it is basically music entertainment that drives them to source for entertainment information on YouTube about Nigeria. The researcher further rephrased the question by asking them whether they use the information they obtain about Nigeria in their home, school, in conversation with friends, or to impress, or to show social/cultural identity? Their response was that the information they obtain about Nigeria on YouTube is purely for entertainment purposes which they use in school to flaunt their new dance steps and to impress their parents who feel they don't want to learn anything about Nigeria. Could that be the reason they seek information about Nigeria? Majority of them said, it's purely for entertainment's sake, because they believe that the American music industry is beginning to embrace what they call Naija music flavor. For them, what motivates them in seeking information about Nigeria is purely for social identity in music. They believe if Nigerian youths are making it in the music industry to the admiration of even the Americans, then they too could do well in the entertainment industry as Nigerian-American. According to them, it's the global commercial success story of Nigeria's movie industry-Nollywood and Nigeria's music industry that triggers their desire for seeking information about Nigeria.

For RQ2: Do demographic variables, including gender, play a role in the choice of communication sources of second-generation Nigerians in the USA? They were asked whether they think their gender plays a role in the choice of their communication source. All of the respondents in the three groups said gender has no role to play in their choice of communication source. According to them, both guys and girls go on YouTube. They suc-cinctly put, "we all do YouTube." Whether their circle of friends influence their choice of information source, all of them said no to this question, as they visit any social media platform of their choice irrespective of their friends' choices. One of them said, "for God sake, this is a free nation, you do your thing and I do my thing." The researcher also asked whether their financial status influenced their choice of information source? They all answered that the internet is cheap and affordable in the US, so their financial status does not really affect their choice of information source.

For RQ3: What level of the historical/political knowledge about Nigeria's nationalists do second-generation Nigerians have? The researcher asked them what knowledge of Nigeria's history/political past are they aware of through the choice of their communication sources they have already identified. All of them said they don't really know so much about Nigeria's history/political past. When asked whether they have ever heard of Nigeria's past nationalists such as Dr. Nnamdi Azikiwe, Ahmadu Bello, Tafawa Balewa, Okotie Eboh, and Sir Herbert Macaulay? They said their parents rarely mention Nigeria's past nationalists to them.They were also asked whether they have ever heard about the past military leaders who ruled Nigeria. One of the respondent's response was "not really, except Abacha." And whether they know the current president of Nigeria, their homeland, "I hear my parents mention his name when they are discussing with other Nigerians about the challenges in Nigeria," were their responses. Each of the respondents from the three groups was also asked their state of origin in Nigeria and the various governors of your state? "My parents have told me about my state of origin, but I can't remember it now; but not my state governor," they all chorused. They added, "if I want to know his/her name, I mean my state governor, I just google it, period." The researcher also asked whether they know the name of the village they hail from in Nigeria? This particular question made them all laugh out loud and cover their faces shyly. They said, "Oh my God, we can't pronounce it because it is some African name. But daddy used to tell us." The question, would you want to return to your parents' homeland someday was asked? When this particular question was asked, they looked at themselves and gave a good laugh. To put it in their words, "we love it here because this is where we have known all our lives. But we can visit Nigeria and return back to the USA. To live there permanently is not possible because we are not used to the environment and of course the culture. We love it here, and some of us would want to be buried here."

CONCLUSION

The result of this study shows clearly a good majority of second-generation Nigerians living in the United States of America between the ages of 13 to 17 years of age go to YouTube channels belonging to Nigerians to source information about Nigeria, and the type of information they seek about Nigeria online is principally for entertainment purposes, new release of Nigerian music and dance steps. For instance, sixteen out of the eighteen participants agree to have very strong social identity ties with the Nigerian identity asides being an American. More so, seventeen out of eighteen of the participants admit that they rely heavily on YouTube to gather information about Nigeria, which is only about entertainment. Fourteen out of the eighteen participants said the type of information they seek about Nigeria online is principally for entertainment purposes—new release of Nigerian music and dance steps for which they use to form their social identity. This is because, according to them, YouTube is more specific in nature than any other media as it groups subjects of interest together. Also, according to them, YouTube gives visual dramatization to any subject they want to learn about online. The result also shows that a good number of them use YouTube and Instagram mostly to source information about Nigeria because of the visual characteristics of this channel.

The result also shows that a good number of them use YouTube and Instagram mostly to source information about Nigeria because of the visual characteristics of this channel. And when this entertainment information is gotten, they use it to form their social identity that is pan-African. Therefore I propose more involvement of Africans in software development that would carry and project Africa's image and identity that Africans in the diaspora would be proud to be associated with. It is observed that a good portion of second-generation Nigerians in the USA are interested in Nigerian homemade music and dance steps viewed from the YouTube channels of some Nigerian bloggers; and this is the only thing that motivates them to seek to know about their homeland. This clearly shows that they appreciate Nigerian music and dance steps to the American music and dance steps. It also shows that these categories (18 years and above) of second-generation Nigerians in the USA are interested in entertainment. Therefore, the Nigerian government should invest in Nigeria's media industry as well as Nigeria's entertainment industry as a way of motivating her citizens in the diaspora to be identified with Nigeria.

Table 12.1. Participants of the Focus Group Discussion and Related Demographic Data. *Source*: Author created.

Name	Age	Sex
Ade	21	M
Adekunle	18	M
Bisi	20	F
Bola	18	F
Emeka	22	M
Ajala	18	F
Uzoama	19	F
Tope	21	F
Bola	18	F
Chukwuemeka	19	M
Tolu	22	M
Yinka	21	M
Eberechukwu	19	F
Fisayo	18	M
Ejike	19	M
Dele	20	M
Fola	18	F
Chika	19	F

NOTE

1. The names of the participants used in this study are pseudonyms. This was done intentionally in order to protect the identity of the respondents.

REFERENCES

Abu-Lughod, J. 1989. *Before European Hegemony*. Oxford: Oxford University Press.

Abu-Lughod, L. 1993. "Bedouins, cassettes and technologies of public culture, Middle East report." *Popular Culture* 159: 7–11; 47.

Adeniyi, A. 2007. "Nigerian Diaspora and the virtual construction of identity." Proceedings of the Institute of Communications Studies (ICS). Post-Graduate.

Agugua, A. 2018. A personal interview with Dr. Augustine Agugua, a lecturer in the Department of Sociology. University of Lagos, Akoka, Lagos, Nigeria.

Akinrinade, S. and Olukoya, O. 2011. "Historicising the Nigerian Diaspora: Nigerian Migrants and Homeland Relations." *Turkish Journal of Politics* 2 (2).

Aksoy, A. and Robins, K. 2003. "Banal Transnationalism: The Difference that Television Makes," in Karim H. Karim (ed.), *The Media of Diaspora*, 89–104. London: Routledge.

Alakija, O. 2016. "Mediating home in Diaspora: Identity construction of first and second generation Nigerian immigrants in Peckham, London." Doctoral dissertation presented to the faculty of the University of Leicester, UK, on November 17.

Alonso, A. and Oiarzabal, P. 2010. *Diasporas in the New Media Age: Identity, Politics, and Community*. Las Vegas: University of Nevada Press.

Altheide, L. and Schneider, C. 2013. *Qualitative Media Analysis* (vol. 38). Thousand Oaks, CA: Sage.

Anderson, B. 1993. "The new world disorder." *New Left Review* 193: 13.

Anene, Austin. 2019. Oral interview with father of three adolescent Nigerian Americans.

Awokoya, J. 2012. "Identity Constructions and Negotiations among 1.5- and Second-Generation Nigerians: The Impact of Family, School, and Peer Contexts." *Harvard Educational Review* 82 (2): 255–281, 325.

Bailey, O., Georgiou, M., Springer, R. 2007. *Transnational Lives and the Media: Re-imagining Diasporas*. Chicago: Routledge.

Balogun, O. 2011. "No necessary tradeoff: Context, life course, and social networks in the identity formation of second-generation Nigerians in the USA." *Ethnicities* 11 (4): 436–466. Accessed June 16, 2022. DOI: https://doi.org.proxyhu.wrlc.org/10.1177/1468796811415759.

Baran, S. J. and Davis, D. K. 2009. *Mass Communication Theory Foundations, Ferment and Future*. New York: Wadsworth, 408.

Blunt, A. 2007. "Cultural geographies of migration: Mobility, transnationality and Diaspora." *Progress in Human Geography Journal* 31 (5): 684–694.

Boyatzis, R. 1998. *Transforming qualitative information: Thematic analysis and code development*. Thousand Oaks, CA: Sage publication.

Brubaker, R. 2005. "The 'Diaspora' Diaspora." *Ethnic and Racial Studies* 28 (1): 1–19.

Brubaker, R. 2009. "Ethnicity, Race, and Nationalism." *Annual Review of Sociology* 35: 21–42.

Chacko, E. 2019. "Fitting in and standing out: Identity and transnationalism among second-generation African immigrants in the United States." *African and Black Diaspora: An International Journal* 12 (2): 228–242.

Christoph, V. 2012. "The role of the mass media in the integration of migrants." *Journal Compilation International Mind, Brain, and Education Society* 6 (2): 97–107.

Clark, M. 2008. "Identity among first and second generation African immigrants in the United States." *African Identities* (6): 169–181. Accessed June, 16, 2022. DOI: https://doi.org/10.1080/14725840801933999.

Codjoe, H., Abdi, A., Hayfron, J., Laryea, S., Deiwert, G., Okeke-Ihejirika, P., Kumsa, M., Yesufu, A., Spitzer, D. 2005. *The African Diaspora in Canada: Negotiating Identity and Belonging*. Calgary: University of Calgary Press.

Cooper, B. 2008. "Women out of Africa Diaspora, gender and identity: Twinning in three diasporic novels." *A Journal of English Studies* 25 (1): 51–65.

Crane, D. 2002. "Culture and globalization: Theoretical models and emerging trends." *Global culture: Media, arts, policy, and globalization*. New York: Routledge, 1–25.

Creese, G. and Kambere, E. 2003. "What Colour is Your English?" *Canadian Review of Sociology and Anthropology* 40(5): 565–573.

Croucher, Stephen M., Oommen, Deepa, and Steele, Emily L. 2009. "An examination of media usage among French-Muslims." *Journal of Intercultural Communication Research* 38 (1): 41–57. DOI: 10.1080/1747575090347.

Curtis, A. 2005. *Nationalism in The Diaspora: A Study of the Kurdish Movement.* Universiteit Utrecht.

Dayan, D. 1999. "Media and Diasporas: Fragile Communities, Particularistic Media." In Gripsrud, Jostein (ed.), *Television and Common Knowledge*, 18–33. London: Routledge.

Dolan, R., Conduit, J., Fahy, J., and Goodman, S. 2015. "Social media engagement behavior: A uses and gratifications perspective." *Journal of Strategic Marketing* 24 (3–4): 261–277.

Elam, G. and Chinouya. 2000. "Feasibility Study for Health Surveys among Black African Populations Living in the U.K.: Stage 2—Diversity among Black African Communities." Manuscript Prepared for the Department of Health. National Center for Social Research.

Elias, N. 1998. *On civilization, power, and knowledge*. Chicago: University of Chicago Press.

Faist, T. 2010. "Towards transnational studies: World theories, transnationalisation and changing institutions." *Journal of Ethnic and Migration Studies* 36 (10): 1665–87.

Fortunati, L., Pertierra, R., and Vincent, J. 2012. *Migration, diaspora, and information technology in global societies*. New York: Routledge.

Georgiou, M. 2001. "Crossing the boundaries of the ethnic home: Media consumption and ethnic identity construction in the public space: The case of the Cypriot community centre in north London." *International Communication Gazette* 63 (4): 311–29. DOI: https://doi.org/10.1177/0016549201063004003.

Georgiou, M. 2006. *Diaspora, identity and the media: diasporic transnationalism and mediated spatialities*. Cresskill, NJ: Hampton Press Inc.

Gerstl-Pepin, C. 2015. "Popular media portrayals of inequality and school reform in the wire and waiting for 'Superman.'" *Peabody Journal of Education* 90 (5): 691–710.

Gillespie, M. 1995. *Television, Ethnicity and Cultural Change*. London and New York: Routledge.

Gilroy, P. 1993. *The Black Atlantic: Modernity and Double Consciousness*. Cambridge: Harvard University Press, 193, 115.

Halualani, R., Mendoza, L., Drzewiecka, J. 2009. "'Critical' Junctures in Intercultural Communication Studies: A Review." *The Review of Communication* 9 (1): 17–35.

Hansen, A., Cottle, S., Negrine, R., and Newbold, C. 1998. *Mass communication research methods*. London: Macmillan.

Harrison, K. 2000. "Television viewing, fat stereotyping, body shape standards, and eating disorder symptomatology in grade school children." *Communication Research* 27 (5): 617–40.

Hernandez, H. 2015. "New African Diaspora." Oxford Bibliographies. Last modified: June 28, 2016. Accessed June, 16, 2022. DOI: 10.1093/obo/9780190280024-0044.

Heyd, D. and Honkanen, M. 2015. "From Naija to Chitown: The New African Diaspora and digital representations of places." *Discourse, Context and Media* 9: 14–23.

Hornik, R. and Kelly, B. 2007. "Communication and Diet: An overview of Experience and Principles." *Journal of Nutrition Education and Behavior* 39 (2): 5–12.

Hume, S. 2010. "Ethnic and national identities of Africans in the United States." *Geographical Review* 98 (4): 496–512. Accessed June 16, 2022. DOI: Onlinelibrary. wiley.com/doi/abs/10.1111/j.1931-0846.2008.tb00314.x.

Ifinedo, P. 2016. "Applying uses and gratifications theory and social influence processes to understand students' pervasive adoption of social networking sites: Perspectives from the Americas." *International Journal of Information Management* 36 (2): 192–206.

Iwuagwu, O. 2018. A personal interview with Dr. Obi Iwuagwu, an associate professor in the Department of History and Strategic Studies. University of Lagos, Akoka, Lagos, Nigeria.

Jenkins, R. 2008. *Social Identity*. London: Routledge.

Johnson, M. and McKay, J. 2011. "Mediated diasporas: Material translations of the Philippines in a globalized world." *South East Asia Research* 19 (2): 181–96. Special Issue. DOI:10.5367/sear.2011.0047.

Jones, A. 2008. "Cyber-extended identity among 1.5 and 2nd generation female Armenian immigrant high school students: A segmented assimilation." A dissertation presented to the Faculty of the Rosier School of Education University of Southern California in Partial Fulfillment of the Requirements for the Degree Doctor of Education Ethnic Studies.

Karim, H. Karim. 1998. "From Ethnic Media to Global Media: Transnational Communication Networks among Diasporic Communities." International Comparative Research Group, Strategic Research Analysis Canadian heritage, WPTC-99-02, 1–22.

Karim, H. Karim. 2003. "Mapping Diasporic Mediascapes." In In Karim, H. Karim (ed.), *The Media of the Diaspora: Mapping the Globe*, 1–16. London, New York: Routledge Taylor and Francis Group.

Karim, H. Karim. 2006. "American Media's Coverage of Muslims: The Historical Roots of Contemporary Portrayals." In Poole, Elizabeth, and Richardson, John E. (eds.), *Muslims and the News Media*, 116–27. London, GBR: I. B. Tauris.

Karim, H. Karim. 2012. "Are Ethnic Media Alternative?" In Kozolanka, Kirsten, Mazepa, Patricia, and Skinner, David (eds.), *Alternative Media in Canada*, 1–18. Vancouver: UBC Press, ProQuest Library.

Katz, E., Blumler, J., and Gurevitch, M. 1974. "Utilization of Mass Communication by the Individual." In: Blumler, J. G. and Katz, E. (eds.) *The Uses of Mass Communication: Current Perspectives in Gratification Research*. Beverly Hills, CA: Sage, 71–92.

Kitzinger, J. 1995. "Introducing focus groups." *British Medical Journal* 311 (7000): 299–302.

Konadu-Agyemang, K., Takyi, B. K., Arthur, J. 2006. *The new African Diaspora in North America: Trends, community, building and adaptation*. Lanham, MD: Lexington Books.

Korhan, O. and Ersoy, M. 2016. "Usability and functionality factors of the social net-work site application users from the perspective of uses and gratification theory." *Quality and Quantity* 50 (4): 1799–1816.

Ledbetter, A., Taylor, S., Mazer, J. 2016. "Enjoyment fosters media use frequency and determines its relational outcomes: Toward a synthesis of uses and gratifications theory and media multiplexity theory." *Computers in Human Behavior* 54: 149–157.

Logan, R. and Deane, G. 2003. "Black Diversity in Metropolitan America." Unpublished manuscript.

Macnamara, R. 2005. "Media contents analysis: Its uses, benefits and best practice methodology." *Asia Pacific Public Relations Journal* 6 (1): 1.

Madianou, M. 2002. "Mediating the Nation: News, Audiences and Identities in Contemporary Greece," (Published doctoral dissertation). London School of Economics and Political Science. Sage.

Madianou, M. 2005. "Contested communicative spaces: identities, boundaries and the role of the media." *Journal of Ethnic and Migration Studies* 31 (3): 521–41.

Madianou, M. 2006. *Mediating the Nation: News, Audiences and the Politics of Identity*. London: UCL Press.

Mitra, A. 2001. "Marginal voices in cyberspace." *New Media & Society* 3 (1): 29–48.

Morley, D. 1980. *Nationwide: Structure and Decoding*. London: British Film Institute.

Mustapha, L. and Wok, S. 2015. "Exploring the agenda-setting potential of homeland online newspapers on perceptions of election issues among diasporic Nigerians in Malaysia." *Intellectual Discourse* 23 (2): 275–298.

Neuendorf, K. 2002. *The content analysis guidebook.* Thousand Oaks, CA: Sage Publications.

Newbold, K. and Campos, S. 2011. "Media and Social Media in Public Health Messages: A Systematic Review." *McMaster Institute of Environment and Health Journal, West* Hamilton. Accessed June, 16, 2022. www.mcmaster.ca/mieh.

Noar, S. 2006. "A 10-year Retrospective of Research in Health Mass Media Campaigns: Where do we go from here?" *Journal of Health Communication* 11 (1): 21–42.

Nwabara, O. 2017. "New Routes to the African Diaspora(s): Locating 'Naija' identities in transnational cultural productions." Dissertation submitted to the faculty of Michigan State University.

Ogunyemi. 2018. "Mediating identity crisis: A discourse analysis of conflict reporting in the African diasporic press in the United Kingdom." "Crossings." *Journal of Migration and Culture* 9 (11): 107–122.

Oh, D. 2012. "Mediating the boundaries: Second generation Korean adolescents use of transnational Korean media as markers of social boundaries." *The International Communication Gazette* 74 (3): 258–76.

Ong, J. 2009. "Watching the nation, singing the nation: London–based Filipino migrants' identity constructions in news and karaoke practices." *Communication, Culture & Critique* (2): 160–81.

Ong, J. and Cabañes, J. 2011. "Engaged, but not immersed: tracking the mediated public connection of Filipino elite migrants in London. South East Asia." *Research* 19 (2): 197–224. DOI: 10.5367/sear.2011.0047.

Onyejekwe, O. 2018. "The necessary step for Nigerians in the USA. The Daily Dose." Ozy. Accessed June 16, 2022. https://www.ozy.com/.

Punch newspaper. 2018. "Trapped between cultures." www.punching.com, November 18, 2018.

Research Base. 2022. "Uses and Gratification Theory." Accessed June, 16, 2022. https://researchbase.com.ng/uses-and-gratification-theory/.

Rivers, N. 2012. "No Longer Sojourners: The complexities of racial ethnic identity, gender, and generational outcomes for Sub-Saharan Africans in the USA." *International Journal of Population Research. Volume 2012.* Accessed June 16, 2022. https://www.hindawi.com/journals/ijpr/2012/973745/.

Roberts, S. 2005. "More Africans enter US than in Days of slavery." *New York Times,* February 21. Accessed June, 16, 2022. www.nytimes.com/2005/02/21/nyregion/21africa.html.

Robins, Kevin and Asu Aksoy. 2000. "Negotiating spaces: Media and cultural practices in the Turkish diaspora in Britain, France and Germany." *Transnational Communities Programme*: ESRC. Available at http://www.transcomm.ox.ac.uk.

Rowley, S. J., Sellers, R. M., Chavous, T. M., Smith, M. A. 1998. "The relationship between racial identity and self-esteem in African American college and high school students." *Journal of Personality and Social Psychology* 74 (3): 715–724.

Sabatier, C. 2008. "Ethnic and national identity among second-generation immigrant adolescents in France: The role of social context and family." *Journal of Adolescence* 31 (2): 185–205.

Sanyu, A. 2018. "New media, diasporic identity and social exclusion: A study of everyday practices of identity negotiation among second-generation Ghanaian women in Hamburg." *Journal of Migration and Culture* 9 15): 29–43, 15.

Schlesinger, P. 2000. "The nation and communicative space." In Tumber, Harold (ed.), *Media Power Professionals and Politics*, 99–115. London: Routledge.

Sehee, H., Jinyoung, M., Heeseok, L. 2015. "Antecedents of social presence and gratification of social connection needs in SNS: A study of Twitter users and their mobile and non-mobile usage." *International Journal of Information Management* 35 (4): 459–471.

Sharkdam, W., Akinkuotu, O., and Ibonye, V. 2014. "The Nigerian Diaspora and National Development: Contributions, Challenges, and Lessons from Other Countries." *Kritika Kultura* 23 (23): 292–342. Accessed June 16, 2022. https://www.researchgate.net/publication/265569685_THE_NIGERIAN_DIASPORA_AND_NATIONAL_DEVELOPMENT_CONTRIBUTIONS_CHALLENGES_AND_LESSONS_FROM_OTHER_COUNTRIES.

Silverstone, R. and Georgiou, M. 2005. "Editorial introduction: Media and minorities in multicultural Europe." *Journal of Ethnic and Migration Studies* 31 (3): 433–41.

Smith, S. 2019. "Purple visions of blackness: Prince's expansion of the depictions of black experiences through his music videos." *Howard Journal of Communications* 30 (2): 180–195.

Spring, R. 2002. "Uses and Gratifications/ Dependency Theory." Accessed June, 16, 2022. http://zimmer.csufresno.edu/~johnca/spch100/7-4-uses.htm#:~:text=As percent20Jay percent20Blumler percent20points percent20out,Blumler percent2024) percent20It percent20is percent20clear.

Sreberny, A. 2005. "Not only, but also: Mixedness and media." *Journal of Ethnic and Migration Studies* 31 (3): 443–59.

Sulaiman, A. 2016. "Nation, Nationalism, and Other Intervening Concepts: The Tensions, Contentions in Their Meanings." *Research on Humanities and the Social Sciences* 6 (12): 81–84.

Terrazas, A. 2009. "African immigrants in the United States." Migration Policy Institute. www.migrationinformation.org/USFocus/display.cfm?id=719. Accessed June 16, 2022.

USA Census Bureau. 2002. "Profile of selected demographic and social characteristics of people born in Nigeria in the United States." Accessed June 16, 2022. www.census.gov/population/cen2000/stp-159/STP-159-nigeria.pdf.

USA Census Bureau American Community Survey. 2010a. B04003. Total ancestry reported 2005−2009. American Community Survey 5-Year Estimates. American Fact Finder.

Vertovec, S. 1999. "Three meanings of 'diaspora' exemplified among South Asian religions." *Diaspora* 7 (2).

Watson, M. 2004. "Africans to America: The Unfolding of Identity." *A Journal of African Migration.* Accessed June 16, 2022. https://www.researchgate.net/publication/26414576_Africans_to_America_The_Unfolding_of_Identity.

Web, N. 2012. "Home across the Atlantic? Views on the maintenance of the Portuguese culture in Port Elizabeth, South Africa." *Society in Transition* 30 (1).

Wiio, O. 2009. *Communication usually fails—except by accident: Wiio laws and the future of communications.* Espoo, Finland: Delta Books.

Williams, P. 2013. *Paul Gilroy: Routledge Critical Thinkers.* New York: Routledge, 93, 113, 114.

Chapter 13

Relevance of Nigerian Traditional Communication Systems in the Digital Space

Des Wilson

African communication systems comprise a complex of multiple channels and media which are used in socialization. In this chapter, I intend to show that it is irrelevant to raise the issue of relevance of Indigenous Communication System (ICS) because they have never been irrelevant in Africa nor in any part of the world where they are used. What we refer to as ICS is a system of indigenous African communication media and channels. These channels and media are only traditional to Africa because they employ devices which may be used for other purposes in other cultures around the world.

In other words, the instruments or devices and channels used in indigenous communication may be used for other purposes in other continents. Thus in ethnocommunicological studies there are traditional communication instruments unique to certain cultures, which help to define the character, nature, and functions of these instruments as they make human communication possible.

DEFINING OUR TERMS

Before I go into greater detail about this topic, let me attempt here to make some conceptual and semantic distinctions between some of the major terms used in this chapter. The key terms in this chapter include the following: Relevance, African Communication System (ACS), Digital Space and Traditional Indigenous Communication.

Relevance is used here largely to reflect "the quality or state of being closely connected or appropriate." Thus when we talk about relevance of the African Communication System (ACS) we refer to the connectedness, appropriateness, applicability or pertinence of ACS in the digital space. So what we are examining is whether the ACS has any appropriate or relevant role or function in our digital world; even though the opposite question can also be asked: Is the digital space relevant to the African communication system? This can be resolved as the paradox of a dichotomous communication perspective. Perhaps what one can talk about here is whether there is the possibility of convergence of the African system with the digital system.

Digital Space is the space created within the world of the internet. Within this space you can develop platforms which other visitors to these platforms can use to interact with other users on the platforms they have developed. It also refers to what is displayed on the screen of digital devices such as laptops, computers, smart phones, television monitors, tablets, Ipads, and so forth.

African Communication Systems is a term which refers to a multimedia system of indigenous, interpersonal communication devices and instruments used in many parts of Africa but which are not necessarily unique to Africa. It is a system of autochthonous communication which employs various African language groups based on an order, code, or practice accepted from the past and handed down through beliefs and customs, and by word of mouth, or by example without instruction. Barber (1997, pp. 1–17) explains that this system, which she refers to as traditional communication (see Wilson 1981, 1988), is "the purely oral communication expressed in exclusively indigenous African languages or images, and coming from or alluding to the pre-colonial past."

Barber (1997), a British cultural anthropologist, goes on to contrast this form of communication with the Euro-American systems which she describes as "elite communication designed for a world formed by higher education, full mastery of European languages and representational conventions, defined by its cultural proximity to metropolitan centers, and addressed to a minority but international audience."

Communication, as we know it, has different facets, skills, and kinds. Traditionally, in the Western perspective, communication has always been seen as being of four kinds, namely, Speaking, Writing (Productive Skills), Listening, and Reading (Receptive Skills). But today, communication has been broken into additional types or kinds namely, Visual Representation, Silence, Nonverbal communication, and Visual literacy, which deals with understanding visual images.

All these aspects are covered in our view of indigenous or traditional communication systems except that less attention is paid to writing and reading because the early African writings, outside the Egyptian hieroglyphics and the over 400-letter alphabet system of Ethiopia, revolved largely around symbolgraphy and the cryptic writing of the "Nsibidi" found in Cross River, Akwa Ibom, Ebonyi, Abia (Nigeria), Western Cameroon, and the Ifa divination signs (Southwest Nigeria), the Vai alphabet system of Liberia and Sierra Leone.

Various terms have been employed to describe the African communication system which is a system of systems. Such terms include: oramedia (Ugboajah 1985), traditional communication (Wilson 1988), nonformal communication, African communication, indigenous communication, folk-communication, ritualistic communication, interpersonal communication, man-media, among other labels which are continuously being used to describe this inchoate new discipline.

Hachten (1971, p. 171) refers to the indigenous type of communication as "informal channels of communication." Ansu-Kyeremeh sees indigenous communication systems as:

> any form of endogenous communication which by virtue of its origin from, and integration into a specific culture, serves as a channel for messages in a way and manner that requires the utilization of the values, symbols, institutions, and other of the lost culture through the unique qualities and attributes. (2005, p. 7)

Despite this, the use of these forms of communication are widespread in Africa and constitute the traditional communication systems of the continent. The digital space which we envisage can be a platform for expanding the scope of our communication enterprise and legitimizing our content. It is through this interface that we can bring a greater credibility to our messages. This represents the foundation of the thinking on integration—that is, bringing African and modern media together in a dynamic, critical relationship in order to make our communication more effective.

Thus media integration is conceived of as a deliberate policy of bringing two or more media systems together to create a mutually beneficial mix. Such a mix cannot be based on a forced parity or balance between the systems. The principle of this integration plan is that the relationship should be based on a balance of strength (credibility, advantages of reach, effectiveness, fidelity, and accessibility).

The idea of media integration was first mooted by UNESCO in the 1970s and although it has been accepted, a standard approach based on the above relationship plan has not been developed. Although the idea is popular among development scholars, the question has been the how and wherefore of the mix. The media integrationist school whose origin is traceable to the early 1970s was responsible partly for the proposals which inspired the agitation for a New World Information and Communication Order. Foremost among these scholars were Herbert Schiller, Karl Nordenstreng, Frank Ugboajah, and the Irish diplomat Sean MacBride.

Integration does not mean the cannibalization of another system or medium by a dominant one. In spite of the advances made in this regard through the efforts of UNESCO in the 1980s and other regional bodies in Africa, Asia, and Latin America, the stiff opposition spearheaded by the Ronald Reagan (US) and Margaret Thatcher (UK) administrations put an end to the quick realization of the goal.

Later efforts by Wilson, Unoh, Nwabueze, and a younger generation of Nigerian and African scholars have adopted this media interactionist approach and extended the frontiers of knowledge. This has given birth to the trado-modern communication model which Wilson proposed in 1988 in a landmark study of the Old Calabar Province which today embraces Cross River and Akwa Ibom states, as seen in Figure 13.1.

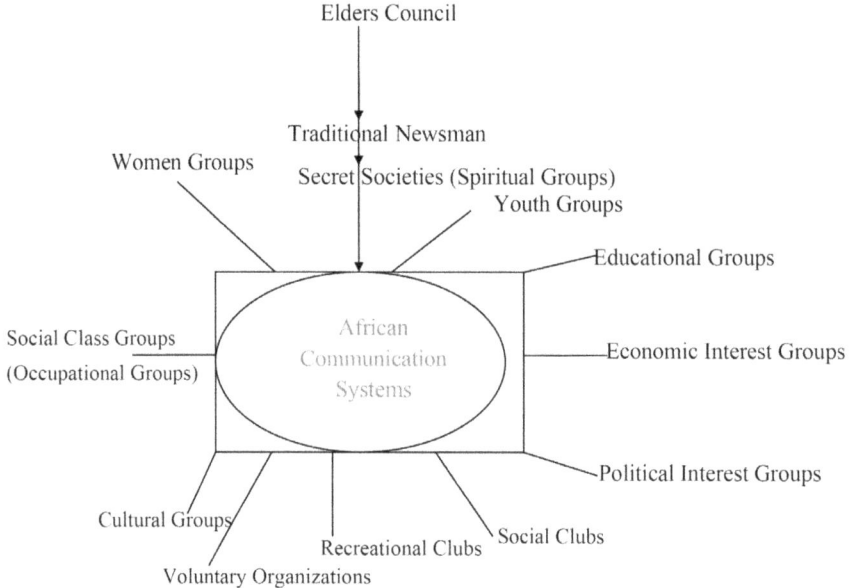

Figure 13.1. Formal and Informal Channels of Communication.
Source: Author created.

TARGET AUDIENCE OF AFRICAN
COMMUNICATION SYSTEM

Under the African communication system, the audience is not as amorphous or variegated as we find in the mass media population. Rural Africa is usually not organized along the formal dichotomous divisions between the more homogenous, homophilous social relationships and the heterogeneous.

Basically, traditional communication is operated largely from the interpersonal perspective and socioeconomically as a monocultural system. In examining this system, we ought to try to understand the nature of traditional society. And this should showcase the organization, leadership structure, legitimation processes, politics, religion, culture, traditional rulership institutions and the formal and informal channels used for communication in the society.

The message from the traditional communication system is not directed at the social isolate watching, say a football World Cup match alone in his living room, or the white-collar worker speeding home from work and other city residents seeking to catch up on prime-time news on cable television, or purring through *Business Day* newspaper.

The audience of the African communication system can be segmented into *rural, rural-urban* (or *semi-urban*) and *urban*. Thus, receivers in large traditional cities such as urban: Lagos, Kano, Benin, Sokoto, and Calabar, and in less traditional cities like Eungu, Jos, Port Harcourt, Eket, and Abuja, who depend on all forms of communication, both traditional and modern, are able to use both systems either independently or in combination to satiate their information needs.

Generally, the audience for traditional communication is made up of the ruralites. It is estimated to comprise about 70 percent of Africa's population. In the rural areas, we find the following groups of audience not necessarily segmented.

a. Rural audience: farmers, fishermen, blacksmiths, tradesmen, cyclists, teachers, traditional artisans and artistes, rulers, peasants, professional messengers, masquerade groups, the unemployed, etc.
b. Rural-urban audience: General receivers, formal and informal groups, societies, traditional institutions, tricyclist, motorcyclists, the unemployed, etc.
c. Urban: industrialists, businessmen, teachers, taxi and bus drivers, tricyclists, civil servants, industrial workers, tradesmen, university and college teachers, political leaders, modern commercial centers (supermarkets, modern markets, a large army of the unemployed, etc).

Communicative activities in traditional society are similar in so many ways to modern communication practices. Communication in traditional society is a constantly changing dynamic function involving exchange of meaning, interaction and sharing of meaningful symbols. African communication is transactional such that a change in one element of the process can automatically alter the other elements of the process.

Thus, communication today can influence the content of future communication messages. We all seem to agree that when a person initiates a verbal communication contact, he is tentatively labeled a source (or sender) and their contact may be called a receiver (or destination). Both of them will be involved in a verbal exchange where each monitors and tries to regulate each other's response such as level of interest, understanding, visual responses like a smile, eye movement, and any other symbolization that will "encourage" or "discourage" or even change the content of the discussion. These reactions are critical elements in interpersonal communication. These reactions or responses are also referred to as feedback because their contents feed the conversation and make it a helpful or unhelpful contribution depending on its nature.

African communication instruments are deployed around events and specific instruments or devices and are used to convey messages that are meant for receivers in groups, associations, societies, institutions, and individuals. Whether in the villages, rural areas, or in towns and cities, messages can be delivered to individuals or groups.

The perspective of African communication, which is often restricted to the use of the "town crier" (the traditional and official newsman), is grossly inadequate in explaining the multiplicity of processes involved in the information traffic between and among rural folks, and between rural folks and the urban/city dwellers.

It is therefore implicit in its operations that the media and channels used in traditional communication are interpersonal in nature, while others may be seen as applicable in group communication settings. They operate as person-to-person, person-to-group, and intragroup and intergroup communication activities.

Thus, the traditional newsman, sometimes generally referred to as messenger because their essential task is to deliver messages to individuals and groups in the communities, often provide an opportunity for feedback as they go round through the village paths and roads to deliver their messages.

In some communities they are known as "town masters" (Liberia), "asua-netop" (geographical south-east Nigeria), "gboun-gboun" (Yoruba of the political southwest, Nigeria), and known in popular communication literature as "town crier." They abound in every community in Africa and are sometimes defined by the instruments they employ to attract the attention of the listener in an oral presentation or visual attention through the use of symbolographs as in the use of icons as message bearers. When oral communication is involved, the instrument used serves as an attention-directing device. Each communication instrument has significance for the community in which it is used.

As has been clearly illustrated in Wilson (2015, p. 37) the various classes of indigenous communication devices perform specific functions and are used for messages directed at various target audiences, as seen in Table 13.1.

Thus, through musical instruments different messages are directed at audiences that the initiators wish to get their messages across to. Performances in town halls, village, squares, stadia, and so forth, apart from eliciting entertainment, relaxation, and opportunities for recreation, pointedly deliver development messages in campaigns for change. Participants at a Majek Fashek concert not only enjoy the rhythm and syncopation of songs like "So Long, Too Long," they relish the change message delivered through the haunting lyrics which move audiences to action. When this is broadcast through radio or television, it becomes mass communication, and this helps to establish the relevance of African communication systems in the digital space.

Table 13.1. Modes of Indigenous Nigerian Communication Media. *Source*: Wilson (2015, p. 37).

S/N	MODE OF COMMUNICATION	MEDIA/CHANNELS USED
1	INSTRUMENTAL	Idiophones—Wooden drum, Metal gong Ritual rattle, woodblock etc.
		Membranophones—Skin drum
		Aerophones—whistle, ivory horn, reed pipes, etc
		Symbology—Bamboo rind, *nsibidi*, tattoo, chalk marks
2	DEMONSTRATIVE	Music—Songs, Choral/Entertainment Music, Griots, Dirge, Elegy, Ballad, Pop, Rap, Spiritual
		Signal—Canon shots, gunshots, whistle call, campfire, drum.
3	ICONOGRAPHIC	Objectics—Charcoal, Kolanut, White clay, egg, beads, flag.
		Floral—Fresh palm frond, Plantain stems, boundary trees
4.	EXTRAMUNDANE	Incantatory—Ritual, Libation, Vision, Prayer
		Graphic—Obituary, In Memoriam
5.	VISUAL	Color—White cloth, red cloth, yellow, etc.
		Appearance—Dressing, hair style, body language.
6.	INSTITUTIONAL	Social—Marriage, Chieftaincy, Festival
		Spiritual—Shrine, masquerade.

In the same vein, the Gambian or Senegalese griot retells the history of his community to villagers or community members, and they learn the art of traditional information storage and retrieval as this traditional historian and literary artist employs literary codas to present the story of their past.

This performance can also be enacted on radio and television for a wider audience. Even the official channel, the traditional newsmen or gongman can also ply their trade using the digital space. The modern media can appropriate the credibility inherent in traditional media practices to boost its own content credibility in a world where fake news in the social media appears to render effect to the content of modern news media in our virtual world.

The relevance of African indigenous systems of communication can therefore be established through what Wilson (1988) had proposed as a trado-modern communication model of communication in which a select group of indigenous instruments can be technically integrated into a modern system and vice versa in order to produce a viable, effective and credible content for a world audience that has become increasingly incredulous about the overwhelming influence of the unverified content in the social and modern media.

The operation of this model has to be determined by experts in indigenous (traditional) communication practices and their counterparts in the modern media, as seen in Figure 13.2.

For this to be feasible, issues of language, technology, economy, and training have to be addressed. For instance, since many African communities have various languages, what language can this model adopt in reaching the homophonous and heterophilous populations especially in Africa? In parts

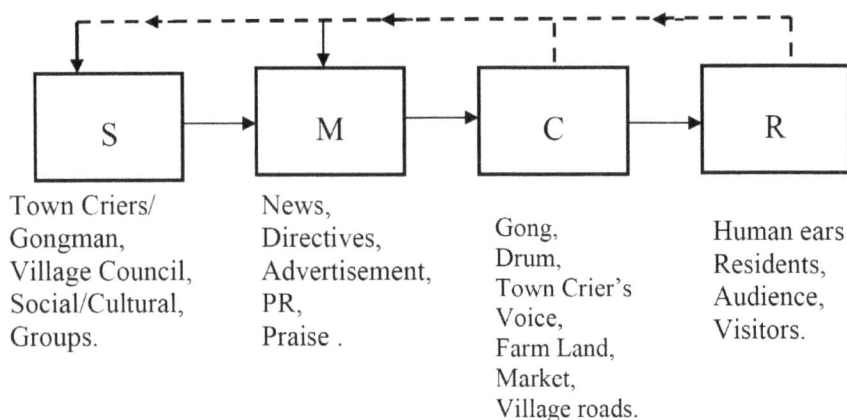

S	M	C	R
Town Criers/ Gongman, Village Council, Social/Cultural, Groups.	News, Directives, Advertisement, PR, Praise .	Gong, Drum, Town Crier's Voice, Farm Land, Market, Village roads.	Human ears Residents, Audience, Visitors.

Figure 13.2 Traditional Communication Process.
Source: Author created.

of Africa where a few languages are spoken across borders as in East Africa (Swahili), West Africa (Hausa/Fulfulde), North Africa (Arabic); this problem could be overcome to a large extent. But in small language communities this may be difficult.

Again, in former colonial territories where a former colonial language has been adopted for a wider use, then we can also speak of the elites being more at home with English, French, Portuguese, Spanish, and Arabic.

Other issues of what form of technology can serve this purpose, the cost of funding this model and the manpower and skill that may be required which are yet indeterminate are daunting issues which the model has to address. Africans therefore have an obligation to develop the appropriate model to serve their respective countries. For in spite of the ubiquity of modern information and communication technologies and the fact that they tend to govern the lives of the people, the indigenous communication systems are, and will continue to be, with us. This view is shared by Cherry (1978) who states succinctly that new media cannot replace the old but can replace some of its functions. For example, is it possible to replace face-to-face interpersonal talk in homes and between husband and wife with discussions on a mobile phone?

The answer is simple. It is not possible except in a situation of estrangement. But can the warm embrace, eye contact, smile on the face, or general touch be captured in a phone conversation? Thus those futuristic prognostications can only excite us to think of a lifeless artificial machine-to-machine communication which can eventually lead to a kind of lost world and lost humanity.

Since human communication is purposive, everything that can make humanity realize its purpose must be employed to make communication effective so that we can realize the kind of meaningfulness and clarity we seek when we communicate with others.

Of course, it is clear that we cannot be communicating about nothing, not even for its own sake. The functions of indigenous African communication systems help to define the target audience for which we may use each instrument, device, or media of communication in order to achieve our objectives.

MEDIA INTEGRATION IN THE DIGITAL SPACE

The philosophy of integrating African media practice into Western media practice is a laudable one. But the challenge is: How can the integration be achieved? Furthermore, other questions can be asked: What are the elements that could be involved? From whose perspectives can the integration plan be driven? As noted earlier, some of the notable challenges that can be faced are: technological, financial, personnel, cultural, sociopolitical, and linguistic.

The technological issues are questions of appropriateness of technology, the type of technology, originating technology in the process, technology dominance, and subject paradigm.

The next is financial. Financial issues are those linked to national resource challenges, cost of technology, budgetary constraints, debt repayment, and resource allocation.

Third are issues of personnel linked to paucity of training facilities, knowledge/technology exchange, level of competence, and general requirements for training personnel for both systems.

Fourth, the sociocultural components of the proposal system, which could address fears of cultural/media imperialism include the fact of the undeveloped cultural inputs of the African system and the existence of a babel of cultural policy objectives.

Fifth, sociopolitical issues also would impact this model. There must be an understanding of the impact of such issues on society. The question can also be asked: Can technology bring about social and political disorientation? Yet there is still the issue of weak political leadership.

Finally, there is the question of language. With over 250 languages in Nigeria, for example, can a nation bring about a new and effective integration? Won't this large number of languages not bring about a babel of voices?

But can we say that media integration can provide the final solution to our communication challenges? Beyond these challenges we can ask further. In the process, what can we integrate? Is it technology, the initiating source, the message, the channel/medium?

All of these complexities can be explained as follows:

Source: Legitimation Process
                     Attribution
                     Type: Organizational source/Individuals and Groups
                     Community and Modern media
                     Consensual/utilitarian status
                     Personnel (traditional and modern) training process,
                     work ethics standard of training, language
                     Village Head
                     President/Governor/Vice Chancellor/Master-Servant

Message: Content, message type
                     News
                     General Information
                     Cultural elements—attitude, beliefs, values, activity
                     value orientation, time value orientation, work ethics

	Villagisation of vision Publicity, Advertisement, Announcement
Channel:	Choice of Medium—Oramedia, interpersonal, Broadcast, Print, Internet Idiophones, Aerophones, Membranophones Chordophones Choice of Technology—Big Media/Small media Technology—modern and tradition
Receiver:	Nature of Audience—Audience demographics and psychographics Characteristics of the audience Rural/Urban

The future of communication and development in Nigeria rests squarely on whether the leaders and drivers of development communication will pay serious attention to the potential integrative processes. Media integration is the successful implementation and efficient use of multimedia applications in society and in a particular communication system or network. It is the process of combining, incorporating, and homogenizing to arrive at an effective media mix.

Media integration is a term which describes the relationship between the units of two or more systems in a social setting and how they are connected by interpersonal communication channels. For example, the relationship or interconnectedness of traditional media and channels with modern communication systems like radio, television, and the internet, or Skype.

TECHNIQUES OF AFRICAN
COMMUNICATION SYSTEMS

As I have already discussed in the section on the target audience of indigenous communication, several techniques, channels, media, and strategies are used to advance the purposes of communication initiators. These include the use of oral/audio means, symbolography, visual media, combination with radio, television, and the internet, and so forth.

In this section my intention is to show the different modes and strategies that are used in traditional African societies to deliver development and other messages to members of the various communities, not from a central point

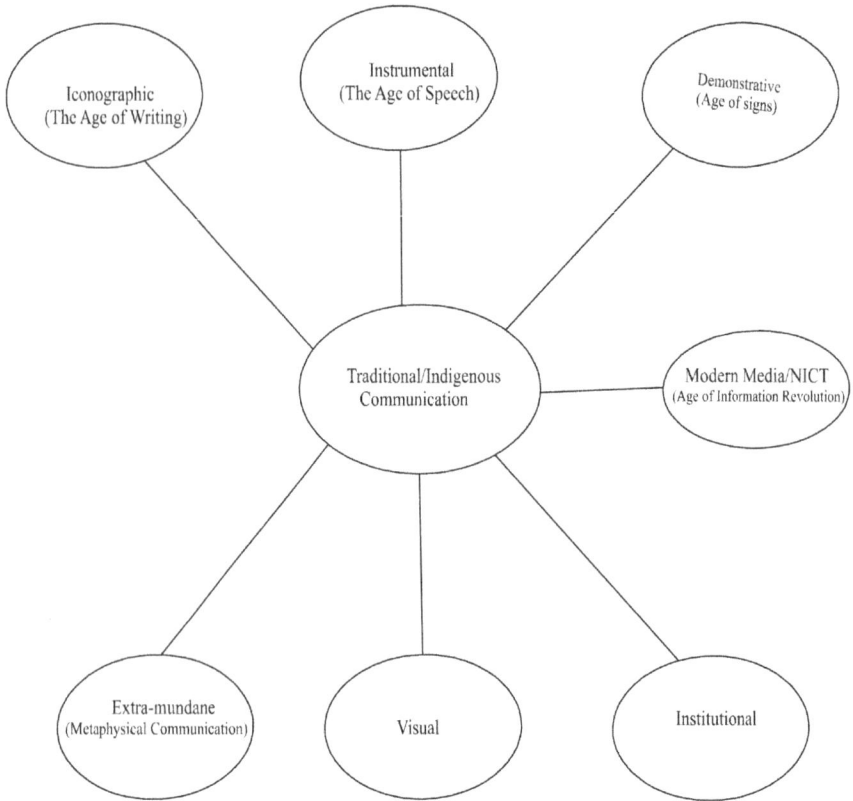

Figure 13.3. Modes of Traditional (Indigenous) Communication.
Source: Author created.

as in broadcasting or other mass media institutions but from decentralized village communication centers to the residents, as seen in Figure 13.3. This will include how the traditional centers deal with information dissemination activities in rural communities. Such activities are conducted through institutional, visual, iconographic, extra-mundane demonstrative and instrumental communication modes.

The media and channels of communication which are used within the above modes of communication are multifarious. Apart from the fact that there appears to be a scholastic bias against most things that come from the Third World, the situation is made worse by African scholars who have themselves abandoned the obligation to think for themselves and smarting from a battery of complexes bordering on intellectual inferiority, they have joined others in disparaging the trajectory of their own development, wishing to be welcomed into the Western school of thought as free agents and racially neutral scholars. Ironically, those who paved the way to these African thoughts were those who, out of curiosity, wished to see what lay in the minds of the people who dwelt in the Heart of Darkness. Indeed, they became the pioneers.

For years scholars and others involved in governance have tended to push for a relegation of the indigenous systems to the rubbish heap of history. Many are still fascinated by technology and have therefore not invested in original research, especially in the area of integrating traditional with modern communication systems whose idea continues to undergo critical changes. One other fact that must be borne in mind is that the African indigenous system is not just about technological mutations, but it is a system of culture, values, faith, education, community development, grooming, and to some extent, the use of technology appropriate to communication.

In its practice, just as marketing communication, public relations, advertising, and other adjunct fields of communication studies all use the mass media for the promotion of their activities; there is therefore no issue with the idea of indigenous communication systems combining as co-equals in the digital sphere. Today, in Africa, indigenous communication has greater credibility which the modern digital technology can leverage on for a more effective communication engagement.

CONCLUSION

I had noted earlier that the issue of relevance is a rather contentious one in the light of our present experience with traditional and modern media. It is reflective of an attitude which seems to suggest that the traditional system is an old paradigm that could perhaps be relegated to the Age of the Troglodytes. This is a product of the misconception and a lack of knowledge of how the traditional system works and how it is structured. A clear understanding of the indigenous communication processes freed from the obfuscation created by the limited perspective of the town crier model, would assure users and scholars of a virile interface between the ancient and modern. This is not difficult to achieve, for apart from the clearly visible challenges posed by technology, economy, language, and manpower, and with the present media mix in a convergent model of communication, it could be easy to deploy African communication systems for use within the digital space.

REFERENCES

Ansu-Kyeremeh, K., ed. 2005. "Indigenous Communication in Africa: A Conceptual Framework," in *Indigenous Communication in Africa: Concept, Application, and Prospects*. Accra: Ghana Universities Press.

Asante, Molefi Kete. 2012. "Marat and Human Communication: Supporting identity, culture and history without global domination." *Communication* 38 (2).

Barber, Karin. 1997. "Preliminary Notes on Audiences in Africa." *Africa: Journal of the International African Institute* 67 (3): 347–62. Accessed August 24, 2020. DOI: https://doi.org/10.2307/1161179.

Berger, Guy. 2012. "Theorizing African Communications: The bad news signaled by broadcast digital migration policy." *Communication* 38 (2).

Cherry, Colin. 1978. *World Communication: Threat or Promise.* Chichester, UK: Wiley.

du Plessis, Danie. 2012. "Introduction, African Communication Media Theory." *Communication* 38 (2): 123–126.

Hachten, W. 1971. *Muffled Drums: The News Media in Africa.* Ames: The Iowa State University Press.

Mutese, Molaika. 2012. "Towards an African centered and pan-African theory of communication: Ubuntu and the oral aesthetic perspective." *Communication* 38 (2).

Ngomba, Teke. 2012. "Circumnavigating de-westernization. Theoretical reflexivities in researching political communication in Africa." *Communication* 38 (2).

Obonyo, Levi. 2011. "Towards a theory of communication for Africa: The challenges for emerging democracies." *Communication* 37 (1): 1–20.

Ugboajah, F. 1985. "Oramedia in Africa," in *Mass Communication, Culture and Society in West Africa*, 165–86. London: Hans Zell.

Uwah, Innocent. 2012. "Identity and Culture in theorizing African perspectives of communication: The case of an African Cinematic model." *Communication* 38 (2).

Wilson, Desmond. 1981. "From the Gong to Electronics: A survey of mass communication in Old Calabar." In MA dissertation of the Department of Communication and Language Arts. University of Ibadan, Ibadan.

Wilson, Desmond. 1988. "A survey of Traditional and Modern Communication in Old Calabar." A PhD thesis of the Department of Communication and Language Arts. University of Ibadan, Ibadan.

Wilson, Desmond. 2015. "Ethocommunicology, Trado-Modern Communication and Mediamorphis in Nigeria." 44th Inaugural Lecture, April 30, 2015. University of Uyo, Uyo.

SECTION V

Communicating Health in the Nigerian Digital Space

Chapter 14

Communicating Health Information to the Rural Nigerian in the Digital Space

Olumuyiwa Odusanya

The World Health Organization (WHO) defines health as a state of complete physical, mental, and social well-being and not just the absence of disease or infirmity. This definition may be a challenge to many people who think of health first in terms of absence of diseases or symptoms such as fever, cough, and diarrhea. The comprehensive nature of the definition is even more important for non-communicable diseases (NCDs) such as cancers, hypertension, and diabetes, which at the onset of such diseases are insidious and the person may be apparently well for some time. Health is not achieved by factors in the health sector alone which focuses on provision of services including availability of manpower. Social and economic factors are major determinants of health. They include peace, justice, education, food, shelter, and employment. They go a long way in shaping and determining the health status of individuals, families, communities, and nations. Health must be seen as a resource for living and not the object of living.

Health literacy is another important concept in communicating health. Health literacy involves more than being able to read medical pamphlets. It includes the processes required to achieve an understanding of the health system, health conditions, and making informed decisions. Kuyinu et al. (2020) reported a 74 percent rate of health literacy in Lagos. Adequate levels of health literacy were found more significantly in females, the use of broadcast media and the internet as sources of information and being more comfortable with the use of the English language. This study highlights the importance of digital sources of health communication. Suka et al. (2015) reported that in

Japan, persons with sufficient information from multiple sources had higher levels of health literacy and were more likely to report good self-rated health. Karimi et al. (2014) on the other hand did not find any significant correlation between health literacy, health status, and health utilization in two districts in Iran.

Access to health information makes health services more accountable, promotes healthy behavior and self-care, and obtains knowledge which may lead to more appropriate use of services and lowers barriers to health services. A systematic review on health research focus in published papers showed that health information was the most frequently studied topic, whereas health literacy was the least. Cancers were the most frequently focused health condition and internet use was the most frequently mentioned technology for obtaining health information (Hu 2015). Without an understanding of and improvements in health literacy it may be difficult to connect with people.

Health promotion, another concept in health communication, is the process of enabling people to take control over the determinants of their health and improving them. The pillars of health promotion include healthy public policy, creating supportive environments, strengthening community actions, strengthening people skills, and reorienting the health services. These are key to health communication to all persons including the rural African.

PROFILE OF RURAL AFRICA

A rural area is defined by the national office of statistics in each country. They often have a low population density and large areas of undeveloped land. Very often government presence and modern facilities are absent. Educational institutions are often few, health facilities are sparse, and the major occupation is small-scale farming and petty trading. There is often a large proportion of the elderly in the population as many young people migrate to urban centers in search of better living conditions.

The rural African as well as the rural Nigerian is dispersed widely over the continent in a wide variety of geographical locations including deserts, mountains, rivers, plains, and in hard-to-reach communities, internally displaced persons camps and conflict zones. The diverse environment makes person to person contact challenging and moreover this is true for static health facility-based interventions. There are not enough health workers to undertake the assignment. Mass media methods have become the only practical means of effective communication to the rural Nigerian. It is tempting to claim that the rural African is illiterate or uneducated but that is an overstatement. Many have a primary level of education and those without can still be reached in their native language. The real challenge may be that of the health worker to effectively transmit health messages.

The prevalent health problems in rural Africa are largely communicable in origin. These include malaria, upper respiratory tract infections, diarrheal diseases, and vaccine-preventable diseases such as measles and whooping cough. The main causes are poor levels of hygiene, stagnant water, poor sanitation, and improper disposal of both liquid and solid waste.

The African continent is also in the grip of NCDS as the pooled prevalence of hypertension is 57 percent (Bosu et al. 2019). Due to the low level of information, many of these NCDs are attributed to mysterious forces. An apparently well person with elevated blood pressure may suddenly slump and die and is likely to be termed a "spiritual attack." The family may not even bother to have a postmortem examination to know the cause of the sudden death or how to prevent or protect themselves in the future. In rural Africa, many work practices are manual and labor dependent. Occupational health problems are also prevalent including snake bites, injuries, and lower back pain. Preventive occupational health services are largely unavailable to the small-scale worker in rural Africa.

COMMUNICATION ABOUT HEALTH

Communication refers to delivery of information. In the health sector, it is more than passive sharing of information. The objectives of health communication are to make health a valued community asset, to promote the health of individuals, and increase the utilization of health services. Health services may be provided but without adequate communication they may be underutilized.

Information required will be about common or prevalent health problems, their symptoms, and simple actions needed to prevent and treat them as well as the adoption of appropriate health behavior and uptake of services. The use of preventive services is of utmost importance. Such services include immunization and screening for cancers and other non-communicable diseases (NCDs). Screening tests lead to early detection, early treatment, and better survival rates. It is well known that breast cancer survival rates are very low in Africa compared with the developed nations (Odusanya, 2006). This is due in part to little information about the condition, lack of access to mammograms, and low uptake of screening tests including clinical breast examination. Whereas, there are opportunities to extend information through female school teachers as documented by Odusanya (2001).

The digital age presents a great opportunity to reach a large number of Africans in diverse places with health messages. The telephone density in

Nigeria, for example, is 88.184 percent and in South Africa 165.6 percent, both figures showing that mobile telephony may be a good starting point for communication. In addition, internet penetration on the continent is 39.3 percent compared to the world average of 58.8 percent and is much lower for the 62.9 percent for the rest of the world. However, for selected countries, the internet penetration is good and varies from 87.2 percent in Kenya, 72.5 percent in the Seychelles, 61.2 percent in Nigeria, 55 percent in South Africa and 48 percent in Egypt (www.internetworldstat.com, 2020).

The infrastructure for electronic communication is improving on the continent and can be leveraged for health. Capacity of mobile telephones can be taken advantage of to increase access to health and disseminate information. Jacobs et al. (2017) reported that one in three adults in the United States of America used the internet to diagnose or learn about a health condition. They noted that although the web is an easily available source of information it also creates inequalities in health information. Digital interventions designed to support decision making, information exchange, and shared accountability have been suggested as strategies to overcome inequalities between black men in the United States of America and their physicians (Sherman and Grande 2019).

There are three agents or parties to effective communication: the sender or expert with the message who may be the health worker or any other person so designated with expertise in communication; the message which is to be shared; and the focus of the message, which can be on understanding disease patterns, disease presentation, uptake of preventive services, utilization of health services, and healthy lifestyles. The messages must be authentic, factual, culturally acceptable, and delivered by trustworthy individuals. The channel of communication is of extreme importance. This will include the use of digital means and platforms. Such platforms or media include the town crier, radio, television, telephone, internet, and social media. Social media such as Facebook, WhatsApp, Instagram, and other chatting platforms are used a lot by young people. The use of video conferencing applications such as Google Meet and Zoom has become widespread.

The key issue is the clarity of the channel to prevent noise and wrong signals. A challenge of social media is availability of data and cost. Mechanisms such as sponsorship or bulk purchase or delivery of messages in formats that consume the least amount of data can be widely deployed. Then the primary focus is the target audience. Formative research must be done to identify audience characteristics such that the message is delivered in a way to have lasting intended impact. There must be monitoring and feedback to know what was understood, the barriers to the message, what worked and what changes need to be made. A few of the media that can be used to communicate with the rural African are further discussed.

CHANNELS OF COMMUNICATION
WITH THE RURAL NIGERIAN

Town Crier

The town crier is still relevant today as in many rural areas; this is the primary form of transmission of messages for the generality of the people. The mechanism is activated by the traditional institution and a schedule for the town crier is known with a provision for emergency dissemination of information as the need arises. The town crier, who is usually a male member of the community, is an important part of the culture and information received through him is seen as authentic and shared from person to person. Announcements concerning rites of passages, celebrations, taboos and warnings are made by the town crier. The health sector can utilize this medium for information through advocacy and training of the town crier. Such town criers can be selected as village health workers and become polyvalent information agents bringing health benefits to the community. A personal experience is known to have been used in a rural part of Edo State, Nigeria, to mobilize women to utilize immunization services.

Short Messaging Service (SMS)

Short message services or text or multimedia messaging services (MMs), where available, is another powerful tool for disseminating information to the rural Nigerian. The SMS requires condensed messages, usually 160 words or less, and can be translated in various official languages. Telecommunication organizations have exploited this tool to advertise various messages and products including songs. These companies can be approached to offer SMS free for the public good. The potential reach and effect of such messages are likely to be huge.

Conventional Media

Conventional media such as radio and television are still useful in reaching Africans. The radio is perhaps the most widely patronized media, especially in northern Nigeria. Torwel and Rodney (2010) showed that most newspaper coverage of health issues in Nigeria was good and provided readers with information and a knowledge base in health which can be used in their daily lives. Most newspapers are now available freely online thus increasing access. The radio was reported to be the most important source of health information for 73 percent of respondents in a survey in Akwa-Ibom State, Nigeria, but failed to convey information about sickle cell disease as the radio station workers were not aware and only 33 percent were adjudged to have adequate knowledge of sickle cell disease (Umana and Ojebode 2010). A further advantage is that most mobile phones come with an FM radio function. This way the phone becomes either a primary tool (for those without a radio) or secondary (for those with radio) for communication. Public information on new happenings, discoveries, important research findings on health and in the health sector, breaking news, short dramas, and drama skits can all be used to convey health messages.

Television is still relevant in rural areas. The Nigerian Broadcasting Commission is in the process of switching to digital broadcasting, which will enhance and make communication easier and clearer. In many houses, there is a television as it is a symbol of not being poor or backward. Many urban dwellers buy televisions for their families in rural areas to enhance recreation and entertainment. Besides, viewing centers for football and other sporting activities are found in many rural areas. This makes the television a useful medium for transiting health information. The additional advantage of visuals on television allows for more audience engagement, more impact, and more vivid messages and longer duration. Documentaries, films, interviews, drama, songs on health and health promoting behavior can be shared.

Social Media

Social media is a very useful tool for communicating health messages. Applications such as WhatsApp, Telegram, Instagram, Twitter, YouTube, and Facebook are readily available. They allow for text, audio, and video messages as well as for chain messages. They are useful for large audiences and for video conferencing. They have been used recently in the control of the Coronavirus pandemic. Users can generate their self-videos as well as voice notes to communicate with an unlimited audience. Drama skits, simple messages on disease prevention and appropriate behavior, and messages by role models and political leaders have all been featured. The problem with social media is validating the veracity of the information shared as it is prone to abuse.

Skype and other conferencing applications are an asset for the same purpose. They can be used for the purpose of e-health and telemedicine. Photographs of health problems and conditions can be shared in real time so that actions can be taken. For the rural African, where connectivity is available, these can be used to communicate with the nearest health facility and health personnel particularly in emergencies or disasters or in evolving health challenges. These facilities can be used to guide the deployment of resources before the health worker reaches the scenario or enroute to the facility.

CONCLUSION

The revolution of the digital age has made it easy for all peoples to receive information about their health. The tools needed are now readily available. Training of manpower, investment in digital infrastructure, initiating mechanisms of fact-checking, deployment of appropriate messages, monitoring and evaluation are important. There is the need for collaboration and training by both health workers and communication and ICT experts to ensure effective and efficient use of the digital media to promote the health of Nigerians. Other recommendations at improving digital communication include creating an enabling environment that will make knowledge easy to share. Lowering the cost of data is very important. Knowledge creation should be inclusive and a focus on open knowledge and research. The poor should participate in developing knowledge (Institute of Development Studies, 2015).

REFERENCES

Bosu, W. K., Reilly, S. T., Aheto, J. M. K., Zucchelli, E. 2019. "Hypertension in older adults in Africa: A systematic review and meta-analysis." *PLoS ONE* 14 (4): e0214934. Accessed March 26, 2020. https://doi.org/10.1371/journal.pone .0214934.

Hu, Y. 2015. "Health communication research in the digital age: a systematic review." *Journal of Communication in Health Care* 8, 260–289.

Institute of Development Studies. 2015. "The future of knowledge sharing in a digital age: Exploring impacts and policy implications for development." Evidence Report No. 123. Accessed September 29, 2020. www.itoca.org.

Jacobs, W., Amuta, A. O., Jeon, K. C. 2017. "Health information seeking in the digital age: An analysis of health information seeking behavior among US adults." *Cogent Social Sciences* 3 (1). Accessed September 29, 2020. http://dx.doi.org/10/1080 /23311886.2019.302785

Karimi, S., Keyvanara, M., Hosseini, M., Jazi, M. J., Khorasani, E. 2014. "The relationship between health literacy with health status and health care utilization in 18–64 years old people in Isfahan." *Journal of Communication and Health Promotion* 3: 75.

Kuyinu, Y. A., Femi-Adebayo, T., Adebayo, B. I., Abdurraheem-Salami, I., Odusanya, O. O. 2020. "Health Literacy: Prevalence and determinants in Lagos Nigeria." *PLoS ONE* 15 (8): e0237813. Accessed September 29, 2020. https://doi.org/10 .1371/journal.pone.0237813.

Odusanya, O. O. 2001. "Breast cancer: Knowledge, attitude and practice of female school-teachers in Lagos, Nigeria." *The Breast Journal* 7 (3): 171–175. Accessed September 29, 2020. http://doi.10.1046/j.1524-4741.1998.410062.x-i1.

Odusanya, O. O. 2006. "Breast cancer: Knowledge, attitudes, and practices in Africa." In *About Cancer in Africa*, edited by Ly, A., Khayat, D. Paris: Institut National Du Cancer, 73–80.

Sherman, L. D., Grande, S. W. 2019. "Building better clinical relationships with patients: An argument for digital health solutions with black men." *Health Services Insights* 12: 1–4. Accessed September 29, 2020. http://doi.10.1177 /1178632919834315.

Suka, M., Odajima, T., Okamoto, M., Masahiko, S., Igarashi, A., Ishhikawa, H. et al. 2015. "Relationship between health literacy, health information access, health behavior and health status in Japanese people." *Patient Educ Couns* 98: 66–668. Accessed September 29, 2020. http://doi.10.1016/j.pec.2015.02013.

Torwel, V. and Rodney, C. 2010. "Newspaper coverage of health issues in Nigeria." *African Communication Research* 3: 235–252.

Umana, E., Ojebode, A. 2010. "The failure of radio to communicate knowledge of sickle cell disorder in Nigeria." *African Communications Research* 3: 253–266.

SECTION VI

Theory and Practice

Chapter 15

Educational Broadcasting in Nigerian Digital Space

Comfort Memfin Ekpo

Education is the right of every child. Great leaders do not toy with the education of their citizens. It is the foundation upon which all other socioeconomic life is built, and it can be achieved through many means, one of them being the use of broadcast media. Broadcasting is a veritable strategy to create necessary ethical sensibilities in a community. It is the simple and cost-effective use of various gadgets to educate and inform members of the public globally. Over the decades, educational broadcasting has made significant contributions to meeting the educational needs of many nations. A typical American child, for instance, would have learned a lot about the world before entering kindergarten through exposure to the broadcasting media. Lately, as the COVID-19 pandemic began to spread across the globe, the majority of nations turned prominently on educational broadcasting.

THE CONCEPT OF EDUCATIONAL BROADCASTING

Conventionally, educational broadcasting refers to the use of television and radio programs that are particularly designed for intellectual stimulation. At times the term applies to other television and radio programs that are for public enlightenment and informative in nature. It is used in providing public service announcements, daily news, weather forecasts, documentaries, and so forth. Educational broadcasting is therefore the broad use of television or radio to educate a whole community. It is a modern tool used in educating members of the world. Educational broadcasting can be received at home or in an educational institution. Learning by oneself in the home through these media is often referred to as "distance education." Other broadcast programs do provide education in the form of entertainment; this too is another way of intellectual development. Examples of broadcast media include television (digital and analog), radio receivers, internet media (websites, personal blogs, podcasts, online streaming, voiceover internet protocol (VOIP), internet telephone, Skype, voice messaging, and so forth.

HISTORICAL BACKGROUNDS TO EDUCATIONAL BROADCASTING

Available literature reports that the first broadcast transmission was from a temporary station in 1895 on the Isle of Wight in the United Kingdom. By 1905/1906, an experimental radio broadcasting of music and speeches intended to reach a dispersed audience started. The year 1932, according to Ogunranti (1988) marked the emergence of educational broadcasting in Nigeria because the first radio receiving station began transmission in Lagos the same year. This had a great influence on education in Nigeria, particularly due to the quality of educational broadcast programs that were available to teachers and pupils. The first educational radio programs were for the English language and were broadcast once a week by the Radio Distribution Service (RDS) under the Post and Telegraphs Department (P&T).

The Nigeria Broadcasting Service (NBS) which was later established in 1951 inherited limited educational programs. This was the situation until 1957 when the Nigeria Broadcasting Corporation (NBC) was established. According to Olushola (1979), television in Nigeria and indeed in the whole of Africa was also introduced in that year. The Western Nigerian government realized that television was a better and more versatile medium than radio for educating the masses. To back it up, it was written in the charter establishing the Nigerian Television Authority, a provision for a fixed amount of time per week for educational television broadcasts. Olushola further confirmed this when he observed that about 50 percent of all the TV programs were devoted to education. Television sets were therefore distributed to the existing schools and colleges. The Eastern and Northern regional governments also followed suit a few years later by establishing their own television and radio stations. In 1969, according to Agun and Imogie (1988), the Northern Schools Broadcasting Unit which was responsible for the production of the content for the broadcast media was taken over by the Federal Schools Broadcast Unit (FSBU) with headquarters in Kaduna. Many African nations have a similar history of simple beginnings in the establishment and utilization of the broadcast media.

EDUCATIONAL BROADCASTING IN THE DIGITAL ERA

Digital era or computer age is merely a historical period that began in the early twentieth century. It is a period that is characterized by a rapid shift in Information and Communication Technology. The COVID-19 pandemic has been one of the biggest disruptions to education and entertainment the world has ever known, affecting more than 90 percent of the world's population of students; hence the twist by many countries to online based distance education, to ensure that learning never stops.

However, according to a recent study by the UNESCO Institute of Statistics (UIS) and the Teacher Task Force, it is observed that about 826 million students of the world's population are kept out of classrooms by the COVID-19 pandemic because they do not have access to a computer at home. Around 706 million students lack access to the internet and 56 million live in areas not covered by mobile networks. With that scenario, many of the deprived countries quickly found effective solutions using television and radio which have proven to be a good alternative in a context where online learning is not possible. It is worrisome to note that at least 9.7 million children globally may not be able to return to formal schooling as a result of budget cuts to education after the COVID-19 lockdown. Education stakeholders are exploring possible roles that educational broadcasting can play in filling the gaps in their circumstances.

Radio broadcasting has gone beyond imagination. With the current technology used by Google Play in Radio Garden that explores live radio broadcasts by rotating the entire world to access local radio stations. This visual of the world map with numerous green spots that provide links to local radio stations trending music and live broadcast is an overwhelming broadcast experience of the digital era.

There is also the use of smart class technology which permits both the learners and teachers to make online presentations, with the learners obtaining feedback from their teachers in less time than in a conventional structured classroom. Previously, students used to be excited as school television sets were rolled into their classrooms for teaching and learning events but with the digital age, learners simply get live stream videos from Google or YouTube broadcasting solutions.

THE SIGNIFICANCE OF EDUCATIONAL
BROADCASTING

Educational broadcasting has a unique role of increasing access to formal education and where the intellectual content has been effectively planned and delivered; they enhance learners' interest towards the learning concepts. Various African nations have tried to catch on the potentials of the broadcast media to meet their peculiar needs. In the Southern part of Africa, the broadcast media have been used to promote their socioeconomic development as well as extend the frontiers of their formal school system. Radio is largely their channel of choice to disseminate knowledge and enlightenment messages in rural areas. It is a more affordable technology and over the years it has proven itself as a dependable developmental tool. With the digital era where video streaming is trending, radio is still the dominant medium of mass communication in Africa. In attempts to bridge the learning gaps created, a lot of broadcast contents are aired using Skype video meetings, WhatsApp voice calls, and Zoom conferencing. Although availability of the requisite technology is still the major setback in utilizing these technologies.

Considering this technological divide, most countries around the world are using television or radio-based programs to implement distance education. Africa seems to be the most active in the efforts to leverage either TV or radio (70 percent), some combining both (34 percent of countries), while Europe and North America seem to be using less radio than other regions, yet very active in deploying TV-based distance education programs (http://radio.garden/live).

The value of educational broadcasts through television and radio also goes beyond the need of students alone. In some countries, these programs are conceived to provide intergenerational learning, including those in local languages. They also include issues such as health and psychosocial well-being, both of which are important in supporting populations affected by the threat of COVID-19.

Educational broadcasting plays vital roles in the education process globally by:

- encouraging a greater understanding of the subject matter because its presentation is done in clear, straight forward, and simple language
- promoting individualized learning because the listener or viewer can learn at his or her pace by listening to and or viewing the lesson personally without having to meet the real teacher
- disseminating large volumes of educational and informative messages to the audience economically

- checking schools' population explosion because it takes care of learners both young and old that could not be readily accommodated by the regular school program
- promoting equal access to educational opportunity for all learners because the mode of presentation is the same and uniform, no matter the number of times the presentation is done
- assisting in population enlightenment programs because of its coverage of a very wide area at a time. Moreover, the beneficiaries could easily be reached at their various locations without being assembled at a point for such an exercise

However, the setting-up and use of radio and television as tools to provide distance education do present major challenges, such as:

- the nonavailability of educational content in audio-visual formats with the use of radio
- difficulties of countries to produce content in quantity and quality in a short time
- the absence of preexisting partnerships for the design and broadcasting of the educational content
- the need for communication and collaboration between education specialists and the professionals of the audio-visual sector to produce quality educational programs
- the lack of the know-how and expertise in monitoring and evaluation of learning.

Reaching students and ensuring the continuity of education is the main goal of the initiative of educational broadcasting in a digital era like this. Most broadcasters would have to design their programs with more interactive components to capture the attention of learners, particularly with the youngest ones. For effective use of the broadcast media in the digital era, the designers require more training and retraining workshops. Several examples of prototype contents should be provided during the workshops to include the use of apps or videos as well as online quizzes.

CHALLENGES IN THE UTILIZATION
OF EDUCATIONAL BROADCASTING
IN A DEVELOPING NATION

Educational broadcasting as it is practiced in Nigeria is faced with a barrage of problems just as it is in most other developing countries. Some of the problems according to Kolade-Oje and Babalola (2004) include:

- Finance: A lot of money is expended on the planning and execution of educational broadcasting. Huge sums of money would have to be spent on purchasing the equipment as well as paying for the required manpower needed. The huge sum of money involved cannot be readily afforded by most developing countries in general and Nigeria where most inhabitants live below the poverty line. The voiceover internet protocol (VOIP) which is growing so much in use globally is not affordable because of its high bandwidth requirement. Individual governments also lack the will power to fully exploit the potentials of the broadcast media.
- Personnel: Lack of qualified and experienced personnel in educational broadcasting as a relatively new field of study has constituted a serious problem in the educational sector. For now, there are not enough personnel on educational broadcasting that could readily meet up with the demands of the teaming population.
- Equipment: The equipment that is being utilized in educational broadcasting is not available locally. It is mostly imported. This has posed a threat to educational broadcasting now that there is a global economic recession, the foreign exchange earnings that might be required might be difficult to get.
- Storage: The problem of storage is prominent in the tropics because most of the gadgets are better stored under cool temperatures. But here we are in the tropics where the weather is hot and harsh. The environment is not conducive for educational broadcasting equipment, which is mostly designed to be operated in the temperate region.
- Distance: Qualitative educational broadcasting could further be hindered by the distance of the listening and viewing centers to the broadcasting station. There might be some problems along with the communication pathway which is capable of hindering the reception of the educational broadcast messages, let alone those that might originate from both the encoding and decoding points of the messages delivered.
- Power Supply: Regular power supply cannot be vouched for at the various listening and viewing centers across some countries. In most developing countries, Nigeria included, regular power supply cannot be

guaranteed, hence the need arises for educational broadcasting planners to make alternative arrangements for power supply to the listening and viewing centers in a bid to ensure hitch-free educational broadcasts.

- Maintenance: The problem of maintenance of the old equipment that is used for educational broadcasting calls for urgent attention. The malfunctioning of this equipment hinders the transmission of educational broadcast lessons. This is due largely to the fact that the technicians who know how to maintain the equipment are often not available locally. More often than not, foreign experts are relied upon to repair the equipment whenever the need arises. Even when the services of the foreign experts are sought, their financial demands constitute another hurdle as there may not be sufficient funds to meet up with their financial demands.

- Climatic Condition: The climatic condition of the tropical region is not favorable to some extent for the educational broadcasting equipment. Unless such equipment is designed to suit the tropical climatic condition, they break down easily, and regularly coupled with the poor maintenance culture, thus hampering hitch-free educational broadcasting.

- Level of literacy: The differences in the level of literacy from person to person and from nation to nation makes educational broadcasting "a nightmare" on one hand and "a reality" on the other hand. Hence, for it to achieve the desired goal, the level of literacy of the audience should be improved upon. Differences in language, value system, culture, economy, and social standing also affect educational broadcasting. They must all be addressed so that educational broadcasting can achieve the desired goals.

- Corruption: Another heartbreaking problem bedeviling effective utilization of educational broadcasting in most African nations is corruption among public and private office holders. This has become extremely difficult to make proper accountability of resources entrusted to them. By implication, funds that are earmarked for the running of educational broadcasts sometimes are misappropriated or circumvented into personal use while the main issue at hand suffers the consequence.

- Internet Connectivity: Consistent internet connectivity cannot be vouched for at the various listening and viewing centers across the region. In some countries, Nigeria included, strong internet connectivity cannot be guaranteed, hence, the need arises for educational broadcasting planners to make alternative arrangements for internet connectivity to the listening and viewing centers in a bid to ensure hitch-free educational broadcasts.

Even at that, the various institutions and government agencies that promptly looked inward during the COVID-19 pandemic to activate various learning platforms met with challenges. For instance, during each learning exposure at the Google classroom, each user is issued a specific code. This makes the use of a very versatile medium clumsy and unmotivated.

CONCLUSION

From all that has been discussed on educational broadcasting, it is no exaggeration to state that if broadcast media are well utilized within and outside organized learning environments, they will go a long way in solving some of the problems that have cropped up in the education industry.

Educational broadcasting can assist in the areas of distance learning, adult education, containing schools' population explosion, making up for the shortage of teachers as well as in promoting self or individualized instruction on the part of the learners. All these are pointers to the fact that educational broadcasting is a veritable tool for combating educational problems.

In view of the usefulness of educational broadcasting in Nigeria, the government, both at the federal and state levels and indeed all other developing nations, should embrace this technology and effectively fund it to transmit quality messages to the unreached rural communities in Africa.

It is pertinent that the government should pay attention to the following:

- employment of experts on educational broadcasting
- training and retraining of personnel in the use of modern technology
- provision of quality equipment
- develop a culture of equipment maintenance
- address the issue of power supply (electricity, solar energy)
- teachers should be encouraged to embrace and facilitate the use of educational broadcasting judiciously

Educational broadcasting in the digital era, especially as it is observed in the post–COVID-19 situation can be regarded as a future direction for education. Teaching and learning have largely left the on-site learning environment to virtual environment, and the increasing use of broadcast media has become inevitable. Consequently, the need to strengthen the role it plays cannot be overemphasized.

REFERENCES

Agun, I. and Imogie, I. 1988. *Fundamentals of Educational Technology.* Ibadan: Y. Books.

Babalola, B. K. 2005. "A Guide to Educational Technology." In Kolade-Oje, O. T. and Babalola, S. K. (eds.). Ado-Ekiti: Tomol Publishers.

Kolade-Oje, O. T. and Babalola, B. K. 2004. *Educational Technology: Theoretical and Practical Approaches.* Ado-Ekiti: Greenline Publishers.

Ogunranti, A. 1988. *Problems and Prospects of Education Technology in Nigeria: Proceeding of A National Symposium in Ibadan.* Ibadan: Heinemann Educational Books (Nig.) Ltd.

Olushola, O. 1979. "Telescope, Some Notes on 20 Years of Television in Africa." Ibadan: Ariya Production.

Radio Garden. Accessed September 21, 2020. http://radio.garden/live.

Chapter 16

The Relevance of Theories in the Development of the Nigerian Media Industries in the Era of Digitization and Globalization

Joseph Wilson

The ubiquitousness of digital technology is influencing every facet of human endeavors, including practices and operations in the media industry and related fields. Interestingly, the twenty-first century has been unprecedented in respect of its impact on the media industry. The last two decades have been eventful, especially considering the extent to which digital innovations have transformed the ways of conceiving the practices and operations in the media industry. The increasing penetration of digital technology into every facet of the media industry and the phenomena of convergence as well as divergence in the industry have necessitated a rethink and shift in practices of the media industry. Likewise, research efforts in respect of the media industry have paid much interest to the transformative influence of digitization on media practices, cultures, and institutions (Albarran 2010). Digitization of media practices of gathering, processing, dissemination, and management have spurred the redefining and updating of old media culture to stay relevant in what is today a globalized media landscape (Gobalo 2018). For example, Ugangu (2012) argued in respect of the Kenyan media, which constitute a part of the African media structure, that the obvious changes in the nature of the media, mostly as a result of globalization, calls for a rethink on the role expected of the media. Buttressing digitization-driven change in the media industry, Gobalo (2018, p. 11) notes that:

the greatest change in media culture has not been just the emergence of the Internet, but the digitalization of culture and communication in general. Most of the films, TV shows and texts we consume today are transmitted in digital format. And even the remaining analogue media objects (paper books and newspapers) we consume—excluding statues, paintings and other fine art objects, of course—are usually produced or printed from a digital file.

The era of digitization and globalization has increasingly directed attention to the need to revisit the theories which facilitate the understanding of journalism and compelling media organizations to master a wide range of practices. Media practitioners are expected to be multi-skilled and to exhibit not only traditional media abilities of news writing, editing, and new media abilities, but to carve their own specialized knowledge as well as adapt to emerging trends in the industry (Takahashi and Parks 2018; Barnes and de Villiers 2018).The emergence of new media, such as social media, and the increasingly ineffective traditional media funding models as well as the highly competitive media landscape have continued to mount pressure on the operations of the media and placed greater professional responsibility on media practitioners to contribute across the media production practices. The demand for such diversely skilled media practitioners places a special burden on individuals who want to stay relevant in the media industry to seek deeper understanding of the emerging trends.

The transformation in the media by several waves of digitization is not new, what has continued to be new is determining ways to realize a thriving media industry. Besides keeping technology at the heart of media practice, other perspectives are expedient for the media to create compelling content and reach new audiences. Interestingly, the reality of digitization and globalization has left the media industry, especially in Africa, with no other choice but to key into the opportunities and culture these phenomena present. As important as keying into this development is, there are accompanying perspectives that contribute immensely to maximizing the opportunities. One of such perspectives is theorization or theories. Theorization is a component of the media and communication discipline, which helps significantly in understanding media practices and cultures, especially when it seeks to understand, and explain the flow, impact, and implications of the way the media operate and how people communicate (Bonney 2013; Real 1980; Davie 2010).

Theorization in the media and communication discipline is not new. There are several studies that have touched on the theoretical perspectives of media practices. In recent times, studies have frequently leaned towards understanding how the new media is impacting on traditional media culture and how the speedy changes being witnessed in the media industry have made existing theories seem inadequate to capture the realities of the new situation and there are limited new theories to replace or transform the old ones (Gobalo 2018). Another perspective is the emergence of what Albarran (2010) described as a "fourth wave" of research endeavors in digital journalism sphere, which theorizes issues such as news ecosystem, news landscape, networked journalism, among others, which have been enthusiastically embraced by many media and communication researchers (Gobalo 2018).

As the endeavors to understand the workings of the media through the lens of the several existing and emerging theories continue to generate interest, it is imperative for media practitioners to explore and harness theoretical provisions to enhance media practices, especially in Africa where the media industry is still grappling with the pace of changes in the global media sphere. "Many African countries have shown strides in the adoption and distribution of digital tools and media. However, there are still challenges in terms of digitization and digital media development in the countries" (Desta 2018, p. 1). At the same time, since digitization and globalization are no longer optional, coupled with the demand to step up professional practices, it represents an opportunity, because media practitioners who seek to expand their knowledge base and develop new expertise might seek among other things the benefits of theories. The present moment, therefore, is particularly a suitable time to highlight the relevance of theories in enhancing professional practices in the African media industry, especially as theory, according to Mierzjewska and Hollifield (2006) represent an advanced level of knowledge and understanding in a particular area and emerging area.

Therefore, this chapter underscores the relevance of media and communication theories in enhancing practices in the African media industry in the era of digitization and globalization. The chapter specifically identifies and explicates how theories would enhance professional practices of the media industry in Africa and looks at the possible challenges.

MEDIA AND COMMUNICATION THEORIES

A theory is primarily the presentation of an idea intended to elucidate a specific concept and to give meaning and to make a phenomenon easy to understand. Theory is regarded as a description of how a phenomenon works and how it applies to a scenario or action, experience based on a systematic observation (Bonney 2013; Davie 2010). Daiton and Zelley (2014) identified three types of theories:

- Commonsense theory, which is usually a creation of an individual's personal experience and found to often serve as a basis for our decisions about how to communicate.

- Working theories, which have been generalized, that could offer the profession the best techniques for carrying out journalistic tasks.
- Scholarly theory usually undergoes systematic research and provides a more thorough, accurate, and abstract explanation for communication. It is usually complex and difficult to understand.

These theories are useful, depending on the areas they are applied, for the understanding and application of communication theories in a variety of professional settings (Dainton and Zelley 2014).

Communication theories explain the relationship between the mass media and the audiences, describe the process of communication and understanding of the extent of the influence of the media on the society (Lamb, n.d.).

Gavin (2010) identified the relevance of theory in the communication sphere. They include explaining and understanding the following:

- the effects of communication on society
- the people's utilization of mass communication (this points to the active role of the audience in the mass communication process)
- how the audience learn from the mass media
- the role of mass media in shaping audiences' values and opinions

Considering mass media information, interpretation, instructive, bonding, diversion, and gatekeeping functions in society, as well as the complexities the digital and globalized era present to media practitioners, understanding and use of theoretical promotions would help streamline media output for impact, as the era demands (Anonymous 2012). It is not surprising that at some point in the evolution of the media and communication discipline the interest in understanding media effect on the audience grew. In line with this development, Lule (2012) notes that the use of propaganda and persuasion dominated early media studies, but the interest of journalists and researchers soon shifted to behavioral sciences to help determine the possible effect of mass media on society. Any time there is such a shift in the media sphere, operations and strategies are expected to change. In recent times, the interest has continued to shift because of the impact of digital media landscape from effect theory to mediatization theory, which highlights media's penetration into all areas of society and into the daily lives of media users (Fourie 2018). Buttressing the impact of change, according to Fortunato and Martin (2016, p. 130), "Every time the communication environment changes, individuals and organizations have to adjust their communication strategy to reach the audience. There is a need to understand the message distribution system capabilities and an understanding of how the audience seeks and retrieves information." Therefore, understanding the relevance theories is one way of comprehending the changes in the media and communication environment, and the effect on society (Gavin 2010).

There are a number of these media theories that would help media practitioners understand the impact of the media on society, including "all factors involved in the communication chain." Some of these theories are spirals of silence theory, media dependency theory, agenda setting theory, framing theory, and so forth (Bonney 2013). Exploring these theories by professionals would undoubtedly impact the media industry and by extension the society.

For instance, Hanson (2009) notes that knowledge of the agenda-setting theory, as a construction that promotes the idea of the media determines what issues the public thinks about, would indeed prevent the media from failing to address a particular issue of societal interest and avoid being marginalized in the minds of the public. Media scholars and professionals with interest in agenda-setting would understand the issue of salience, acknowledge the media power to select and frame content, what causes an issue to be important and how salience regarding such an issue determines its place within the public agenda, which in turn influences public policy creation (Fortunato and Martin 2016; McFadden 2010; James and Rogers 1996).

Similarly, uses and gratifications theory would enable media professionals to explore the rationale for media consumption, consequences and the benefits associated with use of a particular medium. To further assert this position, Papacharissi (2009) further asserts this position by pointing out that knowledge of the reasons for the use and popularity of a particular medium would help determine the roles the medium occupies in the society. The uses and gratifications theories of the media often find expression in contemporary media issues. In line with this thought, McFadden (2010, para. 14) states that:

> the analysis of the relationship between media and violence that you read about in preceding sections exemplifies this. Researchers employed the uses and gratifications theory in this case to reveal a nuanced set of circumstances surrounding violent media consumption, as individuals with aggressive tendencies were drawn to violent media.

It is such an insight that usually encourages a media practitioner to complement a typical youth program on radio with social media posts to make the needed impact on a youthful audience. Symbolic interactionism is another media theory that comes handy in this discourse. This theory points to the idea that symbols are vital in the development of the self, which is a product of human interaction. This implies that the way people act toward others or something is based on the meaning they attach to a person or thing. Hence, people use constructed symbols with shared cultural meanings for effective communication. Symbolic interactionism theory is instrumental in making much sense of the society and the place of the media in this is the crucial role the media play in creating, disseminating, and influencing a shared symbol on the society. For example, the use of cultural symbols in commercial and noncommercial media messages to give a product or an item a shared meaning to make them desirable or admired (McFadden 2010; Jansson-Boyd 2010). Other theories, such as the normative media theory gives a clear idea of the operating environment of the media and clearly outlines media operations in a particular clime. The spiral of silence theory focuses on the power of the majority opinion. Cultivation theory highlights the variation in perception between media users and how media audience perceptions of issues can be influenced by media output. The gatekeeping theory highlights the method to ensure only content that is most relevant to the society is selected and disseminated by the media, thus helping to ignore the large additional data points that are calling for audience attention (McFadden 2010; MCT, n.d). These and many other media effects theories have remained relevant in the changing media landscape. However, the digital and globalized posture of the media environment presents a more challenging practice environment, from the conceptual frameworks that open the theoretical terrains resulting from the penetration of innovative forms of digital media into the daily lives of people, to complexities underlying practices in the media in the era of digitization and globalization. Like its counterparts in other continents, the African media industry is awash with several digital characteristics and obviously operates in a globalized environment. Hence, it is not immune from the complexities the era presents, therefore, exploring media and communication theories as the posture this chapter presents can never be over emphasized.

THE MEDIA IN THE ERA OF DIGITIZATION AND GLOBALIZATION

The era of digitization and globalization presents a picture of a transformed media industry irrespective of geographical location. Currently, the trend in the industry points to enhancements in various segments of the industry. Although the media industry is arguably considered as one of the causes of globalization and globalized industry, influencing global audiences, technology is central in the digitized and globalized transformation visible in the industry (University of Minnesota 2010). According to Albarran (2010) the transformation, propelled by technology among other factors, is far from complete and it is unknown how long it will last. This transformation is "creating chaos and havoc for media managers and officers, while offering consumers new and expanded choices and options for entertainment and information" (Albarran 2010, p. 18). The waves of digitalization are characterized by social and mobile services/platforms, file-sharing, streaming, and increasingly highlighting real-time which have resulted in the impatience or the craving of audiences to access any content from anywhere in the world at any time.

The big data phenomenon, emanating from social media, video-streaming services, and smartphone apps, and with millions of contents being created every moment, media companies are constantly faced with the enormous task of competing for millions of audience attention. This complex scenario has placed the media industry under pressure to deliver content more global yet more precise to its audience. The pressure on the media is captured in the World Economic Forum Report (n.d, p.7) thus:

> in this hypercompetitive market, having great content is no longer enough. Media enterprises need to integrate their content into high-quality user experiences, with customized content, better viewing recommendations, more personalized and relevant adverts, and online tools to recreate those "office water-cooler" conversations about the latest hit TV series. For media organizations to create the right content and present it in the correct context will require innovation and digitization throughout the business, from discovering new methods of creating content (such as crowdsourcing) to experimenting with imaginative ways to distribute it (say, through connected retail apps).

The era of digitization is characterized by interactivity, momentariness, mass authorship, declining physical spaces, and cost reduction, personalization and contextualization, content fragmentation, and partnerships and industrialization (Josephe 2008; World Economic Forum Report, n.d.). All these features require knowledge of the various developments to be an effective player in the evolving media landscape. For instance, the personalization and contextualization feature of the industry entails creating personalized content and personalized advertising within the relevant context to ensure engagement with what is today a global audience that is daily overloaded with millions of information available offline and especially online. This brings to the fore the idea of content fragmentation which ensures that contents are disseminated across the ever-growing media, devices, and platforms and, in so doing, features partnership and industrialization. Media organizations and businesses now partner with the audience to crowd-source material and co-create content as well as automating the content-creation and distribution processes, utilizing the several forms of information delivery platforms and redefining the experience of the end user (World Economic Forum 2016; Pugalia 2019).

Technology is undoubtedly central in the digitization and globalization era. Media industry that desires to make the required impact must key into the trends. Although the African media industry is not left out in harnessing the benefits of the era, the argument hitherto remains that much globalized media content comes from the West, particularly from the United States and Europe, thereby causing foreign cultures to increasingly shape the globalized media landscape and perpetuate predominantly one-way transmission ideas (University of Minnesota 2010; Santos 2001). McGivern (2014) notes that the exchange of technology from core nations to peripheral nations is still leading to several complex issues. McGivern further asserts that, while it is obvious that technological advances are propelling a more level playing landscape where anyone anywhere can be part of the global competition, the reality is such that opportunity still largely rests in advanced or developed climes.

However, there are several theories regarding how society, technology, and media will progress. For instance, McGivern notes that "Symbolic interactionists see the symbolic uses of technology as signs of everything from a sterile futuristic world to a successful professional life" (p. 63). This chapter further finds expression in McGivern's argument regarding the position that knowledge of theories would in no little way enhance several practices in the African media industry. For example, functionalism sees the perspective that technology and media contribute to the stability of society, through the facilitation of leisure time and increasing productivity. Similarly, the technology acceptance theory describes the use of technology because of its ease of use and usefulness, knowledge of which would facilitate the digitization in the media industry (McGivern 2014).

AREAS THAT THEORIES WOULD BE RELEVANT IN ENHANCING PROFESSIONAL PRACTICES IN THE ERA OF DIGITIZATION AND GLOBALIZATION

The media industry is fundamentally shaped around information and communication. It is an industry that thrives on collecting and packaging information for dissemination to the public on different issues and events guided by a determined management procedure. News production is a generic process that includes access and observation; selection and filtering; processing and editing; distribution and interpretation (Domingo 2008, as cited in Hanitzsch and Hoxha 2014). The enhancement in these professional technicalities and management procedures would always have a direct effect on the output of the industry. Therefore, infusing media and communication theoretical principles as a position this chapter aligns with, is one of the ways that would enhance these fundamental professional practices. The fundamental areas media and communication theories can find expression and would enhance professional practices in the media industry in the digitization and globalization are as follows.

News Gathering

News gathering or sourcing is a fundamental component of the media industry professional practice. It is a process of researching events or issues that is worth broadcasting or publishing. It is a product of a professional judgment based on what has been identified as news values or news elements. These elements are: Timeliness—Is it current or new? Proximity—Is it happening nearby? Prominence—Is it well known to your readers? Consequence—Will it affect your readers in an important way? Conflict—Does it involve tension? Human Interest—Is it about other people's lives? These news elements predominantly shape journalists' perceptions and routines of sourcing or gathering information (Hellmueller 2014). The gathering process has been greatly influenced by the evolving digital transformation.

Pugalia (2019) describes the digital transformation as an aggressive digital evolution that has currently made data one of the most valuable products, which has spurred a renewed focus on information gathering, especially in this era of targeted audience, and noting issues of objectivity, privacy, and security. Data holds enormous information that will distinguish a news organization in this era of digitization and globalization. However, there are complexities in accessing or gathering relevant data because of the more complex search environment to consider, both in terms of types of sources to use and search modalities to employ.

Hence, enhancing the news gathering process becomes necessary. Interestingly, there are search models developed to facilitate information gathering in the current age of big data. Bates (1989, p. 5) notes that:

> as the sizes and variety of databases grow and the power of search interfaces increases, users will more and more expect to be able to search automated information stores in ways that are comfortable and familiar to them. We need first, to have a realistic model of how people go about looking for information now, and second, to find ways to devise databases and search interfaces that enable searchers to operate in ways that feel natural.

For example, classical models for information retrieval, information retrieval model and berrypicking model, and click models for web search could be of immense help to media practitioners to access relevant information in the pool of millions of information online (Philippe and Chevallet 2017; Chuklin, Markov, and de Rijke 2015; Bates 1989).

Similarly, knowledge of cultivation theory which focuses on the idea that the views and behaviors of those who spend more time with the media, particularly television, are likely to reflect the media content they have been exposed to, would help in ensuring more relevant news sources for media output that would be more impactful on the audience. The customization characteristic of the media in the era of digitization and globalization calls for a better understanding of the media audience, which the knowledge of the cultivation theory could facilitate its realization and help media set agenda on relevant issues.

News Processing

News processing stage involves selection—filtering, editing, and packaging (making attractive or advantageous). This practice in the media industry can benefit immensely from the theoretical provision of knowledge of theories like gatekeeping theory, framing theory, and priming theory, which would enhance the news processing practice in the media industry. For example, the gatekeeping theory would help the media practitioners whose work falls within this stage, such as sub-editors and editors, and can explore the various provisions of the gatekeeping theory to properly handle selecting and filtering news items based on specific standards for information value. Knowledge and application of the principles of gatekeeping theory would help media practitioners enhance news sourcing, in a way that only items that meet the set standard would be selected.

Similarly, a knowledge and application of the framing theory principles would help media practitioners enhance performance in focusing attention on certain events and then place them within a field of meaning. Another example is the priming theory which provides an explanation on how the information from the media is stored in the minds of the audience and how it influences decision making among the audience. A knowledge of the priming theory would help media practitioners enhance media effect by influencing people to make judgment or a decision based on information from the media.

Audience Analysis

Audience analysis involves identifying the audience and adapting a medium and type of content that would be of interest to them and would be within their level of understanding, attitudes, and beliefs. The knowledge and application of audience related theories, such as uses and gratification theory, diffusion of innovation, cultivation theory, among others, would help enhance performance in the delivery of media content. For example, the knowledge of uses and gratification theory of how the audience will use the media and how it will affect or help them fulfill a particular need. The media richness theory would help media practitioners understand the effectiveness of communication messages based on the effectiveness of media used to convey the message. This would help in ensuring the most appropriate and suitable media is selected for better impact.

Another example is the knowledge of cognitive dissonance theory by media practitioners would enhance their understanding of the interrelationships among competing cognitions (beliefs, opinion, attitudes, values, and ideas) and enhance performance by eliminating dissonance through the media content that would downplay or reduce the importance of the conflicting beliefs, acquiring new beliefs that removes the conflicting attitude or behavior. Understanding the audience would enhance the performance of media practitioners through more suitable news content that takes cognizance of the audience.

Similarly, understanding the principles of the knowledge gap theory would help media practitioners focus on infusion of mass media content into a social system based on the suitability of the content to the knowledge gap of the audience. A more targeted approach to news dissemination would lead to better impact.

In the same light, the media dependency theory would enhance media practices when there is clear understanding of the level of dependency of the society on the media for fulfillment. For example, the potential of radio as a source of information among teenagers is limited when compared to teenager's dependency on social media as a source of information. Thus, for the purpose of media effect on teenagers, the media practitioners would prefer to deploy the social media.

News Dissemination

News dissemination is the process of sharing news content with a defined set of people known as the audience. Digitization and globalization significantly impacts on the process, especially with the emergence of internet platforms that has given the media industry the opportunity to reach a global audience, speedy and cheaper delivery of or sharing of news content. The dissemination platforms are no longer limited to the mainstream media. The internet has ushered in numerous platforms, especially social media. Modernization in the media industry now allows the instant sharing of information and creating a sensation of virtual presence at events that occur far away. Hence, knowledge of theories such as the diffusion of innovation enable media practitioners to enhance their performance of content dissemination by timely adoption of the most suitable media technology for a particular society. The diffusion of innovation theory in this regard is useful in understanding, for example, the breaking news diffusion in the media industry and how propagation features, such as audience matric, influence online media platforms.

Understanding the principles of theories, such as the modernization theory, would enable the media industry to understand the changing ways of communication and media use in traditional and (post)modern societies and ensure that it does not lose sight of emerging media for effective news content delivery.

Media Management

One of the major challenges of the media industry in the era of digitization and globalization is management. The question that readily surfaces in the media environment is how can local newspapers or local radio stations survive in a digital age? One thing that is certain in trying to respond to this question is that the mainstream media must respond to this digital age of media turbulence as quickly as possible.

Although most theories in media management are based in organizational studies, there are fundamental characteristics that relate to the media practices, the organizational structure, market conditions, technologies of production leadership decision making, culture, communication, among others (Mierzjewska and Hollifield 2006). The knowledge of strategic management theories would help practitioners understand the strategy of media market concentration, adapting to changing market conditions, strategic options for media organizations operating in various media markets and regulatory settings, as well as social responsibilities that media need to meet for the good of the society they operate in.

Similarly, structural theories would help practitioners understand and adopt structures that maximize efficiency and enhance financial performance of the media organization. It would further help media practitioners understand the effect of media ownership structures on media content, news managers' professional values and priorities, and how they shape news decisions (Mierzjewska and Hollifield 2006).

Other media management theories include transnational media management theories, which entails how leadership, social networks, and decisions affect global media expansion, content development and the outcomes. Organizational culture theories deal with, among others, the cultural environment within which the media organization operates and the influence of the leadership and the media organization's operating environment (Mierzjewska and Hollifield 2006). Economic theory looks at how emerging media technologies may influence existing media markets and the feasibility of business models for media operations. New product development theory and diffusion of innovation theories explicate the issues of new product development in the media in line with the trends and inject them into the media system. Knowledge of these theories would enhance the professional performance of media practitioners in Africa in this dynamic era.

CHALLENGES OF LEVERAGING ON THEORIES TO ENHANCE PERFORMANCE IN THE MEDIA INDUSTRY IN THE ERA OF DIGITIZATION AND GLOBALIZATION IN AFRICA

The major challenges that could affect the effort to leverage on theories to enhance performance in the media industry in the era of digitization and globalization in Africa are inadequate knowledge, media ownership and control, lack of interest and willingness to explore and use these theories by practitioners.

Inadequate Knowledge

Theoretical principles are in the public domain, but it is an area that attracts more communication scholars than the practitioners. Although some of these theories find expression in day-to-day practices in the media industry, there seems to be inadequacies regarding knowledge of these theories and a conscious effort to use them for professional benefits. Patterson (2013) and Swyter (2014) note that media practitioners' knowledge deficiency is a reason they are vulnerable to manipulation. One of the major challenges of modern journalism is the knowledge problem, which has led to frequent failure to communicate complexity (Patterson 2013; Swyter 2014). By extension, this knowledge problem is likely to affect infusing theory into media practice.

The solution to this is what Patterson described as knowledge-based journalism. A kind of media practice in which journalists at university-based training courses learn everything. It is expected that "the more media practitioners know about a given topic, the better they assess facts for validity, content, relevance, and timeliness" (Patterson 2013). Likewise, the more they know about relevant theories, the better their output. Training and retraining of journalists are fundamental ways to address the issue of inadequate knowledge.

Media Ownership and Control

The political economy of the media is one area where media practitioners are faced with the problem of free operation. Irrespective of a practitioner's creativity, the policies of the organization, which often emanate from the owners of such media, reign supreme. Other initiatives that could distort the routine or does not conform to policies of such an organization are frowned at, thus limiting performance. Sjovaag and Ohlsson (2019) note that one of the concerns with ownership in journalism is market concentration and monopolization, and the undue effects this often has on professional cultures, especially journalistic autonomy, and media diversity. The ownership structure determines the operational structure of the media. Where the independence to initiate creative ideas is restricted, the utilization of theoretical principles, among other ideas, would be restricted. For example, deploying agenda setting theory to the fullest is not completely within the powers of the media practitioner who sources and submits reports, but the editor who is guided by the editorial policy of the organization, which is often a product of the ownership of the organization.

Lack of Interest and Willingness to Explore and Use Theoretical Principles

It is one thing to have the knowledge or be willing to search and use the knowledge. There must be the willingness on the part of the journalists to take interest in knowing these theories and applying them to professional practice. Resistance to change, ownership and control problems, and poor management are largely responsible for the lack of interest in professional practices in the media. Where the motivation is poor, media practitioners are likely to perform poorly on the job, especially in taking steps to initiate ideas that would enhance performance. The complexity of understanding theories and their application is likely to affect the willingness of practitioners to delve into the area of theoretical principles for professional practice. Some would rather stick to the routine of the practice than attempt exploring other areas, such as theories, which some view as a preserve for scholarly research. The solution to this is constant motivation and training and retraining that would help them develop interest.

FAMILIARITY WITH ROUTINE AND RESISTANCE TO CHANGE

Familiarity with routine sometimes leads to resistance to change. Sticking to an old way of doing things usually leads to resistance to innovation. Infusing theoretical principles more consciously into the routine of media practitioners may face the challenge of resistance from either the journalist themselves or the manager. Resistance from media managers would normally discourage media practitioners from fully harnessing theoretical principles; for example, the issue of autonomy to independently set agenda based on public interest may meet resistance from the managers, especially when the public interest goes against the media organization's political or economic interest. The solution to this is a constant campaign for autonomy of the journalist in matters of news content development. Individual resistance could be addressed by training and retraining for journalists in the areas of the benefits and relevance of applying theory to boost media output.

CONCLUSION

As digitization and globalization are transforming the media landscape, various media are changing their practices to meet the trends. Looking towards and adopting theoretical principles in order to enhance practices in this dynamic era is one of several ways to go in Africa. Professional practices, such as news gathering, processing, dissemination, audience analysis, and media management are some major areas that would benefit from the infusion of theories. Although there are likely challenges, such as inadequacies in terms of knowledge on the side of the media practitioners, ownership and control problem, and the lack of interest or willingness to explore and use the theories to enhance professional practices, these challenges are surmountable through training and retraining, and motivation. The chapter concludes that media practitioners in Africa would undoubtedly find expression in the ever-changing digitized and globalized media space when they explore and use theoretical principles to enhance their practices.

REFERENCES

Albarran, A. B. 2010. *The Transformation of the Media and Communication Industries*. Spain: Gráficas Egúzkiza.

Anonymous. 2012. *A Primer on Communication Studies*. Accessed November 23, 2021. https://2012books.lardbucket.org/books/a-primer-on-communication-studies/s15-02-functions-and-theories-of-mass.html.

Barnes, R. and de Villiers, S. M. J. 2018. "Tackling Uncertainty for Journalism Graduates: A model for teaching experiential entrepreneurship." *Journalism Practice*, 94–114.

Bates, M. J. 1989. "The design of browsing and berrypicking techniques." Accessed November 23, 2021. https://pages.gseis.ucla.edu/faculty/bates/berrypicking.html.

Bonney, E. K. 2013. "Media Theories and their Relevance to Communication Practice." Academia.edu. Accessed November 23, 2021. https://www.academia.edu/4979401/Media_Theories_and_their_Relevance_to_Communication_Practice.

Chuklin, A., Markov, I., de Rijke, M. 2015. "An Introduction to Click Models for Web Search." Accessed November 23, 2021. https://staff.science.uva.nl/i.markov/publications/Chuklin_SIGIR2015_Tutorial1.pdf.

Dainton, Marianne and Zelley, Elaine D. 2014. *Applying Communication Theory for Professional Life*. Los Angeles, CA: Sage.

Davie, G. 2010. "What is Theory?" Mass Communication Theory. Accessed November 23, 2021. https://masscommtheory.com/2010/03/06/what-is-theory/.

Desta, T. 2018. "Comments on the Digitalization and Digital Divide in the Horn of Africa (HoA), Kenya and Ethiopia: The Media Perspective." *Global Media Journal* 16 (30). Accessed November 23, 2021. https://www.globalmediajournal.com/open -access/comments-on-the-digitalization-and-digital-divide-in-the-horn-of-africa -hoa-kenya-and-ethiopia-the-media-perspective.php?aid=86823#corr.

Fortunato, J. and Martin, S. 2016. "The intersection of Agenda Setting: The media environment and election campaign laws." *Journal of Information Policy* (6): 129–153.

Fourie, J. P. (2018). "The impact of the digital media landscape on media theory: From effect theory to mediatisation theory." *Tydskrift vir Geesteswetenskappe* 58 (4): 650–668.

Gavin, D. 2010. "What is Theory? Mass Communication Theory." Accessed November 23, 2021. https://masscommtheory.com/2010/03/06/what-is-theory/.

Gobalo. 2018. "Digital Media Culture: Old and New." Marbella International University Centre. Accessed November 23, 2021. https://miuc.org/digital-media -culture-old-and-new/amp/.

Hanitzsch, T., Hoxha, A. 2014. "News Production: Theory and conceptual framework generic and conflict influences on the news production process." InfoCore. Accessed November 23, 2021. https://www.infocore.eu/wp-content/uploads/2014 /12/Theoretical-Framing_WP1_News-Productions.pdf.

Hanson, R. 2009. *Mass Communication: Living in a Media World*. Washington, DC: CQ Press.

Hellmueller, L. 2014. "News-Gathering and Sourcing Routines of DC Correspondents." In L. Hellmueller, *The Washington, DC Media Corps in the 21st Century* (pp. 59–77). New York: Palgrave Macmillan.

James, D. and Rogers, E. 1996. *Agenda-Setting.* Thousand Oaks, CA: Sage.

Jansson-Boyd, C. 2010. *Consumer Psychology.* New York: McGraw-Hill.

Josephe, P. 2008. *La societe immediate*. Paris: Calmann-Levy.

Lamb, B. (n.d). "Communication Theories." Accessed November 23, 2021. https: //lessonbucket.com/vce-media/units-3-4/agency-and-control/communication -theories/#:~:text=Communication%20theories%20are%20ways%20of ,understand%20extent%20of%20media%20influence.

Lule, J. 2012. *Communication, Understanding Media and Culture: An Introduction to Mass.* Washington, DC: Flat World Knowledge.

McFadden, B. J. 2010. "Media Effects Theories." In B. J. McFadden, *Understanding Media and Culture: An Introduction to Mass Communication.* University of Minnesota Libraries Publishing. Accessed November 23, 2021. https://courses .lumenlearning.com/suny-massmedia/chapter/2-2-media-effects-theories/.

McGivern, R. 2014. "Media and technology." In W. Little, *Introduction to Sociology,* 1st Canadian Edition. Victoria: Bcampus.

MCT. (n.d). "Gatekeeping Theory." Mass Communication Theory. Accessed May 20, 2021. https://masscommtheory.com/theory-overviews/gatekeeping-theory/.

Mierzjewska, I. B., Hollifield, C. A. 2006. *Theoretical Approaches in Media Management Research*. New York: Routledge.

Papacharissi, Z. 2009. "Uses and Gratifications." In D. S. Salwen, *An Integrated Approach to Communication Theory and Research* (p. 137). New York: Routledge.

Patterson, T. E. 2013. "Informing the news: The need for knowledge-based reporting." The Journalist's Resource, October 8. Accessed May 20, 2021. https://journalistsresource.org/tip-sheets/research/knowledge-based-reporting/.

Philippe, M. and Chevallet, J. 2017. "Classical models for information retrieval." Accessed May 20, 2021. https://ginf533u.imag.fr/lib/exe/fetch.php?media=m2r_mosig_iar_chapter_02_classical_models_for_information_retrieval.pdf.

Pugalia, S. 2019. "The rise of the digital era in journalism." The Hindu, January 7. Accessed May 20, 2021. https://www.thehindu.com/thread/technology/the-rise-of-the-digital-era-in-journalism/article25733413.ece.

Real, M. R. 1980. "Communications, Media Theory: Contributions to an Understanding of American Mass." *American Quarterly* 32 (3): 238–258.

Santos, J. M. 2001. "Globalization and Tradition: Paradoxes in Philippine Television and Culture." *Media Development* 3, 43–48.

Sjovaag, H. and Ohlsson, J. 2019. "Media Ownership and Journalism." Oxford Research Encyclopedias. DOI: https://doi.org/10.1093/acrefore/9780190228613.013.839.

Steensen, S. 2009. "What's stopping them? Towards a grounded theory of innovation in online journalism." *Journalism Studies* 10 (6): 821–836.

Swyter, N. 2014. "Beyond Carnegie-Knight: 'Knowledge Journalism.'" Knight Foundation, October 3. Accessed May 20, 2021. https://knightfoundation.org/articles/beyond-carnegie-knightknowledge-journalism/.

Takahashi, B. and Parks, P. 2018. "Journalists and Communicators' Perceptions of Their Graduate Training in Environmental Reporting: An Application of Knowledge-Based Journalism Principles." *Frontier in Environmental Science* 5 (94).

Ugangu, W. 2012. "Normative Media Theory and the rethinking of the role of the Kenyan media in a changing social economic context." PhD thesis: University of South Africa. Accessed May 20, 2021. http://uir.unisa.ac.za/bitstream/handle/10500/8606/thesis_ugangu_w.pdf;sequence=1.

University of Minnesota. 2010. "Globalization of Media." Accessed May 20, 2021. https://open.lib.umn.edu/mediaandculture/chapter/13-6-globalization-of-media/.

World Economic Forum. 2016. "Building a media enterprise for the digital age." Accessed May 20, 2021. http://reports.weforum.org/digital-transformation/building-a-media-enterprise-for-the-digital-age/.

World Economic Forum, Report. (n.d). "The media industry: In the vanguard of digital transformation." Accessed May 20, 2021. http://reports.weforum.org/digital-transformation/the-media-industry-in-the-vanguard-of-digital-transformation/.

Chapter 17

Media Templates and the Relevance of Research in the Digital Era

Grace Nwagbara

While in school during my postgraduate studies, several years ago, one of our professors asked us a rather disturbing question in an advanced reporting class. The question was "at the end of your studies as a journalist, would you be able to do everything and everything to get information for a news story?" As students, we made attempts to answer the question, but he told us it was a rhetorical one. He knew we did not fully understand the implication of his question; neither did we have a clear picture of what he meant. He, however, added that we would someday answer the question as practicing journalists in the field. Today, as a communication teacher, teaching journalists and teaching communication research in Africa, I have a better and clearer picture, and understanding too of what that implies.

Practicing journalism in an African setting in this digital era is definitely not the same as practicing journalism in Europe or the United States of America, where modern infrastructures are available and access to information and information sources are better. African media systems evolved from a rather difficult authoritarian background, with inadequate modern facilities for journalists to work with. Access to information is an uphill task and the fear of arrest and the punishment that goes with it is ever present. Sourcing for news in this environment is both risky and difficult. A journalist might be present at an event as it unfolds or sent to cover a beat, and has nose for what makes news, ears that can distill newsworthy information from the cacophony of voices around, and eyes that see news in what other people dismiss as unimportant but does not have the necessary/appropriate equipment to gather information. Sometimes it might seem like a matter of life and death. Even with the Freedom of Information Act that came into force in Nigeria in 2011, access to some records and information in the country is still a mirage. This is contrary to what the act stipulates.

Working with media templates as conceptualized by Western countries, does not make their jobs any easier. News, for instance, has always been conceived by the Western media as something that represents a departure from the everyday pattern of life and tilts towards the novel, odd, or outright ugly. African journalists believe there are more criteria that should guide the content of information if it must be useful to the public, and thus no longer accept such a limited definition of news (UNESCO 1981). To them, news should not only be negative, but also positive and should go beyond an event. It should be more of a process that has a history, a present, and a future. Besides, what makes news should vary according to the needs of each society. Every mass media society defines its templates and operates by them since they can provide journalists with context for news and newsworthy events, encourage understanding of such events, and act as a key reference point for them. Media templates also "serve as rhetorical shorthand, helping journalists and the audience to make sense of fresh news stories. They are instrumental in shaping narratives around particular social problems, guiding public discussion not only about the past, but also the present and the future" (Kitzinger 2000, p. 61). Media templates are also useful when writing about key events and news icons. Bennet and Lawrence (1995) note that templates help introduce icons into stories and open up such news stories to other linkages.

Media templates can pose subtle challenges to journalism by making journalists tend to stick to laid down patterns in news gathering and reporting with little or no allowance made for personal initiatives or diversity in reportage. However, the African journalists still find ways to perform their duty, providing connections between daily events in the society (familiar or unfamiliar), with the lives of the citizens and interpreting those events to the best of their ability. This often involves several levels of interactions between the journalists, the occurrence (event/ source of information) and the people (the news consumers). Some important aspects of these interactions may require the journalist meeting certain key persons on or outside the scene of an incident, asking them relevant and meaningful questions about the occurrence, taking down notes of useful observations made, consulting other sources to verify and validate the veracity of the information gathered. This process may appear simple as described, but the everyday experience of a journalist in the African setting is not. In addition to this job, the journalist also makes efforts to solve whatever problems that may arise in the course of duty.

Generally, before journalists set out to cover a story, they should have sketchy details of what their assignment involves. The major focus of their task is identifying what aspects of the event billed for coverage are newsworthy enough to merit attention. This constitutes the initial hurdle and if properly handled, guides the journalist in the search for information. They might also need to ask the six basic journalistic questions—"what, who, why, where, when and how," also known as the five Ws and one H. Journalists will answer these questions based on the importance attached to the various aspects of the event already identified as deserving attention. This they do as the situation unfolds. They make vital decisions on what to do and how to do it at each crucial stage of the news gathering process. Their decisions are based on their interaction with what is on ground, what they already know and are familiar with as professionals, and the information they have about the audience (the final consumer of the news).

As the journalists perform their duty or carry out their assignment, they are involved in research, though not in the formal sense. From story ideas to news gathering and processing, to reporting and presentation, research takes center stage, though subtly. The idea of fact-finding, discovery, or unearthing hidden matters situates journalism in the realm of research. People sometimes refer to this aspect of media operation as investigative journalism or accountability reporting. Why do journalists need to investigate and what should they investigate? There are a thousand and one things happening in the society at the same time. Some go unnoticed because they do not touch peoples' lives directly. Others are such that they cannot be ignored because they have direct or indirect bearing with lives. Many people may not have the privilege of taking more than a cursory glance at those things and do nothing about them for several reasons, one of which is lack of access to mainstream media where such information could be published.

However, the watchdog role of the media gives media professionals (including citizen journalists) the edge or opportunity to question those happenings, enlighten people in the society about them, or even warn people if need be. This way, people gain more understanding and can relate better with their environment. This role also confers on journalists the privilege of being the conscience of the society, crusaders of what is right and proper by their sustained efforts to highlight issues including the ills in the society. In doing this, they help awaken peoples' consciousness to antisocial behaviors, and keep the society in check, particularly public office holders. Undertaking the duty of society's watchdog requires more than just a narrow or casual inquiry into issues. It demands a broader and more in-depth approach to issues, that is, considering more than one perspective of an issue under investigation. To secure this kind of insight, the journalist might have to interview eyewitnesses, experts, government officials, various stakeholders, and other persons whose opinions are considered useful, in telling a meaningful story (news reporting is storytelling) to his audience. The entire process is not a blind search or a purposeless venture. It involves searching for information with the aim of gaining knowledge and "pushing back the frontiers of ignorance" (Best and Kahn 2006), in what individuals know about their society. This is basically what research is all about.

Surprisingly, whenever the word research is mentioned, what readily comes to peoples' mind is a rigorous, time-consuming exercise involving several steps and procedures in order to achieve an end. This end might be to solve a problem, gain more knowledge about a situation, answer a thorny question, or even discover something entirely new. Research may fit this picture, or it could be less. People make inquiries daily on several issues. Some of these issues are as little as locating a shop in town that offers goods at comparatively lower prices than other shops. It could also be as already stated, a journalist trying to decide on which event to cover because it is more newsworthy than another or trying to put together bits and pieces of information for a news report.

At other times, research could mean arriving at a ground-breaking discovery or invention in science and technology. Either way, questions are asked, and answers are sought. Research is simply asking relevant and meaningful questions about issues and finding answers to them. Being able to ask the right questions determines to a large extent, the possibility of receiving the right answers. Research therefore can be informal with no detailed plan or steps to follow, or it could be formal with defined procedures to follow. However, what is paramount in every research situation is for the investigator to be certain of the issue that constitutes the focus of his search.

At the global level, access to information is currently better and easier with the coming of the internet, than it was some decades ago. People can source whatever kind of information they desire at the touch of a button. All they require is to visit a website or a blog that contains the kind of information that meets their needs. The way people can source information unhindered is the same way they can provide information to others almost unhindered through different social media platforms or websites and blogs. The world is experiencing an information explosion. In fact, the volume of information in circulation on any specified topic at any given time is such that ordinarily it should be an advancement for society. Globalization is thriving because of the ease with which information about different parts of the world circulates among people.

Like a coin, information explosion has two sides. The first and beautiful side is laced with all the advantages it could offer, while the second and ugly side brings out its disadvantages. Media practice has left the traditional environment (media houses) and moved to the digital space where people are at the same time, consumers and contributors of information on this digital highway. Citizen journalism (a situation where nonprofessional journalists also gather and report news stories) has grown out of it and more may still be coming. With this development, some people are questioning the relevance of certain time-honored journalism guidelines in this digital era.

Agreed, the current reality has expanded the journalism base to include "alternative" communication (UNESCO 1981), that is, communication not emanating from mainstream media houses but from different categories of people such as those radically opposed to some status quo in society, those with differing ideological, philosophical, and political leanings, and those who generally think information consumers deserve a more active role in media fare, but is society really better served in terms of content? Yes, in the quantity of information available, not in the quality. The major issue here is that of who controls the content of what the alternative sources disseminate. Alternative communication has a large capacity to defy or evade constraints by state authorities (UNESCO 1981).

This lack of control in what is disseminated to the public is neither healthy for society nor for the journalism profession. The risk of misinformation and loss of credibility is high. A society is guided by the quality of information that flows into it, particularly so, because information is an instrument for social control. Some citizen journalists do not take the pains to search or consult to verify the authenticity of what they push out to the public. The messages that are targeted to inform may end up leaving the people ill-informed, under-informed, or outrightly not informed. Mainstream journalists are likely to be more mindful of what they disseminate because of the different levels of checks their stories are subjected to and the penalty they may face for any misstep. More worrisome is the fact that with so much information at peoples' disposal, they may suffer from information overload or information fatigue syndrome. People become intoxicated with too much information and then they are incapable of reacting logically to the demands of the information they receive. Schaefer (2005) describes it as the narcotizing effect of the media, noting that such influx of information to the public leads to numbness or insensitivity in the audience.

WHAT IS RESEARCH?

Human beings are naturally structured with the tendency to be curious and to want to know and understand their environment. This quest follows us through life from childhood to adulthood. It is by this that we learn about life and live it to the best of our ability. The search for knowledge can drive us beyond our imagination but it will help us build our lives and that of others. Society is built on this search, both from individual and collective efforts. Through this same process, questions are answered, knowledge is gained, discoveries are made, conclusions are drawn, and ignorance is minimized or eliminated. What then is research? Like every useful concept and area of study, research has been defined in several ways by different scholars. We will look at some of these definitions and consider what they emphasize.

According to Keyton (2001, p. 2), "research is the discovery of answers to questions through the application of scientific and systematic procedures." These procedures are step by step search meant to yield dependable answers and solutions to either an observed problem or an envisaged one and to provide explanation or understanding to most of our collective agreements of social reality (Nwagbara 2006). Wrench, Thomas-Maddox, Richmond, and McCroskey (2008, p. 11) define research from a perspective they borrowed from Merriam-Webster's Dictionary as, "studious inquiry or examination; especially: investigation or experimentation aimed at the discovery and interpretation of facts, revision of accepted theories or laws in the light of new facts, or practical application of such revised theories or laws." For Wimmer and Dominick (2011, p. 2) research is basically "an attempt to discover something." Treadwell (2011, p. xv) supports this perspective by noting that research is "a journey from not knowing something to knowing something." This "something" could be as small as figuring out the most direct route to someone's destination, or a little more difficult as determining how effective advertising is on TV, radio, the internet, and in all types of print media work. Chawla and Sondhi (2011, p. 5) consider research as, "an unbiased, structured, and sequential method of enquiry, directed towards a clear implicit or explicit business objective. This inquiry might lead to validating existing postulates or arriving at new theories and models." Research for Kothari and Garg (2014) is as simple as a "search for knowledge" but this search must be scientific and systematic and must arrive at information on a specific topic.

To Ary, Jacobs, Sorensen, and Walker (2014, p. 20), scientific research is a "systematic way to acquire useful and dependable information that bears on a meaningful problem." Although the settings and methods may differ, research in their view, remains a systematic and objective means to gain reliable knowledge on issues. Akpabio (2019, p. 1) on his part finds research as an investigation of a phenomenon, occurrence, process, and so forth, through a systematic, scientific, and an acceptable procedure.

A close look at these definitions point to the following major highlights about research:

1. a search for new information/knowledge about issues through objective and systematic procedures

2. a means of adding to and validating existing knowledge
3. a process of finding answers to questions by inquiring into happenings

Knowledge is an important aspect of human existence. It is what keeps the world moving in the right direction. Contemporary society is besieged by all manners of issues, from the very small to the hydra-headed. Some of them have put humanity under very intense pressure. For instance, when the news of the outbreak of COVID-19 in 2019 first filtered in, people did not consider the virus a serious threat to our collective existence until more information was provided about its potential danger to humanity. Scientists and medical experts went to work on the origin of the virus, its features and characteristics, the conditions that favor its existence, the different ways it manifests, the sickness that it causes and the effect it has on the human body. As the scientists and medical experts were working, the same way the media were working too, interpreting these medical facts to the public, educating and helping people gain new knowledge on the subject and reinforcing what they already knew. In this way, the uncertainties surrounding COVID-19, which may be the result of a lack of sufficient information about it, were reduced, and the boundaries of ignorance in that direction were pushed back. The level of knowledge the public has about any subject matter in the media is directly related to how much journalists themselves know about the issue and can convey the same to their audience.

Knowledge can come in three different ways: through experience, through authority, and by deductive and inductive reasoning. Experience is derived through direct exposure to an issue. It is a very familiar way to gain knowledge about something, but it has its limitations. Sometimes, experience may present just an aspect of the issue. Individuals get to know only that bit and it defines their knowledge of the issue. Journalists, in their day-to-day coverage of events, go through all kinds of experiences with people and the issues involved. Some of these experiences define their approach to news stories and how they report them. That is why journalists must seek information beyond their personal experience in order to present a balanced report, which takes care of all the perspectives.

There are certain things a person cannot know by experience. Such knowledge can only come by interacting with experts and authorities in that area, or people who have had personal experience with the issue. Journalists often resort to this while gathering information for a news story. They usually seek the opinions of recognized authorities in a field as part of their search. This adds to the credibility and authenticity of the story (Itule and Anderson 2003, Nwabueze 2009). Harcup (2009, p. 146) observes that "one of the primary questions of journalism is: 'who says?'" In other words, the credentials of the source of information are important in journalism practice, because it determines whether the public believes the story to be true or not. Authorities invoke respect.

Knowledge can also be sought through deductive and inductive reasoning. In deductive reasoning, a person proceeds from general to specific knowledge through logical argument (Ary et al. 2014). This argument is expected to yield a pattern that might be confirmed through the observations made. An argument is, "a set of propositions in which one follows logically as a conclusion from the other" (Wrench et al. 2008, p.16). The other propositions are known as premises, and they lend support to the main proposition. Arguments are built on syllogism. A syllogism has three parts, two premises and one conclusion. An example of deductive reasoning: "Journalists are usually well informed" (major premise); "Chinwe is a journalist" (minor premise); "Therefore, Chinwe is well informed" (conclusion). In deductive reasoning, it is assumed that if the premises are true, the conclusion should also be true.

It is not always that the premises are true. If that happens, the syllogism will be inaccurate, and the conclusion will be false. On the other hand, inductive reasoning is the flipside of deductive reasoning. Here knowledge acquisition moves from "the particular to the general, from a set of specific observations to the discovery of a pattern that represents some degree of order among all the given events" (Baxter and Babbie 2003, p. 69). Knowledge gain is deliberate and comes through direct observation, and with it the investigator arrives at conclusions based on the observation. But to arrive at a trusted conclusion, the investigator must be prepared to observe all examples. Journalists are always faced with the temptation of drawing hasty conclusions based on what can be deduced from a situation like the example of Chinwe, the journalist or what an authority has said. That someone is an expert in a certain field does not automatically translate to having all the information required to answer some critical questions that may arise in that area of expertise. Someone could be a professional who is not in the mainstream of that profession. For instance, someone could be a lawyer but works as a company secretary. Not being directly involved with the day-to-day running of the law courts might mean not being able to answer certain questions or provide dependable information on what happens in the courts at certain intervals.

The place of information or knowledge in contemporary society cannot be overstressed. Both are instruments of social control. For too long, we have built what we know around tradition. We organize and structure the world around us in specific ways that become entrenched as our reality. We are taught to consider certain behavioral patterns acceptable and some others antisocial. This reality becomes so natural and normal for us that we take it for granted and dismiss it as, "That's life" (O'Shaughnessy and Stadler, 2008). By accepting what is generally known by everybody, we spare ourselves the trouble of having to search for meanings and interpretation to things, explanation to happenings, and trying to understand how they all add up to make human existence possible. Knowledge is actually cumulative. Whatever body of information and understanding that is inherited, that is, passed down from one generation to another, adds to knowledge and helps bring about development (Baxter and Babbie 2003).

When people start questioning or disagreeing with the status quo or things that everybody already understands to work in a specific way, we create an opportunity to gain fresh insight and sometimes better understanding of a phenomenon. Because of our limited understanding of things, usually based on the burden of tradition, our normal and casual ways of inquiry are prone to several errors. They include prejudice, subjectivity, inaccurate observation, overgeneralization, selectivity, and illogical reasoning. Journalists must be painstaking in their quest for knowledge and information about the goings-on in society. That is the only proper way to guarantee factual and accurate reportage. Research, as presented in this chapter, shows a more objective approach to human inquiry, even in this digital era, and thus helps journalists guard against some obvious errors in news reporting.

RESEARCH AND JOURNALISM

Credibility of content is a major issue in journalism practice. Research provides a means to deal with this issue. According to Alao and Olawunmi (2014), research enhances the factualness of news writing by consulting records, documents, and databases. The volume of information at the disposal of a journalist in the field, from which to sift what makes sense is usually enormous. At an accident scene, for instance, there might be conflicting claims from people as to what happened and what has led to what. Before reporting the story, a journalist should check the facts by searching for more evidence. Not everyone who claims to be an eyewitness actually saw what happened. Even those who saw what happened will present it from different perspectives. Some may just be repeating what they heard from others and in the process inject their opinions into the report. If the journalists rely on that kind of evidence, inaccuracies would be introduced into the story. That is why a reconfirmation is necessary. Journalists should start by comparing what they have been told with what they "know" of the world; with their knowledge and experience; asking whether at a commonsense level, it has a ring of truth about it (Harcup 2009). From this point, the journalist consults a higher authority, an expert whose opinion is reliable, and as a source is considered trustworthy. Such authority might even be a routine point of contact for journalists or a new source based on recommendation. What is important in all is the credibility of the source and the information provided. Sandra Mims

Rowe, an editor with *Oregonian* as cited by Itule and Anderson (2003, p. 438) stresses this fact. To her, "credibility is not theoretical, philosophical or remote from our work. It is at the heart of our professional lives. Credibility is not about selling more newspapers. It is about building the quality and integrity of our news."

Research helps the journalist handle the issue of bias and prejudice. Journalists, like all human beings, have the tendency to be prejudiced at different times and circumstances. This can be noticed when they bring preconceived notions or opinions that are not based on any valid reason or real-life experience into their professional calling or reportage. Sometimes, because of political, ethnic, religious, or any other kind of bias, a reporter may decide not to present all the sides of a story. That is not right because news coverage is expected to reflect both the positive and the negative. Nothing should be kept back for personal or selfish interest. There are some basic principles of ethical conduct that should guide journalists as they carry out their daily duty. They are supposed to seek and report the truth in a truthful way, they are to serve the public interest, exercise fair play, and act with integrity. Sometimes all these ideals are thrown overboard making way for unfair and biased reporting. Itule and Anderson (2003, p. 438) note that, "fairness is vital for every story and every newspaper, for the unfair story hurts the credibility of the reporter and the editor and the newspaper." For this reason, they suggest that editors should emphasize fairness in their staff meetings and let reporters know that "stories always need to be framed in ways that are fair to all parties" (p. 432).

Quite often, human beings make mistakes in the way they observe things. Some details about a situation or something might escape their attention or be deliberately ignored due to inexperience, personal prejudices and biases, lack of awareness of their existence, or generally that the individual involved is distracted by some other factors. A situation of this nature can lead to inaccurate observation. Journalists are not shielded from this. Keeble (1998, p.182) notes that "even reporters witnessing an event for themselves may be carrying all sorts of personal or cultural baggage that can impact on what they see as true and what they recognise as facts." Journalists are first and foremost human beings and are naturally affected in their duty by some personal realities. If a journalist, in a hurry to get to the place of assignment, for instance, forgets to take a recording device along, or at the scene of an incident gets distracted by an unforeseen personal emergency, the journalist will likely not be in the proper frame of mind to perform the duty and might just engage in whatever is possible within the limits of the situation.

In that circumstance, one cannot rule out inaccurate observation and it will in turn affect the information gathered and the news report presented from it.

The tendency for the news report to have inaccuracies is high and accuracy is immensely important in any news story. If journalists must gather the kind of information that would ensure accuracy in their reports, they should make their observations more conscious and deliberate, eliminating as much as possible, extraneous, and personal factors that stand in the line of duty. Observation can sometimes be painstaking, requiring undivided attention in order to be able to carry out an on-the-spot recording of minute details of an event as it unfolds. Achieving this involves a lot of preparation (a conscious plan) on the part of the journalist. First, identifying the story and the focus, generating background information on the issue, identifying the location of the event, going to work with the right equipment and frame of mind, ensuring that statistics are well noted, confirming the correct spellings of names, noting the proper honorific, looking out for other important details and lastly looking out for a possible follow-up. All these require extra care from the journalist and with them in place would help minimize inaccurate observation.

Another serious error any journalist must guard against through a deliberate and conscious inquiry is overgeneralization. Under normal circumstances, people are prone to infer or draw hasty conclusions on a matter based on previous experience. Experience may be a familiar and useful way to acquire knowledge, but it is not completely foolproof. How someone is affected by an incident depends on who the person is. That two persons or more get exposed to a similar incident does not necessarily mean they see it the same way. Likewise, no two incidents occur exactly the same way. Two course mates may hold their graduation party the same day/time and in the same neighborhood but with different outcomes. Two robbery incidents might take place in the same neighborhood but with different consequences for the victims.

Journalists have the tendency to search for patterns in what they observe. In other words, they have specific things they look out for, or would want to see when they observe an event as it occurs. It helps them draw lines of similarity to link up one event with the other. This often happens when a journalist has been covering a particular beat for too long and becomes overly familiar with the patterns of occurrences in that area. The temptation is to dismiss issues as déjà vu without finding out what makes one incident unique or different from the other. It is also possible for journalists to draw such lines when they are under pressure to interpret a situation in a manner that will enable the public to arrive at a general understanding of the issue. For instance, if there is a case of an oil spill or pipeline fire outbreak in the Niger Delta creeks, many journalists, without visiting the site to know exactly what happened, may conclude that the spill or fire incident would have happened as a result of pipeline vandalism. Pipeline vandalism may be a regular occurrence in the creeks and could result in oil spills or fire outbreaks. But not all oil spills or fire incidents in the Niger Delta are caused by vandals/vandalism. Some can occur because of worn out pipes or a malfunctioning of the system or for some other reason.

Journalists can guard against overgeneralization by deciding well in advance to treat every "news generating" incident on its merit, be ready to go all out in search for information even when it involves leaving their comfort zone, and always be cautious of unconfirmed rumors because they can destroy the credibility of a media house. One major reason journalists must avoid overgeneralization is that it leads to selective observation, perception, and interpretation. Once journalists have been able to draw lines of similarities among events and establish patterns that might enable them to explain or interpret events, they tend to view other events through this mold and overlook anything that presents dissimilarities.

Some media establishments have the habit of seeking "expert opinions" regularly, from certain individuals they consider knowledgeable in their fields, with no pretense of diversifying or seeking the views of other authorities in that area. Whatever opinions those people hold become the yardstick with which such media organizations measure or judge other "expert opinions" from elsewhere or similar occurrences. Given the African situation where some media houses, particularly government-owned, do not tolerate contrary opinions or may not have the financial resources to support such diversity, they tend to be satisfied with what they have and not bother about consulting widely. There is a need for them to seek wider views to help them provide more insights and better interpretation to happenings.

Another pitfall research helps journalists avoid is illogical reasoning. Several factors influence the way journalists make observations and make decisions on what to report or not. Apart from the traditional news determinants of timeliness, prominence, impact, proximity, human interest, and novelty, Harcup (2009, p.17) adds that legal constraints, regulatory codes of practice, proprietors, organizational routines, market forces, cultural bias, patriotism, professional ethos, gender, racial or class imbalance in workforce, time, sources, subjectivity, audience, and advertisers also constitute a source of serious concern about what is reported and how it is reported. When a reporter is in the field gathering information for a news report and has all these factors to consider, one can imagine how difficult the decision on what to settle for would be. The issue of conflicting loyalties is an everyday experience for every journalist, but the demands of such loyalties seem more pronounced in Africa with a developing and fragile media system which is trying to reinvent itself in this digital era. Sometimes, the pull to tilt towards a particular direction may be so strong that logic in the way information is gathered and conclusions drawn is neglected.

A reporter may be detailed to cover a communal clash between two neighboring communities and coincidentally, the owner of the media house happens to come from one of the communities. The reporter requires extraordinary bravery to submit a report indicting the boss's community, if they are at fault. An organization may be involved in community relations activities in its host community. It may have embarked on road construction projects, rehabilitation of schools and presentation of scholarships to indigent students. As noble as these initiatives may be, reporters can decide to misrepresent the facts either by inflating or underreporting them because of what their media organization stands to gain. Such inconsistencies in reporting would be explained away as being "exceptions to the rule or norm" or "that is what *oga* wants." *Oga* could be anybody ranging from the journalist's immediate boss to the highest authority in government. Their opinions take precedence in many situations. Again, journalists may be sent out to cover an event with inadequate facilities or poor equipment. They bring back only what they could capture and build their stories around it.

That some of these contradictions in reporting may be seen as exceptions does not make them acceptable. No system of logic can prove right what it contradicts. Objectivity should be the watchword for any journalist on assignment, and to avoid the dangers of derailing must use systems of logic consciously and explicitly. Logical reasoning involves both inductive and deductive reasoning as earlier discussed in this chapter. In addition, journalists have their professional tenets and their colleagues to provide the checks and balances they need in their job. Although journalists may always face the dilemma of illogical reasoning, a little determination to want to see things done the right way might just be the beginning of a more logical perspective to news coverage.

SOURCES OF INFORMATION/DATA
AND TOOLS FOR RESEARCH

There are many sources that can yield important and relevant information/ data for a journalist in his assignment. These sources are classified into primary and secondary sources. The primary sources include human eyewitnesses, persons directly involved in an incident, important sites such as archaeological sites, historical sites, and religious sites, cultural festivals/ceremonies, and important artifacts. Secondary sources include libraries, the internet, and documents. To access information from these sources, the journalist requires two major research tools, viz interview and observation.

Interviews are a practical qualitative method for discovering what peoples' opinions are on a particular subject matter. It is a purposeful and deliberate interaction between the interviewer and a source who is considered to have relevant information on the subject of discussion. Journalists use interviews to generate information that can be processed as news stories or used as additional details to such stories or any other journalistic writing. A journalist should be able to determine ahead of time why a particular person should be interviewed. The purpose could be to discover more facts about a situation, ascertain the person's opinion on an issue, or any other reason. After establishing the "why" for the interview, the next step is to determine the "how." There is a need for meticulous planning before embarking on any interviews. This will ensure that the journalist remains in control, that is, always on point and knows what is at stake. An interview could be structured, with prepared standardized questions asked in a predetermined order, and little room for the interviewer to ask follow-up questions. On the other hand, an interview could be unstructured, with broad questions that gives the journalist the freedom to ask follow-up questions to obtain more information. Knowing the kind of questions to ask is very important because a news story can fail if a journalist asks the wrong or insufficient questions.

Interviews should go beyond a simple linear process of asking questions and receiving answers (Keyton 2011). A good interview session should be conversational in nature. This will take away suspicion and foster a better relationship between the interviewer and the interviewee. Itule and Anderson (2003) observe that the key to a successful interview is establishing a good rapport with the source. To achieve this, the interviewer will need to find out some background information about the source, as well as being knowledgeable on the subject matter. That way, sources will be more relaxed and open up when they feel they are talking to journalists who speak with knowledge and authority. Hilliard (2004) gives a few guidelines for an effective interview. First, the interviewer should establish early enough what the reason for the interview is, should not start by asking difficult or controversial questions because that might discourage the interviewee; it should not be a monolog, rather an interaction between the interviewer and the interviewee; should seek depth and lastly should be careful of boring and distracting repetition in questions.

If interviews are properly handled, they can yield very good results. This is because interviews, particularly face-to-face, can help establish a friendly and relaxed atmosphere, and with that a more flexible interaction between the source and the interviewer, questioning will have greater depth and details which can result in access to unexpected information, and more clarification to ambiguous questions and issues. The interviewer also has the privilege of observing some information (especially nonverbal cues) during the interview without necessarily asking a question in that direction. Interviews can be face-to-face, by telephone, through email, via Skype, Zoom, and other internet-based services.

Observation is the second tool a journalist can use to gather information. A keen observation of events and general happenings within the society can expose the reporter to many news ideas and equally provide more insight to news reports. The curiosity sparked by such observations and experiences can lead a journalist to ask more questions about a specific situation. In fact, observations are made to obtain a comprehensive picture of a situation. If a journalist, for instance, attended a friend's birthday party and on the way coming back saw a group of persons gathered by the roadside and two persons lying on the ground unconscious, journalistic instincts will tell the journalist that all is not well and therefore should stop, and find out what the matter is. This will involve conducting some preliminary investigations into the situation by observing the scenario and asking questions. From there, a news story can develop.

The journalist needs to always be alert and very observant of the happenings around the environment. Cozby (2007) notes that the world around us is a rich source of material for scientific investigation, and by extension, a rich source for investigative journalism. Information sought through personal observation makes the journalist an eyewitness of some sort, thus eliminating the subjective bias that could come from an interviewee. Observations involve an on-the-spot recording of events as they happen. The journalist needs to be present at an event to take notes unlike interviews that could be done through telephone or any other means. Observations can be time consuming, expensive, and painstaking because of the things the observer should note. This means the observer must have eyes for details and must also be certain of what information he is looking for. Because it is not possible to record everything that happens in a given situation, Ary et al. (2014) note that the investigator should decide beforehand what information to record and note and record those things as they occur since someone's memory can sometimes fail. Kothari and Garg (2014, p. 91) suggest three questions that can help make observations work more effectively. They are: What should be observed? How should the observations be recorded? How can the accuracy of observation be ensured?

Observations are very important in news reporting. According to Itule and Anderson (2003), they add color to stories, that is, they give an audience a clearer picture of a person or an event. A journalist might write a good story from facts gathered during an interview with a source and will make the audience "hear" the story. But to make them "see" the story, the reporter could include certain nonverbal cues displayed by the source during the interview or add striking features about the surroundings to the story. The observations a journalist makes during an interview complement the information from such interviews and are useful in writing feature articles as well as news stories.

RESEARCH AND JOURNALISM IN THE DIGITAL ERA

From the earliest days of communicating through the mass media to the current digital era, media operations have gone through a series of overhauling and transformation. Baran (2012, p. 33) refers to it this way:

> The mass media system we have today has existed more or less as we know it ever since the 1830s. It is a system that has weathered repeated significant change with the coming of increasingly sophisticated technologies—the penny press newspaper was soon followed by mass market books and mass circulating magazines. As the 1800s became the 1900s, these popular media were joined by motion pictures, radio, and sound recording. A few decades later came television, combining news and entertainment, moving images and sound, all in the home and all, ostensibly, for free. The traditional media found new functions and prospered side by side with television. Then more recently came the Internet and World Wide Web.

These changes have brought a convergence and reshaping that is healthy for the mass media and the growth of the industry but at the same time challenging the status quo. Media consumer behavior is no longer what it used to be some decades ago. There is a complete shift in which the old rules no longer apply. Internet access has opened up a new vista to easily available and affordable information. Anybody can access any kind of communication from any website. Since the cost of creating and running a website is so small, individuals can own and maintain theirs (like blogs). This situation has reversed the traditional pattern of one-to-many communication (one reporter to many audience members) and has given everybody the chance of becoming a mass communicator (Dominick 2009). The challenge media houses face today is to be able to capture a sizable portion of the mass audience that has been fragmented into a million pieces as a result of the numerous media outlets available to them.

The fact that anybody can become an electronic publisher with millions of followers (audience) calls for caution and concern. Very often, contents from such websites are not subjected to any kind of check or verification to determine accuracy or authenticity. Some are mere gossip or rumors, out to malign or slander someone or to cause unnecessary panic. Others are even sponsored contents aimed at defaming a political opponent or business rival. Dominick (2009, p. 16) observes that with such contents, "there are no editors to sort out the credible from the bizarre or distinguish merit from trash." If current experiences with information on such blogs and websites are taken as examples, then journalists must conduct a detailed search for information before publishing or reporting any news item. People post just anything without the fear of being censored or someone altering the content. While there is no guarantee that what is made available on these websites and blogs are accurate and worthwhile, the same should not be said of websites of known media organizations like Channels, Nigerian Television Authority, African Independent Television, among others. The issue of credibility is one major challenge, out of several others, that journalism as a profession faces in this digital era. It stands out like a sore thumb. It is only research that can help handle the issue of credibility. Research will guarantee a confirmation and reconfirmation of stories before they are published.

As earlier noted, news sources have increased with the digital age. There are general news sites that offer video, text, and pictures in diverse areas and topics, both national and international. Websites of major newspapers such as punchng.com or broadcast stations such as channelstv.com fall into this category. There are also what Dominick (2009) refers to as news aggregators (Google and Yahoo) that offer a digest of news from other sources. There are equally specialized new sites for contents like sports and blogs too. Because of the nature of these news sources, information gathering here does not require much of interviews or observations, rather computer-assisted reporting. Here, journalists gather and use information from existing or specially created databases to search for patterns, trends, and missing links that can become the basis for news stories.

The digital era has undoubtedly changed the face of the journalism profession globally. Information seems to be everywhere and access to it is no longer as problematic as it used to be. But does this mean journalists no longer need to do thorough investigations before publishing stories? Definitely not! Those journalistic skills of good interviewing, keen observation, and accurate note taking are still very relevant in today's digital reporting. However, the old skills may no longer be sufficient for today's job. Journalists need to learn new technical skills to be able to cope with the demands of journalism in this digital era. These skills include new ways of collecting information using the computer, conducting web searches, downloading data files, building spreadsheets and using them to analyze the data gathered, using emails and chat programs for collaboration and interviews, and setting up listservs.

With the current state of journalism, reporters must learn new ways to report events and tell a story. After gathering information from a wide range of sources, journalists must use writing styles and visuals and sound clips that meet the demands of digital news reporting. As journalists go for assignments, they need to go along with more than a notebook and a pen or just any kind of recording device to gather data and capture all that is required to tell a story. More importantly, they need outdoor broadcasting vans fully equipped with satellite facilities including telephones, laptop or tablet computers, wireless internet connection, digital cameras, and other digital equipment necessary for outdoor reporting.

CONCLUSION

Journalism should inform society about itself and bring to the public domain what ordinarily should have been hidden or kept private. Taking on this responsibility makes journalists accountable to the society. They can go to where every other person may not be able to visit, see what others may not see, hear what other people may not hear, and smell what everybody may not smell, all these in the bid to collect information and transmit the same to the society. In addition, they must become the conscience of the society. This is a big responsibility they hold in trust for the society. Therefore, it is expected of them to be trustworthy and tell the society the truth always.

The coming of the digital age with its challenges has made this expectation more difficult. There are tens of thousands of blogs and websites and social media platforms that have assigned to themselves the role of journalists, albeit, nonprofessionals, that regularly disseminate information to the society. Sometimes, the information so disseminated is a mélange of falsehood, half-truths, and truths. This is eroding the credibility of the profession. Professional journalism has always depended on research for objective, accurate, and factual reporting. Research may appear time wasting, energy sapping, and intellectually demanding, but it is one major tool to handle the issue of credibility, inaccurate observation, overgeneralization, selective exposure and interpretation, and illogical reasoning which may affect the news reports that journalists present to the society.

REFERENCES

Akpabio, J. 2019. "The Value of Academic Research." In *Handbook of Communication and Media Research*, edited by Obot, C., Nwagbara, G. U., and Batta, H. Ibadan: Ibadan University Press.

Alao, D., and Olawunmi, B. 2014. *News and Beat Reporting.* Lagos: Jamiro Press Link.

Ary, D., Jacobs, L. C., Sorensen, C. K., and Walker, D. A. 2014. *Introduction to Research in Education* (9th ed.). Boston: Cengage Learning.

Baran, S. J. 2012. *Introduction to Mass Communication: Media Literacy and Culture* (7th ed.). New York: McGraw Hill.

Baxter, L. A., and Babbie, E. 2003. *The Basics of Communication Research.* Boston: Wadsworth/Cengage Learning.

Bennet, W. L., and Lawrence, R. G. 1995. "News Icons and the Mainstreaming of Social change." *Journal of Communication* 45 (3): 20–39.

Best, J. W., and Kahn, J. V. 2006. *Research in Education* (10th ed.). London: Pearson Education.

Chawla, D., and Sondhi, N. 2011. *Research Methodology: Concepts and Cases.* New Delhi: Vikas Publishing.

Cozby, P. C. 2007. *Methods in Behavioral Research* (9th ed.). New York: McGraw Hill.

Dominick, J. R. 2009. *The Dynamics of Mass Communication: Media in the Digital Age* (10th ed.). New York: McGraw Hill.

Harcup, T. 2009. *Journalism: Principles and Practice* (2nd ed.). London: Sage.

Hillard, R. L. 2004. *Writing for Television, Radio, and New Media* (8th ed.). Belmont: Thompson and Wadsworth.

Itule, B. D. and Anderson, D. A. 2003. *News Writing and Reporting for Today's Media* (6th ed.). New York: McGraw Hill.

Keeble, R. 1998. *The Newspaper Handbook* (2nd ed). London: Routledge.

Keyton, J. 2001. *Communication Research: Asking Questions and Finding Answers.* New York: McGraw Hill.

Kitzinger, J. 2000. "Media Templates: Patterns of Association and the (Re)construction of Meaning." *Media, Culture and Society* 22 (1): 61–84.

Kothari, C. R., and Garg, G. 2014. *Research Methodology: Methods and Techniques* (3rd ed.). New Delhi: New Age International Publishers.

Nwabueze, C. 2009. *Reporting: Principles, Approaches, Special Beats.* Owerri: Top Shelve Publishers.

Nwagbara, G. U. 2006. "Research Methods/Data Analysis." In Wilson, D. (ed.), *Fundamentals of Human Communication.* Ibadan: Stirling Horden Publishers.

O'Shaughnessy, M., and Stadler, J. 2008. *Media and Society* (4th ed.). Oxford: Oxford University Press.

Schaefer, R. T. 2005. *Sociology* (9th ed.). New York: McGraw Hill.

Treadwell, D. 2011. *Introduction to Communication Research: Paths of Inquiry.* London: Sage.

UNESCO. 1981. *Many Voices, One World.* Ibadan: Ibadan University Press.

Wimmer, R. D. and Dominick, J. R. 2011. *Mass Media Research: An Introduction* (9th ed.). Boston: Wadsworth/Cengage Learning.

Wrench, J. S., Thomas-Maddox, C., Richmond, V. P., and McCroskey, J. C. 2008. *Quantitative Research Methods for Communication: A Hands-On Approach.* Oxford: Oxford University Press.

SECTION VII

Nigerian Sports Communication and Robotics

Chapter 18

Technology for Peacebuilding in Northeast Nigeria

Harnessing Precision of Collaborative Robotics and Artificial Intelligence

Pate Umaru and Joseph Wilson

For a decade, the Northeast region of Nigeria has been engulfed in terror and violent conflict caused by the Boko Haram insurgency. In 2015, the insurgents were halted and defeated by the governments of Nigeria and neighboring countries of Chad, Cameroon, and Niger. Subsequently, developments in the region have now shifted to resettling displaced people, reconstruction of destroyed areas, and relocating displaced persons from camps to their original settlements. In this process, robotics and artificial intelligence technology can be considered as worthy supportive instruments. Absence of precision in operations in the region has led to loss of lives, ineffective humanitarian aid delivery, and poor information flow, among others. At this point in time, the region requires high-level precision in peacebuilding efforts, which requires advanced intelligence to achieve precise results. Technologies that require minimal human intervention, such as collaborative robotics and artificial intelligence are essential to help stakeholders deal with specific needs of the peacebuilding efforts and shape peacebuilding on issues of security, health, shelter, education, humanitarian interventions, and so forth, in the region. The precision in collaborative robotics and the advances in artificial intelligence have undoubtedly complemented human efforts in various fields and their applications in human endeavors are abundant. Considering these and other gaps, this chapter examines the potentials of collaborative robotics and artificial intelligence in peacebuilding in the Northeast region of Nigeria by the major stakeholders (security, humanitarian organizations, civil society organizations, the media, government agencies, and members of society).

Technology is unimaginably influencing everyday activities of the people globally. The increasing desire or yearning for efficiency in societal activities is compelling individuals, groups and organizations to explore the possibilities in adopting and utilizing technology to facilitate the realization of set goals. Fortunately, technological advances now present a number of such opportunities and possibilities globally. There are smart technologies that offer solutions to issues relating to health, education, urban planning, agriculture, commerce, among others, when and if effectively used.

In recent times, the subject of artificial intelligence and robotics is increasingly being adopted and utilized. *UNESCO Courier* (2018, p. 3) states that "there have been spectacular advances in the field of artificial intelligence (AI) in recent years, leading to inventions that we had never thought possible." These inventions center on the use of computers and robots with the ability and capacity to learn "how to improve their own work, and even make decisions—this is done through an algorithm, of course, and without individual consciousness" (*UNESCO Courier* 2018, p. 3). While arguments rage on, as to the impact that AI and robots might be a few years away from influencing or causing any considerable effects on the lives of people globally, Agarwal (2018) points out that "the fact remains that it is already having an enormous impact on us" and they are already affecting people's daily decisions and lifestyles. Similarly, Kumar (2017, p. 7) notes that "we are all using artificial intelligence in our daily life in one way or another. We are using it, managing it and responding to artificial intelligence every hour and minute of the day directly and indirectly." It is the same thing for robotics.

Robotics technology is used routinely to carry out several tasks, from the simplest to the most complex, a scenario Staples (2018) described as a task people don't want to do because of the boredom, complexity, and dangers involved. More recently, collaborative robotics (Cobot) (a robot intended to physically interact with humans in a shared workspace) is gaining relevance, too. According to Elejalde-Ruiz (2018), Cobot has become one of the fastest-growing robotics segments and is becoming an increasingly popular automation tool designed to augment the capabilities of human workers rather than replace them.

AI and Cobots can be programmed to carry out some tasks that are too complex for humans to achieve a more precise result. Although human beings sit to control and program, AI and Cobots perform actual tasks (in area crime fighting, medicine, agriculture, education, security and surveillance) which helps maximize precision (Staples 2018).

Security and surveillance, for instance, are already an issue of serious concern globally and require precision in preventing or mitigating the threats, dangers, and destruction that accompany most security and surveillance breaches. Interestingly, these challenges have not gone without efforts in the technological sector to address challenges associated with security and surveillance. AI and robotics are not left out as possible solutions with capability of maximum precision to security and surveillance issues. Agarwal (2018, p. 21) notes that "While we can all debate the ethics of using a broad surveillance system, there's no denying the fact that it is being used and AI is playing a big part in that." Similarly, Staples (2018, p. 4) points out that "Crime fighting robots are helpful in any situation that would be too dangerous for people." Lanz (2017, p. 1) notes that "new technologies, in particular Artificial Intelligence (AI) and virtual online platforms, can enhance global efforts to prevent conflicts and build peace."

Nigeria, like other nations, is involved in adopting and utilizing technology to address complex issues of interest. It formulated the information technology policy in 2001 and established the National Information Technology Development Agency (NITDA) to drive technology for development (NITDA, n.d.). This effort has led to the diffusion of technology in all sectors of the country. According to Oladimeji and Folayan (2017), the importance of Information and Communication Technology (ICT) to the different sectors of the Nigerian economy, governance, education, and legal system, among others, is enormous. Thus, as the nation grapples with security challenges and explores possibilities to address these challenges, AI and robotics become imperative.

The Northeast region of Nigeria, for example, has been devastated by Boko Haram insurgency and terror since 2009. At the peak of the insurgency in 2009–2015, when the terror group *Jama'atu Ahlis Sunnah Lidda'awati Wal Jihad*, also called Boko Haram (Western Education Is Sinful), was rated as the deadliest terror group in the world, captured a chunk of the Northeast region of Nigeria with about 25 million people and unleashed violence and terror on citizens. It was in the later part of 2015 that the terrorists were halted and defeated by the governments of Nigeria and neighboring countries of Chad, Cameroon, and Niger. At the height of its activities, characterized by bombings, killings, and widespread violence, thousands of people of all classifications were killed or maimed, and towns and villages were devastated. The group killed peasant farmers, fishermen, teachers, women, children, students, politicians, traditional leaders, clerics, traders, professionals, and security operatives.

About 30,000 to 50,000 people have been killed in Boko Haram induced terror in five years in Nigeria (*Guardian*, February 26, 2016). The World Bank had revealed in a preliminary validation report on the impact of the insurgency that Borno State alone, the epicenter of the crisis, had lost 20,000 citizens and suffered property damage of $5.9 billion (₦1.9 trillion) (*Daily*

Trust, March 21, 2016). Similarly, 9,000 police personnel and 600 classroom teachers had lost their lives in the Boko Haram insurgency, while 2.5 million people have been displaced, towns and villages devastated, and property worth billions of dollars destroyed (*Daily Trust*, Oct 5, 2015; *Guardian*, Nov 12, 2015). In brief, the 25 million people of the region were severely affected by the atrocities of the terrorists.

In recent times, developments in the region have shifted to resettling displaced people, reconstruction of destroyed areas, and relocating displaced people from the camps to their original settlements. This is as a result of the gains made by various stakeholders for lasting peace and development. As stakeholders explore possibilities for peacebuilding, technology is obviously an option worthy of adoption in the region to complement other measures, especially in maximizing precision.

Events have shown that precision is posing a challenge to stakeholders in their efforts to end the bloody conflict and build lasting peace. For example, in January 2017 it was reported that airstrikes by the Nigerian Airforce mistakenly killed refugees and injured humanitarian workers in Rann community (Kazeem, 2017; Associated Press, 2017; UN Office for the Coordination of Humanitarian Affairs 2017). Another example is the uncoordinated activities of several nongovernmental organizations in the Northeast, especially Borno State due to "uncoordinated efforts . . . different NGOs to IDPs when the resources could have been better utilized in other areas." That interventions by these NGOs "are based on what their team of assessors see as needs of the communities and not what the people really need" (Sulieman 2017, p. 24, 25).

There is also the issue of precision by the media, a major information stakeholder in peacebuilding. Furnard (2018, para. 1) notes that a team of international journalists, Nigerian journalists, humanitarian workers, and a coalition of civil society organizations disclosed that "most of the news about insurgency from the North East is fake and 'a direct opposite of the actual situation on the ground.'"

Accordingly, this chapter examines the potentials of collaborative robotics and artificial intelligence in the peacebuilding process in the Northeast region of Nigeria. Thus, the chapter is set to examine how Cobots and artificial intelligence can be used for maximum and high level precision application by stakeholders for peacebuilding activities as well as identify emerging challenges in the use of such technologies to maximize precision in peacebuilding activities in the region.

LITERATURE REVIEW

Artificial Intelligence, Collaborative Robotics, and Peacebuilding

Research into AI dates back to the 1950s when issues tied to areas such as problem-solving and symbolic methods became of interest to researchers. Subsequently the US Department of Defense focused on the development of AI in the 1960s and began programming computers to mimic basic human reasoning. In recent times, because of increased data volumes, advanced algorithms, and improvements in computing power and storage, AI has become a popular term and has paved the way for computers being automated and enabled with formal reasoning to augment human abilities (SAS, n.d.).

Artificial intelligence (AI) is an area of computer science that emphasizes the creation of intelligent machines, such as a computer system that is able to perform tasks normally requiring human intelligence, such as visual perception, speech recognition, decision-making, and translation between languages (Techopedia, n.d.).

AI enables machines to learn from human interaction with these machines and adjust to new inputs and perform human-like tasks. Most common examples of AI are chess-playing computers, self-driving cars rely heavily on deep learning and natural language processing (SAS n.d.). AI entails computers to be programmed to accomplish specific tasks through processing large amounts of data and recognizing patterns in the data. This process usually exhibits traits such as: knowledge, reasoning, problem-solving, perception, learning, planning, and the ability to manipulate activities (Techopedia, n.d.; SAS, n.d.). According to Gupta (2017, p. 2):

> artificial intelligence is all about performing tasks by machine that require human intelligence but without the presence of a human being. Artificial intelligence enables devices and not just robots to understand language, solve problems after analyzing it, provide logical reasoning like a human being could and all such possibilities that human beings are capable of.

AI combines large amounts of data with fast, repetitive processing and intelligent algorithms that allow the software to learn automatically from features in the data (SAS, n.d.; Howstuffworks, n.d.). Furthermore, SAS (n.d.) notes that AI, through computer technology analyses, understands and generates human language, analyzes and understands images, captures images or videos in real time and interprets their surroundings. There is a high visibility of AI in question and answering systems that can be used to provide risk notification in various fields, legal assistance, patent searches, among others.

AI applications' effect is most visible in the industry, banking, insurance, health, media, and defense sectors. Several tasks are now automated. For example, in the health care sector, AI applications can provide personal health care assistance through life coaching, reminding patients to take their pills, exercise or eat healthier, X-ray readings and easy interpretation of some medical test results. Marketing is another area that showcases the AI in action. For example, it provides virtual shopping capabilities that offer personalized recommendations and discusses purchase options with the consumer. The constant reminder to buy a product earlier viewed by a customer is a function of AI. In the sports sector, AI is used to capture images of a game and provide coaches with options on how to better organize the game, including suitable strategy. In the manufacturing sector, Smart technologies can help manufacturers diversify into offering both manufactured products and complementary services (SAS, n.d.; Link Labs 2018, Ganascia 2018). Ganascia (2018) points out that:

> Many achievements using AI techniques surpass human capabilities. in1997, a computer programme defeated the reigning world chess champion, and more recently, in 2016, other computer programmes have beaten the world's best Go (an ancient Chinese board game) players and some top poker players. Computers are proving, or helping to prove, mathematical theorems; knowledge is being automatically constructed from huge masses of data, in terabytes (1012 bytes), or even petabytes (1015 bytes), using machine learning techniques. (p.9)

This is in line with Wolverton's (2018) position that there is increasing fear of how artificial intelligence is going to affect society, but at the moment, AI is a lot better at some things than others. For example, Facebook is increasingly relying on AI to monitor its service and identify content that violates its policies and guidelines. It is reported that Facebook is having varying levels of success as a result of the use of AI. Posts that are offensive, posts that promotes nudity, terrorism-related posts from the likes of ISIS and Al Qaeda are easy to police with AI and most recently the use of AI to tackle hate speech (Wolverton 2018). Terdiman (2018) adds that Facebook is using AI to proactively detect eight categories of content: nudity, graphic violence, terrorism, hate speech, spam, fake accounts, racism, and suicide prevention.

New information technologies and the advent of machines powered by AI have already strongly influenced human activities in the twenty-first century, thereby simplifying everyday tasks, and it is increasingly becoming impossible to imagine how most societal activities could be managed without them (Wisskirchen et al. 2017). Increasingly, machines enabled with AI are performing numerous tasks speedily and precisely. Wisskirchen et al. (2017, p.13) note that there a number of such task from the field of robotics and AI.

For example, "'smart factories,' driverless cars, delivery drones or 3D printers, which, based on an individual template, can produce highly complex things without changes in the production process or human action in any form being necessary." This, what Gupta (2017) describes as the intersection of AI and robotics to create what is known as artificially intelligent robots.

Collaborative robotics (Cobots) put robots alongside humans to work, reduce up-front investments, and improve flexibility and productivity. According to Curran (2017) notes Cobots have made it possible that instead of focusing on removing humans completely from a work process, it is seen as an opportunity for humans and robots to work together. Since 2017, Cobot has dominated the robots' market, and it is estimated that by 2021 the market is expected to grow to approximately two billion US dollars and 150,000 units (Gonzalez 2018). This growth is not unrelated to the fact that several industries are looking towards Cobots as a way of introducing the new automation future and because Cobots are cheap, lightweight, easy to program, designed to work alongside humans, and can be introduced into an existing work process without major transformation or expense (Curran 2017; Gonzalez 2018). Emphasizing the growing relevance of Cobot, Gonzalez (2018, p. 2) notes that "Cobots excel because they can function in areas of work previously occupied only by their human counterparts. They are designed with inherent safety features like force feedback and collision detection, making them safe to work right next to human operators."

However, Curran (2017) points out that although there are surprising benefits of Cobots over the long term, especially in providing the opportunity they create to tap into innovation and creativity of workers in various fields, the twist to it is that Cobots would take on more of the repetitive tasks while humans take on the higher-level aspects. This lays to rest the fear that robots will take away human jobs.

Until recently, the benefits of automation in workplaces have been limited in part because there were no clearly defined ways to allow humans and robots to work together and thus led to the adoption of workplace automation in either lights-out automation or robot-centric automation. Curan (2017) noted that the lights-out automation approach completely removes humans from the work process. That is, operations or work can go on unsupervised for weeks at a time without human involvement in the facility.

However, the robot-centric automation approach limits the interaction between humans and robots by enclosing robots behind barriers or a closet and implementing protocols to mediate how and when people can enter a robot workspace. This is because of the dangers involved in having humans working around exceptionally large, heavy, fast-moving robots.

These approaches were considered awfully expensive and cost intensive and required skills to program the robots to do their jobs, which limits work automation's benefits. Only a few business outfits could tap from these auto-mation approaches (the manufacturing industries). However, Cobot, which is synonymous to the human-centric Cobot approach, puts robots alongside human workers. This is in line with the reasoning of Curran (2017) that because robots cannot do everything, collaboration with humans in the same workspace may achieve the best results.

A mix of the enormous possibilities in AI and Cobot could be a useful combination for facilitating the realization of set goals in various fields of human endeavors. For instance, looking at the incessant conflict globally, AI and Cobot can support the conflict management process. Lamb (2017, p. 1) points out that:

> Every day it seems I read an article about the march of robots into our jobs and our lives. They can drive cars, milk cows and make burgers, apparently. And often, enthusiasts claim they will do these jobs better than us flawed human beings. Logically then, let's turn to robots to solve our most intractable problems. Human beings seem unable to kick the habit of fighting and killing one another.

Similarly, Honkela, cited in Nurminen (2017, p. 17), "states that machines and artificial intelligence cannot substitute human beings, but they can provide knowledge, possibilities and support for peace processes. Those processes are often about understanding the language, culture and marginal-ization." Those processes point to the future of a peacebuilding effort devoid of avoidable human errors and unnecessary human risks, especially in a world described by Lamb (2017) as increasingly uncertain where more people's lives are affected by the rising conflicts and increasing humanitarian crisis. However, since daily reports point to the injection of one form of AI and robotics into societal life, focusing on "peacebot" would be a logical way to go in a peacebuilding effort (Lamb 2017; Wisskirchen et al. 2017).

Peacebuilding is generally about developmental action designed to enhance capacities for lasting peace. According to Jennings (2003) it involves sustainable conflict management to enable citizens and governing institu-tions to better attend to the business of everyday life for a more fulfilling and rewarding future. Peacebuilding usually thrives on an enabling environment for the repair of civil infrastructure, good governance, and rehabilitation of education systems, among others, through implementing modalities by which developmental goals are achieved. Similarly, Peinado (n.d.) notes that peace-building thrives on:

- Information: providing information on those issues that directly affect them

- Public Consultation: the population should be consulted on issues that the external actors have perceived as problematic.
- Participation: encourage the people to commit themselves to achieve the objectives of peacebuilding efforts or projects
- Mobilization: the local communities take the initiative, in an independent manner, and the external actors back up the process

All of these usually take place in the dimensions of:

- Political institutions, which entail democratization, state reform, good governance, and respect for human rights;
- Military and security dimensions, consisting of demobilization, demilitarization, disarmament, reintegration of the former combatants and de-mining
- Social dimension made up of the return and reintegration of displaced and refugee populations, rehabilitation of basic social services, attention to the needs of the vulnerable groups, especially women and children
- Economic dimension which deals with the reestablishing of a stable macro-economic framework, reconstructing the basics (Peinado, n.d.).

Larrauri's (2014) perspectives to technology and the future of peacebuilding points to alternative infrastructures such as: digital media tools which provide new and creative ways for local peacebuilders to foster alternative discourses and challenge prevailing conflict narratives. This is predominantly about information and communication among stakeholders (peacebuilders) to foster positive contact in affected communities and possibly conflict groups. Technology can further give power to local peacebuilders to counteract calls for violence and make peace viral. Information and communication are vital in all areas of the peacebuilding effort.

THEORETICAL FRAMEWORK

This chapter is anchored on the Diffusion of Innovation theory and the Push-ICT theory. Diffusion of innovation (DOI) theory, developed by Everett Rogers in 1962, explains the adoption of a new idea, behavior, or product (i.e., "innovation") in stages and establishes adopter categories (initiator, early adopter, early majority, late majority, and laggards). The injection of AI and Cobots in Nigeria's peacebuilding efforts in the Northeast region of the country would be an innovation and a way to address the issue of precision in stakeholder's peacebuilding activities. The key to adoption of AI and Cobots as an innovation is that the government must perceive the idea or product as innovative. It is through this that diffusion is possible. The way this would be speedily accepted is through the Push-ICT theory which stipulates that in a situation where information and communication technologies are considered important or relevant to development of individuals or community, such technologies should be deployed by the relevant organization (government, nongovernmental organizations or individual). (In this case, international organizations such as the International telecommunication Union can ensure the availability of AI software and Cobots for use by relevant stakeholders in the Northeast region.)

• The relevant technology or services (e.g., training) should be made affordable. It can be deployed free or highly subsidized.
• The deploying organization or individual would clearly identify workable benefits of the technology and subsequently coerce the individuals or communities to use the deployed technologies or services.
• The push is usually through a policy framework, cheap and affordable deployment of ICT facilities, social status push and ICT-user push.
• Where ICT remains unaffordable (may be as a result of poor implementation of policy) users also push ICT providers to offer affordable facilities and services.

When there is easy access or availability of AI systems and Cobots, resistance to adopt the use of ICT is highly reduced, while acceptance for use is greatly enhanced and the possibility to use the technology is high (Wilson 2017).

AI, COBOT, AND PRECISION IN PEACEBUILDING IN NORTHEAST NIGERIA

The peacebuilding process in Northeast Nigeria involves the communities and key stakeholders, in this case most affected states of Borno and Yobe which at the moment have a lot of ongoing security and humanitarian activities. It is observable that the peacebuilding efforts by these stakeholders have in one way or the other suffered setbacks in precisely executing their activities to make the maximum impact. The security forces have faced precision challenges, the media and fake news or erroneous reportage leading to erroneous information. Humanitarian activities have been carried out that are observably not the immediate needs of the communities or poorly executed important activities. AI and Cobots can help in addressing or reducing error to its barest minimum. The AI and Cobots possibilities are:

AI and Cobots for peacebuilding depend largely on the availability of the infrastructure (which is primarily the responsibility of government and international organizations involved in the peacebuilding process) to be used in the following areas in affected Borno and Yobe states in the Northeast.

APPLICATION OF COBOTS AND ARTIFICIAL INTELLIGENCE FOR PEACEBUILDING ACTIVITIES IN THE NORTHEAST REGION IN NIGERIA

Peacebuilding efforts are broad with a myriad of activities. This chapter identifies key areas that require the precision of Cobots and AI, which would be of immense importance in helping shape the peacebuilding process in the affected states.

Security

Security is an important and indispensable part of peacebuilding. For example, the Military in Stability Operations is key in ensuring that conflict is brought down to its lowest ebb to allow for other developmental activities, making rehabilitation and the return to stability less problematic. Although security agencies' peacebuilding is no substitute for the expertise and capacities of civilian agencies or organizations, it is an important complement in securing post-conflict peace. As is the case in Borno and Yobe states, while the armed forces and other security forces have recorded successes in decimating the insurgents, there are still attacks that pull back efforts to restore lasting peace in the region. Cobots and AI would be useful in ensuring precision in carrying out stability operations to restore, provide armed escorts to all that is required for rehabilitation, reconstruction, rebuilding, and return of displaced people back to their communities.

- Cobots can help in mine clearing activities; assist in detecting arms hidden in communities and other dangerous weapons (swords, daggers, etc.) among returnees.
- AI can be used to monitor inciting communication among returnees, especially mobile communication. Monitor the informant's communication to insurgents. Monitor insurgent's communication to mitigate possible attacks on rehabilitated communities, help in precession and in stability operation of security agencies: arrest only culprits and not the random arrest as is most times the case.

These roles of Cobots and AI in peacebuilding can be viewed within the purview of Arkin's (2007) moral robots' argument that they may be even better than humans in picking a moral course of action by virtue of them considering more courses of action and carry out operations more ethically than human soldiers are capable of.

- A combination of Cobots and AI in drones technology (unmanned aerial vehicles) can be used for surveillance to track insurgents' movements and conduct reconnaissance in communities prone to insurgents' attacks and possibly assist with mitigation activities, searching and recovering victims, and abandoned weapons.
- Quick data analysis: the security agencies are no doubt flooded with all forms of data from monitored communication, data from surveillance, information from informants, etc. Security agencies need a synergy as to how fast they can analyze this information for immediate use in the peacebuilding activities. Cobots and AI can be used for intelligence system awareness to make information insightful and ready for use by all of the security agencies in the region. According to Joshi (2018) data can be used to create situational awareness by applying such data to deep learning, statistical and probabilistic algorithms.
- Security agencies in Nigeria are obviously embracing digital technology like their counterpart in other parts of the world. Digitization is obviously visible with the various agencies using digital technologies for communication and transmitting peacebuilding efforts in Northeast Nigeria. It is necessary to secure the information stored on these web portals. AI comes in handy by offering cybersecurity options as a response to any external infiltration.
- Early warning Cobots and AI technology can be used against impending attack by the insurgents, since there are always attacks by the insurgents to frustrate the peacebuilding process in the region. Early warning Cobots or AI technologies would be useful in this regard. There has been a report that the new Nigerian Army has invented new technologies in army uniforms that campaign against insurgents in the Northeast. Uniforms that will be worn by soldiers will reportedly be tagged wherever a soldier is located and sends signal when a soldier is in danger (*The Cable* 2018). This precision early warning technology would keep peacebuilders safe to carry out their activities without exposure to unnecessary or avoidable dangers.
- Interaction with the communities or the popular civil-military interaction is key in the peacebuilding process in the Northeast. To avoid rumors, misconception, fake news, or distorted information, especially from the military, AI is necessary to organize interaction processes in line with

the principles of simplicity, standardization, and clearly executable by all whose duties are to interact with the communities.

Humanitarian Activities

Humanitarian activities are central to any conflict. The UN, INGO, NGO, Civil Society, national emergency management agencies, among others, carry out these activities to help alleviate the suffering of victims of conflict. These activities cut across several facets of human needs, especially shelter, food, health, water, and sanitation. In Northeast Nigeria, especially Borno and Yobe states, among the interventions of great interest for the NGOs is food supply, sanitation, shelter, health services, rehabilitation, reconstruction, and resettlement. There are observable precision challenges in humanitarian activities, prominent among which is the poor distribution of relief materials. It has often been reported that these materials are diverted (Edeh 2018; Musa 2017; Haruna 2016). Cobots and AI can be helpful in addressing this by installing robots on trucks so as to provide some form of monitoring of truck movements and report any form of diversion as well as providing information on the locations of the diverted materials. Cobots can be used to monitor distribution in camps through aerial monitoring of whether relief materials remain for use in camps or are evacuated from internally displaced people camps or communities. Cobots can also help in ensuring that only those entitled to get the relief materials get them by providing some form of biometric checks of those who are given relief materials.

- Humanitarian information and the transportation of humanitarian cargo as well as distribution would be greatly impacted by Cobot and AI by making these processes faster and precise. Speed in humanitarian information is important for many aspects of emergency response and recovery. If they are not available when decisions need to be made there is the possibility of complication in effectively delivering humanitarian services. Cobots and AI at this point can speed up things with maximum accuracy from data to decisions in the area of data collection and authentication of beneficiaries of relief materials. Cobot could help in the automation process of registration of displaced people in camps or resettled people in communities. The identification of community members can be facilitated by Cobots through biometric identification of community members and ensuring that only community members or camp members access the collected relief materials. This would prevent the infiltration of communities and camps to access relief materials not meant for them. Mobile service Cobots can be useful in this regard (detection and identification) by using any of the fastest means of either the iris, face, or speech pattern.

- Cobots can help in lifting heavy materials in distribution centers and provide surveillance to warehouses where relief materials are stored. Cobots can be used to ensure that only authorized personnel gain access to the warehouses.
- Reconstruction of the communities: Cobots can be used for mines detection and clearing in building or construction sites, especially in communities that were taken over by the insurgents in the past but retaken by the security forces. Cobots can be assigned tasks of working in dangerous conditions that would remove risks to humans. For example, communities that are considered not safe and workers reluctant to work in such places inspire being declared safe by the security forces. Specialized Cobots can be deployed for carrying heavy equipment, lay bricks and fabrication of building components. There are Cobots that can lay two thousand bricks a day, working collaboratively with masons to increase productivity. This process can help fast-track the community rebuilding process in the region.
- Cobots can help in areas that require precision in the reconstruction, rehabilitation, and resettlement process in the region. Drones are an excellent tool for monitoring construction sites for precision in construction. Cobots can help identify defects in construction plans and draw immediate attention to such defects and ensure a perfect fit every time for all buildings. Cobots can help in facilitating agricultural land preparation by detecting and clearing mines in agricultural land, planting of seeds, weed control and harvesting, shepherding, and herding (use of drones to monitor animals in the field and alert owners of encroaching rustlers).
- Cobots can be helpful in ensuring precision in health care issues in the region. Cobot medical assistant would be helpful in facilitating automation of medical records by automatically entering information into patient's electronic health records for resettled communities and internally displaced people camps across the region. Cobots can monitor patients' vital statistics and alert medical practitioners when there is a need for human presence, allowing the few medical practitioners in the affected communities to monitor multiple patients simultaneously. Cobot can be used by surgeons to assist in carrying out surgeries, even in medical facilities in camps and communities without necessarily embarking on the task for moving patients to facilities in the big cities, or encountering the challenge of precision and success rates in operations. Cobots can help greatly in ensuring speed in simple tasks as

drawing blood, checking patient vital signs and conditions, taking care of patient hygiene, and preparing and dispensing medications.

- Coordination of humanitarian activities: there is a constant challenge of coordination in humanitarian activities (World Economic Forum 2015). Duplication of roles is a challenge in the humanitarian activities in the region. NGOs might as usual claim they work collaboratively but there is observable duplication of activities that complicates the effectiveness of the needed impact. Cobots and AI can be of immense help in this regard by assisting coordinators in the identification and documentation of projects and programs of the NGOs and other actors, as well as making data available for use by all intending actors, and provide an overview of the entire activities and next line of action. Cobot and AI can be handy by providing a map of who is doing what to create harmony and precisely provide what is needed at each point in time. This can be done by automation of all organizations and their various responsibilities and their intending activities, tagging of all humanitarian materials to monitor where it is going or determine where best to send them. Drones could be used to capture imagery of activities in various locations to enable relevant government and other humanitarian actors to instantly know who is doing what. This could help in achieving a more coordinated response and instant approach to logistics such that only relief materials and services needed by communities would reach such communities.

Information: The Media

A conspicuous challenge in the Northeast is information-based. A lot of fake news and wrong information are daily circulated about events as they unfold from the activities of the insurgents, the military, government, and humanitarian activities to the communities. The role of the media is key in this regard. Unfortunately, they serve as channels for propagation of fake news. The media have a role in terms of social education, addressing many issues of concern to the target audience, and in the process helping to reduce tensions and build trust within the society. Without reliable news and information, people in the region are forced to rely on rumors, and rumors invariably spread distrust and stereotypes. Important information can be relayed to the populations regarding various issues in the region (government effort, humanitarian efforts, rehabilitation, reconstruction and resettlement efforts, etc.) and fake news can be checked with some level of precision with the aid of Cobots and AI. AI can be deployed to check fake news and hate speech especially in the media channels through the automatic detect and delete fake news and hate speech AI system; automatic detect and hide fake news and hate speech AI system; automatic detect and block/remove user AI system and filter and review fake news and hate speech AI system. These AI systems can be introduced by media organizations and relevant government agencies like the Nigerian Broadcasting Commission and the Nigerian Press Council to monitor media organizations using this technology to check fake news and hate speech in the media. Getting precise and correct information from the media would help reduce the tension often caused by information managers.

CHALLENGES

There are obvious challenges of adopting Cobots and AI in ensuring precision in the peacebuilding activities in Northeast Nigeria. The major challenge is the sociopolitical factor. This has to do with the usual reluctance that comes with accepting change by the leadership of nations. Ordinarily the Nigerian government can saddle the Ministry of Science and Technology, Nigerian Communication Commission, and Nigerian Information Technology Development Agency with the responsibility of partnering with relevant actors (security agencies, humanitarian organizations, and the media organizations operating in the Northeast) to deploy these technologies. But the political will has always been a challenge, especially in program implementation in Nigeria. Great initiatives in the country often suffer neglect especially when the initiator is no longer in power.

CONCLUSION

Cobots and AI are no doubt a useful alternative for Nigeria to address the never-going-away errors often recorded in the peacebuilding activities in Northeast Nigeria, especially in Borno and Yobe. The recent resurgence of the insurgents' attacks to disrupt the already progressing peacebuilding effort is a thing that can be mitigated through effective use of Cobots and AI. The role of Cobots and AI would facilitate a system that would provide human-like interactions with robots and software and offer decision support for specific tasks, provide mapping for a more organized and coordinated humanitarian activities as well as information devoid of fake news and hate speeches. Cobots and AI could have obvious potentials in the conflict-affected Northeast Nigeria in enhancing precision in all peacebuilding activities. It is therefore necessary for the government and other relevant actors in the peacebuilding process to explore technology options, especially Cobots and AI.

REFERENCES

Agarwal, R. 2018. "10 Examples of Artificial Intelligence You're Using in Daily Life." Beebom, December 8. Accessed September 21, 2018, https://beebom.com/examples-of-artificial-intelligence/.

Arkin, R. C. 2007. "Governing Lethal Behavior: Embedding Ethics in a Hybrid Deliberative/Reactive Robot Architecture." Georgia Institute of Technology. Accessed September 21, 2018. https://www.cc.gatech.edu/ai/robot-lab/online-publications/formalizationv35.pdf.

Associated Press. 2017. "Nigerian Air Force Kills More Than 100 Civilians by Accident in Strike Targeting Boko Haram: Military Official." Accessed January 17, 2017. https://www.nbcnews.com/news/world/nigerian-air-force-kills-more-100-civilians-accident-northeastern-strike-n707876.

The Cable. 2018. "Buratai: New army uniform sends signal when you are in danger." Accessed December 23, 2018. www.thecable.ng/buratai-new-army-uniform-sends-signal-when-you-are-in-danger.

Curran, C. 2017. "Humans and machines: Collaborative robots open a new automation frontier." Accessed January 16, 2017. http://usblogs.pwc.com/emerging-technology/collaborative-robots-open-a-new-automation-frontier/.

Edeh, S. 2018. "IDPs relief materials diverted for commercial purposes in Bauchi." Accessed February 17, 2018, https://www.vanguardngr.com/2018/02/idpss-relief-materials-diverted-for-commercial-purposes-in-bauchi/.

Elejalde-Ruiz, A. 2018. "Manufacturers adopt robots that help human workers, not replace them. For now." *Chicago Tribune.* Accessed October 18, 2018. https://phys.org/news/2018-10-robots-human-workers.html.

Furnard, G. 2018. *Journalism and Society.* Books.com.

Ganascia, J. 2018. "Artificial Intelligence: Between myth and reality." *UNESCO Courier.* July-September, pp 7–9.

Gonzalez, C. 2018. "7 Common Applications for Cobots." MachineDesign, January 18. Accessed January 18, 2018. https://www.machinedesign.com/mechanical-motion-systems/article/21836350/7-common-applications-for-cobots.

Gupta, K. 2017. "Difference between artificial intelligence and robotics: What you need to know." FreelancingGig, September 3. Accessed September 3, 2017. https://www.freelancinggig.com/blog/2017/09/03/difference-artificial-intelligence-robotics-need-know/.

Haruna, A. 2016. "Boko Haram victims dying of starvation as Borno officials steal relief materials." *Premium Times*, June 18. Accessed June 18, 2016. https://www.premiumtimesng.com/news/headlines/205489-boko-haram-victims-dying-of-starvation-a-borno-officials-steal-relief-materials.html.

Howstuffworks (n.d.). "What is a computer algorithm?" HowStuffWorks, May 12. Accessed August 30, 2018. https://computer.howstuffworks.com/what-is-a-computer-algorithm.htm.

Jennings, R. S. 2003. "Military Peacebuilding: Stability Operations and the Strengthening of Peace in War-Torn Societies." Accessed April 15, 2003. https://sites.tufts.edu/jha/archives/844.

Joshi, N. 2018. "4 ways global defense forces use AI." *Forbes*, August 26. Accessed January 18, 2018. https://www.forbes.com/sites/cognitiveworld/2018/08/26/4-ways-the-global-defense-forces-are-using-ai/?sh=6233b388503e.

Kazeem, Y. 2017. "An airstrike by Nigeria's military has killed more than 50 refugees in a tragic error." Quartz, January 17. Accessed January 17, 2017. https://qz.com/africa/887270/nigerias-air-force-accidentally-killed-50-refugees-in-its-search-for-boko-haram/.

Kumar, V. 2017. "Uses of Artificial Intelligence in Daily Life." Klient Solutech, February 28. Accessed February 28, 2017. http://www.klientsolutech.com/uses-of-artificial-intelligence-in-daily-life/.

Lamb, H. 2017. "Can Robots Do a Better Job of Building Peace?" *Huffington Post*. Accessed September 9, 2017. https://www.huffingtonpost.co.uk/harriet-lamb/robots-bring-us-peace_b_18031158.html?guccounter=1andguce_referrer_us=aHR0cHM6Ly93d3cuZ29vZ2xlLmNvbS8andguce_referrer_cs=DTXFA5Smw_e_85OAVuBVrg.

Lanz, D. 2017. "New technologies to prevent conflict and build peace." Basel Peace Forum. Retrieved from https://basel-peace.org/assets/listitem/Critical-reflections/Basel-Peace-Forum-Critical-Reflections-New-Technologies.pdf.

Larrauri, H. P. 2014. "How technology can shape the future of peacebuilding at the local level." *Peace Insight*. Accessed September 9, 2017. https://www.peaceinsight.org/blog/2014/06/technology-future-peacebuilding-local-level/.

Link Labs. 2018. "Indoor Assets Tracking Systems." https://www.link-labs.com/.

Musa, N .2017. "NEMA moves to tackle diversion of relief materials for IDPs."*The Guardian*, June 22. Accessed June 22, 2017. http://www.m.guardian.ng/news/nema-moves-to-tackle-diversion-of-relief-materials-for-idps/.

NITDA. "National Information Technology Agency: Background" (n.d.). Accessed June 20, 2019. https://nitda.gov.ng/nit/background/.

Nurminen, N. 2017. "Could artificial intelligence lead to world peace?" Al Jazeera, May 30. Accessed May 30, 2017. https://www.aljazeera.com/indepth/features/2017/05/scientist-race-build-peace-machine-170509112307430.html.

Oladimeji, T. T. and Folayan, G. B. 2017. "ICT and Its Impact on National Development in Nigeria: An Overview." *Research and Reviews: Journal of Engineering and Technology* 7 (1): 5–10.

Peinado, M. M. (n.d.). "The role of NGOs and the civil society in peace and reconciliation processes." Accessed June 27, 2018. http://www.ceipaz.org/images/contenido/Role%20of%20NGOs%20and%20civil%20society%20in%20peacebuilding.pdf.

Rogers, E. 1995. *Diffusion of Innovations*. New York: Free Press.

SAS (n.d.). "Artificial Intelligence: What it is and why it matters." SAS Institute. Accessed August 30, 2018. https://www.sas.com/en_us/insights/analytics/what-is-artificial-intelligence.html.

Staples, P. 2018. "Robots used in everyday life." Sciencing, June 27. Accessed June 27, 2018. https://sciencing.com/robots-used-in-everyday-life-12084150.html.

Sulieman, T. 2017. "Why Borno Governor Attacked UNICEF, Others." *ICiR*. January 11, 2017. https://www.icirnigeria.org/borno-governor-attacked-unicef-others/.

Techopedia (n.d.). "Artificial Intelligence (AI)." Accessed August 30, 2018. https://www.techopedia.com/definition/190/artificial-intelligence-ai.

Terdiman, D. 2018. "Here's how Facebook uses AI to detect many kinds of bad content." Fast Company, May 2. Accessed May 2, 2018. https://www.fastcompany.com/40566786/heres-how-facebook-uses-ai-to-detect-many-kinds-of-bad-content.

The UNESCO Courier. 2018. "Many voices, one world: Artificial intelligence, the promises and the threats." https://en.unesco.org/courier/2018-3.

UN Office for the Coordination of Humanitarian Affairs. 2017. "Emergency response mobilised following airstrike on Rann locality." Accessed January 17, 2017. https://reliefweb.int/report/nigeria/emergency-response-mobilised-following-airstrike-rann-locality.

Wilson, J. 2017. "Overcoming Technophobia in Communication Education: The Push-ICT Approach." *Media and Communication / Mediji i komunikacije* 1 (7): 19–32.

Wisskirchen, G., Biacabe, B. T. Bormann, U., Muntz, A., Niehaus, G., Soler, G. J., Brauchitsch, B. 2017. *Artificial Intelligence and Robotics and Their Impact on the Workplace.* London: IBA Global Employment Institute.

Wolverton T. 2018. "AI is great at recognizing nipples, Mark Zuckerberg says (FB)." Pulse, April 25. Accessed April 25, 2018. https://www.pulse.ng/bi/tech/ai-is-great-at-recognizing-nipples-mark-zuckerberg-says-fb-id8304794.html.

Wolverton, T. 2018. "Mark Zuckerberg says AI won't be able to reliably detect hate speech for 'five to 10' years (FB)." Pulse, April 10. Accessed April 10, 2018. https://www.pulse.ng/bi/tech/mark-zuckerberg-says-ai-wont-be-able-to-reliably-detect-hate-speech-for-five-to-10-years-fb-id8234732.htm.

World Economic Forum. 2015. "6 ways tech can transform humanitarian response." Accessed December 15, 2015. https://www.weforum.org/agenda/2015/12/6-ways-tech-can-transform-humanitarian-response/.

Chapter 19

Nigerian Sports Media and Globalization

Mining Sports for Competitive Edge

Chuka Onwumechili

In 1981, Thomas McPhail wrote about electronic colonialism when he alluded to four major periods of colonization in human civilization. McPhail argues that electronic colonialism subjugates poorer countries and their peoples, like those in Africa, to the will, dictates, and products of world powers. The subjugation is not only total and intense but also covert and hegemonic, which ensures that those dominated by it are virtually unaware. He argues that this type of colonialism is not based on military conquest and land capture but on creation of a psychological, mind, and mental empire.

McPhail points to electronic colonialism as a fourth-stage iteration of colonialism. The previous three being military colonialism (BC–AD 1000), Christian colonialism (1000–1600) and mercantile colonialism (1600–1950). Presently, there is little doubt that we are in the midst of electronic colonialism. One major area in which this colonialism is quite evident is in media broadcasting of football in Nigeria as well as other African countries. Over the last three decades, content for televised football in African countries has changed dramatically. While local football was televised prior to the 1990s, in today's Africa, televised football focuses on the foreign. The effect has been dramatic. No longer are there fans of local football teams such as Enugu Rangers, Shooting Stars, or Kano Pillars in Nigeria. In their place are fans of Manchester United, Chelsea, and Arsenal. In fact, in Okene, in the heart of Kogi State of Nigeria, fans of Arsenal FC of England annually celebrate an Arsenal day with a huge crowd turning out in Arsenal regalia (Sheen 2016). The effect of this televised European football is that the minds of Nigerian viewers are captured, and they are turned into colonial subjects of European football. It is neocolonialism in full force. But what led to these changes? Are such changes inherently negative? If so, how can the negativity be reversed?

Those questions are central to the chapter's discourse, and they imply the capture of the media struggle that is embedded in ongoing globalization. Sports media coverage, specifically football coverage, amply provides a lens through which we can vividly track the tentacles of increasing globalization and perhaps how local entities may fight back against recolonization and its hegemonic tendencies. In this chapter, I examine those questions with the goal of providing preliminary answers to the difficulties that they project. To do this, it is important to review the status quo of globally televised football as far as it impacts Africa with particular focus on Nigeria. But I do not stop there. Instead, I argue that Nigeria and Nigerians can fight back not simply based on questions of pride but also based on economic necessities. This fight back presents opportunities in spite of the colossal economic advantages of the West. There is and has always been windows of opportunities provided by discovering niches and using them to your advantage. It is that strategy that now provides opportunity. The chapter then concludes by noting the importance of a fight back.

THE CURRENT STATE OF AFFAIRS

McPhail's electronic colonialism is indeed an appropriate theorization that makes clear the contours of televised European football in Nigeria and elsewhere in Africa. Its contours are broad, far reaching in width and depth and on first sight one would consider its hegemonic effect not only undeniable but, just maybe, also irreversible. However, I argue here that its irreversibility is only made possible by inaction and an abdication of a recourse to a solution. It is that abandoned recourse, or maybe it is best described as an *unexamined recourse*, that forms the crux of this chapter. But to get there, that is to detail the recourse, one must first discuss the present.

The current state of electronic colonialism in Nigeria, albeit in the broader area of Africa, is a recent phenomenon. Prior to the early 1990s, televised football in much of the continent involved televised local contests. However, that local dominance was to be jettisoned in the 1990s following an intrusion. The instigator of this inward intrusion was largely the state itself. Prior to that time, the state dominated and in many parts of Africa, most certainly in Nigeria, the state had complete and monopoly control of broadcasting that is, both radio and television. Private interest participation in the mass media was restricted to the print media. This control was at the time rooted in the theory that national development was only possible via state control of mass media, particularly broadcasting instruments. It was the glory years of the New World Information and Communication Order (NWICO) which was a central theme that threatened the very foundation of the United Nations Educational, Scientific and Cultural Organization (UNESCO). UNESCO is charged with developing nations via dialogue in the areas of education, sciences, culture, and communication. At the time, most of East Europe and the developing countries argued that successful national development was only attainable through state control of the mass media in order to lead the implementation of state goals. This view, an anathema to much of the view of the Western world, demarcated the ideological views across the globe. It was, therefore, a great tussle between the East and West with Gorbachev's ascendancy to power in the Soviet Union in 1990 and the gradual dismantling of Russian control of the Union leading to the loss of ideological control of much of East Europe. The idea of media control for national development began to develop cleavages. Those cleavages widened in Africa. The Nigerian state began to loosen its grip over broadcasting. But Nigeria's loosening of the grip was not simply based on the demise of the Soviet Union or the loss of the Union's influence in much of Africa. Instead, the World Bank and the International Monetary Fund (IMF) were critical to the loosening of the state's grip on the broadcast media. The state, tottering under massive loans from international lenders, was forced to rethink its control of broadcasting. It was a way to divest its economic and debt burden (Onwumechili, 1996). At the time, and within a twelve-year period, the national debt tripled from $8.9 billion to $30.9 billion (World Bank 1994). As Faruqee (1994) pointed out, at the time, the bank recommended divestment of broadcast media among other measures.

But the surrender of broadcast media control by the state was not solely due to the global upheaval or its combination with pressures induced by the growing national debt. There was yet a third factor which was technological. Bourgault (1995) and Onwumechili (1996) cite the rapid growth of privately-owned satellite dishes that illegally downloaded signals from international broadcasters and, thus, circumventing the state's control of broadcast signals. The state's iron grip was loosened and importantly it was forced to rethink its total control of broadcast media coupled with pressures from private interests who began to anticipate and canvas for an opening of broadcast media ownership. The dam was finally broken when the state promulgated Decree No. 38.

The opening of the broadcast media environment to private interests in Nigeria, as well as elsewhere, under Decree No. 38 was to have a deep and indelible effect on the broadcasting of sports, especially football, in Nigeria (National Broadcasting Commission [NBC] Decree, 1992). It opened a rush as private interests, who had noted the local appetite for purchasing videotapes of recent English league games, Spanish La Liga, Brazilian

Campeonato Brasiliero, and Italian Calcio, pounced on an obvious oppor-tunity. Led by the South African broadcaster, Supersport TV, these private interests purchased rights to the foreign league games and began to broadcast them live to Nigerians. It was a *fait accompli*. Suddenly, spectators began to disappear from the local stadia as local bars began to televise the games on television screens designed to drive customers to the bars. There was no spigot able to stem the leak, it was a massive flood of football fans deserting local football, perhaps forever. The privatization of broadcasting in Nigeria, just as it was in other African states about the same period, created a situation that was not fully anticipated by the state. The state, in liberalizing the envi-ronment, expected private providers to develop a variety of local programs to compete in a newly liberalized environment. It did not happen. Instead, these new providers sought quicker access to profits and local cultural needs were hindered. The focus became sporting programs and recorded programs, which were easier to procure compared to investing in expensive media equipment to produce original programs locally. The marketplace had won!

The impact is astronomical and demonstrates, especially, the electronic colonialism predicted by McPhail (1981). Onwumechili and Oloruntola (2013) found support for Mcphail's theory in a subsequent quantitative study of football fans in Nigeria. They note: "the colonizing effects of consumption of foreign football images, such as those identified (by this study), are deep" (p. 406). The depth is amply demonstrated when Nigerians have established an Arsenal Day for a team that many of them had never watched in-person and that is based outside the continent and in Europe. But beyond electronic colonialism, there is also a two-pronged concern. The first being the signifi-cant revenue loss to European interests and the second being the devastation of local sport.

The consumption of European football is never economically innocuous. At the lowest level, it denies local sports finances that could have been earned from the gates. The money, theoretically, ends up in Europe because the bars and program providers who take these funds end up paying at least part of it to the providers of subscriptions who use it to buy the rights from European leagues. Although this may constitute tortuous logic for some, in reality, it is the complication of fund movement from the pockets of the locals to Europe.

But the economic deprivation does not stop there. The deeper concern is its asphyxiation of the local league itself. By denying the local league specta-tors, it essentially starves it of both gate-takings as well as potential sales of football-related products. Critically, the denial of spectators means that media interest, even from upstart media, in the league is low or non-existent because advertising interest will also be low since advertisers are only interested when the productions that they support lead them to potential audiences for their (advertiser's) products. It is a cascading relationship that heads towards asphyxiation in the end.

HOW TO NAVIGATE THE FUTURE

So, is there no hope? The answer is "not necessarily." However, hope is based on careful thinking and planning. The carefulness requires thinking outside the current box of television broadcasting and locating an appropriate niche to rescue Nigerian football the way the Nigerian film industry used the VHS videotape to develop a niche that elevated Nigerian movie making and Nollywood. Nollywood currently generates $590 million annually and its movies are exported across the world (Moudio 2013). In Nigeria, it has built a great following in a country that was bound to American, Indian, and Mexican movies barely three decades ago! Why is this comparison important? While an American movie may cost millions of dollars to make, Nollywood could produce one "with typical budgets in the range of $15,000 to $40,000" (Maio 2019, p. 14).

For football, there is much to learn from Nollywood and its entrepreneurship but there are important differences that one should not gloss over. First, let's address the similarities. The most important is that football, like movies, has a latent audience. Like the movie industry before the emergence of Nollywood, football is currently dominated by foreign products. Instead of European or Brazilian football, the movie industry in Nigeria was dominated by Hollywood, Indian, and Mexican movies. Big screen Hollywood movies made with multimillion-dollar budgets were replaced with Nollywood videotape movies made with tens of thousands of dollars. For football, the similarities are that instead of waiting for millions of dollars to sign television contracts for the local leagues, it should find other means to bring live games in front of people and begin to develop the market needed to attract those millions of dollars.

However, there are important differences that have potential to create bottlenecks. What are those? While the Nigerian movie industry, at the time, had no strong centralized regulator, for football, the Nigerian Football Federation (NFF), backed by the International Football Federation (FIFA), has an iron grip in regulating football. It is a grip that can easily ostracize those who seek to administer football outside the NFF. The effect is that much of the development with Nigerian football must go through the NFF. But with the NFF often strapped to an ancient past, innovation is often stifled. It would often require not just innovation but political might in order to overcome the lethargy of the NFF. Beyond the NFF is the Nigerian state and those who feast on its scraps. Here, I am referring to local appointees of the state who do little to enhance football but feed fat on its products including state subsidies to support the clubs, player transfer fees, and other sources of state financing related to clubs. Access to all those soft funds constitute bottlenecks that cannot be ignored.

What then can football learn from Nollywood? First, without a ready audience given the flight to viewing foreign football, local football must reorganize just as the local movie industry did to counter the movies from Hollywood, Mexico, and India. But how? Go to a low budget, develop revenue streams, and then win back the deserted football fanhood. The low budget means a realization that the focus cannot be solely on signing the big television contract that isn't forthcoming.Big television stations know that the fans have long deserted local football. After all, television is primarily interesting because it can calculate the eyeballs that can be marketed and sold to products and services seeking consumers. Instead, the focus for the football league in Nigeria should be to produce its own low budget live games to reach and grow a new and younger audience for Nigerian football. It should package football produced with the younger audience in mind. For instance, it will not only be about the live coverage of local league matches but introducing and cultivating stars of local leagues and introducing and growing them for a digital audience.

The new and young audience can be found not just in Nigeria but in the African diaspora and everywhere else in the world. Additionally, there will be European scouts who will use the products to meet their own goals. In essence, there will be an audience and there will be a huge room to grow more audience just as Nollywood did. The league may establish through Youtube, Facebook, and Twitter live transmission of league games in order to grow viewers that would then attract advertisers and create a growing and reliable revenue stream for both clubs and the league. For the league, all of this can be achieved by creating a league television that is based on this live streaming concept with pay access included for live games. Livestream.com (n.d.) forecasts a \$70.5 billion industry by 2021 with advertised brands expected to spend more than \$100 billion on video content by 2023. Importantly, consumers spent \$12.3 million on streaming content, an expenditure that was expected to rise by 30 percent by the end of 2015. Twitter, alone, hosted 1,300 live streamed events in 2015. Other aspects of the live streaming beyond live games may also be based on a low-fee subscription. This low-fee subscription may include purchasing rights for low-budget Nigerian comedies and Nollywood movies packaged into the same channel marrying football and movies as entertainment packages, a package that is not now offered by the live transmission of foreign football leagues in the country. Part of the non-live programming content would be coverage behind the scenes of footballer's home and social lives, football transfer rumors, among other human-interest stories. The programming ideas are not limited and certainly cannot and should not be only about the footballers but more encompassing to focus on the retinue of subjects involved in the game. This type of packaging is designed to create stars and personalities that can also help attract viewers to watch live-streamed games and eventually bring them back to watch live games in stadiums.

These ideas create a viable niche for mediatized Nigerian football. However, the current state-owned football clubs that are bereft of new ideas will likely fail to compete with private clubs who embrace the concept and develop other ideas to grow their access to revenue, instead of depending on the handouts from the football federation. Therefore, it would also be an opportunity to shake out undesirable state-owned clubs and officials that are currently feeding fat on handouts. This will then privilege those willing to develop revenue streams and create a more capitalistic environment. It will be an economic-based shakeout that favors the innovative after the bureaucratic attempt at shakeout failed to dislodge those that are feeding fat on state funds.

WHAT ARE THE BENEFITS?

What I introduce above is not far-fetched. The video streaming technology, as we are aware, exists already (Pires and Simon 2015; Faklaris, Cafaro, Hook et. al. 2016). What is new is its application to Nigerian domestic football as a way to find a niche in an environment currently dominated by the broadcast of European club football. The brief description provided in the previous section serves as an introduction to how Nigerian football can fight back and carve out a lucrative niche that is viable and similar to the niche already developed in other areas such as the film industry in Nigeria. It is a niche that became successful for both the Nollywood movies and the music industry in Nigeria.

But what could be the benefits for Nigeria's football? There are several. They include growing a sustainable niche support at home for the local game and among varied audiences, expanding the market and support for Nigerian football beyond the country's borders, and building a strong financial base for the professional game.

To compete against the hegemony established by European leagues in Nigeria requires thinking outside the box. What is important, therefore, is not simply replicating the strategy of European football broadcasting. Instead, it requires creating a niche that allows even those who now support European football to look towards the local game. This can be accomplished by packaging the Nigerian game differently. This repackaging will include using different and unique media and creating human-interest story lines designed to pull in not just football fanatics but other viewers that seek drama among other attractions. For instance, these story lines may be designed to attract women and children with the eye of future market targeting. The whole goal is to expand the market beyond the diehard football fans. For instance, football players may be co-opted in their off-season to participate in Nollywood movies and comedies where they are introduced to newer types of audiences who may then choose to follow the football subject to actual games. In addition, there could also be coverage of beyond-the-field lives of the footballers. Such coverage could include their homes, their families, and their off-the-field stories. This type of coverage does not have to be restricted to the footballers. It could also include activities of other notables in the game including managers, team officials, referees, and notable fans of teams. Ultimately, this type of media coverage creates new beyond-the-field stars that viewers become attached to. In Nigeria, this is especially important given the fact that footballers are likely to migrate to higher paying leagues leaving their fans without a star to follow. Thus, by creating non-playing stars associated with football, the new followers can be kept attached to football even when a footballer exits his Nigerian club.

Furthermore, marketing the game via the use of streaming media will bring the game to a wider reach beyond what the Nigerian local game has ever experienced geographically. You may wonder how this is possible when the current problem is that less people are watching the local game. Yet, the presence and ubiquity of low-cost streaming technology makes this possible. There is no need for the huge expense associated with broadcast television. Instead, Twitter, Facebook, Youtube, and similar platforms can be effectively used to introduce the local Nigerian game to a worldwide audience and grow the game. In this sense, Nigerian football is coming to the game quite late. Its Nigerian counterparts such as comedy, music, and movies already utilize this in many ways. The only difference is that those counterparts do not have to produce and stream live shows. For football, it is important that the games are streamed live to a worldwide audience via those less expensive platforms for low fees. Already, there is a known but small audience for such live streams among internationally-based Nigerians. This audience is factual, given the numbers that follow the Nigerian national team in Europe and the Americas. That audience is going to be the first mover in terms of accessing local Nigerian league games via social media platforms. In fact, by hosting this platform, the Nigerian Football Federation (NFF) or its designated rights holder would have access to diversified audiences with an upward growth trajectory.

Ultimately, the goal of all this is building a strong financial base for the local game. The options identified above point to several potential financial sources for the local professional football league. By reintroducing local football fans to televised Nigerian football and developing an international market for the league, a new revenue source will be gradually cultivated and opened. For the football itself, a small fee may be charged to those who seek to access the games that are live streamed. Additional revenue may then develop from selling access to this growing viewership base to marketers/advertisers who seek to reach a huge and growing audience. One thing is clear, recent data from Nielsensports.com (n.d.) shows that Nigeria has the world's most engaged football market globally. Nielsensports.com reports "an incredible 83 percent of people are interested in football and even more remarkable as the Nigerian participation rate of 65 percent, was ahead of any other nation" (p. 2). The opportunity for diversified revenue and one that would have potential for further growth can be developed from relationships that were already discussed with Nollywood, music, and other shows including off-the-field coverage of footballers and other major names associated with the Nigerian game. These shows can be offered through subscription streaming with major revenue arising from advertisements on those shows.

CONCLUSION

Mediatized coverage of local football in Nigeria has faced major challenges since the broadcast environment became liberalized in the country in the 1990s. Instead of local sports experiencing increased coverage, the opposite occurred. Private broadcasters found it was easier to accumulate profits by redistributing European and South American football-content to a Nigerian audience rather than budgeting for live production of local football. The result is a Nigerian consumer weaned on foreign football broadcasts and creating a football fandom that is groomed to watch broadcast football at home and in bars rather than visiting the stadium for local football. It was the confirmation of electronic colonialism predicted by Thomas McPhail.

However, this chapter argues that Nigerian football can fight back by creating a niche in this environment. To do this, Nigeria must look beyond traditional television and instead seek a less expensive alternative that provides access not only to local fans but to a global audience while also increasingly raising revenue for football. This alternative is rooted in the new media consisting of Facebook, Twitter, and YouTube live streaming. It suggests that entirely new ways can be developed to package local football. This packaging shall go beyond live streaming of games to include relationships with Nollywood and local music while creating visibility for football players and football personalities, including managers and others, via other related shows. It argues that creating such a niche can catapult local Nigerian football to building a global audience while raising revenue. It is a strategy that has the opportunity to revive local football the way Nollywood revived local Nigerian movies or how local music videos successfully countered a previously entrenched American pop music, reggae, and other foreign music genres that dominated Nigeria up until the early 1990s.

REFERENCES

Bourgault, L. 1995. "Nigeria." In L. Gross (ed.), *The international world of electronic media* (pp. 233–252). New York: McGraw-Hill.

Faklaris, C., Cafaro, F., Hook, S., et. al. 2016. "Legal and ethical implications of mobile live-streaming video apps." MobileHCI '16: Proceedings of the 18th International Conference on Human-Computer Interaction with Mobile Services and Services Adjunct, September: 722–729.

Faruqee, R. 1994. "Nigeria: Ownership abandoned." In I. Husein and R. Faruqee (eds.), *Adjustment in Africa: Lessons from country case studies* (pp. 238–285). Washington, DC: World Bank.

Livestream.com (n.d.). "47 must-know live video streaming statistics." Accessed August 17, 2020. https://livestream.com/blog/62-must-know-stats-live-video-streaming#:~:text=2.,surges percent20inpercent20viewershippercent20throughout-percent202018.percentE2percent80 percent9D.

Maio, A. 2019. "What is Nollywood and How Did it become the 2nd largest film industry?" *Studiobinder*. Accessed August 15, 2020. https://www.studiobinder.com/blog/what-is-nollywood/.

McPhail, T. 1981. *Electronic colonialism: The future of international broadcasting and communication*. Newbury Park, CA: Sage.

Moudio, R. 2013. "Nigeria's film industry: A potential gold mine?" *Africa Renewal*. Accessed August 15, 2020. https://www.un.org/africarenewal/magazine/may-2013/nigeria's-film-industry-potential-gold-mine.

National Broadcasting Commission Decree. 1992. *Decree No. 38 (24th August 1992): Supplement top Official Gazette Extraordinary No. 33, Vol. 79, 4th September 1992–Part A*. Lagos, Nigeria: The Federal Ministry of Information and Culture Printing Division.

Nielsensports.com (n.d.). "Global interest in football." Accessed August 17, 2020. https://nielsensports.com/global-interest-football/.

Onwumechili, C. 1996. "Privatization of the electronic media in Nigeria." *The Howard Journal of Communications* 7 (4): 365–372.

Onwumechili, C., and Oloruntola, S. 2013. "Transnational communications, attitudes and fan identity: Studying Nigeria post-media reform." *Soccer and Society* 15 (3): 389–410.

Pires, K. and Simon, G. 2015. "YouTube live and Twitch: A tour of user-generated live streaming systems." MMSys '15: Proceedings of the 6th ACM Multimedia Systems Conference, March: 225–230.

Sheen, T. 2016. "Ooh to be a Gooner: Arsenal fans in Nigeria celebrate Arsenal Day for the 10th year in a row as hundreds turn out in Okene." *The Sun*. Accessed 12, 2020. https://www.thesun.co.uk/sport/football/2501713/arsenal-day-pictures-nigeria-fans-arsene-wenger/.

World Bank 1994. *World development report: Infrastructure for development*. New York: Oxford University Press.

SECTION VIII

Organizational Communicational in the Nigerian Digital Space

Chapter 20

Exploring Digital Options in Information Dissemination for External and Internal Publics in Organizations

Iniobong Courage Nda and Aniebo Samson

The world revolves around information. Imagine a society without information; everywhere will be in a state of despondency. Information is life without which life will be at a standstill. Information is of the essence, hence, the reason companies and organizations invest huge resources to have a fortified communication system that enhances the flow of information within and without itself. In fact, the success, growth, and development of an organization are dependent strongly on its information dissemination role. This is because communication is the means through which employees are linked together for the achievement of a common purpose or goal.

From time immemorial, information and communication has played an essential role in influencing people's attitude and behavior towards a given course. Rooting communication as the process of exchanging meaningful ideas, values, and opinions, this brings to bear the construct of the human mind. Hamilton (2011) describes communication as the process of people sharing thoughts, ideas, and feelings with each other in commonly understandable ways. Curran (2014, p. 3–4) noted that "the ongoing transformation of communication technology in the digital age extends the reach of communication media to all domains of social life in a network that is at the same time global and local, generic and customized in an ever-changing pattern." Communication creates insight and understanding to issues, it helps in developing self-awareness thus leading to the ability to reconcile differences, influence others, make decisions and solve problems. Communication is indeed all-encompassing.

The world is dynamic; it's ongoing and ever-changing, and so is the organizational space. Organizations have been reshaped through innovations in communication technology. Embracing digital technology is no longer an option for organizations as it allows organizations to embrace the digital space. Change is one actuality that organizations, individuals, and groups must come to terms with, especially in the face of digital options that modify organizational realities. The changes that come from new technologies also affect business models and established industries, which often see the upstarts as threats to their dominance (Paulik and McIntosh 2011). Every fabric of an organization needs digital communication which today has outpaced previously existing communication systems and broken the barriers of language, time zones, and borders in a bid to connect the world. Decades through decades, efforts to change have paid off as information dissemination has moved from the drudgery ways of achieving a goal or task to a more dependable, easier, and faster way of message dissemination within the shortest possible time and with the speed of light. Change has become the only means for organizations that are willing to move with the times in order to survive with widespread technology, accelerated knowledge, exponential growth and innovations. The internet too has presented a wide range of options. That is why Dominick (2009) opines that it has changed so fast that it is hard to predict its future. He explained further that digital technology and the internet triggered a revolution in the way information is stored and transmitted, thus, making the traditional mass communication media find themselves in uncharted waters and having to figure out how to cope with the drastic development. To Ober (2006), it is a vast information system that connects millions of computers worldwide, allowing them to conduct many types of business transmission, such as online banking and shopping.

Organizations exist in competition; therefore, communication becomes the tool to promote opportunities, services, objectives, and collaboration with its competitors and other external publics. The success or failure of organizational collaborations is hinged on the quality of communication between the parties involved. Also, organizations exist around a web of seen and unseen communication networks where members must effectively make meaning of the other's communication to be able to move forward. Where information does not flow freely within the organization, the external publics suffer. An efficient and effective dissemination of information is paramount for the attainment of an organization's mission and vision statement. Insufficient, lack, and dearth of information in an organization results in an obsolete knowledge base and failure in proper routes of communication. However, when there is a free flow of information, more explanation is gathered, more enlightenment, a process well illustrated, or a concept better promoted. Organizational publics are furnished with unlimited new channels for interaction.

Wood (2014) explains that digital media are electronic modes of communication that store and manage data in digital form. Communicating on a face-to-face basis does not require digital communication. However, email, Facebook, instant messaging, among others, is transmitted directly from the message originator to the destination through computer technology that converts the message into digital forms that are transmitted to the respective destinations. Digital technology has brought an end to the notion of territorial boundaries between countries. People who were once separated by distance and considered to be strangers have become friends and coworkers due to the digitization of the world. This brings to fulfill the prophecy of Marshall McLuhan who predicted many years ago that the world will become a global village. We are now linked physically and electronically to people around the world. There are no more digital divides as the presence of the internet has shrunk the information gaps that previously existed between countries with high technology and those without. Information has been made widespread with this development. Digital communication has changed the world; what we say, see, know, hear, how we interact and our view of persons, events, or things, have been transformed with the entry of digital communication. New media technologies impact our culture by offering new lifestyles, creating new jobs, and eliminating others, demanding new regulations and presenting unique new social issues (Straubhaar, LaRose, and Davenport 2014).

In our climes, how many organizations, companies, ministries and government parastatals have digital presence? There is a great dearth of digital communication channels; only a few international conglomerates can boost global coverage through digital communication. The publics are daily questioning statistics, calling for records of activities, scorecards of achievements from organizations and even the government, however, they find none due to the absence of any digital storage. Due to this knowledge gap, most organizations/governments make unfound claims about projects and data. Where these organizations or agencies embrace digital technology especially in transmitting information, information will be commonplace. During the COVID-19 lockdown in Nigeria for instance, the federal government made an unsubstantiated claim about feeding children in their home-feeding program. Contrarily, there is no record of this activity anywhere. Where this information should be found on the government website, no update is found. For some organizations, available updates are stale, say from two to five years ago.

It is an already established fact that information plays an all-important role in a given organization. Digital communication has transformed the working lives of employees in organizations. Apart from an improvement in work pace, employees can remain in contact with corporate intranet locations not-withstanding. Most organizations in our environment are yet to move with the times or embrace all the packages digital technology has to offer, especially in the organization space. Surprisingly, items like computers are still treated like demi-gods in most organizations as they are offered elevated platforms on a well decorated table covered with a tablecloth. Sad isn't it, especially in this century? Consequently, the older version of the computer—typewriters—is still given pride of place in these systems. Reason being that the computer system may go bad and the guilty party may be queried. Messengers are still utilized in some of these organizations even when they pose a challenge in communicating information as received by the source. While digital tech-nologies allow for clarity, authentication, and speed, the messenger on the other hand is constrained with the human factor where information is leveled, sharpened, highlighted, over-emphasized, and distorted.

EMERGING TRENDS IN ORGANIZATIONS

The organizational space has moved to a new communication realm where tasks are carried out digitally to a widespread audience who interact globally. These have created changes in the transmission of information through the improvement in telephony, vast array of information, technologies options, which has resulted in the expansion of available media in the organiza-tion. Contemporary organizations have moved with the times; they make use of several communication channels such as letters, reports, telephones, face-to-face conversations, brochures, reports, emails, videoconferencing, among others. As most of these organizations lay off the use of facsimiles, more opportunity is open to emerging trends to ease information gathering and disseminations in organizations. Miller (2015, p. 235) sums it up thus:

> Consider the changes that have taken place in workplace communication over the past hundred years. To create a simple document, we have moved from handwriting to typing to word processing. To produce multiple copies of that document, we have moved from copying the document by hand to carbon paper to high-speed copying machines. To store those documents, we have moved from boxes to file cabinets to floppy disks to hard drives, servers, CDs, and flash drives and now to cloud storage. To send those documents over long distances, we have moved from stagecoaches to airmail to express mail to facsimile to PDF files. To exchange messages over long distances, we have moved from messengers to telegraphs to telephone to voice mail and electronic mail. To get together as a group, we have moved from formal meeting rooms to conference calls to video conferencing to computer conferencing and online chat rooms. To

keep in touch with a wide array of contacts, we have moved from newsletters to blogs, Facebook, and Twitter. To prepare presentations, we have moved from paper flipcharts to overheads to PowerPoint. In short, the workplace in the early twenty-first century bears little resemblance to the workplace of the hundred years ago, and many of the workplace changes we observe are the result of technology innovations.

Long-standing corporations, institutions, and entire industries are being turned upside down by the digital revolution. Businesses built on analog technologies of production and distributions are trying to figure out how to adapt in the digital age. New efficiencies of creating and delivering content in a digital, networked environment are emerging throughout the world (Paulik and McIntosh 2011). These exponential growths in digital technology have altered information dissemination arrangements giving way for organizations to restructure their communication system to embrace a rapid transformation aimed at reducing the scale and scope of tasks in the organization for optimal results. Employees are linked in formal and informal networks with members of the organization. These networks may be physically involving colleagues and virtual networks which are becoming common in the workplace.

Technological innovations have changed the face of organizations by creating an explosion in information dissemination channels and formats. With digital technology, employees combine digital technology with interactivity to make choices, provide responses, clarify issues, give feedback, and feed forwards, to move the organization forward. For instance, digital technologies erode time and space. Top business executives no longer need to make frequent trips to distant locations for meetings. Today, webinar, internet, computer-mediated machines, among others, have brought about an astonishing manipulation of time and space as these business executives can now "be there" without actually being there.

Furthermore, as cyberspace evolves, "people all over the globe can, according to many proponents of electronic interaction, become 'virtual' neighbors through space-bridging technology of the internet" (Croteau and Hoynes 2003, p. 305). Accordingly, organizational base communications can be contracted in the virtual world of computer networks either with or without face-to-face interactions, often with members who may never have met outside the virtual environment. Croteau and Hoynes (2003) further noted that "high-tech jobs no longer need to be located in an office in a particular geographic location. A growing number of employees and professionals are finding ways to 'telecommute' to work using several digital routes such as phones, fax, and computer networks so they can work from any location, say at home." This bridges the gaps between people in the organization and makes less distance between people.

COMMUNICATION CHANNELS AND
DIGITAL TECHNOLOGY

The debut of new forms of information dissemination, communication events has been transformed. Gamble and Gamble (2010, p. 12) noted that technology continues to speed up communication as it brings the world into our living rooms and bedrooms, offices, and cars. According to them, technology has also given us the ability to interact in more ways, more quickly, and with more people than ever before. As the world evolves, it is translating into better ways of doing things, relating with others like in the workplace, adding to knowledge through learning. Verderber, Verderber, and Sellnow (2014) say channels are both the route traveled by the message and the means of transportation.

The channel of communication influences the way the source encodes a message and this in turn influences the way the receiver decodes the message and responds to it. The success of your message may depend not only on the consistency of your codes but also on the channel you select (Hamilton 2011). Words delivered through several channels do not constitute the same message, hence, the need to use appropriate communication channels in communicating messages. The channel of communication transforms things; messages have channels that best apply in delivery. The message and its content, the channel selected, determines the success or failure of the communication. Riggio (2008) noted that the selection of the proper channel can have an important effect on the accurate flow of communication as well as affect the impact of the message. According to the author, using multiple channels to present complicated information will increase the likelihood that it will be attended to and retained. To this end, employers of labor must critically determine the channels that best apply to their publics, whether internal or external.

Communication channels also have a relationship with job satisfaction, work performance, and efficiency. While some employees may prefer face-to-face communication, others may prefer computer-mediated communications. It is important that a sender chooses the medium that is most likely to correspond to the type of message that needs to be sent and understood (Griffin and Moorhead 2007). To be an effective employee, manager, client, or consultant, it is essential to communicate effectively with others. Messages can be interpreted in different ways based on the channel used to communicate it (Aamodt 2010). Whatever be the case, channel selection should be borne with the unique characteristics of the employees in mind. Some of the digital options available for information disseminations in organizations are:

1. Email: Electronic mail is used primarily to exchange general and timely information, ask questions, and increase access to information and enhance faster retrieval. Several organizations use email to communicate with its members within and outside the organization and employees learn to use the email more rapidly. Emails are not private and could be retained for a longer period; they do not convey bodily language as seen in face-to-face communication. They are usually brief and sometimes usually not with the same concerns for formal documents. Another problem is that email is typically written "on the fly"—composed and sent while keyboarding (Ober, 2006).

2. Blogs: Blogs allow a low-cost way to present new products and brands (Hewitt 2005). Through blogs, organizations find out what the external publics say about them, their products, competitors, organizational politics, among others. Care must also be taken on the nature of information put on the blog because it may sometimes generate unnecessary controversies, especially for the external publics.

3. Instant Messages: IMs allow information to be shared at the spur of the moment. IMs sometimes have an informal undertone especially when there are no careful checks for punctuations, spellings, tone, clarity, double barreled words, among others.

4. Tele/Video Conferencing: Teleconferences are used to engage people in a call from diverse locations. It saves time and money. Videoconferencing on the other hand is used by multiple-location companies to communicate with their employees—for training, business updates, to introduce new products or procedural changes, or just to keep employees from feeling isolated (Hamilton, 2011). According to Fulk and Collins-Jarvis (2001), on the characteristics of videoconferencing in comparison with face-to-face meetings, discussants show less emotion and experience less conflict during meetings, participation is more organized and orderly which may account for shorter meetings, decision-making quality is generally equal to face-to-face groups except when bargaining or negotiation is required. Also, participation is more equal (status differences are less noticeable and less threatening) and discussants find videoconferencing less satisfying than face-to-face meetings.

5. Telecommuting: There are occasions where employees either on a full-time or part-time basis work from home rather than from the office. They are linked to their supervisors and colleagues through computer terminals, phones, and fax machines, among others. Schaefer (2005) puts forth this question: "What are the social implications of the shift towards the virtual office?" According to him, from an interactionist perspective, the workplace is a major source of friendship; restricting

face-to-face social opportunities could destroy the trust that is created by "handshake agreement."

6. Telephone calls: Telephone serves as one of the easiest routes for information sharing. The advancement in technology today has made it possible not to share a call with only one person per time but also to connect with others (conference call) who need to receive the information too. This digital route is however limited with the absence of nonverbal cues.

7. Social networking: Organizations and even employees in the organization utilize the social networking sites such as Twitter, WhatsApp, Facebook, Telegram, Instagram, and so forth, in a bid to get information as well as share it. Technology has allowed the internet to be carried in pockets, bags, thus making it ubiquitous. Robbins and Judge (2013), however, warned that to get the most from social networks and avoid irritating your content, it should be reserved for high-value items only— not as an everyday or even every week tool. This is because a superior might check your Facebook entries and the contents may be displeasing not only to others but to the organization you represent. It can result in grave consequences at work.

8. The internet: This is another aspect of internet technology that has radically changed the way organizations operate. For the individual worker, the web can be used to gather relevant technical or policy information, to check on the activities of partners and competitors, to access timely news on a minute-by-minute basis, or to shop for something. For the organization, the web serves as a forum to promote a desired image, to communicate with customers, and to conduct business of all kinds (Miller 2015). Contrarily, heavy reliance on the web can drain the productivity of the employees as they spend more time surfing the net.

COVID-19 REALITIES IN ORGANIZATIONS

Towards the end of the year 2019, it dawns on the whole world the impending danger with the soon ravaging novel coronavirus. Though the news of its debut was taken with kid gloves, the reality that came with it is untold. Every facet of life, every sector of our economy, every organization, group, family, has in one way or the other felt the spank of its attendant effect. The world has recorded scores and scores of deaths, businesses have met their waterloo, the educational system has witnessed a major setback, organizations have had to restructure and downsize while some workers have had to go off pay. All these have made life generally difficult, especially with the skyrocketing cost of living. However, for the health institutions, social media, telecommunication industries, telecommuting, it was business as usual.

Although COVID-19 came with its negatives, it brought a major awakening into the organizational space. Prior to this time, organizations did not show heavy reliance on digital communication tools to disseminate information to its internal and external publics; it was basically an all-traditional means of communication affair such as face-to-face discussions, memos, newspapers, circulars, reports, newsletters, telephone calls, magazine, radio, and television, which do not all have the same capacity to carry information. Top conglomerates and organizations, religious organizations, government ministries, agencies, and parastatals, have had to go digital; huge amount of money previously spent on travel expenses to seminars, meetings, and conferences at distance locations have been replaced with audio/video conferencing, webinar, telecommuting, emails, and the like. Once displaced and ignored, digital communication routes by some organizations have today become a major avenue of reaching out to organizational publics at their diverse locations. Organizations today are faced with two options—go digital or perish!

Organizations have come to welcome modifications to keep in progress; most employees now work remotely, decision-making has received speed, major adjustments have been made to work schedules, boundaries have shrunk, bureaucratic bottlenecks removed, once difficult tasks accomplished with great results, training for unskilled personnel on the use of digital technology and innovations, and increased organizational pace, among others. However, the end is not yet in sight. Large scale changes and exponential growths are envisaged for organizations in the coming years. No more retrogression, rather, organizations are seeking ways to scale greater heights in order to keep at pace with the rest of the world. Life indeed has generally had a twist as many persons have embraced skill development such as make-up, fashion designing, cooking/baking, and entrepreneurship, among others, through e-learning. Also, several governments and nongovernmental organizations (NGOs) have instituted loan schemes for micro, small, and medium sized enterprises (MSMEs), all in a bid to cushion the stress occasioned by the pandemic.

DIGITAL TECHNOLOGY AND THE WORKPLACE

We cannot only dwell on what a new technology does to an organization but on what people within an organization do with new technology. Miller (2015) noted that technologies do not determine particular outcomes and that the effects of any communication technology depend on the manner it is employed or its appropriateness to the users. The coming in of new technology has disrupted the existing tradition in the workplace and has reshaped general ways of fulfilling organizational goals. The senses of employees have been reworked to accommodate relegated parts for greater productivity. Digital technologies have brought about a new phase to the information environment. It allows organizations to discharge tasks seamlessly across its system. Previous patterns and barriers often faced in job deliveries have been removed. Information flows faster as spatial connections are bridged. Whether one is emailing, sending instant messages, visiting a chat room or blogging, they come in permanent forms as online messages tend to be in a permanent form.

The instantaneous nature of computer-mediated communication has resulted in an increasing growth in organizations in an incomparable manner to information dissemination in the past. Griffin and Moorhead (2007, p. 297) noted that "the real increase in organizational productivity due to information technology may come from the ability to communicate in new and different ways rather than from simply speeding up communication patterns." The abundance of information generated in organizations is stored, retrieved, and referenced as and when due. Digital options have significant capabilities that differentiate it from previous or traditional ways of transmitting information in organizations. Employees now do much more than receive information; they can also respond to the message received, send out their responses on the message received, and select messages to store for easy retrieval. The new communication technology also helps to create enclaves of similar minded people (Schaefer 2005).

According to Wood (2012) digital media also cultivate convergence. Voiceover internet phone conversations are possible because the technology for transmitting sound and the technology for transmitting visual images are both digital and, thus, they can be managed on a single network. The use of multiple channels in organizations helps the internal and external publics to digest the message content whether in the form of text or graphics. For instance, sending an email or SMS and following it up with a phone call. This can have an effect in reinforcing the message, especially persuasively laden messages. Contrarily, inconsistencies may arise where the verbal messages are in contradiction with the written ones. Blundel (2004, p. 46) says "organizations often exert tight operational controls on their communication channels in an effort to minimize this kind of problem. However, there are difficult trade-offs between the degree of control exercised and the organization's ability to engage more flexibly with its multiple stakeholders."

Griffin and Moorhead (2007, p. 289), stress that "the primary purpose of communication in organizations is to achieve coordinated actions, share information, and make decisions." Businesses, organizations, and corporate bodies use digital technologies also for videoconferencing where employees or top management officials are brought together through a screen that may be thousands of miles apart. Through digital technologies, audio and video images are stored and shared, other competing organizations are monitored, ideas and resources are shared, the limitation of time and space are eroded, speed of communication is increased, more communication channels are encouraged, interactive communication is guaranteed, individual user control is allowed, previously separated forms of communication are interconnected for greater results, several options and choices are guaranteed, a well of information resources is assured, employee participation is rejuvenated, among others.

Baran (2010) stressed that technology has an impact on communication. At the very least it changes the basic elements of communication. The coming in of digital technologies into the organizational spheres does not imply an end to communication problems. This is because even with its portability, increase in capacity, faster channel, output quality, among others, the effectiveness of its communication depends ultimately on the communicative practices adopted by its users. Where the channel is inappropriate or ineffectively used, communication tends to fail.

INFORMATION DISSEMINATIONS AND INTERNAL PUBLICS

Organization is the architectural alignment of people and processes around which enterprises are designed (Cook and Hunsaker 2001, p. 80). To this end, it manifests a combination of digital technology and wireless telecommunications that unites people independent of time and geographic locations through interactive databases, emails, teleconferencing, and the internet, among others. Digital technology has transformed work and organizations. It has brought about electronic miniaturization; more power and speed have been configured into microprocessor packages that enable transmission of data, pictures, audio/video effects in no time.

Workers vary greatly in their ability to receive, decode, and understand organizational messages (Riggio 2008). This indicates the need to analyze employees in the organization to understand their personal preferences and feelings towards any channel of communication (Locker and Kaczmarek 2007). With the increasing use of electronic communication in organizations, there is the absence of nonverbal cues which makes it difficult to convey emotions. To a greater extent, nonverbal communication complements communication, the absence of which may result in lack of depth in the communication process. With the flow of communication in work organization's upward, downward, and lateral flow, a number of communication channels are used in this process.

An organization that is gearing for the top must ensure an effective flow of communication for the organization to operate smoothly and productively. It is clear that communication technology, such as emails, cellular phones, and web-based communications, have had an important impact on increasing workers productivity, although workers can waste their valuable work time on personal email communications and non-work-related web surfing (Langan-Fox 2001).

INFORMATION DISSEMINATIONS
AND EXTERNAL PUBLICS

The external publics are those who have one relationship or the other with the organization. Without the external publics there would be no organization. This is so because the success and importance of the organization is dependent on the audience or the external publics. Despite the explosion in the production of information, there is evidence that citizens are no better informed (Attallah and Shade 2006). Their relationship with the organization and their decoding skills can also affect the communication process.

When communicating with the external publics, the choice of channel is also very important. Usually, a channel that is least expensive and can reach the publics and is appropriate for the communication, say to sell a product or idea, should be used. Here, research will reveal the characteristics of the external publics and the best channel that will inexpensively and appropriately be used to reach the publics. Locker and Kaczmarek (2007) say successful communication depends on the common ground between the organization and its audience. Even if the audience is spread over a wide geographic area and the members don't know one another, we will still find that the audience is somewhat distinctive in terms of age, gender, income, political party, formal schooling, race, and ethnicity (Schaefer 2005).

DIGITAL COMMUNICATION:
EMERGING CHALLENGES

Digital communication creates instantaneous interactions through phone calls, emails, data transfers, and so forth, however, with mixed results. This is because heavy reliance on digital communication may not facilitate independent employee critical thinking as they depend solely on it to think for them, thus deadening their thinking. Individuals, groups, and organizations in an attempt to communicate are sometimes misunderstood or the meaning in the communication is lost. This may lead to failure in the communication process and may be expensive not only in terms of the resources wasted but on time wastage too from both ends of the communication process (sender and receiver). This places a key responsibility on the sender who must reflect carefully on the needs of the people he is trying to engage with, their characteristics and the relevance of the channel used. Sometimes messages are not delivered due to technical failures.

Croteau and Hoynes (2003, p. 330) noted that, "some people, though, will make use of the full range of capabilities offered by the new media. For these individuals, new media technology can offer a significantly different way of accessing, manipulating, and using information. But any communication advantage provided by the new media is likely to be distributed unevenly, replicating existing information inequalities." Those who are already better educated, more familiar with emerging technologies and better able to afford devices such as sophisticated home computers will be precisely the people who benefit most from the new media. New media may inadvertently expand the gulf between the technological "haves" and "have nots." Wood (2012, p. 267), noted that "if access to new and converging technology is limited to individuals and groups that are already privileged by social, professional, and economic status, we will see an increasing chasm between the haves and the have-nots."

Relating this to the organizational space, several organizations that belong to the "haves" have moved on due to their information gathering and dissemination advantage while the "have nots" are left behind. It has been widely observed in our settings that only an organization with a strong financial base can embrace and sustain digital technologies. The present economic forces have left several organizations to take critical decisions about their well-being if they must survive and stay in business. The aftermath is that most organizations are reluctant in coming to terms with the present reality and as such are slow in expanding their information reach. Paulik and McIntosh (2011, p. 97) noted that "uncertainty prevails in the largely digital world. Converting to digital production and distribution costs a lot of money, and the returns are not guaranteed." This, however, does not mean the end to digital technology; the new digital world brings with it new business opportunities. It means new markets that were formerly restricted by political, economic, and geographic boundaries have been flung open by digital technology.

Ultimately, digital technologies have made physical distances no longer a barrier as information is shared instantaneously and meetings are held without physical presence. It compels employee commitment to reinvigorate participation in organizational tasks and goal attainments. Change is constant. An organization that intends to succeed must embrace change and move with the times. Digital technologies have presented varied options for organizations. Information has become digitized in the workplace, bearing with its profound changes that when accommodated, moves the organization forward. Looking at emails for instance, large volumes of emails received by members of an organization may create stressful working practices and sometimes access to the email system is restrained by network challenges. Although email and text messaging have increased human communication, they may be limiting others. This is due to the heavy reliance on it to the detrimental effect of other communication routes.

Another resistance to effective utilization of digital communication routes in the workplace is noise. Noise is "anything that either interrupts or distorts an encoded message, so that it fails to reach the receiver in its original form" (Blundel 2004, p. 5). Receiver's responses to messages in organizations are influenced by irregularities and sometimes unpredictable. This can be attributed to the presence of noise in the communication process. People respond to messages either through face-to-face encounters or machine mediated channels in a variety of ways. Their perception of the message influences their reaction towards the message. This is due to other contending factors struggling for their attention; as a result, feedback may be confusing and may impede mutual understanding. The end result will then bear grave consequences in the organization.

Although digital communication presents a veritable means of sharing information within and without the workplace, the use of videoconferencing among other digital routes of communication does not result in a comparatively high performance as derivable when people are together. These digital routes may be good for the sharing of salient information like notices but are not very good for knowledge transfer, resolution of organizational problems/ crises, among others. Physical presence still plays a vital role in several organizational activities like recruitments, employment appraisal, employee relations, public relations, organizational innovations, among others, due to the nature of these exercises. For example, the web, as a communication channel, provides access to information about new products, organizational progress, and news on special events, and so forth, however, very many organizations find it difficult to access and develop the web. Organizations therefore must focus on creating, designing, and implementing their web presence that will appropriately increase audience reach and market share.

Internet use affects person-to-person interaction and sociability. "Some observers believe that the internet advances sociability by creating another medium of communication with colleagues, friends, and family as well as by providing opportunities to forge new relationships. Others counter that it is socially isolating and a poor substitute for social activities and face-to-face interaction. Critics contend the more we use the internet, the less time we are likely to spend face-to-face with friends and family members" (Gamble and Gamble 2010, p. 13). Rodman (2006), however, noted that the internet is changing the way people communicate around the world, and it is changing the way the world does business.

Consequently, digital technologies cannot override or replace previously existing communication routes in an organization but rather complement them. They act as lubricant for the older information routes. For instance, the email saves time and also wastes time. Although it is easier to understand and does not necessarily demand huge knowledge to understand, management of organizations could use it to make unnecessary demands for meetings with employees. The loss of face-to-face communication and networking (e.g., tea breaks, impromptu meetings, after work parties, etc.) are absent in a remote work location. This is because these activities add up to office life and cannot be duplicated from a remote environment.

Managers now have a firm grip on their employees through computer-enabled devices to monitor and control employee work activities. "With the expansion of broadband connections, employees can obtain real-time access to corporate intranets in many locations including their home-based offices. It has also become cost-effective for organizations to provide their staff with the equipment needed to enable remote working; additional costs (i.e., capital equipment and line rental) are more than offset by the substantial reduction in corporate office overloads" (Blundel 2004, p. 153). Allowing an employee to work from home can lead to perceived loss of power by the superiors. The distance can lead to loss of motivation and loss of focus by the remote employee. In the absence of an agreed code of conduct, this process may be subject to abuse.

Digital options are tied to the availability of electricity supply which is still a mirage for several businesses. Accessing the internet in most organizations is impeded by the lack of or the nonavailability/unreliability of electricity and this creates a major setback for organizations. Today, organizations generate their independent power to avoid frequent interruptions or a complete absence of power from the regulating authorities.

What then must organizations do in order to survive in this information age?

- The communicator (sender) and the receiver are responsible for the success of the communication process irrespective of the channel in use. While the source ensures the message as sent is as received, he must frame the message bearing in mind the preexisting behavior, expectations, and the level of involvement of the receiver in the communication process. Most organizations churn out volumes of information to its external publics without recourse to their presence. Background research could enable the sender to know what the receiver already knows about the topic, their disposition towards the topic and the organization from which the message originates.

- Organizations must make efforts to manage their information flow especially as digital communication keeps workers tethered to work at all times. Digital technology encourages a flood of information from various channels which may sometimes be confusing or stressful thus leading to information overload. There are usually two sides to every-thing; while you enjoy the benefits that come with it, plans must be put in place to cope with the challenges too. A flood of information can be choking the employees who may get drowned by the volume of informa-tion received if coping strategies are not put in place. Sometimes there is the need to unplug the system and relax.

- Digital technologies are designed to save time, improve work efficiency, and generate greater results. However, it makes employees available at all times even with very detrimental outcomes such as health hazards, physical constraints, among others. Managements of organizations must exercise choice over how digital media affects their employees by choosing only the digital technologies that fit into their schedule and not just joining the bandwagon. Employees should be allowed to participate in the decision to regulate their use of digital technologies.

- Several organizations which are in competition with others tend to get all the communication channels available even when they do not have the financial strength to do so. Not everyone can get onto the informa-tion highway (Schaefer 2005). Organizations in a bid to survive the times should take one step at a time rather than take up more weight than they can carry.

- White-collar crimes have been perpetuated through technological advancements. Today, it has become easy to gain access to a computer from any location. It is also easy to carry out embezzlement or electronic fraud without leaving a trace. From the foregoing, digital communica-tion routes if not properly managed can become a threat to information society. Security is a huge concern that cannot be taken for granted by any organization, therefore, tight checks should be enforced if excesses must be checked.

- Managers should be cautious on their choice of channels for communi-cation as not all information is appropriate for all channels. This is due to the risk of misunderstanding. For instance, negative messages should not be communicated through emails. Face-to-face communication could shed off most misunderstandings.

CONCLUSION

World over, organizations have traveled decades into decades in search of appropriate channels to communicate with their internal and external publics. While some have fallen by the wayside due to mistakes, others have excelled in their endeavors. As important as communication is, organizations require it to effectively and efficiently carve a niche for themselves in the business world. To reach the world, digital communication then becomes the tool. The traditional media alone could not achieve this; this places a huge demand on digital communication routes to transmit information across the nations of the world.

Subsequently, organizations have witnessed several emerging trends that have been used and abused by some organizations. Although technologically mediated communication has shaped the way people collaborate at work through audio-video equipment (projectors, whiteboard, flip charts, video players, etc.), tele/audio conferencing, the internet, computers, and the likes, caution must be applied in their usage in order not to fall prey to the numerous excesses that comes with strong reliance on it. With digital communication, there is no going back for any organization that intends to reach the world with its goods and services. However, a word of caution—choose wisely!

REFERENCES

Aamodt, M. 2010. *Industrial/organizational psychology: An applied approach* (6th ed.). Belmont: Wadsworth Cengage Learning.

Attallah, P. and Shade, L. 2006. *Mediascapes: New patterns in Canadian communication* (2nd ed.). Australia: Thomson Nelson.

Baran, S. 2010. *Introduction to mass communication: Media literacy and culture* (6th ed.). Boston: McGraw Hill.

Blundel, R. 2004. *Effective organizational communication: Perspectives, principles and practices*. Harlow: Prentice Hall.

Cook, W. and Hunsaker, P. 2001. *Management and organizational behavior* (3rd ed.). New York: McGraw-Hill.

Croteau, D. and Hoynes, W. 2003. *Media society: Industries, images and audiences.* London: Sage Publications.

Curran, J. 2014. *Media and society* (5th ed.). London: Bloomsbury Publishing Plc.

Dominick, J. 2009. *The dynamics of mass communication: Media in the digital age* (10th ed.). New York: McGraw Hill.

Fulk, J. and Collins-Jarvis, L. 2001. "Wired meeting: Technological mediation of organizational gathering." In *The New Handbook of Organizational Communication: Advances in Theory, Research, and Methods. Edited by* F. M. Jablin and L. L. Putman, 624–663. Thousand Oak: Sage.

Gamble, T. and Gamble, M. 2010. *Communication works* (10th ed.). New York: McGraw-Hill.

Griffin, R. and Moorhead, G. 2007. *Organizational behavior: Managing people and organizations* (8th ed.). Boston: Houghton Mifflin Company.

Hamilton, C. 2011. *Communicating for results: A guide for business and the professions* (9th ed.). Boston: Wadsworth Cengage Learning.

Hewitt, H. 2005. *Blogs: Understanding the information reformation that's changing your world.* Nashville: Nelson Business.

Langan-Fox, J. 2001. Communication in organizations: Speed, diversity, networks and influence on organizational effectiveness, human health, and relationships. In *Handbook of Industrial Work, Organizational Psychology. Edited by* N. Anderson, H. K. Sinangil, and C. Viswesvaran, 188–205. London: Sage.

Locker, K. and Kaczmarek, S. 2007. *Business communication: Building critical skills* (3rd ed.). Boston: McGraw Hill.

Miller, K. 2015. *Organizational communication: Approaches and processes* (7th ed.). Stamford: Cengage Learning.

Ober, S. 2006. *Contemporary business communication* (6th ed.). Boston: Houghton Mifflin Company.

Paulik, J. and McIntosh, S. 2011. *Converging media: A new introduction to mass communication* (2nd ed.). New York: Oxford University Press.

Riggio, R. 2008. *Industrial/organizational psychology* (5th ed.). New Jersey: Pearson Prentice Hall.

Robbins, S. and Judge, T. 2013. *Organizational behavior* (15th ed.). Boston: Pearson.

Rodman, G. 2006. *Mass media in a changing world: History, industry, controversy.* Boston: McGraw Hill.

Schaefer, R. 2005. *Sociology* (9th ed.). Boston:McGraw Hill.

Straubhaar, J., LaRose, R. and Davenport, L. 2014. *Media Now: Understanding media, culture and technology* (8th ed.). Boston: McGraw Hill.

Verderber, K., Verderber, R., and Sellnow, D. 2014. *Communicate!* (14th ed.). New Zealand: Wadsworth Cengage Learning.

Wood, J. 2012. *Communication in our lives* (6th ed.). Australia: Wadsworth Cengage Learning.

Wood, J. 2014. *Communication mosaics* (7th ed.). Australia: Wadsworth Cengage Learning.

Index

About the Contributors

Dr. Olubunmi Ajibade is a senior lecturer at the Department of Mass Communication, University of Lagos, Lagos, Nigeria, where he obtained the bachelor of science, master of science and doctor of philosophy degrees between 1987 and 2010. He had worked variously as reporter, senior reporter, assistant news editor, deputy news editor, and editor-in-chief of several newspapers and a specialized magazine in Nigeria before joining the faculty of the department in 1997. His areas of specialization are print journalism, media management, new media, media law and ethics, communication theories and development communication. He has worked on multi-sector projects and with a number of international organizations across Nigeria.

Abiola Ajibola is an accomplished broadcast engineer who left the federal civil service as the director, National Broadcast Academy (the training arm of the Federal Radio Corporation of Nigeria), Lagos, Nigeria. He is also the convener of Digital World Forum.

Dr. Unwana Samuel Akpan, a media scholar-practitioner with over two decades of broadcast experience. He has been a visiting scholar at the Department of Communication, Culture and Media Studies (CCMS), where he completed his postdoctoral studies in the School of Communication and Media Studies, Howard University, Washington DC, USA. He is the editor of the *University of Lagos Communication Review*. He started his career with The Federal Radio Corporation of Nigeria, and was deployed to the National Broadcast Academy, its training arm, after obtaining his PhD in mass communication. He's presently a lecturer in the Department of Mass Communication, University of Lagos, Akoka, Nigeria. He has publications in the form of book chapters and research articles in prominent national and international journals. He has delivered several research papers at international conferences. His classes are where research, teaching, and learning interface, and he's dedicated to making students succeed in the classroom and

343

beyond. His research and teaching investigate and explore broadcast contents, sport communication, African communication systems, diaspora communication studies, media aesthetic.

Kelechi Okechukwu Amakoh is a graduate assistant in the Department of Mass Communication, University of Lagos, where he graduated with a first class honors. At present, he holds a joint degree in media, journalism and globalization from the University of Amsterdam, the Netherlands and Aarhus University, Denmark; a program funded under the Erasmus Mundus Scholarship. He has had freelance stints with leading national media organizations in Nigeria such as *The Nation Newspaper, Media Career Services* and *Campus Daily.* He was also the editor-in-chief of two campus publications: *Unilag Sun Newspaper* and *Masscope Magazine.* He is a member of the International Association for Media and Communication Research (IAMCR).

Azuh Arinze is the publisher/editor-in-chief of *YES!* international magazine and convener of the *YES!* International Magazine Annual Lecture. A member of the Nigerian Guild of Editors and Guild of Corporate Online Publishers, he served as the editor of *Encomium Weekly* between 2003 and 2011. Before that, and as a twenty-six-year-old, Azuh edited *Reel Stars* magazine. He plays ambassadorial roles for Nigeria's Federal Road Safety Corps (FRSC), National Drug Law Enforcement Agency (NDLEA), and the Lagos State Government (Ministry of the Environment). He has a BSc in public administration from the Lagos State University (LASU) and a Higher National Diploma (HND) in mass communication from the famous Institute of Management and Technology (IMT), Enugu. A prolific writer, his books, *The CEO's Bible* (volumes 1 and 2), *Tested and Trusted Success Secrets of the Rich and Famous, Encounters and Success Is Not Served A La Carte* are all doing great.

Dr. Nasir Danladi Bako is a television broadcaster, a former director general of the National Broadcasting Commission, NBC, Nigeria, and a former governorship aspirant in Nigeria.

Dr. Comfort Memfin Ekpo is a well-researched scholar who was the first female professor cum first female vice chancellor at University of Uyo, as well as the second female vice chancellor to head a federal university in Nigeria after Professor Grace Alele Williams of University of Benin. She has served in several educational reform boards in Nigeria and has been a mentor to a lot of upcoming scholars around the world.

Ray Ekpu is a veteran journalist and a cofounder of *Newswatch* magazine (with the late Dele Giwa and others). He is a prose craftsman, prolific writer, renowned columnist, analyst, and informed commentator. As far as journalism is concerned, Ray is a pacesetter and role model, and a shining star in the media firmament in Nigeria. He has published numerous books such as *Moving in Circles*. His edited works include: *Newswatch Best*, *Jogging in the Jungle: The Newswatch Story*.

Babatunde Adeshina Faustino is currently a doctoral student in the Department of Mass Communication, University of Lagos. He has participated in several research activities within and outside the department. He is an associate member of the Nigerian Institute of Public Relations (ANIPR) and Associate Registered Practitioner of Advertising (ARPA); and member of the Association of Communication Scholars and Professionals of Nigeria (ACSPN). He is a laureate of Bloomberg Media Initiative Africa (BMIA).

Teslim Olusegun Lawal, a seasoned journalist, joined the services of the University of Lagos in 1998 as a lecturer in the Department of Mass Communication, where the World Bank Center of Excellence in Multimedia and Cinematography is domiciled. He obtained his first and second degrees in communication and language arts at the University of Ibadan; and at present winding up his doctoral thesis in film-media at the same university.

Dr. Iniobong Courage Nda is a lecturer at the Department of Communication Arts, University of Uyo, Uyo, Akwa Ibom State, Nigeria, where she has taught communication and media studies since 2012. As a scholar who has garnered practical expertise from both the print (*The Sensor* newspaper) and broadcast media (the Nigerian Television Authority [NTA]) respectively, Dr. Nda has been able to integrate her field experience with the classroom demands for effective and efficient teaching of mass communication and has published her research in several national and international journals including contributing chapters to books. She is an active member of the African Council of Communication Education (ACCE), Nigerian Institute of Management (NIM), and the Nigerian Union of Journalists (NUJ). Her research interests are in business/organizational, health and development communication.

Professor Grace Nwagbara passed on in the last quarter of 2021. Dr. Nwagbara was a professor of media research at the Department of Communication Arts, University of Uyo, Nigeria, where she taught communication research, advertising, and other mass communication courses. She had more than twenty-seven years teaching experience at the university. Her research interests were in advertising, communication research and gender issues in communication. She has published in several journal articles and book chapters and coedited a book: *Handbook of Communication and Media Research* (2019—a publication of the Department of Communication Arts, University of Uyo). She held membership in the African Council for Communication Education, Nigeria Institute of Public Relations, Gender and Peace Research Group and International Association for Communication and Media Research (IAMCR). May her soul rest in the bosom of her creator.

Dr. Olumuyiwa Odusanya is a professor of public health at the Department of Community Health and Primary Health Care, Lagos State University College of Medicine (LASUCOM), Ikeja, and consultant public health physician at the Lagos State University Teaching Hospital (LASUTH), Ikeja. He is a fellow of the Faculty of Public Health of the National Postgraduate Medical College of Nigeria (FMCPH) and holds the master of public health (MPH) and the MB and BS degrees from the University of Lagos. Professor Odusanya was promoted to professor in 2008. Professor Odusanya's research interests are in clinical epidemiology, rational drug use, vaccine development, clinical trials, and health management. He has published over one hundred papers in Nigerian and international peer reviewed journals of repute. In November 2012, Professor Odusanya delivered his inaugural lecture (the 48th edition of Lagos State University) titled "Health in the Interest of the Public."

Chukwudi Ogbuaja is a veteran broadcast presenter and trainer. He has also attended high-level training in broadcast management and journalism.

Dr. Abigail Odozi Ogwezzy-Ndisika is the first female professor at the Department of Mass Communication, University of Lagos. At different times, she has served as the head of this department. She is an expert in development communication, public relations and advertising, with research interest in the gender dimension to development and strategic communication. She has worked on multi-sector projects and with a number of international organizations across Nigeria. She is a recipient of ELF Petroleum Coy Ltd. and British Chevening scholarships; laureate of the Council for the Development of Social Science Research in Africa (CODESRIA), laureate of the African Association of Political Science (AAPS)/Harry Frank Guggenheim (HFG); laureate, Pulitzer Center on Crisis Reporting, Washington, DC; Erasmus+ Staff Mobility grant for teaching at Birmingham School of Media, Birmingham City University, Birmingham, United Kingdom; and 1991 best graduating student in Department of Linguistics, University of Port Harcourt. In addition, she is a fellow of the Nigerian Institute of Public Relations (NIPR); Associate Registered Practitioner of Advertising (ARPA), member, Association of Communication Scholars & Professionals of Nigeria (ACSPN), and member,

International Association for Media and Communication Research (IAMCR). She has attended various local and international conferences; and published articles and books locally and internationally.

Dr. Ngozi Okpara is the current head of Mass Media and Writing Department and acting dean, School of Media and Communication, Pan Atlantic University, Lagos, Nigeria.

Bimbo Oloyede was employed as an assistant producer (TV) in 1975 and became a pioneer NTA network newscaster in 1976. Since 1980, she has been an independent radio and TV producer, presenter, and moderator. She established the Women's Optimum Development Foundation (WODEF) in 1999, and for fifteen years partnered with international agencies including UNFPA, UN Women, UNIC, USAID, the British Council, and so forth, using the media to promote development initiatives across Nigeria, with particular focus on gender equality. From 2002 to 2015, she anchored the news at Channels Television, Lagos, and was honored with a lifetime achievement award for journalistic excellence by the Wole Soyinka Center for Investigative Journalism in 2015. For the last twenty-five years, Bimbo Oloyede has trained various professionals in elocution, public speaking and communication skills, publishing *Strictly Speaking: Pronunciation Made Easy* and *An Oral Guide for Schools and Colleges.* Today, she is the lead consultant at Strictly Speaking, an educational consulting firm that specializes in developing and deploying transformational learning solutions.

Dr. Chuka Onwumechili is professor of strategic, legal, and management communication at Howard University in Washington, DC (USA). He is the author of more than ten books focusing largely on several communication issues that pertain to Africa. These books touch on varied subjects including sports, telecommunications, culture, and development. His most recent book is *Africa's Elite Football: Structure, Politics, and Everyday Challenges.* His other works on similar subjects have been published in peer-reviewed academic journals. Presently, he serves as editor-in-chief of the *Howard Journal of Communications* and serves on the editorial board of the *Communication & Sport* journal. It is important to note that before joining Howard University, Dr. Onwumechili served as vice president for the Digital Bridge Institute (DBI) in Nigeria where his brief included executive visioning, managing and overseeing training programs at different levels for employees in both the Nigerian telecommunications industry and other interested markets.

Dr. Ijeoma N. Onyeator was born in Nairobi, Kenya, in 1976 and she is the first to hold a PhD in media and communication from Pan-Atlantic

University, Lagos, Nigeria. She also holds an MA in media communication and technology from Brunel University Uxbridge, United Kingdom (2003); and a BSc in mass communication from the University of Lagos, Nigeria (1999). She is a member of the Association of Communication Scholars and Professionals of Nigeria since 2013. She is also a member of the International Association for Media and Communication Research and received certification from Birmingham City University for research leadership in 2017. She has publications in the form of books and academic journals and has delivered research papers at prominent international conferences. Ijeoma is a scholar-practitioner with nearly two decades of broadcast journalism experience at Channels Television. She also has years of classroom experience as an adjunct lecturer, School of Media and Communication (SMC) Pan-Atlantic University and Caleb University; as well as mentor and facilitator, Professional Education Department, School of Media and Communication (SMC) Pan-Atlantic University. Her main research interests include journalism studies, new media, alternative media and media philosophy.

Dr. Aniebo Samson is a senior lecturer at the Department of Communication Arts, University of Uyo, Nigeria.

Femi Sowoolu is a broadcaster par excellence. A qualified journalist, who graduated from the Nigerian Institute of Journalism, he joined the Ogun State Broadcasting Corporation in 1977, rising to the position of principal presenter when he left in 1990. He then joined Grant Advertising, Nigeria, a leading Nigerian advertising agency and member of the McCann Erickson Worldwide Group, where he was simultaneously media and radio/television production manager. After three years at Grant, he left to set up FM Productions, then producing mainly radio commercials, and doing voiceover presentations. He again submitted to the lure of the radio environment when he was invited to join Rhythm 93.7, Lagos, upon inception in 1996, guiding the station to an enviable number one position on the ratings. He left Rhythm, after six years, as station manager, to face the challenges of broadcast management consultancy, radio and television programming, production of advertising material, media planning and conceptualization of programming ideas for companies and organizations. Femi has produced, or assisted in the production of, broadcast and advertising materials, including programs, commercials, documentaries, and television series for a wide scope of companies and corporate organizations, and his voice is still heard on many radio and television commercials and documentaries. He has also performed variously over the years as a master of ceremonies at many first-class events. He has been narrator of the Gulder Ultimate Search since inception and served as both narrator and head writer in season 3 of the series; head writer, *Star Quest* music reality

TV shows; head writer, *Maltina Dance All Family* reality show; producer\ presenter, *Calypso Jazz Show*, Benson & Hedges Golden Tones; *Fine Tunes*; *Top Moments—Inspirational Talk* series; and producer, *Inspired Moments* (motivational syndicated talk series on selected Nigerian radio stations. He is also the voice behind the Globacom Nigeria and Ghana current advertising material and is a Glo ambassador. Femi has also written five books: *There Are No Heroes*, an autobiographical instructive for the modern broadcast debutante; *The Last Autumn and 76 Other Poems*, a poetical reflection on society; *Voices In My Head*, a compilation of essays, articles, quotations and political commentary on Nigerian issues in recent history; *Chatterbox*, a book of talk topics and show prep for radio presenters and producers; and a novel on high stakes political intrigue and corruption titled *A Kiss before We Die*, which is also intended to be produced as a movie. He has also contributed features and articles on behavioral, environmental, political, and media-related themes in various Nigerian newspapers, magazines, and blogs. He is the president of FMP Lagos, a mass media consultancy. After serving in a consultative capacity for a new radio station, Unity 102. 3 FM in 2007, helping to redesign, reengineer and refocus the G65TV/Unity media outfit, he was appointed director of Radio Services at the re-branded Radio Continental (now Max FM), the radio arm of Continental Broadcasting Services (TVC). In less than three years he employed his clout and experience to bring the station to a leading position in the Nigerian broadcast environment. He was afterward appointed general manager of Smooth 98.1 FM, further also leading that station to greater prominence in the Nigerian broadcast space. He has numerously consulted for a number of radio and television stations across Nigeria. He retired in 2020 as managing director/CEO of Jamz100.1 FM, an Ibadan based radio station, which in his three-and-a-half years at the helm became the most listened to radio station in the entire Southwestern region of Nigeria. Femi was chairman of the Media Committee for the Senator Ibikunle Amosun Campaign Organization, (SIACO) for the 2015 Ogun State Gubernatorial election, a role in which he served diligently and excelled creditably. To reflect that performance and further his contributions to the advancement of media services in Nigeria, he was appointed to the board of directors of Voice of Nigeria by His Excellency, President Muhammadu Buhari. in March 2018, for which he successfully and diligently served his constitutional two-year term.

Shamusi Olarenwaju Tiamiyu is a prolific broadcast news editor and retired from the services of the Federal Radio Corporation of Nigeria (Radio Nigeria) as a deputy director. He's also an author.

Dr. Pate Umaru is a Nigerian media scholar and a professor of media history. Umaru Pate is a one-time head of the Media Studies Department, University of Maiduguri, also was the dean of Faculty of Communications, Bayero University, Kano, as well as the dean, School of Postgraduate Studies at the University of Maiduguri. He is the president of the Association of Communication Scholars and Practitioners of Nigeria (ACSPN). He has been elected vice chancellor of the Federal University in Kashere, Gombe State, Nigeria.

Kingsley Datubor Uranta is the assistant general manager operations of Channels Television, Lagos, Nigeria, with the sole responsibility of driving strategy/innovation, partnership, training, and corporate communications. Kingsley is the provost of Channels Academy, a high-breed media training institute set up by Channels Television to provide training for journalists and the larger society. He has a robust career in communication spanning over twenty years in a variety of functional and managerial roles in broadcast journalism, corporate communication and engagement, journalism training, and television production. From 2011 to 2016, he was the manager media and communications of the Rivers State Sustainable Development Agency (RSSDA). He had earlier worked at Channels Television between 1992 and 2003, and helped to fashion out the station's operational philosophy. He rose to the position of editor, chief correspondent, controller news and producer. By 1996, Kingsley won the highly recognized Nigeria Media Merit Award as Best Television Reporter and was a member of the first generation of African journalists to contribute to the *CNN World Report* in the early years of Cable News Network. In 2004, Kingsley joined British American Tobacco as corporate communications manager.

Dr. Des Wilson is a professor of ethnocommunicology and African communication systems. He is currently the acting vice chancellor of Obong University, Akwa Ibom State, Nigeria.

Dr. Joseph Wilson is a professor of communication and journalism. He is the current head of Mass Communication Department, University of Maiduguri, Borno State, Nigeria.

Ingram Content Group UK Ltd.
Milton Keynes UK
UKHW020156040523
421189UK00003B/10